D0030875

MORE . . .

FATHER, SON & CO.

MY LIFE AT IBM AND BEYOND

THOMAS J. WATSON JR.

AND PETER PETRE

BANTAM BOOKS

NEW YORK • TORONTO • LONDON • SYDNEY • AUCKLAND

FATHER, SON & CO.

A Bantam Book
Bantam hardcover edition / June 1990
Bantam paperback edition / June 1991

Photo sections designed by M 'N O Production Services, Inc.

ISBN 0-553-29023-1

Published simultaneously in the United States and Canada

PRINTED IN THE UNITED STATES OF AMERICA

OPM   0 9 8 7 6 5 4 3 2 1

For Olive
and our children
Tom, Jeannette, Olive, Lucinda, Susan,
and Helen

And for
Major General Follett Bradley
(1890–1952)
who gave me confidence

INTRODUCTION

When my father died in 1956—six weeks after making me head of IBM—I was the most frightened man in America. For ten years he had groomed me to succeed him, and I had been the young man in a hurry, eager to take over, cocky and impatient. Now, suddenly, I had the job—but what I didn't have was Dad there to back me up. I'd heard so many stories about sons of prominent men failing in business, and I could imagine their devastation at finding themselves unable to fill their fathers' shoes. I worried I'd end up the same way, but after my father had been dead a year I announced to my wife: "I've made it through twelve months without the old boy around!"

I went another year, and then another. The computer era was beginning and IBM was able to capitalize on it: while I was chief executive the company grew more than tenfold. I like to think that Father would have been impressed with the $7.5 billion-a-year business I left behind when I resigned in 1971. He had always predicted it would someday be the biggest business on earth.

I was so intimately entwined with my father. I had a compelling desire, maybe out of honor for the old gentleman, maybe out of sheer cussedness, to prove to the world that I could excel the same way he did. I never declared myself winner in that contest, because many of my decisions were based on policies and practices learned at his knee. But I think I was at least successful enough that people could say I was the worthy son of a worthy father.

It could have turned out very differently. The kind of privileged upbringing I had—private school, world travel, wealth—often leads to disaster for a son. I knew I was supposed to follow in my father's footsteps, but I did not see how that was possible. I was in awe of the man, yet we both had such hot tempers that it was hard for me to be in the same room with him, much less try to learn from him how to run a company.

I didn't have much motivation as a youth. At Brown University, I spent so much time flying airplanes and fooling around that I barely graduated. In the yearbook you had to have a line next to your photograph. The only thing in mine was the name of the prep school I'd gone to. There was nothing else to say. I had no distinctions, no successes of my own, and only a vague notion of how to be sympathetic and understanding to others. I was totally qualified to be either a playboy or an airplane bum.

If it hadn't been for World War II, I might never have become my own man. After 1939 my favorite recreation, flying, suddenly became serious business. I joined the Air Force as a pilot and learned to be responsible for an airplane full of men. The military took me far outside my father's influence, and by 1943 I had made it to lieutenant colonel. Though I never got promoted beyond that, I came back from the war confident, for the first time, that I might be capable of running IBM. But I'd been so unimpressive before the war that it was hard for my father to believe it. It took him years to convince himself that I'd changed, and I don't think he was ever completely sure. You can see that in the photograph of us that appeared in the *New York Times* when he turned IBM over to me. It shows us in our pin-striped suits, shaking hands in front of a bookcase. On my face is a look of great self-assurance and I'm obviously enjoying the occasion tremendously; but on Dad's face there is a faint, uncertain smile.

He ran IBM for forty-two years and I ran it for fifteen —all told, nearly six decades of Watson management. My job was to lead the company into the computer business, but it was he who put IBM on the map. By the time I joined the Air Force he had built the business from almost nothing to revenues of nearly forty million dollars a year. IBM was still really an insignificant part of the American industrial scene, but thanks to T.J.'s genius for selling, it was fast growing and highly profitable, and it attracted a lot of attention. Father knew how to project an image as well as any salesman who ever lived. At the New York World's Fair of 1939 there was a General Motors Day, a General Electric Day, and an IBM Day—two elephants and a gnat all getting the same treatment. We even had Mayor La Guardia as our guest at the Fair. President Franklin Roosevelt, whose confidant Father had become, sent a greeting by telegram.

During the ten years after World War II Father taught me his business secrets as we worked together. It was a stormy relationship. In public he would praise me lavishly, and I'd hear from other people the nice things he was saying about my shrewdness and brains and talent as a manager. But in private Father and I had terrible fights that led us again and again to the brink of estrangement. These arguments would frequently end in tears, me in tears and Dad in tears.

We fought about every major issue of the business— how to finance IBM's growth, whether to settle or fight a federal antitrust suit, what role in IBM other members of our family ought to play. From around 1950 my goal— one of the things on which we never saw eye to eye—was to push into computers as fast as possible. That meant hiring engineers by the thousands and spending dollars by the tens of millions for new factories and labs. The risk made Dad balk, even though he sensed the enormous potential of electronics as early as I did.

When I finally took over I was excited about change. Computing was a brand-new industry, and I always felt that if IBM didn't grab the opportunity, somebody else would. So we taught ourselves to ride a runaway horse, expanding on a scale that no company has ever matched. We grew so fast that some years we had to cope with the problem of training twenty thousand or more new employees.

I kept myself where employees could see me, out in front, setting a fast pace. I had learned from my father that by seizing opportunities for dramatic action—personally answering an employee's complaint, slashing the price of a new computer that failed to perform as promised—I could set an example of how IBM should do business. At the same time I had yearnings outside the company that would have been hard for my father to understand. In the top drawer of my desk I kept a list of adventures, like climbing the Matterhorn and retracing the South Sea voyages of Captain Cook, for which I simply had no time.

All that changed in 1970, when I had a heart attack. I was only fifty-six, and I think many executives would have been back in the office before their triple-bypass scars had even healed. But my experience at the hospital changed my life.

I had a chest pain in the middle of the night and drove myself to the emergency room. They put me on a monitor, but early the next morning I stopped the doctor and said, "Look, I've got to get out of here. My best friend is dead and I've got to go to his funeral, then I have to fly right out and give the inaugural address at the Mayo Clinic medical school, then—" He told me, "You're not going anywhere. You're having a heart attack." They moved me into intensive care.

The doctor, Marc Newberg, was someone I grew to like very much. Over the next three weeks we had long discussions, and finally one morning he looked me right in the eye and said, "Why don't you get out of IBM right now? I think you've proved just about everything you can up there."

He left. I didn't want any lunch, it was such a shock. By dinnertime I started thinking about the responsibilities I'd carried for so many years and all the things I could do outside business. The next morning I woke up at dawn and got a cup of coffee at the nurses' station. When I got back to my room, sunlight was streaming in the window and I felt better than I had in decades. It was as if somebody had lifted a heavy pack off my back.

Before I left the hospital I told the people at IBM that I was thinking of getting out. The board of directors did everything in the world to keep me in the company. They came to me individually and as a group. But I knew I was doing the right thing. I wanted to live more than I wanted to run IBM. It was a choice my father never would have made, but I think he would have respected it.

This is the story of my father and myself, of my years alone at IBM's helm, and of what I've done since leaving the company. Father and I played out our rivalry and our love for each other in the great American business that he created. I helped build it and then left it behind me twenty years ago. Along the way I learned a great deal about power: being subject to it, striving for it, inheriting it, wielding it, and letting it go. I learned lessons for fathers who have dreams for their children and for children burdened with parental expectations. Lots of sons ask me if they should follow their fathers into business. My answer is: If you can stand it, do it.

CHAPTER 1

I n the spring of 1987, not long after celebrating my seventy-third birthday, I took my helicopter out to follow the scenes of my childhood. I went by myself, the way I often fly when there is something that I want to see. Helicopters are noisy and sometimes hard to handle, but they can take you exactly where you feel like going. You can land on a flat rock only ten feet by ten feet far out in the sea, or tuck into a garden behind the house of a friend. On that spring day I wanted to learn what remained of the world in which I was raised.

I flew down the Hudson River alongside Manhattan, swinging west off Broad Street, where my father would catch the ferry after work. On the New Jersey side of the river Dad would get on a train. I followed the railroad west over the rolling hills and fields of New Jersey, where he'd ride talking politics with other early suburbanites like Malcolm Muir, the founder of *Business Week* magazine, and André Fouilhoux, an architectural engineer who was one of the chief designers of Rockefeller Center.

I spent my boyhood in the village of Short Hills, twenty miles from New York. In the 1920s it was a fashionable little community populated mainly by the families of commuters like Dad, called "downtown men." It had a train station, an Episcopal church, a private school and a public school, and the houses were large and set on three- or five-acre tracts. It was easy for me to spot the big gabled place where I grew up. It sits on top of a low hill, a near duplicate of our first house on that site, the one my father accidentally burned to the ground. It happened when I was five, and Dad was still in his early days of struggle and debt. The fire started when he was trying to demonstrate the use of a fireplace. He became very

1

conscious of fireproofing after that; the roof of today's house is made out of slate.

In back of the house we'd had chicken coops, a big vegetable garden, and a pony corral; all of those were gone now. But I saw the long winding driveway where my mother taught me to drive a car when I was eleven. Nearby I spotted the two ponds that were a big part of my boyhood. That part of New Jersey was so rural in those days that right near our town there were people who made a living running traplines in the local swamps. No one lived around those ponds when we moved in. There was only a big wooden icehouse, where horse-drawn sleds would haul huge blocks of ice in the winter. When I was eleven or twelve, my friends and I used to take girls behind the icehouse to play kissing games.

I wanted to set the helicopter down and walk around. But now the banks of the ponds are covered with houses and there was no place to land. So I climbed up and flew out along the winding road we used to drive to get to Dad's country place: a farm he bought in 1927 when he was feeling the first flush of wealth after running IBM for thirteen years. The farm, which we called Hills and Dales, was near the town of Oldwick, twenty miles west of Short Hills. I found Oldwick quite easily, but when I looked for Hills and Dales outside the town, there were so many highways and corporate headquarters that I never found it.

In Short Hills I was known as Terrible Tommy Watson. Whenever there was trouble, I seemed to be involved. Youthful rebellion was not in fashion in the 1920s, so I was not at all popular. Most of the kids in my school could see that at the slightest opportunity I would goof off, and none of them thought I would amount to a hill of beans. I had only a handful of friends. The other kids thought they were superior. Worse still, I was very sensitive about the fact that they avoided me.

When I was ten a friend named Joe and I were fooling around near a house being worked on in our neighborhood. The door to the screen porch was open and we could see cans of paint and brushes and turpentine. We took a couple of cans and somehow ended up painting a street.

Mother asked us about this and we confessed that the paint was stolen. She had lectured me before about swiping things, to no avail, and I think this time she decided that unless she did something dramatic, I was going to end up a felon. Usually Mother was mild and sweet tempered, but if she thought things were getting out of hand, she would move with real force. So she took us to the police station. She must have called the chief beforehand. He shook our hands and said, "It's nice to see you. I want to tell you about who we have locked up here. We have people in here for murder and robbery, but most of the people who come in are petty thieves."

Our eyes were wide open by this time. They had a thing in this police station such as I've never seen since: a stand-up cage about half the size of a telephone booth. The front would swing open, you'd straddle a bar, and they'd lock you in. It must have been for questioning suspects. You could move a little bit but you couldn't get out. I remember the feeling of that. Then the chief took us to the back and put us in a cell.

"Once you're in jail, it's a terrible place to be," he said. "Most people turn into repeat offenders, and then there goes your life." I dreamt about it afterward: getting caught and going to jail when I hadn't done anything wrong.

Mother really had her hands full with us. She married late, at age twenty-nine, and then had four children in the space of six years—me, my sisters Jane and Helen, and Arthur, whom everybody called Dick. Even though I was the oldest, Mother did not expect me to help look after my brother and sisters, so I was pretty much on my own as a boy. I loved Dick, but he was too young to be an interesting companion. Helen, the second youngest, was always a cozy friend. If she saw me with a bag of stolen candy, she'd want to know what it was, but I could always trust her to clam up around our parents. My relationship with Jane, who was closest to me in age, was more difficult. She would sometimes join in one of my escapades, but then she'd feel guilty and confess to Dad, getting me in trouble. Worse, Jane was Father's favorite. He went far out of his way to accommodate her and she always called him by the odd name "My Joy" instead of Daddy or Father. This started as an endearment, but she kept it up as long as she lived. Mother thought it was inappropriate for Dad to play favorites, but there was very little she could do about that relationship.

The fact that *I* wasn't Dad's favorite did not surprise me. From very early in my life I was convinced that I had something missing. I was never able to connect completely with what other people were doing. There is a film of my first-grade play in 1921, photographed by my father. The boys were all dressed as bumblebees and the movie shows us buzzing in and out among little girls dressed as flowers. I'm the tallest, long boned and ungainly, and you can spot me easily: while the other boys all have their wings neatly spread and pinned, mine are flapping around, all awry. I keep reaching back trying to set them straight.

My lack of polish didn't seem to hinder my father, who was on the rise in Short Hills society. He joined the tennis club, the school board, and the board of directors of the local bank, and may have been the only man in Short Hills who took his family to Europe every other summer, albeit on business. Dad quickly became a pillar of the Short Hills Episcopal church in spite of his roots as a humble Methodist. A few families saw him as *nouveau riche* and turned up their noses, but most of our neighbors admired Dad.

He was a tall man, unathletic but fairly lean, and always impeccably attired. When we were very young he knew how to loosen up and have fun with us. I have films of him dressed in his three-piece suit marching with us and tooting a horn in a backyard parade. Dad loved to ham it up when our aunts and uncles and cousins visited for Sunday dinner. Sometimes he'd disappear upstairs with Mother and she'd help him struggle into one of her dresses. He'd come tottering down the stairs all decked out in a hat and veil and high-heeled shoes, clinging to the banister on one side with Mother steadying him on the other. When I was little I thought he was the liveliest father imaginable. But for some reason his playfulness gradually diminished, and by the time I was ten or eleven Dad acted quite formal and aloof. This loss of warm companionship made me sad, but looking back I think the cause was mainly age. Dad was thirty-nine by the time I was born, and the fact that he was ten years older than most other boys' fathers made it difficult for us to be pals. He wasn't one to come out and play ball, or invite me for a hike around the local reservoir.

Father must have known he had an uncontrollable temper that might feed on itself, because when there was punishing to be done he made Mother do it. These punishments became a sort of ritual. I would go up with the two of them to their big white-tiled bathroom. Father would stand over near his basin to observe, I would hold on to a towel rack, and Mother would do the switching.

I quickly developed a sense of what is fair and just, which these punishments, to my mind, sometimes were not. I'll never forget one switching I got when I was ten. It was March, the snow was melting, and my parents had given me new rubber boots. I rushed right out of the house and, to test the boots, stepped down into a hole that had water in it. It was deeper than I thought and water poured in over the tops. Mother and Dad insisted that I had soaked myself on purpose. Soon I was facing the towel rack, thinking I was getting rooked.

Switchings didn't stop me from getting into trouble, however. The following winter I kept asking Father for a leather coat. They made double-breasted leather coats for kids in those days that came down to about mid-thigh. Finally my father presented one to me, with great pride, for my eleventh birthday. Coming home from school the next day, some buddies and I made a fire—it's fascinating to make fires when you're young. I'd been reading about Indians and smoke signals, so I took that beautiful leather coat that had been on my back only once and used it with another guy to make signals from the fire.

Then I tried to clean it up and couldn't. There were big burns all through it. I felt awful about what I'd done, but that made no difference when I told my parents. They switched me anyway.

Life didn't go much better for me at school. My brother and sisters and I went to Short Hills Country Day School, a rustic-looking turn-of-the-century brick-and-shingle structure within walking distance of our house. The curriculum was conventional and not very demanding, and in most classes I would watch the clock. The school clocks came from Father—IBM had a time division, and he donated a system that rang the bells to change classes. There was a master clock in the headmaster's office and classroom clocks throughout the building. These did not move smoothly from one minute to the next. They would stay on 9:04 until the main clock got to 9:05; then they'd all go CLICK CLICK and move up one minute. It would get to 2:56, and I'd be thinking "Just eight more clicks and I get out of here."

My report cards were always a jumble of Ds and Fs with an occasional A or B. I learned much better by doing than by reading, probably because words on a page seemed to swim around whenever I tried to read. It was years before I learned how to compensate for whatever flaw in my vision kept me from reading normally. In school, deportment was the area in which I really stood out—my conduct marks were the worst. You could get fifty demerits a semester at Short Hills Country Day School without being thrown out; I'd always have more than thirty and sometimes more than forty. To work off demerits you had to run laps around the building on Saturdays, in full view of passersby. I sometimes had to run fifty laps while other people were doing ten.

For some reason, being punished only drove me to greater mischief. When I was about twelve, I met Craig Kingsbury, an outdoorsman type, not much older than I, who went trapping in a nearby swamp. I sought him out for advice about how to skin a squirrel I had shot. When he mentioned that he sometimes skinned skunks it didn't take me an instant to zero in. "What do you do with the stink glands?" I asked. It turned out that Kingsbury knew how to extract skunk juice and put it in bottles. I bought some from him.

At school just before assembly I sneaked down to the furnace and examined the ducts going off in various directions. I thought that if you put something in the main vent it would spread through the whole building. So I dumped in the entire bottle, ran upstairs, and went to the assembly hall. A hundred kids were sitting there, along with the teachers and the headmaster, Mr. Lance, a straitlaced disciplinarian who knew me well.

There was a terrible stink, and the longer we sat the worse the stink got. Finally Mr. Lance said, "Is there anyone who knows anything about this detestable smell?"

There was a long silence. We had an honor system, so eventually I raised my hand.

"Watson!"

"Yes, sir."

"Stand up!"

"Yes, sir."

"What do you know about this?"

I explained what I'd done, how I'd gotten the skunk juice, and I pulled the bottle out of my pocket to show him. Everyone backed away a little.

Then the teachers opened all the windows and tried to fan out the smell. Finally Mr. Lance decided the school had to close. It was my moment of ultimate triumph. Whatever happened to me as a result was worth it.

Mr. Lance didn't know how to deal with me. His first idea was to tie the empty skunk-juice bottle around my neck. But that was too minor a punishment, because I was getting used to the smell by then and it didn't bother me very much.

His next move was more effective. There was a school board meeting that night. Mr. Lance waited until it convened and then described my transgression—to the chagrin of my father, who was on the board.

By the time he got home Dad was in a fury. He began by saying it was wrong for me to have forced the school to close, thereby depriving my sisters and other honest children of the opportunity to learn. Father never struck me, but this time he came close and I bolted. He chased me and roared, "I don't need to discipline you! The *world* will discipline you, you little skunk!"

CHAPTER 2

My father went from rags to riches, but what impressed me was how close he came to staying in rags. He was the only son of an immigrant Scots-Irishman who made a meager living cutting lumber and farming in New York State, which was still quite primitive in the 1880s when Dad was a boy. Dad had four sisters, all older than he, and the family lived in a cramped four-room cabin with no running water near the town of Painted Post. Dad's first job, at age seventeen, was selling pianos, organs, and sewing machines to farm families off the back of a wagon. Salesmanship was his ticket into the world, and he loved talking about those early days as a peddler. "Everything starts with a sale," he'd say. "If there's no sale, there's no commerce in the whole of America." As a salesman Dad wasn't a back-slapper; he had a thoughtful manner that people responded to. You'd be attracted by his good looks, his slightly reserved way of speaking, his attentiveness—and before long you'd find yourself sold.

His first boss took advantage of him. Dad worked for a local hardware dealer named W. F. Bronson, who loaned him a wagon and paid him twelve dollars a week. Dad thought this was a stupendous amount—he was making more than the cashier at the Painted Post bank, for example—until one day a sales agent for the organ company said, "You're certainly selling a lot of instruments. What's your pay?" When Dad proudly told him, he said, "That's awful!" He explained that salesmen usually earn commissions, not salaries, and that on a commission basis Bronson ought to be paying Dad around sixty-five dollars a week. Dad quit the next day. From then on, he always wanted to be paid by commission, so he could be sure of getting his just reward.

My father used to say his ambition grew in stages. The more he saw of the world, the more he wanted to achieve. He could remember standing on a muddy roadside as a boy and watching Amory Houghton Jr., the founder of the Corning Glass Works, ride past in his carriage, which made Dad want a team and rig of his own. Dad got another glimpse of wealth after he had moved up several notches and was selling cash registers: a Chicago lawyer he had met invited my father to his grand house on the shore of Lake Michigan. The lawyer remarked that he, too, had started out on a farm, so Dad raised his sights again.

For the first several years he seemed predestined to fail. He went to the city of Buffalo to find work when he was nineteen, but selling sewing machines to farmers wasn't very good preparation for what he encountered. Buffalo in the 1890s was a sprawling, rough, unfriendly place in the middle of a recession. Jobs were scarce and soon Dad was hard up. He told me that at one point he was reduced to sleeping on a pile of sponges in the basement of a drugstore. He had only one suit to his name, and when he could afford to get it pressed he had to wait in the back of the tailor shop in his underwear until it was ready.

The first man in Buffalo to recognize his talent was a salesman named C. B. Barron, who took Dad on as his assistant. Barron, unfortunately, was a flamboyant city slicker who sold stock in the Northern New York State Building and Loan Association up and down the shores of Lake Erie. Dad thought Barron was the most worldly and charming fellow he'd ever met; he was too naive to see that the guy was a crook. When Barron came into a town he'd rent the finest room at the local hotel and then say to the bell captain, "I'm C. B. Barron. I want to be paged three times during dinner. I have reasons for it, not important to you. Here are a couple of dollars." Soon word would get around that there was an important stranger in town who had come to sell shares in the

Building and Loan. The stock itself was legitimate; investors paid for it in installments, like a savings plan. Barron would keep the first payment as his commission, which enabled him to live pretty high.

A photo of Dad from that period shows Barron's influence. My father is sitting on a stump and looks like a caricature of the turn-of-the-century traveling man, with his silk hat, frock coat, high-button shoes, striped socks, and ridiculous handlebar mustache. His share of the building-and-loan commissions amounted to more money than he'd ever seen, and Dad decided to go into business for himself on the side. He opened a butcher shop in Buffalo, intending to use future proceeds from his work with Barron to start more and more stores. Chain stores were just beginning to spread around America then, and the idea of running a retail empire appealed to my father. But in less than a year, it all fell apart. Dad woke up one morning on a sales trip to find that Barron had taken off with their funds; since Dad had no savings to fall back on, instead of being able to open his second butcher shop, he had to sell the first.

My father had the ability to overcome setbacks that would have sent other young men back to the farm. Later on this optimism came out in slogans that everybody in IBM had to learn—"Make Things Happen," "Ever Onward," "Beat Your Best," and so on. He knew how to find opportunity where none seemed to be, such as in the remnants of his butcher shop business. He had bought a cash register for the store on the installment plan, and when he went downtown to transfer responsibility for the payments to the new owner, he used the occasion to talk his way into a job with the National Cash Register Company. That was the lucky break that made his career. The Cash, as it was called, was one of America's best-known companies. It belonged to John Henry Patterson, a fierce little tycoon from Dayton who was on a campaign to make the cash register an indispensable fixture in every modern store. Having used a cash register himself, my father thought he could convince other store owners of its virtues and he was right—he soon became one of the top salesmen at the Cash.

Patterson, who shows up in business histories as "the father of modern salesmanship," was in effect my business grandfather. Dad worked for him for eighteen years and learned from him many of the ideas that built IBM. Patterson's genius was to figure out how to take crude, partly educated, ambitious commercial travelers like Dad and mold them into America's first national sales force. He made his salesmen memorize and use standardized sales pitches, inspired them with revival-like meetings, and challenged and bullied them into hitting sales quotas that were sky-high. One of his innovations was to break up each sales region into exclusive territories, so no salesman had to worry about others from the company stealing his prospects. Since the Cash had a virtual monopoly on the cash register business, these territories were valuable indeed. Patterson paid extraordinarily well—it wasn't unusual for a man with only a few years' experience to make one hundred dollars a week, which had the buying power of fifteen hundred dollars today. Being a salesman at the turn of the century was an ignoble job, but under Patterson it became almost a profession.

My father rose through the ranks at the Cash Register company, and by the time he and Mother met sixteen years later, he was Patterson's second-in-command. Tall, handsome, and well-turned-out, Dad was also Dayton's most eligible bachelor. He could be seen driving around town in a fine Pierce-Arrow automobile given to him by Mr. Patterson. He had plenty of money—enough so that when his father developed diabetes and died, Dad was able to take over as head of the family and support his mother and sisters in style. He set them up in a fine stone house in Rochester, New York, where he'd run a sales office, and he found successful salesmen for my aunts to marry. But he put off getting married himself, he explained to me, because he had seen successful men who married without much thought of the future and then found themselves burdened with wives who couldn't keep up as they rose in the world. Such men would suffer their wives or get divorced. He'd had girlfriends before Mother —he said he'd thought of marrying one who was an opera singer in Philadelphia—but he wanted a real lifetime partner. So he waited until he could find someone who would provide both an intellectual and a social boost.

Dad liked to tell the employees at IBM that convincing Jeannette Kittredge to be his wife was the finest sale he'd ever made. Mother's family was prominent in Dayton. Her father headed the Barney and Smith Railroad Car Company, a maker of railroad passenger cars, and Mother told stories from her girlhood of riding in beautiful new cars with varnished interiors. She used to say she first noticed Father at a country club dinner, when she looked down the table and saw that he was the only guest besides herself who had left his wineglass untouched. Her father was a strict, teetotaling Presbyterian, and she knew she'd need his consent for any mate she picked. Mother was capable of making great leaps of sentiment and she immediately thought, "That's the man I'm going to marry." Her father approved of the match, and so did Mr. Patterson, who always liked the idea of his employees' gaining status in Dayton society. When my parents came back from their honeymoon—a combination sightseeing and business trip to the West Coast—Patterson surprised them with the keys to a house he'd put up for them near his own. Dad's life finally seemed to be turning out the way he dreamed. But the following year, just after I was born, my parents were forced to leave Dayton under painful circumstances. After building my father up for so many years, Patterson turned around and pushed him out of the Cash Register company.

Dad probably shouldn't have been surprised. The way he described Patterson, it was hard to imagine a more arbitrary and eccentric boss. Patterson managed his people by pressure and fear. Once, when he thought the men weren't paying attention during a long sales meeting, Patterson grabbed a fire ax and chopped a cash register to pieces onstage. Executives who were his favorites got extravagant rewards, but on the other hand, Patterson punished people he didn't like, sometimes with real cruelty. Dad told the story of an executive who showed up for work one morning not knowing Mr. Patterson was angry with him. On the grass in front of the Cash he found his desk and the contents of his office, soaked with kerosene and set on fire. He left without ever going into the building. Even though Dad later became famous for his autocratic style at IBM, compared to Patterson he was mild.

Patterson was always firing his best men. He owned almost all of National Cash Register's stock, but he was irrationally afraid that an employee would somehow take the company away from him. The end came for Dad after a vice president named Edward Deeds whispered to Patterson that my father was developing quite a following among the rank and file. In 1913, as Dad addressed a sales convention, Patterson went to the podium and interrupted the speech. He began lavishly praising the other people present, and ignored Dad completely. Dad's desk never got set on fire, but after a time he was no longer invited to meetings or consulted on important decisions. He felt devastated, and after a few months he resigned. Oddly, Dad never complained of this treatment and revered Patterson until the day he died. He used to say, "Nearly everything I know about building a business comes from Mr. Patterson." The man Father hated was Deeds, for setting him up. He encountered Deeds later on several occasions, but he never spoke to him again.

The winter of early 1914 must have been pretty grim for my father, although he was far from broke. After pushing him out, Patterson had given him a massive fifty-thousand-dollar severance payment, and also let him keep his Pierce-Arrow car. But Dad's carefully built-up security was gone. He was out of work and about to turn forty. He had a new wife and son to support and no place to live—the house in Dayton belonged to Patterson. There was no other job for Dad in town, and he took Mother and me with him to New York in order to hunt for work.

I've always been impressed with how picky he was about what he'd do next. He once explained this by saying he was sure he'd find a job because he had a reputation for being able to sell almost anything. Quickly he rejected offers from the Electric Boat Company, a maker of submarines for the navy, and Remington Arms. With war coming in Europe these would have been very lucrative positions, but Dad figured that both firms would shrink as soon as the fighting stopped. He rejected a job at Dodge Motor because the Dodge brothers would not give him the sort of contract he was after—he wanted to be an entrepreneur like Patterson, with a share in the company's profits, and not simply a hired manager. Yet he had no capital to buy his own firm and no promising ideas of his own to commercialize.

Eventually Dad might have gotten anxious, but before even two months had passed, he met Charles R. Flint, the founder of what was to become IBM. In those days Flint was known as the hottest financier on Wall Street. They called him the Trust King. He was a little man with a goatee and sideburns, about sixty-five years old. He'd played a key role in the creation of the United States Rubber Company, had investments in the automobile and the airplane, and had made and lost fortunes trading arms. During the Russo-Japanese War of 1904, he had been a purchasing agent for the czar.

Flint recruited my father to manage the Computing-Tabulating-Recording Company, or CTR, a little conglomerate he had assembled in 1911. It sold a grab-bag of products that Flint saw as roughly "allied": scales, time clocks, and tabulating machines. The concept of the business was sound, but Flint had loaded the balance sheet with so much debt that the company was in danger of collapse. Its twelve hundred employees were confused and demoralized, and the board of directors was talking grimly about liquidation. Flint, who was also on the board, decided to step in and find a manager who could turn CTR around, or at least enable the stockholders to salvage a few cents on their dollars.

What intrigued my father about CTR was the products that did the work of clerks. This meant the time clock and, in particular, the tabulating machine. An engineer named Herman Hollerith had invented the tabulator to help tally the results of the 1890 U.S. Census. By the turn of the century a few primitive Hollerith machines had made their way into the accounting departments of railroads and insurance companies. Father saw ways to improve the machine and he imagined broad commercial possibilities. American industry was growing to unprecedented size, and if huge corporations were to keep from drowning in their own paperwork, they had to find ways to automate their record keeping and accounting.

One of Dad's first moves at CTR was to call on the Guaranty Trust Company, the company's biggest creditor, and ask for an additional loan of forty thousand dollars to pay for research and development. When the banker pointed out CTR already owed the Guaranty Trust four million dollars and that the condition of the business did not justify further loans, Dad said, "Balance sheets reveal the past. This loan is for the future." It was one of his greatest sales pitches. The Guaranty Trust coughed up the money, and the resulting improvements on the tabulating machine enabled CTR to greatly expand its market.

Dad used some of Patterson's techniques to light a fire under CTR's ragged work force. He created CTR slogans and CTR songs, a CTR newspaper and a CTR school, all modeled on those of the Cash. Whatever seemed good about Patterson's way of doing business, Dad copied; whatever seemed bad, he boldly reversed. His code of discipline for CTR employees was just as rigid as that of the Cash, but his philosophy of management was far more humane. Patterson loved to make heads roll, but when Dad arrived at CTR he made a point of firing no one. He told the men that he was going to depend on them, and that his job would be to build them up. Since he'd worked hard to pull himself up from the farm, Dad knew that the way to win a man's loyalty is by bolstering his self-respect. When I joined IBM many years later, the company was famous for high pay, generous benefits, and the intense devotion of the employees to Dad. But back at the beginning, when there was hardly any money, Dad gained their loyalty with words.

My father loved to recall his and Flint's discussion of compensation on the day Flint offered him the job. He said to Flint, "I want a gentleman's salary, so that I can support my family. And I want a percentage of the profits that remain after the stockholders get their dividend." Flint went right to the heart of it and said, "I understand. You want a peck of the corn you harvest." When Flint presented this arrangement to the other directors they were incredulous, because it was hard to imagine that there would ever be surplus profits to divvy up. But by the time I was in college, a version of the formula they agreed to would make Dad the highest-paid man in America.

Late in his life my father would take a pencil and do scratch calculations of his own fortunes, toting up his net worth. He carried these scraps of paper around. Sometimes I'd find them and throw them away; sometimes I'd keep them. They show that not until the mid-1930s was he in a position to stop worrying about debts. He was sixty years old by the time he was really on Easy Street.

The chances he took with money are amazing to me. For the first eight years of his married life, he was pretty much on a shoestring. At any point he probably owed at least one hundred thousand dollars. He never accumulated any capital. The first two summers he took us to Europe, in 1922 and 1924, we traveled on borrowed funds as he planted the seeds of the IBM World Trade Company.

As soon as he'd get a little cash, he would buy CTR stock. He felt it was a damn good buy. He bought on margin in the beginning—those were the days when you only had to put up ten percent of the stock price. As the stock went up, his broker friends would say, "Tom, you ought to take some profits." And he'd come home indignant that someone was suggesting he should sell. More than once this investment strategy, if it can be called that, looked like a big mistake. CTR nearly went broke in the recession of 1921 because Dad had expanded too rapidly. Only by heavy borrowing did he manage to keep the company and himself afloat. He had another close call during the Depression. The company, by then known as IBM, weathered the initial stock crash in 1929 relatively well, but by 1932 the stock had fallen more than two hundred points and Dad had to borrow on everything to keep up his margin payments. He told me that if the stock had gone down just another three or four dollars, he would have been wiped out. There just wasn't any place left to go for money.

Though he never owned more than about five percent of the company, virtually his entire fortune was in IBM. If the company failed, he failed too. His only hedge was a farm in Indiana that he bought in the late 1930s when war seemed likely. He thought it was remotely possible that some unforeseen catastrophe might wreck IBM, and he told me he wanted our family to be able to return to the land. Other than this, he had absolutely no impulse to hoard or even worry about money. He wanted to rise in the world, so he knew he had to spend. He never panicked when the money was low; I think it never occurred to him that he couldn't make more. If it came in, it went out, and that was fine with him. Father used money purely as a tool—to express his generosity, to cement his family and company, and to ease his passage upward in society.

CHAPTER 3

My mother wasn't necessarily cut out to be married to a socially ambitious businessman. In spite of her upbringing and her boarding-school education, she was strong on prairie virtues that were unusual in Short Hills. She was so frugal that at home she'd walk down two flights of stairs to turn off a single light, and so unpretentious that she didn't care much for the Paris dresses Dad insisted on buying her. I have a photograph from the 1920s that shows her looking lovely and regal in a Short Hills community play. But the way I remember her is as an overworked mother, trying to raise four little kids and manage that big gabled house the way Father wanted it run. She struggled constantly to keep peace among the help and play hostess to all the guests Dad would bring home. But she was very game. One night a stuffy businessman from Switzerland stayed at our house and left his shoes outside the guest room door. "He thinks this is a palace!" Mother said. Then she laughed and polished the shoes herself.

My father owed her a great deal. By the time they met, he had already learned how to dress and how to give a speech, but the nuances of gentle living sometimes escaped him. She helped greatly with that. When we were young, she'd correct Dad's English, watch his table manners, and caution him not to lose his temper. Her lessons to him could be pretty brisk. After he was making a lot of money in the 1930s, he came home one day and proudly gave her a big diamond ring. It was the first expensive piece of jewelry he'd ever bought—not a really good diamond, just big, as big as an aspirin. It must have weighed two carats. Mother pointed out that it was flawed and that she would have preferred a smaller diamond that

19

was perfect rather than a larger diamond that wasn't. This stung Dad. He took the ring back and some years later produced one that was equally large, but perfect. It must have cost a fortune.

Mother was short, maybe five feet four, and fairly thin; and she always kept her gray-brown hair long and pulled back into a bun. Her hands were naturally calloused; to make them soft she worked on them every night with a pumice stone. She had a gentle mouth, appealing eyes, and a straight, interesting nose. Even though Dad often overshadowed her, we children always knew she had a powerful streak of fun. When the Charleston was popular, around 1925, she invited some of her friends and had a dance instructor teach the Charleston in our cellar. There were clotheslines strung along the ceilings that Mother and her friends held on to to steady themselves as they practiced.

Because she was more handy than Dad, Mother did many of the "man's" chores around the house. When a fuse blew, she changed it; when coal needed to be shoveled, she did that too. Much later she told me that this arrangement started soon after they got married. They were going to bed one night and she said, "You ought to go look at the furnace."

Dad said, "Why?"

"Because my father always looks at the furnace before he goes to bed."

That must have rubbed Dad the wrong way. He was still a little profane in those days and he said, "The hell with the furnace!" So Mother went downstairs and checked the furnace herself, not knowing what she was looking for. Later that week she had someone come in to teach her all about it.

Our worst family disaster happened on a cold February night in 1919 when this division of labor between my parents didn't stick and Dad burned down the house. He was trying to break in a new houseman and said to Mother, "Carlo doesn't know how to build a fire. I'll show him." So he piled the fireplace high with kindling and wood and touched it off. An hour or so later I started wailing upstairs. I was only five and often cried after being put to bed, so Dad said, "Now, Mother, I'll settle that young man." He started up the stairs and heard me yelling, "I see a funny light in my room!" The fire was right outside the window: sparks from the chimney had set the whole shingle roof on fire. Mother never blamed Dad for that, even though the fire burned up all her heirlooms from Dayton.

Until I went to boarding school when I was fifteen, Mother was the biggest presence in my life. She was much more accessible than Father, and always made us feel protected and loved and wanted. I think she understood that at the root of my odd and mischievous behavior was a lack of self-esteem, because she was forever inventing ways to get me involved and interested in the world. When I joined the Boy Scouts, earning merit badges gave me a boost, and Mother was pretty deft at capitalizing on this civilizing influence. For instance, one day I decided to go for a cooking merit badge and she went with me out to the vegetable garden. I built a fire, got a couple of potatoes, and threw them in. She stayed right there with me, watching the whole procedure. It takes an hour, so we walked around a bit. Finally I took a black, charred potato out of the fire and broke it open. I didn't even have a spoon; I used a stick. Potatoes taste quite sweet baked that way. I gave her a piece. "Oh" she said, "Tom, it's wonderful." That was the beginning of my love of cooking.

The closer I got to my mother, the more upset I was at the way I thought Dad treated her. This was when IBM was at a critical stage, demanding a lot of Dad's attention. In his office he could press the button on his desk, a fellow would come in, Dad would say, "Send a letter," and boom, it would happen. When he wasn't thinking, he expected Mother to obey him in the same way. She found that hard to put up with, so in the years when Dad was most intense about his work, there was enormous tension in our household. I remember incessant arguments between them. The door to their bedroom would be closed but my brother and sisters and I would hear angry, muffled voices rising and falling. Father would be rude to her, and then half an hour later he'd give us a lecture about how we ought to be good to our mother. I never had the guts to say, "Then why aren't you?"

Father would sometimes act as though he'd completely forgotten how much he had depended on Mother in the early days of their marriage. He'd call from the city and say, "Now, Jeannette, I've asked all the district managers to come out tonight for a little supper." That would mean eight guests, and this news would be delivered at three in the afternoon. Mother, who didn't have nearly his stamina to begin with, would get physically fagged. He was also becoming active on the social scene in New York, and often pressed her to go with him to dinners or the opera. Another big source of strain was money. It was torture for Mother, as frugal as she was, to see the style in which they were living and the debts he was running up.

Then, after about ten years of strife, around the time I was fourteen and the other children scaled down to nine, Mother suddenly seemed to capitulate. This shocked me —I thought she'd stopped standing up for herself. But many years later she confided that, in fact, she had asked Dad for a divorce. "I told him I couldn't stand it any longer," she said.

This was terribly poignant for me to hear. I said, "What happened?"

"Tom, he looked so shocked, so upset, that I realized how deeply he loved me—and I never brought it up again."

After she made that conscious decision to preserve the marriage, she never complained. When a crowd of guests would suddenly arrive and she had no one to help in the kitchen, she'd simply smile and say, "The cook is off today, but we have some sandwiches and fruit."

Everybody seemed to get along better when we were away from Short Hills. Father and Mother were constantly rounding us up, along with any friends or cousins who might want to come, for trips to Washington, to the

seashore, to great exhibitions. Often we'd travel in a two-
or three-car caravan, and descend like a wild tribe on
relatives or IBM managers along the route. On weekends
we'd drive out to Dad's Oldwick farm, and in summer
we'd go to the Pocono Mountains or Maine, where Dad
would join us on weekends. Being on the road gave
Mother freedom that she lacked at home, and she loved
it. As for Dad, he had started out as a traveling man and
never really stopped. Throughout his life the simple motion of a car or train calmed him down and made him
less demanding.

In spite of the hundreds of thousands of miles they
covered, my parents chose to leave the pioneering of air
travel in our family to me. My lifelong passion for flying
began before I was even old enough to ride a bicycle. I
used to love our visits to Mother's family in Dayton,
because Dayton was the home of the Wright brothers and
the Army Air Corps had an airfield there. In that area,
airplanes were almost as common a sight as cars. I have
an old newspaper photograph of Mother and her sister
that bears the heading "The First Aerial Callers." It
shows the Kittredge girls posed not far from their country house with two spindly-legged army aviators who are
lolling against the framework of a stick-and-canvas con-
traption called a Wright Flyer. Aunt Helen was being
courted by an aviator named Major Kirby. They never
got married, but I thought he was tremendous because he
talked airplanes.

Dad became scared of airplanes during a Sunday out-
ing to a county fair in the early 1920s. We passed a field
where there was a Jenny, back from World War I, and a
pilot taking people up for five dollars. Since he'd spent so
many years in Dayton, it would have been odd if Dad
had never been curious enough to go up. He'd even met
the Wright brothers. So he bought a ticket and joined the
line. But as he stood there waiting, we kids started yap-
ping at him, "You promised to buy us ice cream!" Father
said we were right, and asked the flier if he could come
back in half an hour for his ride. By the time we came

back, the plane had crashed and three people had been killed.

He took that as an omen that he should never fly. I have to admit that in those days there was every reason for him not to. Before World War II airplanes were crashing all the time. Anyone who was a sportsman had to have an airplane, and often the plane would malfunction or he'd make a mistake, and he'd be killed. But Dad's superstition never made me hesitate. A year after the Jenny incident, a fellow announced with placards that he was going to land an airplane on a golf course near Short Hills. He would perform and then give rides for one dollar per minute. Father was having a district managers' meeting at our house, and I badgered those men privately and got a buck from each. Although Father was annoyed when he found out, he said patiently, "I'm not going to let you go up in that airplane. I think they're still getting them improved. But if you'll give these gentlemen their money back, we'll go see it." He took me over and paid the guy a couple of bucks to let me climb in the cockpit and feel the controls. After that I would sit in Mother's kitchen doing flight simulations using a broomstick and a board balanced under my feet as a rudder.

When Father had business to do in Europe, all of us went; and during my boyhood we made five long trips there. CTR accounting machines were sold in most countries by independent agents, but Father, convinced that Europe was going to be a big deal one day, disliked this arrangement. He gradually bought out the middlemen, bringing foreign sales under the company's direct control.

Europe had a special meaning in our family. It was the place where all of us could unbutton a little. In London, Mother would take us to the joke store near the Savoy Hotel to buy itching powder. Then she'd try to keep her face straight as we liberally sprinkled the chair of the fat wife of one of IBM's Scandinavian managers. Dad would make a show of admonishing us not to play hotel slot machines, lecturing about the evils of gambling—and then he'd play them himself.

It was in Europe that my parents finally let me fly. It had to be the greatest thrill of my entire childhood. In Paris in 1924, when I was ten, Dad took us to Le Bourget field and we walked around an air exhibition with thousands of people. I got more and more excited, listening to the roar of engines running up. They were selling rides in a converted French bomber, a great big hefty biplane called a Breguet. It was the same type of plane that the great French pilot and writer Antoine de Saint-Exupéry later used to start the first air mail line, from Toulouse to Dakar. It had only one engine but enough room in back to tuck in four seats. The Hancocks, a young couple traveling with us, wanted to go up, and I pleaded to go along. I'm sure Dad and Mother were worried, but they knew how much I wanted to. We bought three rides, and the Hancocks and I got in with one other passenger. Two sat backwards and two sat forwards. The whole cabin smelled of castor oil, then the best lubricant for difficult jobs. The pilot sat up above and forward, where we couldn't even see his legs.

As we taxied out, the engine, which was probably four hundred horsepower, just rumbled and stumbled. Then he opened it up to take off, and we were engulfed with noise. It seemed to take over, until there was no other sensation. We were rolling on grass, so the undercarriage was bumping pretty hard. Then suddenly everything except the noise stopped, and a terrific smoothness took over. I watched the ground fall away. We had big windows on both sides so we could see everything.

After we went around a few times we headed down. Then the engine noise dropped and was replaced by a singing. Few people today have ever heard that sound—it comes only from old biplanes with many wires between their wings that sing as the wind passes. To keep the engine clear, the pilot opened the throttle every once in a while. As the ground approached, the whistling got quieter and the tail was dropping and dropping. Finally we made a smooth landing and I could feel the wheels thumping on the grass again. I was overwhelmed. I knew airplanes killed people, but the sensation of freedom, the noise, the unseen bumps that pushed the airplane up and down, the ability to choose one's own angle of bank and make one's own decision to climb or descend—all these combined to give me a powerful desire to learn to fly.

I pleaded to go right back up. But I had to wait a few years before my second flight, again in Europe, in the fall of 1927. This time I actually went somewhere. I was wandering around a hotel lobby in Basel and saw an air schedule next to the desk. There was a four o'clock flight to Paris! My family was eating lunch nearby with a friend named Mrs. Mangan. I came racing in with this announcement, and before Father could send a negative signal Mrs. Mangan said, "Oh, how thrilling! I'll go with you!"

We bought tickets and flew. Everyone else was to follow by overnight train. Paris was about two hundred fifty miles away, and the flight took almost four hours. We arrived early enough in the evening for me to go to the movies. As it happened, they were showing *The Jazz Singer,* the first film with sound. In a single, fantastic day, I'd become the first Watson to travel by air and the first to see a talking picture.

CHAPTER 4

I never remember, when I was growing up, Father coming right out and saying, "I'd really like to have you follow me in this business." In fact, looking at me then, he probably found it hard to imagine a less likely successor. But I got it into my head that the old man wanted me to come into IBM, take it over, and run the whole deal. The very idea made me miserable. One day after school, when I was about twelve, I sat on a curb thinking about my father. What precipitated it I don't know, but by the time I got home I was in tears. My mother asked what was wrong and I said, "I can't do it. I can't go to work at IBM."

She said, "But nobody asked you to."

"Yeah, but I know Dad wants me to. And I just can't do it." She said I shouldn't worry and put her arms around me. When Dad came home Mother told him how I felt. He gently said to me that his own father had wanted him to become a lawyer and that I should do exactly what I wanted. From then on he was always offering me alternatives.

This happened at a time when everything was out of kilter for me, even more so than for most adolescents. I was tall and gangly and thin, having grown to a man's height much too fast. My father's power and success in the world were mushrooming just when I was trying subconsciously to match myself with him man-to-man. I was subject to terrible emotional lows that lasted weeks at a time.

No matter what he said about alternative careers, Dad's real hopes for me are obvious in a 1927 photograph of us. He and I are standing together, shoulder to shoulder, almost equal in height. We are dressed exactly alike, with heavy, somber suits, overcoats, and derbies. We were on our way to a sales convention in Atlantic City; I was thirteen, a little young for business clothes.

My first memory of IBM is from when I was five and Dad took me through the Dayton factory where we made scales. I remember the acrid metallic smell of the assembly line, and the smoke and noise of metal casting. From then on, Dad often brought me to IBM meetings, which were quite small in those days because the whole company was small. Sometimes the chauffeur would pick me up in Short Hills and take me to Dad's office downtown. This was in the early 1920s, before IBM started filling up buildings in midtown Manhattan. The company occupied a couple of floors near Wall Street, in the same building where Mr. Flint worked. Those rooms at 50 Broad Street seemed gloomy, because the receptionist sat in the center of the building. You'd step out of the elevator, go through a glass door, and there she was. There were no windows to be seen; some lights, but not very many.

Normally the receptionist would say, "Oh, hello, Tommy, are you looking for your father?" He had a corner office with an Oriental rug and a big mahogany desk that has belonged to me ever since he died. Around the room were a picture of Dad shaking hands with Nicholas Murray Butler, the head of Columbia University and Dad's first important friend in New York; a couple of medals Dad got for joining some society; a few mementos of his boyhood; and maybe a stone or two from faraway places for paperweights. The place smelled of cigars.

Usually I would make a beeline for the machine room, a few floors below. This was where they used punch-card machines to keep records of IBM's own sales network. In those days the network was pretty thin: in fact, the Los Angeles salesmen had to cover a region that stretched all the way to El Paso. Clerks would be shoving stacks of punch cards into tabulating machines and vertical sorters, and sometimes I'd accidentally knock the cards over and foul up their work. Keypunch machines produce terrific confetti—the tiny little rectangles of cardboard that result when you punch a hole in the card. Those little cutouts would collect at the punches and then would be sold back to paper manufacturers. But if there was a parade on Broadway, many flights below, the clerks would dump some of this stuff out the window. I loved to throw handfuls of it whenever I got the chance.

All sons at some point have the idea that their father is the most important man in the world. But that impression is hard to outgrow when your old man's photograph is in every office and everybody around is bowing and scraping and trying to ingratiate themselves with him. Everything he did left me feeling inconsequential by comparison. The worst was when he was doing something that he thought would make me happy. Once, knowing my interest in flying, he decided to introduce me to Charles Lindbergh, whom he didn't even know. This was soon after Lindbergh's transatlantic flight in 1927 and Dad bought tickets to a banquet in his honor. Dad led me right up to the dais and introduced himself as head of IBM, and then me. He had such astonishing brass. I think I stammered, "Congratulations."

In self-defense, I developed an internal streak of skepticism about my father's world. The first glimmer of this had come several years earlier, on the winter day in 1924 when IBM got its name. I was only ten at the time, still in knee pants. Father came home from work, gave Mother a hug, and proudly announced that the Computing-Tabulating-Recording Company henceforth would be known by the grand name International Business Machines. I stood in the doorway of the living room thinking, "*That* little outfit?"

Dad must have had in mind the IBM of the future. The one he actually ran was still full of cigar-chomping guys selling coffee grinders and butcher scales. That didn't stop him from trying to raise the tone as best he knew how. The top showrooms, like the one at 310 Fifth Avenue, always had Oriental rugs. I guess Dad thought linking Oriental rugs and meat scales was splendid, but I found it embarrassing.

While Dad was willing to delegate much of my upbringing to other people, he was the one who taught me
how to look and act like a gentleman. To him these were
among the most important skills in life, and he had
worked hard to master them. His favorite method was to
take me on trips—to upstate New York, for example,
where his family had lived, to see a relative or visit a
grave.

He knew all about railroads—I suppose he'd spent
hundreds of nights on trains. On the first such trip, when
I was about twelve, Dad showed me how to use the lad-
der to get to the upper berth, and how to button the
curtains for privacy. Then he took me into the men's
room. It was called the smoking room and had a long
bench. The men waiting to take their turns at the two or
three basins would sit, often just in an undershirt with
their suspenders down. Our train was rattling along and
Dad waited until all the others were gone. Then he said,
"Now Tom, this is a public room. Everyone who uses it
has to be careful, because the person coming after you
will judge you by how the place is left. Here's the way
you do it."

The basin was pretty clean when he stepped up to it.
He said, "I take a towel, get some water on it, and first
clean the thing all up so there are no whiskers or soap or
toothpaste or anything around it. And I clean the front
so there are no splashes there. I throw the towel away in
this receptacle, and now I start clean.

"I lather my face, I shave, I brush my teeth." I wandered off while he went through this fifteen-minute routine. He called me back when he was finished and said,
"Now here is the way you leave it." And he cleaned it up,
clean as a whistle. He said, "That's it. Then the next
fellow has the same chance you had."

I noticed he always tipped the porter on these trips.
On a trip to Chicago he tipped the man ten dollars, a hell
of a lot of money in those days. The porters would always
say, "Mr. Watson, sir, nice to see you," and it wasn't
until I noticed those tips that I figured it out.

I said, "Dad, that's an awful lot of money to give a Pullman car fellow."

"I do that for two reasons, Tom," he said. "First, that fellow has been up all night in his little cubicle and I feel sorry for him.

"The second reason is that there is a whole class of people in the world who are in a position to poor-mouth you unless you are sensitive to them. They are the head-waiters, Pullman car conductors, porters, and chauffeurs. They see you in an intimate fashion and can really knock off your reputation."

These trips always seemed as if they might be the start of a warm and intimate friendship between Dad and me. But when we got home Dad would always become aloof again. I could never understand why he retreated. Maybe he really was too old to remember what it was like to be a boy, or maybe just too busy.

When he couldn't spend time with me himself, my father would farm me out to an employee. Most often this would be his personal secretary, Mr. Phillips. George Phillips, who started life as an accountant, ended up as president and then vice chairman of IBM after World War II, during Father's declining years. Phillips was the perfect man Friday. He first went to work for Dad in 1918 and had my father's complete confidence. If Father had a poor aunt he was sending money to, Phillips knew all about that aunt, where to send the money, how much, and so on. Phillips was on his way to making a large fortune in IBM stock, but he never owned a car until 1926. When he decided to get one, he went to Dad and said, "Mr. Watson, I have enough money to buy a car but I would like your permission before I do it." Dad used to make Phillips take me sightseeing—to the Statue of Liberty, to Fraunces Tavern, to the Brooklyn Bridge. As soon as I was old enough, Phillips taught me how to shoot. Hunting was possibly the only enjoyment Phillips got out of life, and we went shooting together until he died.

• • •

Most of the time my father praised me, telling me what a great fellow I was going to be. But as I look back, I think he must have been awfully worried. Around the time I was thirteen, I began to suffer recurring depressions so deep that no one knew where they were going to lead. The first one started with an attack of asthma. Just as I was beginning to feel a little better, all my willpower seemed to evaporate. I didn't want to get out of bed. I had to be urged to eat; I had to be urged to take a bath. Such behavior today would probably be seen as a symptom of clinical depression, a serious mood disorder that causes a lot of suicides. But at the time my parents had all sorts of doctors in to see me, and no one knew what the problem was. The best doctor we had said he was sure the trouble was connected to my being an adolescent, but he didn't know what to prescribe.

After about thirty days I recovered. But six months later, the same thing happened. For the next six years, until I was nineteen and started college, twice a year I'd be severely depressed. Unless you've had such a depression, you can't imagine what you go through. The fear is totally irrational, your whole thinking process goes awry, and everything you see seems unreal. I would look, for instance, at a knot in a ceiling beam. For some reason I'd tell myself, "That's a plain board. There are no knots in that beam. I'm going crazy, I see a knot." Then I'd slip from that stage, of thinking I was going crazy, to a stage where I didn't know what was going on around me. I couldn't read a book and couldn't talk to anybody. When the doctor came I would give him one-word answers.

Mother had the idea that if she got me to exercise I'd come out of it. So she bought me a medicine ball. I remember forcing myself out onto the driveway, having peculiar thoughts and wanting to lie down. Meanwhile the chauffeur would be throwing me this ball, back and forth, back and forth. Nothing helped, and I was afraid I'd never feel right again. These times must have been rough on my family, especially my brother Dick. He looked up to me, and I'm sure it was confusing to see me become suddenly helpless. I got horribly depressed at a camp in Nova Scotia where he and I both went one summer. I was barely functioning, getting up for camp activities but going back to my bunk as often as possible. Dick was only about nine, but I felt so lonely and desperate that I finally took him aside and tried to tell him what I was going through. I said, "Stick around, help me, and if I die be sure to tell Mother and Dad that it's not their fault."

CHAPTER 5

The crash of the stock market when I was fifteen seemed to fit right in with my periodic feelings of gloom. Two Short Hills men committed suicide and the community was pretty shaken. Father's own fortune was hurt too, of course, but he managed to keep the damage on paper. After the suicides he made a gesture that I still admire today: he took over the school bills for the dead men's children.

When the Depression really began to bite in 1932 and IBM's stock slumped, the company's profits stayed quite high. So did Dad's income, since it was pegged to the profits. Word that he was still solvent got around, and neighbors would come at night to ask if he would lend money. I suppose he gave a hundred thousand dollars to people who were caught short. He never turned anybody away, even those he didn't know well. I think it bothered him that several people in Short Hills never paid him back after they had money again.

Like many businessmen, Dad thought the downturn was temporary. He would have applauded if he had been present when President Hoover declared a few weeks after the crash, "Any lack of confidence in the economic future or the strength of business in the United States is foolish." Dad believed that renewed prosperity was just around the corner, and his answer to the Depression was to expand production. In hard times, he saw opportunity. When there weren't enough sales to keep the factories occupied, he ordered the warehouses filled with spare parts to be ready when demand picked up. He urged the sales force to sell harder and he hired more salesmen. Years later he loved to tell about visiting an art gallery and running into Jim Rand, the head of Remington

Rand, IBM's chief competitor in the tabulating machine business. This was in the very depths of the Depression, 1933, and Rand must have thought Dad was losing his grip.

He said to my father, "Well, Tom, are you still hiring salesmen?"

Dad said, "Yes, I am."

"That's amazing!" Rand said, shaking his head. "Businesses are laying people off all over, and you're hiring salesmen. That's something."

"Jim, I'm getting along in years," said my dad. "You know I'm almost sixty now. A lot of things happen to men at that critical age. Some of them get to drinking too much. Some of them are interested in girls. But my weakness is hiring salesmen, and I'm just going to keep doing that."

In any other business he might have ended up bankrupt. But as far as IBM was concerned, he was right—and lucky besides. IBM more than doubled in size during the New Deal. When the National Recovery Act passed in early 1933, businesses all of a sudden had to supply the federal government with information in huge and unprecedented amounts. Government agencies needed IBM machines by the hundreds too—it was the only way to manage Roosevelt's welfare, price control, and public works programs. Social Security, which was enacted in 1935, made Uncle Sam IBM's biggest customer. One of the few things you could do to keep from getting swamped was call IBM. The vital statistics of the whole country went onto punch cards.

While my father was achieving phenomenal success at IBM, I barely made it through high school. It took me three schools and six years before I finally graduated at age nineteen. Even before I started, Dad suspected that I was going to have trouble, and decided to keep me close to home. My friends went away to boarding school, but he insisted on enrolling me at Carteret Academy, an old, dingy place only twelve miles from our house. For two years I settled into an odd and lonely existence. I'd com-

mute to Carteret every day, often starting out on the
same train as Dad, and take another train back at night,
barely speaking to anyone.

Since I was a failure academically, I longed for some
other kind of recognition. I went out for all the sports,
but while I was skinny and taller than most other kids, I
was no athlete. My eye-hand coordination was terrible,
so I hated baseball. I tried out as a goalie in hockey—
although it was very exciting to have people shooting
pucks at me from every direction, I didn't make the first
team. In football I was also pushed quickly onto the second string. The coach, Balky Boyson, was impressed with
me—not because of anything I did on the field but just
because I showed up. He knew that I faced a long commute home after practice.

The difficulties I was having seemed to bring out a
warmth and gentleness in my father that were not otherwise obvious. He knew I was drifting, but he never gave
up. He was constantly telling me that childhood wasn't
the happiest stage of life and that I had much to look
forward to. He said, "No matter what happens, it is a
time of great change and nobody coasts through it without lots of problems. There is no need to worry about it."
Sometimes he would bring up my bad grades. He'd say,
"I wish you were better in school, and I'm sure you do,
but at some point, something will catch hold and you are
going to be a great man." I always thought, "That's impossible."

Dad became more and more tolerant of the scrapes I'd
get into. Not long after I started at Carteret I teamed up
with another boy and secretly bought a Model T from a
schoolmate. Neither of us was old enough to drive and I
don't know how we got the license plate. We were driving
around Short Hills one day when Father came home
from work unexpectedly and caught us with the car. We
saw him coming and tried to sneak away by cutting
across a neighbor's field. But Dad saw us and flagged us
down.

"Very interesting car," he said, walking all around it.

"I used to have trouble with these cars. But very interesting. Do you own this car?"

My friend started to say, "Well, not exactly, Mr. Watson," but we finally admitted we did. He asked where we kept it and we said in the backyard of Carteret. "Well, if I were you," he said, "I'd take it back there and sell it or get rid of it. That car will get you in trouble." He could have made a big to-do, but he didn't, and we sold the car a few days later.

It was a big event when Dad let me transfer to boarding school. I spent a year at a place called Morristown, and then moved on to the Hun School in Princeton. I wanted to be a Princeton man, and by going to Hun, which had close ties to the university, I figured I was as good as in.

Hun was filled with playboys. I'd see them with the hip flask, the raccoon coat, the babe on their arm, driving the Stutz Bearcat roadster like hell down the street. It was a style of life for which I felt to some degree qualified. It meant that studies were not particularly important, that you had a little more money than the average fellow, that you were always out with the girls, and that you owned a car. Mine was a really hot-looking black and red Chrysler that I got on my seventeenth birthday.

Prohibition was still on. Speakeasies didn't monitor the age of their customers much, and I used to take girls dancing at the Blue Hills Plantation outside of Short Hills. My luck with girls was at best uneven. Part of my trouble might have been that I didn't drink, which was another sign of Dad's influence. I did try marijuana once, however. In those days nobody knew much about drugs, although people did say that the black bands played wonderful jazz because they smoked a kind of cigarette called reefers. These supposedly stretched out time so much that the musicians could play eighth notes instead of quarter notes. A racy guy at Hun by the name of Moore came around with a couple of reefers for sale. I bought them with another guy named Tom. Today he's a pretty staid fellow around New York, and I never greet him without saying, "Remember the time we smoked marijuana cigarettes?" It really irritates him.

We locked ourselves in Tom's room and each smoked a whole reefer. At the end I honestly felt no different from when I started. Neither did Tom. I looked at him and said, "I don't feel any different at all, do you?" And he said, "Not at all." Then he began to laugh. I began laughing too—it was uncontrollable laughter—and we both realized this was abnormal as hell. We thought we'd walk it off so we went out in the hall. I remember feeling so tall that it was hard to keep my balance, and I ran into a wall. We were so afraid we'd get caught in this condition that we decided it would be prudent to sleep the drugs off, and that's what we did.

My performance at Hun was no more impressive than at my first two high schools: academically I was still a zero. But I had one great success, the first of my entire life. The day I arrived at Hun a fellow told me, "We've got a crew here, they use the Princeton boathouse." Rowing out of the Princeton boathouse seemed exciting to me. As soon as I got down there and made the first crew, things started to pick up.

Rowing in a crew is a pretty simple motion. I wasn't good at throwing or hitting, but this involved pushing hard with the legs—I've got strong legs—and pulling hard with the arms. It got you out on the water and I love water. I was mad for that sport and all the next year worked hard at it. The crew during my final year was good enough to qualify for the international regatta in Henley, England. We got our parents to put up a couple of thousand dollars—a round-trip steerage ticket in those days cost only one hundred dollars—and the whole crew went over.

While I was engrossed in crew, Dad and his friends were trying hard to get me accepted to Princeton. I had taken the college admission tests a year before and got very uneven scores. I was at or below the passing level in most subjects, but had the highest mark in New Jersey in physics. I loved the subject; my teacher gave vivid demonstrations on such things as how pulleys make lifting easy. When the results came in this teacher said to me, "You're a funny guy. Most of your marks are lousy, so how did you score so well in this?" I couldn't explain it. I just have a sense of why mechanical things do what they do.

The man to whom Dad turned for leverage was Benjamin Wood, a professor of educational research at Columbia University. Wood was a strange genius, a self-educated Texan who was the pioneer of standardized college entry tests. He and Dad discovered each other in the 1920s, when Wood was desperately looking for a machine that could help score and process hundreds of thousands of tests. As soon as Dad heard what Wood had to say, he supplied Columbia with free equipment by the truckload. Wood believed that anything of value could be quantified and that numbers were going to play an increasingly important role in civilization—music to the ears of a tabulating machine maker.

It is ironic that the great advocate of quantitative testing should be called upon to write a recommendation for somebody with grades and test scores like mine. I barely knew Wood but I think I would have liked him. His letter to Dean Radcliffe Heermance, the Princeton director of admissions, was very dignified and at the same time warm and generous. Here is how he tackled the question of my grades:

In mind and character I do not hesitate to place him in the highest ten per cent of secondary school graduates. I am not acquainted with his high school record, but my inference would be that his strictly academic record would not adequately indicate his real mental capacity and intellectual originality and persistence. His is the type of mind that, in my experience, would not be adequately or justly measured by the ordinary tests and examinations used for college entrance, regardless of how high or low his marks may be.

The letter didn't work, but it must have gratified my father, because a copy of it was still among his papers when he died.

Dad went personally to plead my case with Dean Heermance during my final spring at Hun. When he came back, all he said was that it wasn't likely that I'd get in. Not until years later did he tell me what happened at that meeting. The dean laid my records from Morristown and Hun on the desk and said to Father, "Mr. Watson, I am looking at your son's record and he is a predetermined failure."

Not knowing this, I was everlastingly hopeful. I told my father that my final grades from Hun would show great improvement. When I got back from Henley, I joined Dad and the rest of our family at the big summerhouse he owned by then in Camden, Maine. My marks were waiting for me—I still have them somewhere. A couple of them were good, and three were bad. Finally I had to admit that my chances for college that fall seemed pretty slim.

Two mornings later Dad had his big Packard touring car in front of the house. I said, "What's the car for?"

"You and I are taking a trip. We're going to look at colleges. There must be some college we can find that will accept you with your marks." This was just like Dad. I can see it now from his point of view. When something had to be done he'd do it.

I was deeply in love with a girl there in Maine and didn't want to be away from Camden very long. So I immediately thought of an acquaintance who went to Brown University in Rhode Island. I said, "Why don't we go to Brown?"

We drove to Providence, checked into the Biltmore Hotel, Dad called the admissions office, and up we went the next morning. He said to the admissions officer, "I'm Thomas Watson, I run the IBM company, and my son would like to consider coming to Brown. By the way, who is the president of Brown?"

The admissions guy said, "Clarence Barbour."

"That's very interesting," said Dad. "He was my pastor when I lived in Rochester, New York." In those days Brown's charter required that the university president be a minister.

We went to Clarence Barbour's office, said hello, and Barbour got somebody to show us around the campus. When we returned, the admissions officer was looking at my record. He said, "He's not very good but we'll take him."

CHAPTER 6

The girl I wanted to get back to in Maine was Isabel Henry. I wanted to marry her, even though I was only nineteen and had yet to start college. Loving this girl was the only deep attachment I had until five years later, when I met the woman who would be my wife. Isabel was socially prominent, two years older than I, and already going out with a wealthy guy who had just graduated from Harvard, the very handsome John Ames. I met her with the help of an impetuous blond-headed fellow named Conway Pendleton, a friend from the Hun School whom I'd invited to Camden that summer.

Conway and I were at a dance at the golf club one night when Isabel and Ames turned up. Everybody stopped and looked at them when they came in. She was the loveliest girl I'd ever seen. She had blond hair, dark eyebrows, a square face, and wonderful carriage—she walked with her shoulders back. Ames looked pretty impressive in a black dinner coat, a white shirt, a black tie, and white flannel pants. To me they were high society, way up out of reach. But my friend Pendleton cut right in on them. I couldn't wait to get him off the dance floor and debrief him. "What was she like, Conway? What was she like?" I said.

"Oh hell, Tom, she's just another girl! She's great, a lot of fun."

Isabel's family was a power unto itself in that summer community. They were from Philadelphia and lived in a different way from what I had ever seen. Isabel's grandfather had bought a small peninsula jutting out into Penobscot Bay and had turned it into a private compound for all the cousins. Isabel's mother was a Biddle. Their house was modest looking outside but very cosmopolitan inside. I noticed lots of foreign magazines around. They played backgammon, which I'd never heard of before.

I got Conway to introduce me to Isabel and waited impatiently until John Ames left town. Then I began to court her. We saw each other on and off for four or five weeks, and finally I put my arms around her, kissed her, and said, "Isabel, I love you."

She said, "I love you too, Tommy. God knows I've tried not to, but I do."

I should have started worrying right then. Instead I went home with my heart singing and couldn't get to sleep. I began to see her all the time. Isabel's father was a nice guy, very intelligent, but subdued. Mrs. Henry ran the roost. They'd invite me out overnight on their yacht or to dinner at their house. At the table, Mrs. Henry would start cutting me down. She'd be describing some garden party and say, "The Lionel Smiths were there . . ." and then, turning to me, "Of course you wouldn't know them." I'd leave those dinners with my tail between my legs.

Father was delighted with Isabel: he thought she was a queenly woman and that the Biddles were a great family. But if Isabel and I had gotten married, it would have been a disaster. Mrs. Henry would never have let up on me. In fact, I don't think Isabel saw much ability in me either. We were out riding one day when she said, "I have money and you do too. I don't think you ought to work. We ought to just pool our funds and travel."

For two years we were very close. She lived with her parents and we dated while I went to Brown. The crisis finally came when I was twenty-one, in the summer of 1935. I picked up Isabel in Boston, intending to drive to Maine. When we got as far as Rockport, we came over a hill and there was a fork in the road. She said, "Tommy, let's not stop at Camden. Let's drive right to Montreal and get married." It was very tempting. But then I thought about who I'd be alienating—her family and my family. I said, "I don't think we should do that. Your family would be forever annoyed. My mother would be upset."

So we drove on into Camden. A few weeks later, Isabel told me it was all over. I was terribly hurt. I went back to Brown and stayed away from eligible girls for more than a year. Mrs. Henry succeeded in getting her daughters married to appropriate men and lived to be about ninety-five. She was always wealthy and spent a month each fall at the Ritz in Paris, buying her gowns. Many years later I ran into her there. I walked down the hall and said, "Mrs. Henry, how are you?"

She said, "Tommy Watson, you've become terribly important. You must come to Philadelphia. I'll give you a dinner."

If you'd visited Brown University in 1933, the effects of the Depression would have been obvious. The campus looked run-down and a good number of students seemed undernourished. Many of them commuted by bus from places like Pawtucket, because they couldn't afford to live at school.

However, I fell in with the minority of students who had the money to behave as if the 1920s had never stopped roaring. I belonged to the Psi Upsilon fraternity, which was known for its fun-loving ways. Every night of the week our crowd would head downtown to drink and dance at the Biltmore Hotel. We had apartments, cars, and a pretty fast life. On weekends we drove off to ski resorts in Vermont or to Smith or Vassar for girls.

Living this way, I was even more at odds with myself than most aimless undergraduates. I was behaving like a playboy, but I could see that the country was in an economic mess. I felt anxious to make something of myself, yet unable to lift a finger to try. I was a rich kid among other rich kids, but my friends' fathers were Republicans while mine was an outspoken New Dealer.

Dad and I were not at all close during those years. At age sixty he was just beginning to gain international recognition and was busy with social and business commitments. Every few weeks he would write me a long moralizing letter filled with the same slogans he'd post on the walls of IBM sales conventions: "Do right," for example, or "We are a part of all we have met." I'd read these things and throw them away.

I had plenty of money for fooling around. My monthly allowance was three hundred dollars—about double the income of the average American family in those years. Out of that all I had to pay for was my college bills and my clothes. Dad never asked for an accounting. When we saw each other he'd say, "You're probably a little short, son," and pass me an extra hundred dollars. I spent every nickel. But oddly, I never knew if I was really rich. I had a trust fund consisting, naturally, of IBM stock, but Dad never told me how much was in it. Each year his accountant would come around and have me sign income tax forms that were blank. He'd make an excuse that he hadn't had time yet to fill them out. This kept up not only through college but ten years beyond, until I was a grown man with children of my own.

My first marks came in after three months, just before Christmas of 1933. I got a phone call asking me to report to Dean Sam Arnold, whom I'd met with my dad. Dean Arnold was fat and had a nice, round, smiling face. "Well now, Mr. Watson," he said, "these marks are not very good. It doesn't look promising for you in college. You've got to do better." Serious talk, but with a twinkle in his eye. The dean and I had at least one visit like this each semester. I was a terrible student but he tolerated me. Dad, however, put virtually no pressure on me to perform in school. Later, when I asked him why he let me stay in college with the horrible grades I was producing, he said, "I thought it would be better for you to be unmotivated in an orderly situation than unmotivated and allowed to create your own situation."

I had barely gotten to Brown when I fulfilled my great dream: finally I learned to fly. In September of my freshman year I soloed after just five and a half hours of instruction, which must be some kind of record. What a feeling! I was good at flying, instantly good. I plowed everything I could, mentally, physically, and financially, into that mad pursuit, and gained a lot of self-confidence. Sometimes I'd get out of bed in the middle of the night, drive to the airport, and fly for an hour. The airport managers were pretty reckless with the students—they didn't object if we flew in the dark. That first winter my biggest adventure was to join the Red Cross airlift of food to Nantucket Island. New England was having a long siege of cold weather, and the Nantucket harbor froze solid for the first time in more than a decade. For a while the only way to get food to the island was by air. I picked up several loads of supplies in New Bedford and took them across.

Dad never complained when he found out I was flying. I suppose both of us realized subconsciously that airplanes were something we were bound to differ on. He simply passed along some advice from Lindbergh, with whom he was now friends: " 'Tell your son never to fly when he's tired.' "

By the time I arrived at Brown, Father and Mother had moved from Short Hills to New York, where they joined the city's elite. During the social season, from October to May, their lives became a regular round-robin: Monday night at the opera with a few other couples, maybe two dinner parties and a charity banquet during the week, and then, every few weeks, an IBM dinner. Father wanted to know everyone important in New York, and eventually he succeeded. In the early 1930s he became head of the Merchants Association of New York and began socializing with people like John D. Rockefeller Jr. and Henry Luce. He joined the Explorers Club and got to know Lowell Thomas and Admiral Richard Byrd, whose expedition to the South Pole Dad helped underwrite; Byrd named a mountain range in Antarctica the Watson Escarpment. He was around my parents' house a lot. I was awed by him, and impressed that the first man to fly over the North Pole seemed genuinely to like my father, not just to cultivate him for his money.

Dad loved to collect autographed pictures of important people and kept them on a grand piano in the living room. There was one of Charlie Schwab, the great steel man, that said, "To Tom Watson, master business machine." There was also a picture of Mussolini, from the days when Mussolini was still well thought of, at least in some quarters—it disappeared as soon as Dad became aware of the viciousness of Italian Fascism.

My father's most influential friend while I was in college was none other than President Roosevelt. Dad contributed money and advice to Roosevelt's 1932 presidential campaign, and that earned him access to the White House after Roosevelt beat Hoover in a landslide. Dad later told me that his first visit to the president practically destroyed his welcome. It was the summer of 1933 and the Merchants Association was alarmed at the wage and production controls Roosevelt was trying to impose on business under the National Recovery Act. So Dad volunteered to go to Washington and ask the president to ease up.

He greeted Roosevelt and said, "Mr. President, I'm here to tell you that the people in New York think you're going too far with regulation. Business should be well regulated, but we also believe it should be well treated. If you go much further, you will decimate what little there is left of business, and we'll end up with nothing."

Roosevelt shook his head and said, "Look here, Tom. You go back and tell your banker and businessman friends that I don't have time to worry about their future. I am trying to save this great nation. I think I am going to be successful. If I am successful, I'll save them along with everyone else."

These words turned Dad around completely. He saw the monumental job Roosevelt had on his hands and wanted to help. It was the last time Dad ever spoke for the conservative side. He used to tell me: "The average businessman's opinion of what is right for the country is almost always wrong."

Later that year Dad put himself back in Roosevelt's good graces by taking a public stand in favor of opening diplomatic relations with Russia. Roosevelt was getting criticized for being soft on the Bolsheviks, and Dad was one of the few business leaders to back him up. After that he and the president grew quite friendly. Once or twice a month Dad would send him suggestions—sometimes solicited, sometimes not. At times Roosevelt's men would even ask for Dad's appointment schedule, in case the president needed to contact him in a hurry.

I saw many of the letters that President Roosevelt wrote back to Dad. Father was so proud of these that he would keep them in his pocket and show them around. Often Dad and Mother went to Hyde Park for tea, and on a couple of occasions they were invited to spend the night at the White House. That was a big event in our family.

Roosevelt was appreciative enough of Dad's support that in the mid-1930s he offered to make him secretary of commerce or even ambassador to the Court of St. James's —the job Joseph P. Kennedy subsequently got. Father said no to both offers because he didn't want to leave IBM. Instead he served, unofficially, as Roosevelt's representative in New York. If, for example, Gustaf, the crown prince of Sweden, was due to visit the United States, one of Roosevelt's aides could call Father and say, "Wouldn't you like to give a luncheon for Gustaf?"

All Father had to do was press a button. He had a whole department that did nothing but set up company dinners and other functions. They'd produce a guest list, and between one hundred and two hundred people would be splendidly entertained at the Union Club, all at IBM's expense. Dad saw this as a smart and dignified way to publicize the company, refine our top executives—and help the president. Cardinal Spellman would be on hand to give the blessing. There would be a dais, several tables with magnificent centerpieces, and a menu with crossed American and Swedish flags on the front and a description of the guest of honor. I'm sure the menus alone cost seventy-five cents each. Dad hosted a number of these lunches for visiting dignitaries. Roosevelt once said: "I handle 'em in Washington, and Tom handles 'em in New York." Dad was very flattered by that.

CHAPTER 7

I was a college junior in 1936 when the government released a list of the leading salaries in America and Dad's name was right at the top. He was making more money than even Will Rogers: $365,000 a year. Newspapers nicknamed him the Thousand-Dollar-A-Day-Man and he was denounced as the Captain Kidd of Industry and the Last of the Robber Barons. Dad got really upset at that. He felt his salary reflected the value he was generating for IBM's stockholders; in fact, the company was doing so well that every few years Dad made a point of having the board adjust his percentage of the profits *downward,* so that his pay did not become even more spectacular. Being the son of the Thousand-Dollar-A-Day-Man didn't bother me at all. I was still trying to get over Isabel, and when the stories about Dad appeared, a lot of girls suddenly found me more interesting than before.

From my vantage point, both Roosevelt and the Depression seemed remote. Except for telling me over and over that Roosevelt was a hero, Dad rarely discussed politics with me. But his liberal principles gradually rubbed off, and I began to develop a sense of social justice. The more I thought about the federal relief programs, the better they struck me. By 1936 I was getting into arguments with members of my fraternity who wanted Alf Landon for President. Then, at the beginning of Roosevelt's second term, I went to Cuba with some of my fraternity brothers for spring vacation. We took a cruise ship from New York and had a tremendous time. Havana offered every kind of vice, and if you wanted to raise hell, that was the place to do it. But when I got home I began thinking it was awful for the Cubans to have their country turned into an amusement park for rich Americans.

New Deal values weren't the only thing I picked up from Dad. Somehow, through his moralizing, his example, and his impressive tolerance for my misbehavior, the old gentleman got to me. Sometime around my sophomore year at Brown I started learning how to police myself.

My roommate that year was an interesting fellow from Pittsburgh with a very wealthy father. His name was David Ignatius Bartholomew McCahill III. I called him Iggy. We had an apartment on Waterman Street, a sort of half-cellar, and we were carousing and staying out late with every girl in town. Iggy really didn't give a damn. Maybe his father didn't mind if he flunked out. At any rate, Iggy was wild: he had a Great Dane that he didn't want to bother feeding, so he bought a meal ticket from the greasy-spoon cafeteria at the end of the block and tied it under the dog's collar. Whenever the dog was hungry it would trot down to the cafeteria and paw the door. Somebody would feed the dog a hamburger and punch the ticket for two bits. That caused quite a stir in the neighborhood. Some people said the meal ticket ought to be taken from the dog and given to a poor student.

Toward the middle of sophomore year, I had another of my visits with Dean Arnold, who said, "This time you're really headed out the door. I like your father and I like you. I'm sorry to see you go."

"I'm not a great student," I said, "but I don't want to get kicked out."

He said, "You'd better knuckle down."

I went to Iggy and told him, "I can't live here any more, because I've got to stay in college." He understood. He went on to flunk out that January. I took a single room in a dormitory and really tried hard. But exam time was coming and I knew I would flunk. Instead, I developed a pain in my right side that turned out to be appendicitis. Getting operated on gave me a chance to postpone taking the exams by six weeks, so I was able to study and pass.

During that same period I wrestled with the question of alcohol. Drinking was a charged subject in our family, going back to when my parents first met by not touching their wine. Dad never served liquor in the house during Prohibition, and his attitude made drinking seem sinful. He avoided alcohol like he avoided airplanes. Once Mother was trying to give him a dose of castor oil. She had a way of making it less revolting by mixing it with soda, lemon juice, and whiskey. Dad got the stuff right up to his mouth, then put it down on the basin and said, "I'd rather not do that, Jeannette." He washed the glass out, poured in straight castor oil, and drank it down.

At IBM, drinking was taboo, and the repeal of Prohibition in December 1933 made no difference at all. The official policy was that employees did not drink during the workday and that no liquor was allowed at IBM gatherings or on IBM property. The unofficial policy was that excessive drinking, even done on your own time, could ruin your chances of promotion. In Endicott, our factory town, the saying was that a prudent IBM man would draw his shades before having a cocktail with his wife. Father did nothing to dispel this myth, although I don't think he ever meant to intrude on people's private lives. He just wanted IBM to be beyond reproach. But his subordinates concluded he was averse to all merrymaking, and they sometimes got carried away in pressing that view on the employees.

It's not surprising that I preferred spending the holidays away from home while I was in college. I'd go home for Christmas Day, then the rest of the time I'd visit my fraternity brothers and their families. One night just before New Year's of 1935, some of us were drinking beer at a country club in Scranton, Pennsylvania. I was twenty years old. One glass led to another and the drinks seemed to improve my dancing, so I had a marvelous evening.

The next day I had a crisis of conscience. On my way back to New York I began agonizing over my gaiety and my father's feelings about alcohol. I felt so guilty that I decided to confess to Dad. Later that day I took some difficult steps into the library of our apartment where he was sitting. "Dad," I said, "I want to talk about something." I outlined the previous evening, which hadn't really been anything more than a few beers and a lot of fun.

Dad must have found my confession very reassuring. He shook my hand and said, "Thank you very much for telling me, son. Can you sit down for a few minutes?" Then he said, "I tried a few beers when I was young, and a few beers led to stronger stuff, and it never really worked out for me." Later I heard a story that, to my knowledge, he never told anyone, not even my mother. It came from an old friend of his. When Dad had gone to Buffalo at age nineteen to seek his fortune, his first job had been like the one he'd left behind in Painted Post: selling sewing machines off the back of a wagon, this time for a manufacturer called Wheeler and Wilcox. One day Dad went into a roadside saloon to celebrate a sale and had too much to drink. When the bar closed, he found out that his entire rig—horse, buggy, and samples—had been stolen. Wheeler and Wilcox fired him and dunned him for the lost property. Word of this got around, of course, and it took Dad more than a year to find another steady job. This anecdote never made it into IBM lore, which is too bad, because it would have helped explain Father to the tens of thousands of people who had to follow his rules. At the time he must have felt as though his life was over. I don't know how much Dad drank up until then, but losing his wagon and his sewing machines was enough to put him off liquor for the rest of his life.

My father began to exercise a profound influence on me, something like the way religion affects some people. I'd go out night after night with pretty girls, dancing and having some drinks. But after about a week of this, I'd start to sense him. Maybe he was four thousand miles away, but I'd feel him like the keel of a boat, pulling me back upright again. I never exactly rushed back to my room to start studying, but I'd take a new tack of trying to live better.

My poor performance at school made it hard for me to see what I was going to amount to. But gradually I reached the conclusion that I might do all right if I worked the whole spectrum of things I was reasonably good at, mainly having to do with people. I knew how to turn down a drink, how to keep myself well turned out, how to show respect toward older people. To some degree I was copying Dad. He wasn't well educated, but he had assimilated enough knowledge of the world that his lack of formal learning was never a handicap. So I began to work hard at making and keeping friends. I learned to focus on the other person during a conversation and to ask myself constantly, "Am I out of line with this fellow? Am I doing right by him or am I offending in some way?" The friends I made in college are still my friends today.

When senior year rolled around I flirted with the idea of dropping out of school to fool with airplanes full time. A friend and I had a little aerial photography business. But I was afraid of what might happen to me if I went entirely out on my own, and I said to myself, "I've already put in three years—I might as well graduate." I took all the gut courses I could find and made a mighty effort to pass. In the end, however, I owed my graduation to Dean Arnold. He must have decided, "This guy is improving a bit. Best give him a diploma and wish him well." Twenty years later I endowed several fellowships at Brown in Arnold's honor.

During my senior year I also began to have surprisingly prudent thoughts about life after graduation. I still had no idea what I wanted to do, except that I thought I needed the discipline that a job could provide. Only one solution seemed possible. I called up Dad and asked, "How do you go about getting a job at IBM?"

No doubt my father privately rejoiced, although he also may have been wondering what kind of employee he was getting. He quickly arranged for me to start as a sales trainee the following October. The prospect of my working at IBM also inspired Dad to write me even more letters than usual. For my part, I stopped throwing them away and I still have a handful today. One of my favorites is a five-pager from December 1936. He was thinking about moral lessons all the time, and he could not write a letter without giving a lecture. This one was meant to inspire me to pass my remaining courses and graduate:

> . . . always remember life is not as complex as many people would have you think. And the older you grow, the more you will realize that success and happiness depend on a very few things. I list the important assets and liabilities as follows. [Here he drew a line down the middle of the page, and wrote in two columns:]

Liabilities	Assets
Reactionary Ideas!	Vision
Love of money!	Unselfishness
Unwholesome companions!	Love
Lax character!	Character (Good)
Lack of love for others!	Good manners
False friends	Friendship (Real)
	Pride in Record

I had always disliked hearing such stuff, but it now seemed pretty well intentioned.

Many of our letters dealt with our summer plans. The summer of 1937 was shaping up as a big one for the Watsons. Father had been appointed president of the International Chamber of Commerce and was going to Europe to accept the honor, taking Mother and my sisters with him. He had been invited to meet the king of England on the way there. Dick was getting his diploma from boarding school, and big things were in store for me too. I got my first unsolicited job offer, from a journalist friend of Dad's named Herbert Houston. He was an expert on Japan and had been engaged by the directors of the 1939 World's Fair to make a trip to the Orient selling pavilion space. He wrote to ask if I would be his secretary for the summer. I was delighted by this offer and flattered that someone had thought of me for a job that was going to involve "hard travel and hard work," as Houston said. I gladly canceled plans for a sailing trip with my fraternity friends and agreed to join Houston in Berlin, which was where the International Chamber of Commerce was going to meet at the end of June. We would watch Dad get installed as president and set out for the Far East from there, via Moscow and the Trans-Siberian railroad.

One consequence of all these events was that my parents missed my graduation and Dick's because they had to leave for England. As a family we Watsons put great stock in ceremonial occasions, and all of us were upset by this, Dad more than anyone else, I think. But there was nothing to be done. So on commencement day I collected my degree alone, with only the beaming, round face of Dean Arnold looking on. I joined some friends and their families for photographs and then, afterward, drove to Hotchkiss to watch Dick's commencement. I was glad to serve as an older brother for once, by making sure Dick did not feel entirely like an orphan.

CHAPTER 8

W
hile I was on the boat to Europe my father proudly attended the first morning reception given by George VI, the new king of England. I have a photograph of Dad striding across the courtyard of Buckingham Palace decked out for this event. He is wearing civil court dress, with knee breeches, black stockings and patent-leather shoes, and on his chest is a row of medals that had been given to him by various countries where IBM did business. T. J. Watson, the former sewing machine salesman, had arrived.

Meanwhile I'd met a beautiful woman on the way over, a model from Chicago who was on a tour with her mother. This girl just swept me off my feet. As we pulled into Southampton I went to tell her good-bye and ended up covered with lipstick. It was about seven in the morning and as I came walking along the deck, all ready to go on shore, everybody I passed started laughing. I'm glad there were no cameras around to witness that event.

I caught up with my parents and Herbert Houston in Berlin, where the 1937 Congress of the International Chamber of Commerce had already begun. The ICC in those days was thought of as the business counterpart of the League of Nations. Its goal was summed up in a slogan invented by Dad: "World Peace Through World Trade." The congress that year had fourteen hundred delegates and attracted attention all over the world. Many people were hoping that international businessmen like Dad would be able to keep war from breaking out.

The atmosphere in Berlin was highly charged. Hitler had already remilitarized the Rhineland, and a massive arms buildup was under way. Right after I arrived Mother told us that her friends the Wertheims, who owned one of the biggest department stores in Berlin, were leaving the country. In the summer of 1935 theirs had been one of the businesses hit when Nazi gangs ran wild in Berlin's streets, smashing the windows of Jewish-owned stores. The Germans we knew pooh-poohed the incident at the time, saying, "Oh, it's too bad, but you know how young people are," but Mother had been shocked. To protect the business, Mr. Wertheim had transferred ownership to his wife, who was a certified Aryan, but they feared for their future and decided to get out. The fact that this family felt forced to abandon a great business because of politics was incomprehensible to me. They ended up selling the store for next to nothing, putting all their possessions in six railroad cars, paying everybody off, and taking the train into Sweden.

I remember walking down Unter den Linden, the city's main avenue, with a manager from IBM's local office. We passed the Reichschancellery building and I saw soldiers in uniforms and helmets. A little further on I spotted the office of Intourist, the Russian travel agency. I needed some information in connection with my trip East, so I walked in. The IBM man followed me absent-mindedly, but when he looked around and realized where he was, he dashed back out the door. There was a lot of animosity between the Germans and the Russians and he didn't want to risk being seen there. I also visited the Japanese embassy, where Houston took me to a reception. It was a beautiful house, and we stood in the garden sipping tea while a German diplomat told us proudly that the place had belonged to a rich Jew who had fled the country. Nobody took exception, but I wondered how the Jewish man felt about having his house taken over. The callousness of the Germans made me very uneasy.

Dad's optimism blinded him to what was going on in Germany. Even though the Germans welcomed the Congress, they didn't like the idea of increased trade. They kept insisting that too much international commerce would ruin their self-sufficiency, which they needed in case of war. But Dad believed his German businessmen friends, who assured him they had Hitler in check. A lot of people made the same mistake, but not everyone had a chance to ask Adolf Hitler point-blank what he had in mind. On the third day of the congress my father had a private meeting with Hitler, and Hitler fooled him completely. When Dad talked to reporters afterward he praised Hitler's sincerity. According to Dad, Hitler said, "There will be no war. No country wants war, and no country can afford it."

At the end of the Congress the Nazi government gave Dad the Merit Cross of the German Eagle. This was a medal that had just been created for "honoring foreign nationals who have made themselves deserving of the German Reich." I was present at the ceremony at which Hjalmar Schacht, Germany's economic minister, draped the thing around Dad's neck. It was a white cross framed in gold and decorated with swastikas. Dad willingly accepted it at the time, but in 1940, after Hitler had taken over much of Europe, Dad sent the medal back with an angry note:

Your Excellency:

At the time of the Congress of the International Chamber of Commerce in Berlin in June, 1937, at which I was elected President of that body, we discussed world peace and world trade. You made the statement that there must be no more wars, and that you were interested in developing trade with other nations.

A few days later your representative, Dr. Hjalmar Schacht, in the name of the German Government, conferred upon me the decoration of Merit Cross of the German Eagle (With Star) in recognition of my efforts for world peace and world trade. I accepted this decoration on that basis and advised you that I would continue to cooperate in the interests of those causes.

In view of the present policies of your Government, which are contrary to the causes for which I have been working and for which I received the decoration, I am returning it.

Yours truly,
Thomas J. Watson

My father somehow found time in Berlin to give me advice about my trip to the Far East. We both thought of this as my first exposure to the real world, and he must have been worried that I'd fall right into the fleshpots of the Orient. He warned me not to fool around with women of other nationalities, because cultural differences made it hard to distinguish between well-bred women and those less well bred. Though Dad never talked about sex, he found an indirect way to mention that too. He said, "Tom, you're going into very unusual territory. There are all sorts of diseases out there. If I were you, I'd be very careful to always use a clean towel. If you cut yourself shaving or something, and you use a towel that isn't absolutely clean, you can get a serious infection."

We said good-bye on July 3, and when I stepped off the train with Herbert Houston in Warsaw the following morning, it felt like my personal Independence Day. Here I was, twenty-three years old, knowing nothing about the world, absolutely on my own. Over the next ten weeks I intended to prove myself the world's best secretary. Houston's plan was to journey northeast to Moscow, board the Trans-Siberian railroad, and start selling pavilion space as soon as we reached Manchuria, which in those days was a puppet state controlled by Japan.

I liked Houston at first because he'd picked me for the job, but we never grew close. He was in his sixties, like Dad, yet he already seemed to be an old man—very formal, hard of hearing, and constantly nodding off. He knew a lot of important people in the Far East and had made his name editing a journal of foreign affairs called *World's Work*. It did well enough in its day but had fallen on hard times. Now Houston was nearly destitute and Father had helped him get the World's Fair job.

At the Russian border we had to change trains, and the guards looked through everything we had. As I soon found out, Russia was in upheaval. Under Stalin people were being executed left and right, or simply dropping out of the picture. There were news stories about a field marshal and fourteen top army officers accused of spying. They had been found guilty in eight hours of secret trial and immediately shot. Among people who knew the country, the assumption was that a great many other people were dying as well, although no one guessed the extent of Stalin's purges.

Unlike many Americans who made pilgrimages to Russia in the 1930s, I felt no special sympathy for Communism—I was just passing through on my way to Tokyo. But the Russian Revolution was only twenty years old, and I was curious to see for myself whether the new system was working. I thought about this on the train while Houston dozed. It bothered me that back home, even talking about Communism was becoming an act of heresy. Why wouldn't sensible people be willing to talk about *any* approach to distributing the wealth? In fact, the way money was distributed in America didn't seem entirely fair. Mother had always told us, "Your father works hard and that's why he's a success," but I could think of other people who worked just as hard and got nowhere. Perhaps some other system might be better; I was prepared to believe there might be some good in Communism.

When we pulled into Moscow, a man from Intourist met us at the station and drove us to the Metropole Hotel, Moscow's finest. The place was badly run down, and I was fascinated to learn that many rooms were occupied by the piecework champions from local factories—I wondered what rewarding top achievers had to do with Lenin's slogan "From each according to his ability, to each according to his need." Another Metropole resident was Gene Schwerdt, a Dutchman working as IBM's Moscow representative. We did substantial business with the Soviets, who relied on IBM machines to manage vast quantities of statistics for their Five Year Plans. Schwerdt saw that I was naive, and he invited me to his room for a crash course on Russia. "Be careful here," he told me.

"They'll try to set you up with a woman. They also mike your room, so don't say anything." While that sank in, he told me that Moscow was in a state of terror, even though none of the Russians mentioned it for fear of being shot. Stalin had established his power through executions right from the beginning, and then—Schwerdt put it in sales terms—he steadily increased his quota until shooting had become as common in Russia as traffic tickets in the U.S.A. I sat for two hours hearing about propaganda, spies, the black markets, the terrible housing shortage, and the bureaucracy that paralyzed everything. By the time I left I was shocked.

At the U.S. embassy they welcomed Houston and me when we showed them our letter of introduction from Secretary of State Cordell Hull, a friend of Dad's. Everybody I met on the embassy staff damned the Russians to some degree. The man who made the deepest impression on me was second secretary George Kennan. He was a thin, intense, dark-haired fellow, only thirty-three. He described Russia as a dictatorship with a Communist façade, and told me that he had come to Russia thinking that Communism was the world's ultimate solution and had slowly reached the view that it was an utter failure as it was being practiced.

After a day or two I wrote my father a letter, saying Russia was a terrible place. When he got it I think he was frantic that I would shoot my mouth off and get into trouble. Somehow he got a reply to me within three days. It said simply,

> I am sure that you will find conditions in Russia much improved for the masses, as compared with pre-war times. Furthermore, you must keep in mind that every country is in a position to figure out what is best for its own people. It is not our duty to either criticize or advise them in these matters.

I got the hint, and toned down my criticism of the Soviet government as long as I was there.

The Intourist people worked hard to put a good face on things. We made a two-day trip to Leningrad, where they showed us the art treasures the czars had hoarded and the palaces they had built while ordinary Russians suffered. To give us an idea of the ideal Communist state, Intourist took us on a bus to a collective farm outside Moscow. It looked more or less like an ordinary U.S. farm, but what did impress me was the way they cared for the children in clean, bright nurseries. I annoyed my guide by paying more attention to the kids than the farm. When I offered money to one little boy, the guide said angrily, "They don't want money. They have plenty." Nonetheless I gave the boy some in secret and he leaped at it.

While we were in Moscow I was surprised at how little Houston asked me to do, even though he was spending a lot of time at the Japanese embassy making plans for our trip east. After about a week he stunned me by saying that we were going to wait for another man my age to join us. This was Peter Weil, nephew of a prominent New York investment banker. When I asked why he was coming, Houston said, "To be my secretary, like you." That riled me, because I didn't think Houston needed two secretaries. I pressed him until finally he told me that Peter Weil's trip was being paid for by his family, and that the same went for me: Dad had secretly arranged to reimburse the World's Fair for my salary and expenses. This was a terrible blow to my pride. I would never have taken the job if I had known that my father had created it. I felt as though he had deceived me; I was angry with myself for not seeing through it sooner, and I resented Houston for going along with it. If Houston didn't need me, then I would spend the trip fooling around on Dad's money, just as I had done for four years at Brown. But my anger and embarrassment weren't that easy to shrug off. The next eight weeks were among the most confused of my life.

Peter Weil and I shared a compartment on the train across Siberia. He was a nice enough fellow and seemed perfectly gentlemanly. We would play backgammon late each night and sleep until midday. By the time we got to Manchuria I owed him about forty dollars, which made me mad, especially when I caught him reading a book called *Winning at Backgammon* he had hidden in his luggage. I always kept an eye on him after that, although we continued to get along. The train went very slowly and stopped a lot. I spent long hours looking out the window at the taiga, the endless forest of evergreen and birch trees. My fantasy was that if a good airline could get a permit to fly across that vast land, it could be the most profitable route in the world: Berlin to Tokyo in five days. I felt curious about the Siberian people, and whenever we stopped I'd explore the little towns and haggle in the shops. That was about the only fun I had in six long days, apart from singing and talking with a group of Germans and some English girls we discovered riding among the peasants in third class.

Crossing into Japanese territory from Siberia meant reentering the modern world with a jolt. To reach Tokyo we had to cross Manchuria, travel down the length of the Korean peninsula, and take a ferry from Pusan across to Japan. I was amazed at the work the Japanese had done all along the way. In Manchuria, which had been under their control for just six years, we rode on a first-rate train, called the *Asia,* that was air-conditioned, completely streamlined, fast, and as smooth as a boat on a calm sea. The only unsettling thing was that everywhere we saw evidence of Japan's military buildup—troops and staff cars at the train stations, battleships in harbors. I was so impressed by Japan's modernity that I didn't pay too much attention to this—even when a Japanese plainclothesman on one train claimed we'd taken pictures in a forbidden zone and confiscated our film. But it was only a few days later that Japan launched the full-scale invasion of China that some historians call the beginning of World War II.

When we reached Tokyo we set up shop in the Imperial Hotel. Houston was hopelessly disorganized and so secretive that he wouldn't let Peter or me open the mail or even keep track of his appointments. Yet somehow, thanks to his connections, the pavilion space got sold. By tagging along with him we met many prominent Japanese, including Ginjiro Fujihara, a paper manufacturer who later became the minister of munitions. He invited us to a tea ceremony at his home and afterward talked about the invasion of China and how it might affect relations with England and the U.S. Fujihara said openly that Japan was no longer afraid of England, as she was a very old nation and Japan was a young one. When Houston asked, "What about the United States?" Fujihara smiled and said, "We like President Roosevelt's Good Neighbor Policy." I took that at face value—it would have been hard for me to believe that Japan thought of the U.S. as a rival. On the contrary, what impressed me most in Tokyo was the extent to which U.S. and Japanese interests seemed entwined. I had always thought of Japan as very remote, but I kept running into familiar faces—men who knew my father, recent Ivy League graduates I either knew or had heard of, and even a Japanese count who had been Princeton's biggest dandy during my years at the Hun School.

By this time I was considering a major change of plans. My IBM training was due to start in the fall, but Peter was making arrangements to go on to India after we finished in Tokyo, and I decided I wanted to go too. I wrote to my father asking his permission to extend my tour. His reply practically scorched the telegraph wires:

From standpoint of future you cannot afford to consider trip. Company rule [requires] fall school. You would not want a special ruling to cover your case. . . . Your own judgment will tell you to return with Mr. Houston as planned. Do not handicap your future or disappoint me. Dad.

I didn't have the nerve to challenge him any further—at least not directly. So I did my work, and after three weeks in the Far East, when Houston told us we'd be free during our remaining time in Japan, I looked for a way to end the trip with a bang. The Japanese had just captured Peking, and I suggested to Peter that we go there to look up a couple of English girls we'd met on the Trans-Siberian. We talked Houston into helping us arrange official permission to visit China for two weeks.

I don't think we really understood that Peking was a war zone. My father certainly did: when Houston informed him where we'd gone Dad was furious and poor Houston bore the brunt of it. Our situation first became clear to me when we got to the Tokyo station and found it jammed with soldiers and their relatives. Watching the ritualistic way those families said good-bye to their sons really opened my eyes to Japan's militarism. They came down to the station about an hour before the train was due to leave, got the boys on safely, and then for maybe fifteen minutes everyone shouted "Banzai!" continuously. They were all waving miniature Japanese flags. Then, just as they were getting hoarse, someone started a song. The singing went on for another fifteen minutes. Then they gave three cheers over and over again. In the last few minutes before the train pulled out there was delirious shouting on both sides. Everyone looked exhausted by the time we left.

The trip to Peking took five days. Once we crossed the Chinese border there were signs of war everywhere—soldiers with machine guns on top of the station houses, wrecked equipment, shell craters, and trenches. Instead of being scared I was excited. It took all night to cover the short distance between Tientsin and Peking on the last leg of the trip, but I barely noticed because I was surrounded by so many exotic characters. There was a company of soldiers in the car, a Tibetan prince with his wife and small children, and a beautiful White Russian woman on her way to join her husband in Peking. One of the soldiers watched me closely for a while, then came over, pointed to himself, and said, "Sing in English!" He'd been to missionary school and knew the old spiritual "Massa's in de Cold Ground." Afterward he sang some Kabuki opera songs which were quite beautiful.

We checked into the Grand Hotel de Pekin and looked

up our English friends from third class on the Trans-Siberian. One girl I met was living with a guy, a Marine officer from the U.S. embassy, which was a new idea to me. No bones about it—they just lived together. Everybody was doing it in Peking, which was a hedonistic place, like no city I'd ever seen. You didn't need much money to live an enchanted existence there. A good servant cost ten dollars a month, a rickshaw and boy a dollar eighty a week, and everything else was comparably cheap. Because of this, Peking attracted many Westerners, including dregs from nearly every country. At one dinner party I found myself sitting with a debutante from New York at one elbow and a French heroin addict at the other. The Japanese occupation of Peking hadn't slowed the social scene at all. One of the most popular night spots was the rooftop bar at the Grand Hotel. You could order a gin gimlet, sit back, and watch the artillery flashes to the west of the city, where the war was going on.

Peter and I got to know two brothers named Fahnstock, who were from Long Island and really knew their way around. Peking was full of war rumors, and one night the Faunstocks proposed that we go and see for ourselves what was happening on the city's outskirts. Early the next morning they hired a car and driver, got a large American flag and draped it over the hood, and off we went. First we visited a place where two hundred Chinese had been ambushed and massacred by the Japanese two weeks before. Each side of the road was covered with graves, and the smell of death was overpowering.

Then, at my urging, we went to the airport. To our surprise we were able to drive right up to the edge of the field without being challenged. We watched Japanese bombers returning from their missions. The planes were old and looked ready to fall apart—I guessed that the Japanese weren't using their best equipment for this war, and I felt sorry for the pilots because the field had been bombed and craters in the runways made landing dangerous. I decided to take a few pictures and got out of the car with my camera. Then I heard something go *clank,*

clank behind me. I turned around. A Japanese sentry had just charged his machine gun and was pointing it squarely at my chest. Up until then it had never occurred to me that the American flag was no guarantee of total protection. The incident rattled us all. I jumped into the car and we headed back into town meekly.

The rest of my time in Peking was spent constructively —in the shops. I love to buy things. I started out with four hundred dollars in my pocket, and after a week I ended up practically broke, with two trunks full of all kinds of stuff. I bought antique Mandarin skirts for my sisters, brocaded silk bathrobes with the wool of unborn lambs inside, and countless carvings of jade and lapis lazuli. I was so popular with the merchants that on the morning I left, several of them sent their sons or shop boys to the train station with small gifts to see me off. The ride into Peking had been an adventure, but the ride out was harrowing. Japan's invasion had bogged down in Shanghai, and the Japanese I met along the way were tense. Near me sat two soldiers solemnly carrying the ashes of their general back to Tokyo. The custom was to cremate men killed in battle and put the remains in a labeled box, which was then carried home in a cloth ritually folded to make a kind of sling. The box sat on the table in front of these two men for the entire trip.

At the border of Korea, an official insisted my visa wasn't valid and demanded a hundred dollars. When I refused to pay, he shouted "No argument!" and called in two soldiers. They came up and pointed bayonets at my stomach. I paid right away. I was angry and afraid, and I brooded for the rest of the day. I decided, "These bastards really are ready to make war!" and it suddenly seemed to me shameful that the United States and Great Britain hadn't intervened on the side of China. On the way out of Tientsin, I'd seen the Navy destroyer *U.S.S. Ford* in the harbor. The ship was there to pick up Americans who were leaving Peking, and it had certainly looked good to me, with American flags painted all over it. Now I wished I'd been aboard.

CHAPTER 9

W hen I got to IBM's sales school in Endicott, New York, I was hoping that people would treat me like any other Joe Blow just starting out. How I could think that was possible, I don't know. Dad was such a tremendous force in that town that as I walked down the street with my books under my arm, people would point and say, "Mr. Watson's son." During the first week I caused a stir by going into a bar after school to get a drink. The bartender said, "Doesn't your father have a big policy about liquor?" I started to explain that the rule only applied to drinking on the job or on IBM property, but there was no point. I stopped going into the bars after that and began to think Endicott was a very unpleasant place.

Even though IBM headquarters was in Manhattan, the company's soul was there in Endicott. That was where IBM built its punch-card machines, showed customers how they were used, and taught recruits like me how to sell them. Endicott is a little river town in the western part of New York State, not far from where Dad got his start selling sewing machines. In winter the weather is perpetually gray and damp, and whenever the wind blew over the tannery of the giant Endicott-Johnson Shoe Company, all of Endicott stank. Yet I think to Dad it was the most beautiful place on earth.

I spent two miserable winters there in 1937 and 1938. IBM in those days trained salesmen in two steps. New recruits would come to Endicott in October for machine school, where they learned the ins and outs of the product line. They'd spend the following spring and summer as junior salesmen helping veterans in the field. Then it was back to Endicott for another winter, to learn sales techniques. Finally they'd become salesmen with territories of their own and the chance to make a respectable living. In salary and commissions Dad paid the average salesman about forty-four hundred dollars a year—which is like earning thirty-eight thousand today—and top salesmen made several times that. The men in my class were an impressive group, mostly college graduates. We lived and ate at a crude old wooden hotel called the Frederick, which catered to IBM. Each morning we'd grab our books and walk three blocks up the main street of town, turn right onto North Street, and enter Dad's world.

I have to admit he had a lot to be proud of. When he first came to Endicott in the spring of 1914, all CTR had there was a small factory manufacturing time clocks. The rest of North Street was lined with bars and greasy spoons. By 1937, thanks to IBM's success, that end of town was totally transformed. Dad had bought up those greasy spoons and replaced them with modern white air-conditioned factories and an imposing research and development center with colonial pillars across the front. There was tremendous company spirit and vitality that anyone could feel just by walking through the plant. IBM's employees earned well above the national average, and they worked in clean shops with spotless machinery and polished hardwood floors. In the hills behind the factory there were signs that Dad was giving employees the best benefits he could think of. He had bought an old speakeasy and turned it into a country club—liquor-free, of course—with two golf courses and a shooting range. Any employee could join for a dollar a year. Three nights a week the country club served dinner to give IBM wives a break from cooking. Dad also provided free concerts and libraries, as well as night courses to show employees how to get promoted. He believed in management by generosity and he was right: morale and productivity at Endicott were high, and in that great era of industrial unionization, IBM employees never found any need to organize.

Some of this Dad created himself, but many of his

ideas came from a legendary businessman named George F. Johnson, the founder of the Endicott-Johnson Shoe Company. Long before Dad arrived, Johnson was a towering figure in Endicott. He had started out as an uneducated boy making boots in a factory near Boston, and he became famous as one of the most progressive businessmen in history. When his business boomed at the turn of the century, Johnson set out to make Endicott a model of what he called "industrial democracy." He built the town center, a school, parks, athletic fields, swimming pools, a library, and a golf course, and donated them all to the town. He built stone arches on the highway leading in and out of Endicott, carved with the words "Home of the Square Deal." He paid employees' medical bills and offered them low-interest loans and good land near town so they could build their own houses. Johnson built his own modest house right in their midst. Even though he employed twenty thousand people in that valley, Johnson always thought of himself as a working man, the same way Dad always thought of himself as a salesman.

Johnson took Dad under his wing from the very beginning, welcoming him to Endicott and encouraging him to build up the CTR operation there. He taught Dad as much about employee welfare as John H. Patterson had about running a sales force. But in 1937 the Depression was causing Johnson's magic to fade. The shoe business went bad, and he didn't have enough cash flow to cushion his workers from the downturn. He had to lay off thousands of people. Meanwhile IBM kept getting stronger, and many of the sons and daughters of Endicott-Johnson families went to work for Dad. But my old man never lost his admiration for Johnson and used to visit him even after Johnson was very old and confined to bed. On one of these visits Dad took my brother, who was then going to Yale. Johnson, the great old progressive, took one look at Dick, the perfectly tailored undergraduate, and then he rose up from his pillow and hollered, "Well, what are you going to do about it?" Meaning, the world.

The IBM School House sat on North Street in the

midst of Dad's enterprise. Not many companies had real schools in those days; Dad copied the idea from the Cash and improved upon it greatly. The school's aim was to produce future officers of the company, and Dad always talked to us trainees as if we were colleagues. Everything about the school was meant to inspire loyalty, enthusiasm, and high ideals, which IBM held out as the way to achieve success. The front door had the motto "THINK" written over it in two-foot-high brass letters. Just inside was a granite staircase that was supposed to put students in an aspiring frame of mind as they stepped up to the day's classes. Engraved on the risers were the words:

> THINK
> OBSERVE
> DISCUSS
> LISTEN
> READ

In class the first thing we did each morning was to stand up and sing IBM songs. We actually had a songbook, *Songs of the I.B.M.* It opened with "The Star-Spangled Banner," and on the facing page was IBM's own anthem, "Ever Onward." There were dozens of songs in praise of Dad or other executives, set to tunes everybody knew. One of my favorites was to Fred Nichol, who started out as Dad's secretary at the Cash, came with him to IBM, and most recently had been promoted to vice president and general manager. Making rousing speeches in praise of my father was one of Nichol's specialties, and his success showed how far loyalty could carry a man at IBM. The song was sung to the tune of "Tramp, Tramp, Tramp, the Boys Are Marching":

> V. P. Nichol is a leader,
> Working for the I.B.M.
> Years ago he started low
> Up the ladder he did go
> What an inspiration he is to our men!

A lot of outsiders thought our singing custom was odd, but the man in charge of our class didn't make a big deal out of it. He said, "We have these company songs. We think they build morale. Here is the way they go. Mr. O'Flaherty here at the piano will sing it through for you first and then you'll all sing it."

The teachers were veteran company men, all dressed, as we were, in regulation IBM clothes—dark business suits and white shirts with stiff collars. Dad believed that if you wanted to sell to a businessman, you had to look like one. There was a big picture of Dad looking watchful on the wall behind the lectern. The rest of the classroom was decorated with his slogans, and, as in every office of IBM, there was a "THINK" sign prominently displayed. Magazine cartoonists used to make fun of these signs, and IBM's critics thought they were ridiculous: how could anybody really *think* in a company that was such a one-man show? But to everybody inside, the message was crystal clear: you would sell more machines, and advance faster, if you used your head.

I used to marvel at how willingly new employees embraced the company spirit. As far as I could tell, nobody made fun of the slogans and songs. Times were different then, and I suppose being earnest didn't seem as corny in 1937 as it does today. And, of course, jobs were awfully hard to come by in the 1930s, so people would put up with a lot. As for me, I was pretty used to the IBM culture because I'd grown up at the source. It only bothered me when Dad let things get out of hand—as in 1936, when he commissioned an IBM *symphony*.

They gave us twelve weeks to learn everything about the products. We didn't have to worry about scales or meat slicers, because Dad had sold off that division while I was at Brown. In its place he had bought a small company that was trying, without much success, to pioneer the electric typewriter. We studied those and the whole line of time clocks. But the bulk of our course work was on punch-card machines, which were in great demand

and already accounted for more than 85 percent of the revenue of the company.

At first I was thrilled to get my hands on punch-card machines. I'd grown up around those things, and the basic concept fired my imagination just as it did Dad's. In the history of industrialization, punch-card machines belong right up there with the Jacquard loom, the cotton gin, and the locomotive. Before punch cards, accounting and record keeping were clumsy operations that had to be done manually by clerks. Punch-card systems took away a lot of the drudgery—such as copying ledger entries and writing bills—and they did the work cheaply, reliably, and rapidly. This obviously was the wave of the future, and IBM was starting to attract high-caliber people because the machines were exciting to work with.

My father always said that those punch cards were what attracted him to IBM when Charles Flint approached him with the job. He had seen his first punch-card installation while he was still selling cash registers in 1904. A friend of his was using Hollerith machines at Eastman Kodak to keep track of the company's salesmen. The way this worked was pretty simple. Each time a sale was made, all the information about it would get punched onto a single card. Those cards would be sorted and tabulated once a month to yield all sorts of information: what each man had sold, which products were selling best in which regions, and so on. Dad used to make a wonderful sales talk about the punch-card concept. He'd hold one up and say, "You can put a hole in this card representing one dollar—a dollar of sales, perhaps, or a dollar you owe someone. From that point on, you have a permanent record. It can never be erased, and you never have to enter it again. It can be added, subtracted, and multiplied. It can be filed, accumulated, and printed, all automatically." Dad believed that here was the world's answer to problems of accounting. All he had to do was keep developing this thing and IBM would revolutionize business. Whenever someone would use the term "punch cards" he would say, "These are *IBM* cards!"

Punch-card machines had become pretty sophisticated

by the time I got to Endicott. They could sort four hundred cards a minute, print out paychecks and address labels, and duplicate, at very high speed, all of the accounting functions that companies were still doing by hand. I liked the idea that one set of cards enabled a customer to use the same data ten or twelve different ways, and I was pretty sure I'd be able to sell that. However, I quickly found out there was more to IBM school than appreciating what a punch card was. Everybody had to learn how to program the machines to do specific tasks. This involved arranging wires on a "plugboard," which looked something like an old-fashioned telephone switchboard. We each had a plugboard to work with, and it soon became obvious that I was much better at understanding the potential of the machines than at actually plugging them up. After only two weeks I had to be assigned a tutor so I wouldn't fail. I spent many nights with that guy in the deserted schoolhouse, trying to learn to hook up those little wires.

Before long IBM school felt even worse to me than Carteret or Hun or Brown. Not only was my performance poor, as usual, but I couldn't escape being seen as T.J.'s son. Everyone in the school was trying to guess what Dad wanted done with me—without any regard for what I wanted myself. The head of the school, Garland Briggs, had been headmaster of the Hun School when I was there. Dad had picked him, in his simplistic way, because he needed an educator and Briggs was one he knew. I always thought Briggs was way out of his depth in that job. He had the big idea that it would please Dad if I were elected class president. So he put the other students up to it, even though they all knew I needed tutoring to get by. Unfortunately for me, I lacked the force of character to say, "I won't have this."

Endicott seemed more and more bleak. The place didn't offer much in the way of fun, and even if it had, I felt obliged to behave soberly and responsibly. Usually I ate with my classmates at the hotel; if we went out it cost money, and most of them were poor. Besides, there was no place to go. Endicott's restaurants were working-class

Italian places, and the food they served always gave me heartburn. Once in a while I'd talk some of the Scandinavians in the class into going skiing for a weekend, but the local slopes weren't very good. Soon I'd be back in my room at the Frederick trying to focus on some big black textbook with a title like *Machine Methods of Accounting.*

I complained constantly to my college friends outside the IBM school, and Nick Lunken, one of my fraternity brothers, decided I was a sitting duck for a practical joke. He called up one day and said he wanted to fly to Endicott to see me. I was delighted. He said, "If you have any friends in class who might like to have a ride in my airplane, bring them along." So I got the vice president of the class and the treasurer, both of whom were trying hard to make their way in IBM. Nick was a little late, and we waited at the Endicott airport, which is very small. Finally a red plane landed and I could see Nick in the cabin with a huge grin on his face. The door opened and out came a pair of silk legs—really good legs. They looked to me like they were about four yards long. Then the rest of the woman came out, and she was very hot-looking. To this day I don't know how Nick set it up. The woman hopped down and made a beeline for the side of the field, where a kid was standing with a horse. The door of the plane opened again and a racetrack tout came out, a guy in a long blue double-breasted chesterfield coat and black derby. He had a bottle of Scotch in his hand, and my two classmates began backing away from the scene. The woman got on the horse and started galloping around with her skirts up to her hips. Finally Nick stepped out of the plane.

I said, "For God's sake, Nick, what is this?"

"I knew you'd want to meet Grandmother Verne," he said. "She'll get off that horse in a minute, but she's very fond of horses. And this fellow's here in case you want to lay a bet."

I didn't know anything about horse racing. But by then the other two officers of my class were disappearing around the airport building. They didn't want to be connected with whatever terrible thing was going on. I bought Nick and his friends lunch at a hot-dog stand, and it seemed like hours before I could get rid of them. Finally I stood watching the plane disappear, and went resignedly back to my schoolbooks.

About once a month, Dad would show up. The local managers would get tense, because Dad was great at spotting something wrong that no one else had thought of and blowing up about it. No matter what aspect of the business he examined, he insisted on having a hand in the details and was always bristling with ideas and questions, forcing people to be on their toes. Often he gave orders without warning and it could happen at any hour, which meant that managers didn't dare leave their offices or their houses when he was in town. Dad's unpredictability would sometimes produce odd behavior in people. Garland Briggs, for example, tied himself in knots over whether to leave me at my studies or order me down to the train station to greet my father. Generally I took it upon myself to be there, standing dutifully on that cold platform as the train pulled in, shooting steam.

Dad's favorite spot in Endicott was the IBM Homestead. This was a square old lovely Italian-style house with dark green tiles that originally belonged to the town's founder. Dad had added a long wing with forty room-and-bath cubicles for guests, and that was where customers would come for one-week courses on how to use punch-card machines. The master suite was always reserved for Dad. From his window he could look out and see it all—the IBM golf courses, the shooting ranges, the country club, and the factory buildings down below. He would inspect the factory during the day—walking through the plant, putting his foot up on the stool of a guy at a drill press, and getting into a conversation that would sometimes last half an hour. Then he'd come out and bark orders to his secretaries based on what he'd heard. Dad was always alert to what the factory man needed. In 1934, after one of these tours, Dad overruled his factory managers and abolished piecework, saying it distracted people from producing high-quality goods.

At night Dad would go into the Homestead dining room, sit down next to some customer—they all wore badges that said who they were—and start a conversation. When dinner ended more people would draw up to the table and he might have fifteen or twenty to talk to. It was easy to see he was a great salesman. His words would come out in a dignified way, he'd make a few simple gestures, and whether they agreed with him or not, people would listen. After a while he'd say, "Gentlemen, let's go into the living room and continue this conversation." He'd talk until one or two in the morning. It was all right for him, but terrible for me if I was there. I was usually bored but I always had to stay to the end because he would feel hurt if I walked out.

There was no better way to learn about IBM than to be present when Dad visited a class. Some of the things he said didn't mean much; he sermonized a lot about self-improvement, as in his letters to me at Brown. But he also told stories to illustrate his management principles. The most important story involved how he learned to sell cash registers. Dad got hired as a salesman for the Cash in Buffalo, New York, in 1896. During his first couple of weeks he failed to close a single sale. Finally he reported this to the branch manager, a tough old-timer named Jack Range, who blew up. He lit into Dad so hard that Dad used to say he was just waiting for the tirade to die down so he could quit. But when Range decided he had pushed my father as far as he could, he suddenly turned friendly. He reassured Dad and offered to help him sell some cash registers. He told Dad, "I'll go out with you, and if we fall down, we'll fall down together." They loaded a big, fancy machine onto the wagon and sold it that same day. Range showed my father how to hit the right notes in talking to businessmen and how to improvise on the canned sales pitch that Patterson required all his salesmen to use. Range let my father watch him close several more sales, until finally Dad caught on.

My father carried that lesson in his bones. He wanted

his managers to be on sales calls with a guy three or four times before labeling the man a failure. And he believed that each employee was *entitled* to help from those above. He would say "A manager is an assistant to his men." That personal relationship between the individual and the supervisor became the IBM equivalent of the social contract.

I never disagreed with those lessons Dad taught, but I'd heard them all a hundred times before. Generally I tried to keep my distance during his visits. Although he never said anything about it, I was sure he was unhappy that I wasn't earning top grades. All the same I persevered, and finally school was done. As a sort of graduation, the whole class went to Manhattan to attend the Hundred Percent Club. This was IBM's annual sales convention, one of the morale-building techniques Dad had learned from Patterson. Hundreds of IBM men who had made their quotas were brought to New York, at company expense, for a huge banquet at the Waldorf. There were songs and awards and testimonials as each salesman stood at the podium and said a few words. It went on for hours. At the end I had to give a little speech. On behalf of the new graduates I gave my father a book of yachting prints, and he and I were presented to the audience as the newest members of the IBM Father-Son Club. This was something Dad had founded back in the 1920s, on the firm belief that nepotism was good for the business.

CHAPTER 10

Fresh out of sales school, I was handed one of the company's prime territories in Manhattan—the western half of the financial district, including part of Wall Street. People eager to curry favor with Dad were constantly tossing business my way. I sold plenty of accounting machines and always beat my quota, but I got more and more depressed. At one point I made a feeble protest to one of my father's top men. He said, "Oh, go on, young man. We help all of our salesmen. You're doing a great job, and ninety-nine percent of what's happened is yours anyway." My three years as an IBM salesman were a time of sickening self-doubt.

I lived with my parents during this entire period, in their beautiful townhouse at 4 East Seventy-fifth Street. Every morning I would walk to IBM headquarters on Madison Avenue and punch in—IBM made time clocks, so everybody including Dad punched in. Then I'd go downstairs and have coffee at Halper's, the drugstore on the corner. A lot of the young people did that; once in a while, my father would walk in and the place would clear out. I got along with my colleagues well enough—mainly because I think they expected worse when they heard the boss's son was coming. I even made a few friends. But I was far from the image of a successful salesman. When I went to meet customers, I was bashful and not sure of myself at all.

My very first sales call was at a tall old office building on Broadway next to Trinity Church. I was supposed to be prospecting, calling cold, and I stood in the lobby looking at the directory and wondering where to start. In my hand I had a printout showing the calls that had already been made at that address. There had been very

few. Suddenly on the directory I noticed the Maltine
Company. I recognized the name because I knew one of
their products: cod liver oil spun up with a grain deriva-
tive and given to children as a tonic. It came in a brown
bottle with a wide neck so you could get a big spoon into
it. The stuff had the consistency of honey, and it tasted
very good.

I went up the elevator to the Maltine Company. Inside
the front door of the office was a low oak fence with a
gate, and a receptionist sat on the other side. I said, "I'm
Thomas Watson. I'm a sales representative from the International Business Machines Corporation, and I wonder if I could see your chief financial officer to talk about
punch-card accounting."

"I'm sure you can't," she said. "We're very busy here
today."

"Would you mind just presenting my card to that individual? If he can't see me today I'd be glad to come back
some other time."

She took the card, and when she came back she said,
"Come right in, young man." I was thrilled. I walked
right into this executive's office and he got up from his
desk and shook hands. He said, "It's nice of you to call."

"Well, sir, I like Maltine tonic," I said. "I used to take
it as a kid, and my mother set great store by it. I'm a new
salesman and I was looking at the register and thought I
should start with a familiar name. And that's why I'm
here."

"Are you the son of Thomas Watson, the head of your
company?" he asked. I said I was. "Let me tell you a
little story," he said. "I had a friend with his own business, and he brought his son into the business with him.
This son liked to live pretty high on the hog and he didn't
really want to work. Finally he became a drunk and the
father had to fire him."

I heard him out and said, "Thank you for telling me
that. I will give it some thought. But now I'd like to tell
you about the punch-card method of accounting."

He said, "Aw, hell, I'm not interested in that. I just
heard you were T. J. Watson's son and I thought you

ought to know that a lot of people in your shoes fail. So nice to meet you, Mr. Watson." And he showed me the door. I was tempted to abandon my IBM career on the spot. I had no idea why the man had made those remarks, and when I told my father about the incident, he couldn't explain it either. He simply said I'd had a very sorry first call.

My luck improved somewhat after that. When I could catch a prospect's interest, I found selling very exciting. The first thing we always tried to do was bring the prospect to a demonstration. Then we'd ask if we could make a survey of his business. That meant going into his office and figuring out how to apply punch cards to his book-keeping. We'd look for procedures that were easy to automate. Punch cards were especially good for handling billing, accounts receivable, and sales analysis, because they all depended on the same data. It was easy for us to show how the equipment used for doing those things would more than pay for itself.

The cheapest installation we had was something called the International 50. It included a card-sorter, a key-punch, and a non-printing tabulator, all for fifty bucks a month. We could tell the customer, "It's fifty dollars a month and it'll probably replace a girl. You're paying the girl ninety dollars." If that whetted the guy's appetite, you could push him along and say, "For a couple hundred dollars, we can give you an installation that prints. That will do all your bills and checks for you and will cut labor costs even further."

What made the job at IBM unusual was that we didn't actually sell our punch-card machines. Most of what we called sales in IBM were really rentals. What we pitched was a complete service—the use of the equipment plus the continuing assistance of IBM's staff. This way of doing business went back to Herman Hollerith, who came up with it out of pure pragmatism. His early machines broke down so often that people were reluctant to buy them; so Hollerith rented them out and promised to keep them in good shape. When Dad took over, he saw that here was something magic. The rental system required a big field force and large amounts of cash, but it made the business stable and essentially depression-proof. If you didn't sell a single machine in a year but worked hard at pleasing the customers who already had installations, you would bring in the same income as the year before. The rental system was one of IBM's greatest strengths.

All the equipment was on one-year leases, and signing the new lease gave us a pretext to call on the senior executives of the companies we sold to. We were always taught to aim high—in sales school they said, "Call where the decision is made! Call on the president!" Dad equipped us with plenty of tools for cultivating executives. *Think* magazine was the most unusual of these. It was a general-interest monthly magazine, very well put together, and the only way to tell it was from IBM was by reading the very small print at the bottom of the opening page. Every issue opened with an editorial on world progress, written by Dad. If a sales prospect was about to show you out, you might say, "Mr. Jones, I can see that you're not very interested and these machines don't fit everywhere. But while I'm here, let me give you a magazine that may interest you. This one, for instance, has speeches by Franklin Roosevelt and Tom Dewey, and an article by Lee De Forest, the inventor of the radio tube. I'd like to leave this with you, along with my card. If you like, you can have a subscription free. Just let me know and I will get you on the list." *Think* was distributed to everybody who had an IBM machine. But it didn't stop there. The press run was close to one hundred thousand, and we only had thirty-five hundred customers. Dad had copies sent to anybody whose goodwill might possibly help IBM, including high school teachers and ministers and rabbis in the areas where we did business, all college presidents, and all members of the House of Representatives and the Senate.

My father never praised me for my work as a salesman. It was so easy for him to deprive me of my self-confidence with just a word. We'd be having a casual conversation at home and he'd say, "What do you think of the new sales plan?" or "What do you think of Mr. Jones?" No matter how I responded, he'd listen for a minute and then come back with something terribly cutting like: "You know, you are really not experienced enough to have an opinion on Mr. Jones." I think Father must have enjoyed these petty emotional exercises. Maybe he was trying to test me, but it was a test no one could pass.

The better I got at selling, the less I worked. There was a salesman I knew, named Vic Middlefeldt, who liked to fly. We'd make a couple of calls in the morning and then drive out to the airport. The New York office manager was Lotti Lomax, a delightful lady I knew pretty well, and she covered for us. I'd tell her, "I'm going flying with Middlefeldt. If anyone wants to reach me, tell them I'm on a call and I'll be home by six o'clock at my parents' house." I didn't care what kind of impression my behavior was making. By 1940, I was spending half the days flying airplanes and half the nights in night-clubs.

My parents knew I was staying out late a lot and sometimes coming home with a few drinks in me, but they rarely said anything about it. I must have been in the Stork Club three or four nights a week, always with a girl and usually with a whole group of people. The Stork Club was one of the big cafe society nightclubs, El Morocco being the other. At the Stork Club a velvet rope separated the bar from the rest of the club. You'd go to the rope and ask for a table, and if you'd been spending as much money there as I had, you'd get shown to a good one right off the bat.

What drew me to the nightclubs was not so much drinking as loving to dance. Most everybody was doing the rumba and the tango in those days, and there was a craze for the conga, which was really for exhibitionists— normally I didn't get involved in it. I made friends with a dance instructor named Teddy Rodriguez, whose business card said "Professor of the Dance." He gave lessons in his apartment, which had mirrors on all the walls. We'd often go out with Teddy and I'd pick up the tab for him and his girlfriend. He was a decent fellow but sometimes talked too much. One Saturday morning I woke up at home around ten-thirty after a long night out with the crowd. When I came downstairs Mother was waiting for me, looking very stiff. She said, "You certainly ought to think about the kind of friends you're with and how you're spending your time."

"What do you mean?"

"A Latin man called here about nine o'clock and said he found your wallet on the table of a nightclub. He seemed to think I was out with you last night. He made remarks about the wonderful way I danced. He told me I was beginning to get it with the hips in the rumba." In spite of herself Mother began to laugh. Teddy had mistaken her for one of the women in our group.

Needless to say, my nightclubbing created a stir around IBM. When I took a drink, I never tried to hide it. This was a way of saying, "I'm not going to let IBM run my life." Of course my father saw things very differently. But instead of simply saying I should knock it off, he made his point by telling me another of his stories. This one involved J. P. Morgan and young Charles Schwab. It was 1901, right after Morgan organized U.S. Steel and talked Schwab into taking the top job. Schwab went to Paris to blow off steam, and stories about his hell-raising soon filtered back across the ocean. When he got back to New York, Morgan called him into his office and told him to stop acting like a fool.

Schwab said, "Mr. Morgan, you're being unfair. You know perfectly well I'm not doing anything you don't do yourself, except that you do it behind closed doors."

"Mr. Schwab, *that is what doors are for,*" said Morgan.

In his own life, Dad set a great example and in fact never had much to hide. But he believed that the business leader who covers his imperfections by keeping them private is better than the one who says, "This is how I am. Let it all hang out." Dad probably would have pressed this point harder if I'd been really reckless in the way I lived. But as much as I loved a good time, I kept myself out of the gossip columns and was never involved in a scandal. I was with girls constantly, but I avoided the raciest women, partly because they scared me. A lot of cafe society women in those days ran around with so many men that they had no idea where their emotions lay. I'd already been hurt by one beautiful and well-bred girl, so I knew that women were capable of inflicting great pain even when they didn't mean to. I hate to think what might have happened had I not known Isabel Henry before being turned loose in New York.

I never got truly involved with anyone until I met Olive Cawley on a blind date in early 1939. A schoolmate of mine from Hun set it up for the two of us to join him and his wife on a ski weekend. They picked me up at the Plaza Hotel, where I went down the steps and saw a little Ford with a ski rack and an astonishingly lovely girl in back. Vermont was a six- or seven-hour drive, and Olive and I talked the entire way. She was such a beautiful and sunny woman. She came from a good family but didn't have much money. I found it appealing that she was earning her own way and making her own decisions. She lived at the Barbizon Hotel and worked as a model for the John Robert Powers agency, which was the best in those days. She had been on magazine covers and in lots of ads, such as one for Lucky Strike that showed a picture of Olive holding up a leaf in a tobacco field. Her face was known; when we were out together people would often stop her on the street and say, "You look so familiar." At one point, when we had had a falling-out, I found I couldn't get her out of my mind. Her picture was always in some magazine to remind me. Olive had a way of doing small kindnesses that revealed her gentle and giving nature. I'd gone around with a lot of beautiful girls, but none of them had the unending generosity I found in her. She was somewhat frivolous, but so was I, and I thought about her seriously from the very start.

When my parents heard from my sisters that I was seeing a model, they hinted that they thought I was making a mistake. But I wanted somebody who would give me sweetness, love, and support—and somebody who wasn't going to feel upstaged if I actually managed to accomplish something in my life. When I started bringing Olive to family occasions, Mother kept her distance at first but Father unbent and welcomed her. He could be very pragmatic about matters of the heart.

The longer I worked at IBM, the more I resented my father for the cultlike atmosphere that surrounded him. I'd look at *Business Machines,* the IBM weekly newspaper, and there would be a big picture of Dad and a banner headline announcing something really mundane like "THOMAS J. WATSON OPENS NEW ORLEANS OFFICE." The more successful Dad became, the more people flattered him—and he soaked it up. Everything flowed around him, he was snapping out orders, and there was always a secretary running behind him with a notebook. He would work on his editorials for *Think* magazine as though it were *Time* and he were Henry Luce and millions of people were waiting to hear what he had to say.

My disdain came out during family dinners, which were dominated, as always, by Dad. When he held forth everyone would be very attentive except me. I'd behave in the most sullen and insulting way. I'd light a cigarette, slouch in my chair, roll my eyes, and look at the ceiling. Olive was shocked by these antics, and my sisters and brother thought I was a nuisance. Dad never gave any indication that he noticed, but I think he decided I was in need of more attention. He started giving me breaks from my sales duties, calling me away from the office to travel with him or just to consult. For example, he brought me along to watch when he went down to testify before Congress in 1940. The hearing was about "technological unemployment"—the question of whether automation was stealing jobs from workers. Father took the position that automation would expand the economy, spur consumers, and create new demand. He quoted Henry Ford to that effect.

Dad also got me involved in the preparations for IBM Day at the 1939 World's Fair. This was the same fair that Herbert Houston sold pavilion space for. What Dad envisioned was the biggest event in company history. He was bringing ten thousand guests into Manhattan—including all of IBM's factory men, field service men, salesmen, and their wives—and putting them up in hotels for three days. A lot of these people had never been in the city before. There were ten chartered trains from Endicott, one from Rochester, one from Washington, and additional chartered Pullmans from all over. To announce the event, Dad took out full-page ads in the New York papers. The headlines read, "THEY ALL ARE COMING." No one had seen anything like it since the troop movements of World War I. Of course, when it came to ceremonies Father always went flat out, but IBM Day was daring even by his standards. It cost a million dollars, about ten percent of the company's profits for the entire year. He was operating on this grand scale because he wanted to convey the idea of IBM's bigness.

Dad almost had a tragedy on his hands instead of the triumph he was counting on. The night the guests were en route, we got word of a terrible accident. One of the trains loaded with IBM families had crashed into the back of another in upstate New York. It wasn't clear how many people were hurt. Dad climbed out of bed at two in the morning, got in a car with my sister Jane, and drove up to the town of Port Jervis, where the accident had happened. They found out nobody had been killed. But four hundred of the fifteen hundred people on board were hurt, and some were hurt seriously. Dad and Jane spent all the following day in the hospital, talking to people and making sure they had the best medical care. Dad was also giving orders by phone, and executives in New York started scrambling. Extra doctors and nurses were sent up to Port Jervis. A new train was arranged for the people who hadn't been hurt or who were well enough to continue the trip. When they arrived in New York, IBM had a fully staffed field hospital set up for them in the Hotel New Yorker. Dad finally got back to Manhattan in the middle of the night, and the first thing he did was order flowers for all the families in the wreck. He had his executives get florists out of bed so that bouquets could be delivered to the hotel rooms before breakfast. Nobody ever forgot the way my father handled the Port Jervis wreck. I was on the sidelines, but he made a deep impression on me. I saw how far you had to go to serve the company. IBM needed that kind of personal involvement from its managers to survive.

IBM Day came off with all the fanfare Dad had intended. Mayor Fiorello La Guardia gave the opening speech, and Dad had a special greeting to read from President Roosevelt. In the IBM pavilion, along with the predictable displays of electric typewriters and tabulating machines, there was an international art show, with a painting from each country in which IBM did business. The opera stars Grace Moore and Lawrence Tibbett sang, and the Philadelphia Orchestra played Bach, Sibelius—and the IBM Symphony. The program was carried on radio networks, where Dad paid to make sure IBM Day got broadcast. It seemed to me at the time that he'd gone completely overboard. But in fact, IBM Day was a public relations coup.

CHAPTER 11

On the first business day of 1940, I became the company's top salesman when U.S. Steel Products, an account that had been thrown into my territory to make me look good, came across with a huge order. With one day's "work" I filled my quota for the entire year. There were headlines about it in the company newspaper: Thomas J. Watson Jr., first man in the 1940 Hundred Percent Club. I felt demeaned. Everybody knew that I was the old man's son, and that otherwise I never could have sold so much in such a short time. From then on, even though life outside of IBM seemed impossible to imagine, all I could think about was finding a way out.

I might never have reached this turning point if there hadn't been a war on in Europe. It seemed inevitable that America was going to get involved, and I wanted to be in the military, flying airplanes, when war came. Qualifying as an Air Corps pilot wasn't as simple as it sounds. To begin with, I wanted to avoid flying school, because I thought the military discipline would cause me to wash out. I was no twenty-year-old kid; I was twenty-six, an experienced pilot, and not about to trade one situation in which I had to take a lot of guff for another. When I learned that Hap Arnold, the commanding general of the U.S. Army Air Corps, was giving a speech to a young men's group in New York, I went to ask him what to do. Arnold was a very direct and impatient man. At the start of the question-and-answer session I raised my hand and he said, "Yup?"

I said, "I have about a thousand hours of civilian time, and I'd like to know how to get into the Air Corps without going to flying school."

"There isn't any way. Go to the flying school. Next question."

But I stayed standing and said, "But, General, it seems like a waste of the government's money to get trained all over again."

"It's an entirely different kind of flying and your civilian time is no good." He just about ordered me to sit down. Well, I did sit down and said to myself, "I'm going to get around him."

I had a second reason for wanting to skip flight school. Something was wrong with my eyes. I confirmed this by going privately to a doctor who put me through the Air Corps eye exam. One of the instruments was for testing muscle balance. When you looked into it, one eye saw a dot and the other eye saw a line. The idea was to superimpose one on the other by turning a knob. After I did this, the doctor shook his head. "You'll never make it," he said. "You'd crash an airplane right away. You have absolutely no depth perception."

"But Doctor," I said, "I have over a thousand hours in the air and I've been flying for seven years!"

"Well, it's highly dangerous, highly dangerous." He explained that I had extremely unbalanced eye muscles. My left eye looks down and my right eye looks up, with three times the amount of divergence allowed by the Air Force. But I wasn't about to give up my flying career. Instead I bought one of those testing machines and practiced setting those dots and lines at home. I became so adept at it that once I made it into the Air Force I passed the test every year for five years.

In the springtime I found out that the way around flight school was to join the National Guard. All they required of pilots was three hundred hours civilian time and a flight test. I signed up right away, and before the year was out I had my wings and a commission as a second lieutenant in the 102nd Observation Squadron. Weekdays I'd mark time at IBM, and every weekend I'd go out to the squadron's airfield on Staten Island and practice.

My father hardly talked to me about the war, but a

couple of weeks after I enlisted he returned his Hitler medal. I knew he'd pinned an awful lot on the idea of World Peace Through World Trade, and the coming of war left him somewhat muted. He wasn't a pacifist, but he was very ambivalent about whether the United States should get into the fight. That was reflected in the way he treated munitions work. Some companies, like North American Aviation, had started shipping warplanes abroad even before Hitler invaded Poland. But Dad didn't like the idea of turning Endicott into an arms plant, and he wasn't happy when the War Department pressed a contract on IBM, in the autumn of 1940, to manufacture machine guns. He set up a subsidiary company in Poughkeepsie, New York, for this work and kept that whole enterprise at arm's length. Of course, when war finally came IBM went all out and Dad put our name proudly on the weapons we made.

In September 1940, Roosevelt mobilized the National Guard and finally I had what I wanted: I was a full-fledged military pilot. My squadron soon moved to Fort McClellan near Anniston, Alabama, for training. Anniston made Endicott seem like a garden spot; it was hot, wet, and boring. But I didn't mind because I was free from IBM, was flying every day, and I had college friends in nearby cities to see on weekends. After having toed the line at IBM for three years in New York, I indulged in some terribly immature behavior. I remember one wild night in Cincinnati, in which I was the only man in uniform at a dinner party, and it suddenly occurred to me that all these people were fiddling while Rome was burning. The host was wealthy, about my age, and he had a marvelous family in a marvelous house in a marvelous town. Somehow I had the idea that he ought to enlist.

I stepped outside to get some air and noticed a garden hose hooked up to the side of the house. I've loved hoses ever since I was little, and this seemed like the perfect way to express what I thought of these self-satisfied people. I turned it on, went back into the dining room, and sprayed the entire dinner party. Two big guys came to life and started after me, but I ran back out and dove into the pool. They'd have thrown me in, anyway. For years after that people would come up to me and say, "Aren't you the guy that hosed down the dinner party at So-and-so's house?" And I'd say, "Gee, I don't think so."

On some level, I think I must have understood it was high time to grow up. Whenever Olive visited for the weekend my behavior improved. We had terrific fun together, and I could sense a depth of emotion in her that more and more made me want to forget the pranks and get serious. We were both still seeing other people, but as war came nearer, marriage seemed more and more appealing. I knew she dreamed of starting a family, and the thought that I might get killed made me want one too. So in November 1941, I visited New York, took her dancing on Starlight Roof at the Waldorf, and asked her to marry me. I had a diamond ring in my pocket. Earlier that day I'd gone to the jeweler Harry Winston in my rumpled uniform, with a plea of poverty, and he gave me a pretty good deal. That was one big difference between me and Dad—he'd have taken out a loan to buy a nice engagement ring, but I preferred to take the cash I had on hand and bargain for one. Olive and I had a big engagement party in Locust Valley, at the home of her aunt Olive Shea, who was married to Ed Shea, the head of the Ethyl Corporation. We scheduled our wedding for the day after Christmas.

I always thought it would be Hitler who'd bring us into the war, but the Japanese beat him to the punch. I was in a car on my way back to the base with my squadron mate John Gwynne and his wife when the news of Pearl Harbor came over the radio. We thought it couldn't be true, but several stations were broadcasting the same report. For a while we sat quietly and finally someone said, "This means major changes in our lives." We knew we'd never stay in Anniston; probably they'd retrain the squadron and send us out to fly bombers.

At the base everyone was very grim. Many people thought the Japanese were going to attack the West Coast any minute. Within a week we got orders transferring the squadron to California. When I heard that, I didn't waste

any time. I called Olive and said, "You have to come
down here so we can get married right away." At first she
cried and said her dress wasn't ready, but she rose to the
occasion. She spent that afternoon in stores and got on a
train with her mother that night. I called my family and
they followed the next day. I asked my father to be best
man, which wasn't the conventional thing to do. I could
have gotten Gwynne or one of my college friends, but
these were men he hardly knew. At that point, Dad was
very much on my mind. Underneath all my resentment
and underneath all the he-bores-me, he-embarrasses-me-
with-his-folderol-about-IBM-Day attitude—underneath
all that was a great love and respect. I couldn't have
resented him as much as I did unless it was based on
some much deeper emotion. The war was upon us and I
thought I might be killed. In that moment of great
drama, I put all my resentment aside. That's why I invited him to be my best man.

The only place for everyone to stay in Anniston was a
cheap hotel near the base that literally had spittoons in
the lobby. I couldn't get away from the base at all, so
Olive had to buy her own wedding ring. At the post
chapel they were banging out a wedding every fifteen
minutes. We nearly missed our slot when the sentries
wouldn't let Olive onto the base—I'd forgotten to give
them her name at the gate. By the time she finally got in,
everybody was upset. We rushed up the aisle together—
the whole wedding party in a bunch—and Olive and I
were married. I knew she was disappointed, getting married in such rough circumstances, and I was determined
that our honeymoon would show some imagination, even
though I only had two days' leave. I'd found a brick
cottage in Anniston that had ivy-covered trellises, rented
it, and stocked it with food and champagne. Dad came
through with one of his thoughtful gestures. There was
no florist in Anniston, so he called one in Atlanta, and
when I carried Olive over the threshold, the cottage was
filled with roses.

·　　·　　·

When you get married, you wonder how long it'll be before your first fight. Everything was speeded up in our case so we only had to wait six days. By then the squadron was on its way to California. I had to fly, and Olive was driving cross-country with Marge Duval, the wife of another lieutenant. They went in the Duvals' convertible, and I'd hired a high school teacher to follow them with my car. It was a slightly used Lincoln that I'd bought from my commanding officer at the base, figuring that cars would soon be impossible to come by. Before we said good-bye, I gave Olive careful instructions: "There are three things I want you to remember. Don't speed. Don't pick anybody up. And don't lose sight of my car. If it gets smashed up or lost we can't replace it. I'll see you in California." We are both pretty independent, but I knew a lot more about the world than she did, and I thought I could save us trouble by telling her exactly what to do. I had no idea what I was getting into. Right off the bat she and Marge found it hard to keep the two cars together, going through towns with stoplights. By the time they reached Texas on the third day, they'd completely lost track of the high school teacher and my car. Then they pulled up at a gas station and the man running it asked, "Would you mind giving my son a ride to the next town? He has to catch a train and he's going to be AWOL unless he can get there." So they let the boy climb in back. Finally they started to speed, because the road was long and flat and they were worried the high school teacher had gotten ahead of them.

Meanwhile my squadron had flown only as far as Midland, Texas, where we had to stop because the weather ahead was bad. I looked on a map at the route the girls would take, and thought, "Olive might come by here today!" So I got an old crate and a Sunday paper and sat down beside the highway, near a railroad crossing. Within an hour, along they came—two beautiful girls in a blue convertible with the top down. I threw the papers up in the air and yelled, and they stopped—quite a distance down the road, because they'd been going so fast. That was number one. As they backed up, a lonesome-looking private sat up in the backseat, where he'd been asleep. That was number two. I was awfully mad. I asked Olive what he was doing there and ordered the poor guy out of the car.

Suddenly it dawned on me that my own car was nowhere in sight. I started hollering, "Where's my car? Where's my car?" Olive became so flustered that she couldn't say where she'd seen it last. Probably she was thinking about divorce. In the midst of all this, a train rumbled by, and by the oddest coincidence it was the train carrying our squadron's enlisted men and ground equipment. They recognized us and started yelling and hanging out the windows. If I hadn't been in such a fury it would have been funny. As it was, we went to a hotel and I called the state police; the schoolteacher had reported in to them and of course the car was fine. We drank champagne that night and I finally stopped being sore.

Our base in California turned out to be an unlit, unpaved airfield at San Bernardino, about fifty miles from Los Angeles. We spent Christmas there in tents. It was terribly bleak; not many of the men had their wives nearby. Luckily Olive had gotten a room at the Mission Inn, quite a nice hotel where I'd stayed with my parents long before. On Christmas Eve she and I got some bourbon and about ten gallons of milk, and we went to the tents and served milk punch to the whole squadron.

At first the squadron sat on that field with no idea what to do, but on the fourth day after Christmas we got our orders. Our mission was to fly up and down the coast looking for Japanese submarines. The flight plan never varied. We would go straight over Los Angeles, out to sea about ten miles, then parallel to the coast at four thousand feet for maximum underwater visibility. When we got as far north as Salinas we went inland, refueled, and came back the same way. We were flying clumsy airplanes called O-47s. The O-47 carried a pilot, an observer, and a gunner. It looked like a pregnant animal with the observer down in the belly peering out of small windows. It had one .30 caliber machine gun, which we

weren't supposed to use if we spotted a submarine because it would just scare the Japanese away. Instead we
were supposed to orbit the thing and radio March Field,
just east of Los Angeles, where they had loaded bombers
ready to attack. Our airplanes were ludicrous for the job.
You needed to be able to go slowly and spot, but to do
that in such heavy, high-speed machines was very difficult.

In my time off I had a lot of fun. Right after New
Year's I rented a little stucco cottage in town for Olive to
share with John Gwynne's wife. It was a two-bedroom
cottage with cheap rugs and motel furniture, and we
shared a bath and kitchenette—pretty primitive living.
The squadron would drop in for parties on the patio, and
we'd serve booze, ginger ale, and sandwiches. One night I
had all thirteen officers there and things were really hoot-
ing when the police came and told us to quiet down. We
started our excuses by saying, "Well, we're going off to
war. . . ." The cops took off their hats and guns and
joined the party.

Near our place was a resort in the San Bernardino
Mountains called the Arrowhead Springs Hotel, and on
days off Olive and I would drive there. I remember seeing
movie people, like Lana Turner. We were ordered not to
go more than thirty miles from our post, but once, when
Gwynne and I had a twenty-four-hour leave, the four of
us went to Los Angeles. I guess they hadn't seen many
aviators there. John's wife Cornee was good looking and
so was Olive, so someone took our picture and it appeared on page two of the Los Angeles *Times*. Luckily
nobody picked up the fact that we were off limits by
twenty miles.

In the first two months of the war, it looked like the
Japanese were overrunning the entire Pacific. They at-
tacked and conquered Hong Kong and captured much of
the Philippines, until Bataan and Corregidor were all that
was left. Far to the east, they took over Wake Island and
set up a base. It wasn't hard to imagine that California
would be next. But I don't think our squadron sighted a
single submarine. Los Angeles had an air raid scare in

which all the lights in town went out and machine guns fired into the sky at nothing. But gradually it became obvious that the Japanese were overextended and they weren't coming. Sub patrol began to seem meaningless and our morale began to sink.

I had to go out of my way to avoid confrontations with Major Nelson, our commander. Our first run-in had been back in Anniston, where I was the squadron safety officer, and he thought I took my responsibility too seriously. It made no difference to him that the airplanes we were flying were hard to maneuver and that the runway on our field was dangerously short with a mountain at one end. Whenever I'd make a suggestion to improve our procedures, Nelson would make fun of me. He thought I was a spoiled rich boy; I thought he was about the poorest leader I'd ever met. After we'd been in California a few weeks they started to pluck men out of our unit to replace crews that had been shot down in New Guinea. The way Nelson let us know about this was by getting the squadron together one morning, calling off three names, and saying, "Let that be a lesson to the rest of you guys. Straighten up or you're next!" I thought, "This is no way to send men off to fight." It would have been great if the Army had kept us together, given us decent airplanes, and made us a bomb squadron. We had working relationships with each other and we all knew our jobs. But it was obvious they were just going to pick us to pieces, and our commander was complying instead of trying to get the best deal for his men.

I decided to use every tool at my disposal to transfer out of there before Nelson got me. Ever since then, when I think trouble is coming my way, I've always taken evasive action. Even if it means making a mistake, I never lie dead in the water. I sent wires to everyone I knew in positions of command, saying I wanted to fly bombers. I went to our group commander and tried to convince him that the military could use my experience elsewhere, but he didn't rise to the bait. Meanwhile three more crews got selected. Every time Nelson lined us up I'd think, "It's going to be Watson." Finally I was desperate; I called my father. I told him, "I'm not shirking. I want you to help me get into bombardment, and I want to join a squadron that's just being formed so I can go through training and know the people I'm flying with."

Dad was quiet for a moment and said, "Tom, I'm reluctant to do this. I'm concerned I might get you into a position worse than the one you're in now. But I'll tell you what—I'll have Mr. Nichol go see General Marshall."

I said, "Oh, that'll be high enough." George Marshall was nothing less than the army chief of staff; Fred Nichol was the executive we'd sung about in IBM school, Dad's trusty number-two man. Just like they taught us in Endicott, Dad was aiming high—calling at the top.

I never thought Nichol would get anywhere, but about a week later I was called to the adjutant's tent and handed a telex ordering me to the Command and General Staff School at Fort Leavenworth, Kansas. I had no idea what that was. I said, "Gee, I don't know whether I want to do this or not. . . ." A colonel from another unit, who happened to be standing nearby, said, "Hell, let me have that telex. I'll see if I can go!" That's how I knew I really had something. As it turned out, the Leavenworth school was one of the most coveted assignments in the Army. The top brass had all been there, and generals chose their aides directly from the graduating class.

Within two days Olive and I were in the car headed for Kansas, with our dog and three or four ginger ale boxes that contained everything we owned. We'd now been married two months and she was pregnant. Somehow we'd gotten gasoline tickets for the trip, and we took advantage of the drive to do a bit of honeymooning. On the first night we stopped at the Grand Canyon and saw the lovely scene of snow coming down through dim moonlight. When we got to Leavenworth we moved into a big old house downtown. The house had been divided up into apartments with beaverboard partitions. It was so primitive that I could talk to Olive while she was taking a bath and I was in the kitchen cooking dinner, but to us it was fun.

I was the only lieutenant in a class of about one hundred. The rest were majors and captains and lieutenant colonels, and people like Marshall and Eisenhower came to lecture us. Thanks to Dad's help, I'd gotten myself in way over my head. My classmates were mostly career army officers already familiar with battle tactics. The Command and General Staff School built on that. We studied things like how you place your machine guns if you've got a valley to defend. None of this had anything to do with flying, but the Army was putting Air Force officers through the school because there was nowhere else to train them.

We had thirteen papers to do, and if you failed three, they threw you out. The grading system was called USA: Unsatisfactory, Satisfactory, and A. By some miracle my first paper was an A, but the second one was a U. That scared me, and I told Olive, "This is serious. Two more of these and I'm out. I'm really going to have to work at this." So I moved out of our apartment and into the room I'd been assigned on the base, and I started studying like hell. I saw older men, senior artillery and cavalry officers, packing their bags, crying because they'd flunked out and their careers were ruined. I got a second U right away, but somehow I pulled through without a third.

Olive put up with living alone without a murmur. This girl I'd married for her beauty and kindness saw with great clarity how desperately I needed to avoid another failure. She also seemed to have a sixth sense about my relationship with Dad. I learned about that one night when my merry friend Nick Lunken—the one who had played that amazing joke on me at IBM school—came to visit. He'd just failed his army physical, I'd just earned another S on a paper, and we were both in the mood for fun. We went to a candlelight dance and Nick said to me, "These are metal chairs we're sitting on. Let's sneak under the table and put candles under a couple of people!" I thought that was a terrific idea, so we did it. I had just about made it back to my place when the people we'd picked screamed and jumped out of their chairs. Then I felt someone tap me on the shoulder. It was the aide of the assistant commandant of the base. He said sarcastically, "I thought you'd like to know that Colonel Shallenberger is amused by your antics."

Olive witnessed this and gave me a pretty strong talking-to later on. "You've got to watch this business," she said. "When you graduate your father's going to be here, and you don't want to be the class clown." She caught me completely off guard. Two months earlier I'd been giving her hell for being irresponsible with my car, but when it came to Dad's expectations, she had a better idea than I did about what constituted the straight path. From that night on, she helped keep me on it.

Dad did come to my graduation. He was proud of my accomplishment, although it seemed to me he was a little subdued. While he was in town, he got a fellow from the Kansas City Art Institute to paint my portrait—IBM had some connection there. The painting wasn't so hot, and once I figured out why Dad had had it done, looking at it made me uneasy. He knew that by graduating I'd just moved closer to the war, and he was preparing himself in case I got killed.

CHAPTER 12

Finally I felt in a position to do something that counted. My war was going to involve flying airplanes, the one thing I knew I was good at. The Air Force was bursting with activity, expanding from three hundred fifty thousand men to more than two million. The Battle of Britain had made it obvious that no one was going to win the war without mastering the air; from now on airplanes were going to be as important to victory as battleships or tanks. I was thrilled to be part of this, and even though in the end I didn't get promoted as far as some people, or come back with as many medals, my successes were my own. For the first time in my life, I wasn't worried about being overshadowed by Dad.

At the time I left Leavenworth one of the big jobs facing the Air Force was transporting heavy bombers to England. The U.S. Eighth Air Force, which was based there, was getting ready to start daylight raids against the Nazis, and American factories were churning out new planes, such as B-17s, by the thousands. These airplanes couldn't hold enough fuel to make it directly across the Atlantic to their bases in England. They had to skirt the ocean, flying up the Atlantic seaboard to Newfoundland, across with stops in Greenland and Iceland, and finally down through Scotland. The airplanes' jumping-off place was New England, part of the territory of the First Air Force, and that was where I was assigned.

My first job was a minor one. In those days most army pilots didn't know how to fly on instruments, and there were numerous crashes. A pilot would enter a cloud bank, lose his sense of direction, and fly right into the ground. I was supposed to help remedy this by promoting the use of Link trainers. These were crude flight simulators, and if a man spent enough time in one he could learn to fly blind. All the air bases had them and the trainers would have helped a great deal, except that most pilots didn't know about them. I was supposed to change that. It was basically a sales job, and I worked hard at it because it was my first chance in the Army to shine. I flew to bases from Presque Isle, Maine, to Philadelphia, preaching Link trainers. I badgered commanders for statistics on trainer usage and showed them how theirs compared with the records of other bases. I got senior officers to write letters recommending the things. I went totally overboard—but usage of the trainers went up by a factor of six and I think I saved some lives.

This modest success caught the attention of Major General Follett Bradley, the head of the First Air Force. In June 1942, he asked if I would become his aide-de-camp. His offer took me by surprise and posed a real dilemma. If I said no, it might hurt my chances in the Air Force; but if I said yes, I might be getting into a personal service job that I didn't want and didn't know how to handle. There was also Olive to think about, because the wives of generals' aides always end up working as aides to the generals' wives. But we decided that the job was a step forward, and I took it. It was the best thing that could have happened.

I have worked for two great managers in my life. My father was one and the other was Follett Bradley. Bradley was one of the pioneers of the Air Corps, having been, among other things, the first to make a radio transmission from an airplane to the ground. He joined right after World War I, when the Air Corps was known as a place for daredevils, ne'er-do-wells, and drunks. But Bradley was a skillful flier and a natural leader. Like Billy Mitchell and Jimmy Doolittle he understood that the Air Corps was going to become really important. He was about fifteen years younger than Dad, nearly bald with only a fringe of white hair, and he had a round face with deep-set penetrating eyes. He smoked from a long cigarette holder and wore pince-nez which he kept in his left breast pocket, attached by a black ribbon around his neck. A fine-looking man, fun to talk to, and a great builder of morale. He took a couple of rides with me in his twin-engine B-23 to make sure I was competent, and immediately made me his pilot. After that he'd frequently ride down in the plane's nose, chatting with some other officer while I sat proudly at the controls, gaining confidence by the minute. I wanted to be as much help to him as I could.

Bradley was busy making inspections around New England, trying to get the bombers overseas faster. There were problems with overcrowding and delays at airports along the transport route. At the first field we came to, in northern Massachusetts, he and a couple of other men toured the base while I stood waiting near the plane. Before they came back I said to myself, "This is a great waste of time." I needed to assure myself that I was something more than an aerial chauffeur.

By our next stop, Hartford, I had decided that I'd follow the general everywhere unless he told me not to, and that I'd write him a complete summary of each inspection. In these reports I discussed the officers we met, supplies that were needed, and my own recommendations about operations. I noted right away that part of the bomber-delay problem was psychological. The longer a bomber group stayed at an airport in the U.S., the longer they wanted to stay. If they moved directly through New England and out to Gander in Newfoundland or Goose Bay, Labrador, they'd go on and finish the trip in a week. But if there was not constant pressure on the group to move, move, move, the delays piled up. That was the sort of observation I'd write. On these reports Bradley would often scrawl, "Thank you very much" and sometimes "Excellent" or even "Splendid"—small compliments that drove me to do an even better and more vigorous job. My months with Bradley were among the most important of my life because he showed me that I had an orderly mind and an unusual ability to focus on what was important and put it across to others.

After only a couple of weeks, Bradley took me to Washington. When I asked what we were doing, he said we were going to get me promoted to captain. He knew how much this meant to me: after finishing the paperwork, he walked me to the PX in the old Munitions Building, bought captain's bars, and pinned them on me himself.

In early summer Bradley was ordered to Moscow to oversee a much more ticklish transport problem: getting airplanes to Stalin. Russia was in desperate need of weapons and supplies from the U.S.: the Germans had Leningrad under siege in the north and were closing in on Stalingrad and the oilfields near Baku in the south. One of the biggest headaches was how to deliver P-39 and P-40 fighters and A-20 light bombers. Because of their short range, the only possible way to deliver large numbers of these planes quickly and safely was to fly them to Alaska and then, in short hops, five thousand miles across Siberia. Bradley's job was to get this ferry route set up—a matter of great strategic importance. When he asked if I would come along, my immediate reply was: "Nothing would please me more." But in fact I was filled with dread. The war had reached its grimmest point, with the Axis powers dominant on every front, and I was committing myself to an indefinite stay abroad, possibly for years. Olive and I spent sleepless nights wondering what was going to happen and how she was going to get through her pregnancy alone. At that point I couldn't even tell her where I was going—we'd been ordered to refer to our destination only as "Plainfield."

Getting ready for that trip was the biggest job I'd ever undertaken. Bradley said we might be in Moscow as long as eight months, and that we'd be lucky to get food and housing. Everything else we might need had to be brought along. I spent three hot weeks working in an IBM apartment in a Washington hotel, writing directives for each of our ten crew members and lists of supplies— arctic kits, materials to coldproof an airplane, recreational reading material, and so on. Anything that was forgotten was going to be my fault. We drew a brand-new B-24, the most advanced heavy bomber, and Bradley hand-picked the crew, including Lee Fiegel, an experienced bomber man, for pilot. Even though I'd organized the trip, Bradley demoted me to copilot because I had no experience in four-engine planes. I have to admit that the B-24 awed me. Before the service I'd flown nothing but little puddle jumpers and navigated with a road map. In the National Guard we still had single-engine planes, and it was big stuff to fly from Alabama to New York—seven hundred miles, or about three hours. Now suddenly I was flying one of the biggest airplanes in the world—a gross weight of twenty-eight tons, a crew of eight, gun ports, and a range of twenty-six hundred miles when equipped with extra fuel tanks. Lee spent a lot of time showing me how things worked and we became lifelong friends. Two days before we left, my parents and sisters visited; Dick would have been there too but he had enlisted in the Army himself and was stationed at the Aberdeen Proving Ground in Maryland. Bradley let me take Mother up in the bomber. She'd never been flying before, but she seemed to enjoy it while Dad stood by nervously on the ground.

Even in a B-24 the wartime flight to Moscow was a tremendous undertaking. Getting there took ten days. We had to go south to Brazil, cross to Africa, and then wend our way up avoiding the colonial territory controlled by the Vichy government. Then north via Cairo, Palestine, and Teheran, and over the Caucasus mountains into Russia. Like many aviators in those days, I was very nervous about flying over water, far from any airfield in case we had trouble.

We crossed the South Atlantic on a full-moon night, with cumulus clouds billowing up in ghostly pillars. Halfway across, I made a routine check on the crew. I climbed down from the flight deck into the nose where the navigator worked. We didn't have the experienced man Bradley had picked for the job, but a last-minute substitute. He was almost completely bald, and I could see his head slumped down on the big navigating table in front of him. I touched him on the shoulder and he jumped. "How's it going, Bill?" I said.

"I don't know. I just can't get started."

I looked on the floor and there were about twenty little balls of crumpled-up paper. "What's all this?"

"I can't get any of the sights to work out."

"What do you mean! We're in the middle of the Atlantic!"

"Yeah, but this is the Southern Hemisphere—I really don't know these stars."

I went back up and said to Lee, "I think it's too late to do anything but stay on the course this guy has set, but he says he doesn't know where we are!"

Lee went down and talked to him for a while. There was no point in bawling him out so we didn't do that. We were heading in the right general direction but it was impossible to tell exactly where we were. At dawn we started looking anxiously for land and didn't see any until an hour after we were supposed to. By the time we finally put down at Accra in what is now Ghana, the gas gauges were at zero.

That wasn't our only close call on the trip. A few days later, when we crossed into Russia and were about to stop for fuel at Baku on the Caspian Sea, I climbed down into the belly of the plane directly beneath the flight deck to check the nose wheel before landing. I was still in the middle of this routine when Lee absentmindedly pushed the landing-gear control to the "down" position. It was totally out of character for him to make a mistake like that, but this time he did. To my horror the giant wheel I was inspecting began ponderously to drop through the ever widening opening in the floor of the compartment. I leaped toward the navigator's deck and almost made it, but one of my legs got pinned. I screamed at the navigator to give me his headphones, and forced myself not to panic as I described my situation to Lee: "I'm caught— one leg between the landing-gear door and the side of the aircraft, and the other side of the door is resting on top of the nose-wheel strut. If you land now, the travel of the nose wheel will cause that door to cut my leg off." I was spread-eagled over the open door with the oilfields of Baku a thousand feet below. The radio operator came down, took a look at my situation, became faint, and had to be pulled back into the safety of the bomb bay. Then General Bradley came down wearing his pince-nez. He took a long look and called for a hacksaw. Within five minutes he sawed through the hinge at the rear of the landing-gear door and it fell loose, freeing my leg.

When we reached Moscow in August the tide of the war was about to turn, but that was not discernible to the Russians or to us. Hitler's best armies were hammering at them for the second year, and the casualties at places like Leningrad and Sevastopol must have been appalling even to Stalin; already millions of Russians were dead of wounds and starvation, and millions more had been captured. The year before, the Nazis had come so close to Moscow that they could be seen from the towers of the Kremlin. Most of the government, along with the Allied embassies, pulled back to the town of Kuybyshev, five hundred miles to the rear. The Russian winter and the courage of the Red Army had thrown the Nazis back, but when we got there Moscow was still officially in a state of siege. We moved into the National Hotel overlooking Red Square. In the moat next to the Kremlin, which was visible from our rooms, there was a fleet of small trucks loaded with file cases. Those were the archives of the Russian nation, ready to be evacuated if the Nazis reached the gates again. All day long clerks would come out to the trucks, pick out files, and run back inside. The people you'd see on the street showed obvious signs of malnutrition—red eyelids, sunken cheeks, and fat bellies from eating nothing but bread. They were so poor and transport was so short that mourners on the way to funerals carried their dead, wrapped in sacking, in their arms.

Scarcely a week after we got to Moscow, Winston Churchill flew in. Stalin had been pushing for an immediate invasion of Europe by England and the U.S., and Churchill came to tell him face-to-face that this wasn't going to happen anytime soon. In his memoir Churchill compared this to "delivering a large lump of ice to the North Pole." It took him three days to calm the Russians down, and when he took off for Cairo on the morning of

the fourth day, we were his armed escort as far as Teheran. The night before I'd had the great experience of attending a diplomatic reception and shaking the prime
minister's hand.

Unfortunately the flight with Churchill was the occasion of a major blow-up between me and our crew. We'd
only been away from home three weeks, but already a
pattern was developing: every time we really needed these
men, some of them were drunk. It was my job to collect
the crew on mornings we had to fly. If we were supposed
to take off at 8:00 A.M., I'd get up at 5:00 and go into
their rooms and drag them out. On the morning we were
supposed to fly with Churchill, I found the master sergeant and the crew chief playing strip poker with a bunch
of Russian babes. On the way out I jumped all over the
sergeant: "God damn it, you don't have to fly more than
once every few days, and every time we fly you're
loaded!" He claimed he was doing more card playing
than drinking, but I didn't believe it. When we got to the
plane he had to inspect the engines, and he forgot to
screw the covers back on after checking the oil. So just as
we broke ground on the runway, sections of cowling flew
up on all four engines and eventually tore away. I'm sure
Churchill's pilots saw that and wondered what the hell
was happening to our airplane. I really bored in on the
sergeant for that.

General Bradley's discussions with the Soviets didn't
go any more smoothly than Churchill's. I wasn't in on
the meetings, but among my other duties I was the mission's code clerk and saw all the messages that went out.
The behavior of both sides was pretty disillusioning. The
Russians were as annoying as they sometimes are today;
we were trying to do them and ourselves a favor, bringing
airplanes across Siberia, and they were giving Bradley
guff about the type of rubber in the tires. Bradley had to
have interminable discussions with them about the airplanes' specifications, the schedule on which they'd be
available, the number of pilots the U.S. would use to
deliver them, and so on. Even then, the Russians were
convinced we mainly wanted to spy, so they decided to

use their own pilots to fly the planes across Siberia. Now it was the War Department's turn to be intransigent. When it heard that Russia wasn't going to let U.S. pilots in, it cut from forty to ten the number of transport planes being offered to bring pilots back to Alaska on the return leg of the ferry route. That was very hard for me to accept as fair. There was no question about the qualifications of the Russian pilots, so how could we justify making it hard for them to do their job?

This tedious debate went on and on, and I spent many hours sliding small strips of paper back and forth in metal racks, which was the method we used for coding and decoding telegrams. If nothing else, I demonstrated to Bradley that I had a certain evenness of temper and an ability to work in a sustained way. Before long the general started turning to me when he had a decision to hash out. In retrospect, I think that he may have seen me as sort of a son. His own boy had been killed demonstrating a B-17 over England before we got into the war.

There was another bond between us: we were both unhappy because we weren't getting any letters from our wives. I missed Olive desperately and our first baby was on the way, but unluckily for me, she and Mrs. Bradley had become friends. Mrs. Bradley was famous for getting "inside information" that was wrong. I had told Olive exactly how to address her letters to me, but Mrs. Bradley said, "Oh, no, that's wrong, here's the way you write them." As a result Bradley and I didn't get any mail while everybody else in the crew was getting letters every week. Homesickness and longing for my wife hit me in waves. I was never without these emotions, but sometimes I'd feel as if there were a knife twisting in my chest. At those moments I'd damn Hitler and Hirohito and dream of settling down to married life in a home of my own.

Life in Moscow got pretty slow during the three months it took Bradley to settle things with the Russians. The heavy autumn rains that slowed down Hitler's armies came and went, and then the temperature dropped well below zero. The Russians had kept their ballet and opera companies going in spite of the war, and we saw some good performances; a number of us even took Russian lessons. Periodically we'd be sent down to Teheran, where you could buy anything, and we'd come back with the bomb bay full of food and other necessities for the embassy staff. Llewellyn Thompson rode along on one of those trips, and became my friend—he was a junior diplomat then, but went on to become perhaps the greatest U.S. ambassador to the Soviet Union. I was also friendly with some of the foreign correspondents like Eddie Gilmore, Walter Kerr of the New York *Herald Tribune,* Henry Shapiro, and Ben Robertson. Our primary source of news was the BBC, which carried reliable war coverage every afternoon. I was eager to hear about the battle for North Africa, because I was convinced that the fight against Rommel would foretell the outcome of the war. The British made slow progress at first, but when they beat the Germans at El Alamein, and when the Americans landed in Algeria and Morocco a few days later, the mood brightened considerably at our nightly poker games.

I was the only one of our crew who had been in Moscow before, during the summer of 1937 after graduating from Brown, and I was tremendously curious to see how the city had changed. Whenever I got loose, I'd find another crew member and walk for five or ten miles. Women constantly introduced themselves to us. We figured they were informers, but we'd have gone stir-crazy not talking to anybody but each other for three months. Mostly the married men stayed straight, but things got pretty complicated for some of the crew. At one point three of them were all seeing the same girl, whose name was Ludmilla and who claimed to be a ballerina. I made friends with a nurse called Tanya who somehow got my name and telephoned me at our little office. We talked with the aid of two dictionaries and spent a fair amount of time together, although the relationship was platonic. After a few weeks we were able to communicate pretty well, and she took me to visit her apartment. There were three different families living there. Tanya had what looked like the maid's room, next to the kitchen, but each of the other rooms housed a whole family. They owned almost nothing. I asked Tanya to show me what she had to wear and she opened her wardrobe. Inside were a winter dress, a summer dress, a big padded overcoat and some clumsy high felt boots, a pair of flat shoes, a pair of high heels, a sweater, and some blouses and underwear. That was it. Whenever I went down to Teheran I'd bring back stockings or shoes or some such for Tanya and other Russians I'd gotten to know.

By early November airplanes from the U.S. were finally flying in across Siberia, and we packed up to leave. Bradley thought we'd be back in Russia soon, since Americans would be needed to help oversee the transport operation. The Russians were pleased enough that they gave us permission to fly home by the route that best suited our needs—southeastward into China, where Bradley had to confer with another U.S. general, then across Siberia to Alaska. This was a great privilege—as it turned out, we were one of the few American military crews to fly eastbound across Siberia during the war. To celebrate our bond with the Russians, Bradley named our airplane the *Muscovite* and had it painted on the nose in Cyrillic characters.

I was terribly excited to see China again, especially when our flight path paralleled the Great Wall in Kansu province. When I realized that I'd seen a part of this same wall near Peking in 1937, I was amazed. Peking was about a thousand miles away. We landed at the ancient city of Ch'eng-tu, near Chiang Kai-shek's wartime capital of Chungking, and got rooms at a little hostel called the Society for Moral Endeavor near the airfield. It was clean and neat and my room overlooked a very pretty garden. Everywhere I could see the charm that made me want to return to China again and again.

We lay over for a few days to get the airplane ready for flying in the Siberian winter. Bradley put me in charge, and I sorted out the tasks and assigned them to the men. Toward the end of the first day I mentioned to them that we'd almost certainly have another mission to Russia. To my surprise the men said, "Don't count on us," and bluntly told me that they'd rather have combat assignments than go through another trip with me.

It was one of the rudest shocks I've ever experienced. Here I was, well into my Air Force career, the son of a famous manager, and I still hadn't learned how to handle the men working for me. By being so eager to please Bradley, I had antagonized everybody below. They complained I was too demanding, never relaxed the pace, and insisted on getting every job done perfectly. They thought I was petty, and they were right: petty criticism is not useful if people are doing a reasonably good job. If their energy level is high and their aim is fairly close to the target, it's better to let things jog along.

I said to myself, "I can't get anywhere if I can't manage these men." I decided to do what I could to win them over. For starters, I drove them twenty-four miles into Ch'eng-tu where I bought them the best dinner I could find and thanked them for all they'd done. On the next leg of our flight, I tried to ask each man how his spirits were and whether he'd gotten any mail while we were in China. I also presented the crew with little pieces of pewter I'd bought in Ch'eng-tu. The men's morale was improving because we were on our way home; there was no way to tell if my efforts were having any effect.

Our flight through Siberia took us to the remote town of Yakutsk on the Lena River, where it was minus 22 degrees Fahrenheit when we arrived. I had to admire the Russians for maintaining a real town this far north—even if one of its main industries was a prison. Yakutsk was used as a place to exile people from Moscow, and is one of the coldest spots on earth. Its only communication with the outside world was down the Lena River, which empties into the Laptev Sea in the Arctic. At one point I took off my glove, not thinking, and froze my finger on the propeller controls.

The following night we took off, hoping to push straight through to Nome, Alaska, two thousand miles to the east. But it was about 40 below and the cold was affecting the way the engines cooled and lubricated themselves. My job as copilot was to manage the engines, and our number-four engine was only delivering about half power. I had to push the three good engines beyond their safe settings to get us into the air. We climbed very well through moonlight and broken clouds for about twenty minutes, and I began to think we might make it. But about half an hour after takeoff, the oil temperature on number four went up and its oil pressure went down. When that happens, something is seriously wrong and you have to act fast because the engine will catch fire once it gets hot enough. I said, "I think we ought to shut down that engine."

There was no immediate response. None of us was thinking terribly clearly because the flight-deck heaters were broken and it was so cold. Fiegel didn't say much and the general, who was standing between us, didn't either. I said, "I don't want to be an s.o.b. here, but if we don't do something about that engine, we may not be able to shut it down. I recommend we shut down the damn engine!"

The general said, "Yeah, I think you'd better do that, Tom."

There was a big red button and I punched it and the engine stopped quite nicely. We didn't have full power on the other three, because number two was a little sick as well—maybe we had 65 percent power altogether. We were in real trouble—picking up ice, unable to hold our altitude, but still headed for Nome, eighteen hundred miles away. We were making no effort to turn. I sat that out for maybe one minute. Then I said, "Hey, fellas, don't tell me we're going to fly to Nome on three engines. We're getting ice right now, and we'll get further and further out here where there's no airport and we'll have a hell of a time." Finally Bradley said we should turn back.

The lights of Yakutsk were one of the grandest sights I have ever seen, because I thought we would never make it back alive. By now it was snowing hard. Our flaps didn't work and we could barely get the landing gear down. We started to sink at an alarming rate and I pushed the two good engines past their limits to check us. The plane was so heavy with ice that it took all the strength of both Lee and me at the controls to handle it at all. We made our last turn just off the ground and it looked to me as though we were going to crack up, but we finally straightened out for the runway, which was dimly visible through the snow. We were still sinking. I saw trees ahead and yelled at Lee but he couldn't see them because of the ice on his windshield. So I pulled back on the wheel and blasted the throttles. The boys in the cabin told me that at that point the general covered his eyes. We zoomed over the trees and hit the end of the runway without much of a bump. I think we were all as pleased as if the war were over.

We were back in town before dawn, very glad to see our warm rooms with their rough-hewn timber walls and coal stoves. Our plane was finished for the winter, and we were stuck in Yakutsk for a week before the Russians could arrange a cargo plane to take us out. Most of the crew were content to sit around their rooms but in spite of the cold I got out every day with Harley Trice, our interpreter, to see the town. Whenever we walked, one or two of the local commissars would join us and a crowd would gather. I'll warrant that fewer than twenty-five foreigners who weren't also prisoners had been there in fifty years. The west side of Yakutsk seemed to be one big prison camp, though they never let us get close enough to be sure. The town was full of Poles who were ex-prisoners and still too poor to leave, and many of the people we met spoke French or German.

The place also had a strong native culture, which I found much more charming than the Communist culture. The natives, called Yakuts, looked like a cross between Eskimos and Chinese, with slanted eyes and fierce mustaches. They wore felt boots and fur garments and drove little Siberian ponies or reindeer. We froze until they supplied us with leggings, gloves, and boots, and I bought a fur coat for my soon-to-be-born baby. At the town museum, which was unheated, we saw a mastodon that had been dug up nearby and the mummy of a native princess dressed in very rich furs and beads. There were

Dad in his early days as a traveling salesman. He started out peddling sewing machines off the back of a wagon. (IBM Archive)

John H. Patterson, owner of National Cash Register, around 1900.
(IBM Archive)

After a few years working for Patterson, Dad learned how to dress like a businessman. (IBM Archive)

My mother and father at the time of their marriage, 1913.

Dad rallying the National Cash Register sales force in 1913. (IBM Archive)

An installation of Hollerith machines. This primitive punch-card equipment was what attracted Dad to the Computing-Tabulating-Recording Company in 1914. (IBM Archive)

Myself at age four. I have no recollection of the checked coat, but I loved canes—my father always carried one.

I'm mad; he's mad. I can remember him saying to my mother standing by the photographer, "Jeannette! No more!"

(IBM Archive)

Dad was an early home-movie buff. He had his chauffeur film us playing skin-the-cat.

Dick, Helen, Jane, and I during our first trip to Europe. Mother and Father parked us with a governess in Bournemouth, England, and traveled all over the Continent setting up small sales offices.

My brother was so proud to be photographed with Dad and me. Even when Dick was little he showed neatness and flair; I was sloppy and could never get my clothes straight.

Our family returning from Europe aboard the ocean liner Aquitania *in 1929, one month before the stock-market crash.* (IBM Archive)

I was all of thirteen years old in this picture. My father insisted that I dress in a man's suit and go with him to an IBM sales meeting.
(IBM Archive)

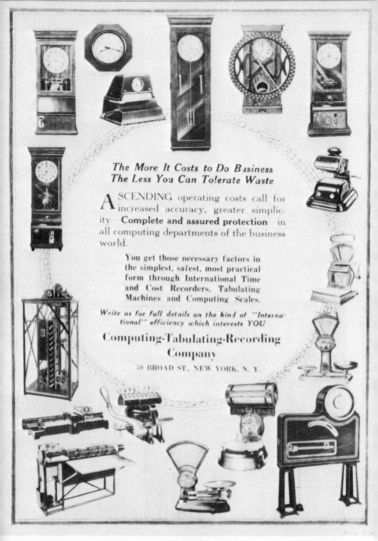

The More It Costs to Do Business
The Less You Can Tolerate Waste

ASCENDING operating costs call for increased accuracy, greater simplicity **Complete and assured protection** in all computing departments of the business world.

You get those necessary factors in the simplest, safest, most practical form through International Time and Cost Recorders, Tabulating Machines and Computing Scales.

Write us for full details on the kind of "International" efficiency which interests YOU

Computing-Tabulating-Recording Company

50 BROAD ST. NEW YORK, N. Y.

The CTR product line in 1920. The machines are laid out clockwise in order of how much money they made: time equipment was most profitable, scales second, and punch-card machines, at lower left, were just a small business then. (IBM Archive)

The 1925 Hundred Percent Club convention in Atlantic City. Probably my father barely knew the salesman he was greeting, but he shook the fellow's hand as though he were the last man on earth. (IBM Archive)

A company luncheon in Cuba, 1931. Dad is at the far end of the table. He nurtured sales operations all over the world with the vision that IBM would someday be big. (IBM Archive)

The IBM country club at Endicott, New York. Any employee could join for a dollar a year. (IBM Archive)

A local sales office in 1924, the year IBM got its name. Both storefront and men look sharp, the way Dad liked. (IBM Archive)

A FEW OF IBM'S MORE THAN 700 AIDS TO MODERN ENTERPRISE

The IBM product line in 1933, the year I started college. By this time, tabulating machines had risen to the top, and scales were at the bottom. We'd added meat slicers and coffee grinders, but Dad eventually became embarrassed by them and sold the division off.
(IBM Archive)

The IBM exhibit at the 1939 World's Fair. Enshrined in the bubble is a tabulating machine; along the back wall is an art exhibit dreamed up by Dad to impress visitors with IBM's size—it featured a painting from each of the countries in which IBM did business.
(IBM Archive)

My first airplane was a Fairchild 24, which I bought in 1935. That's real joy on my face—I'd finally discovered something I was good at.

My first try at business. I did the flying while the photographer shot pictures of yachts out the side door. We tied a rope around his waist to keep him from falling out.

Just out of college in summer 1937, I traveled across Asia as secretary to a man selling pavilion space for the 1939 World's Fair. A high-speed Japanese train carried us through Manchuria.

Dad on his way to meet King George VI in June 1937. He missed my college graduation as a result. (IBM Archive)

The "Steps of Learning" at the IBM school building. This is what I faced in autumn 1937, when I returned from my world tour. (IBM Archive)

After fumbling around IBM for a couple of years I left to become a military pilot. I loved being outside Dad's realm, even though I was initially assigned to fly clumsy observation planes. *(IBM Archive)*

Olive Cawley often came down from New York to visit me at Fort McClellan in Alabama, where I was training. We got married a few days after Pearl Harbor.

Loading our B-24 for the 1942 mission to Moscow, where we arranged for the delivery of Lend-Lease warplanes to Stalin. General Follett Bradley made me second pilot and mission supply officer—more responsibility than I'd ever had in my life.

The Bradley mission to Moscow.

(G. D. S. / Jeffrey L. Ward)

My friend General Bradley, flanked by two commandants and a secret-police officer near the Soviet city of Tashkent, in November 1942. The Soviets let us fly home across their country to Alaska.

A brief respite with Olive in New York, 1944.

implements that indicated a very old civilization. On our third day in Yakutsk we went out to watch ice cutting on the snow-covered river. There one really got a picture of the frozen waste of Siberia. The river plain was flat and snowy and dismal. In the distance I could see the town belching dense clouds of coal smoke in a vain effort to fend off the cold. It was so penetrating that it froze our eyelashes.

That night the general asked me to come up to his room. We talked about everything under the sun. Eventually he brought up the next mission into Russia, saying that Lee Fiegel didn't like staff work much and wasn't interested in going again. He said, "Tom, I am going to make you first pilot. You have worked hard and you've learned a lot and I'm very pleased. You can depend on this." If he had given me a million dollars I couldn't have felt better.

That night I went right down to the crew chief's room, told him I hoped he didn't feel as bad as he once had about me, and asked if he'd stay on. He said yes. So did the rest of the men. The efforts I'd made with them saved me the great embarrassment of having to tell Bradley that his crew had rejected me as its leader. The funny thing was that once I'd really started thinking about the men, I found it easy to make them reasonably happy. The old angle really worked—a little recognition, a few pats on the back.

We finally flew out in a Russian cargo plane that took us over the sharp, leaden peaks of eastern Siberia. The fields where we stopped to refuel were already full of brand-new American-built warplanes destined for the Eastern front. Bradley's Alaska-Siberia ferry route, or Alsib, was a great success—by the end of the war nearly eight thousand planes made their way along it to Russia. Even our own B-24 made a contribution after the Russians got it flying again. In the official records of aircraft turned over to Russia during the war there are a lot of fighters, light bombers, and transport planes, and *one* heavy bomber. That was ours—a little monument to the Bradley mission.

• • •

I got back to New York in time for the birth of our first son just before Christmas 1942. But two months later this great joy turned to tragedy.

I was making a practice flight one afternoon in a DC-3 near Washington when a call on the radio said, "Captain Watson, land immediately." At the field I found an IBM man waiting in his chesterfield and bowler. He said, "Tom, I've got bad news. Your baby's very sick. Your father called and you've got to go to New York." I ran back to the DC-3. Those were pretty informal days. Over the radio the flight sergeant gave me permission to borrow the plane. An hour later I landed at La Guardia field and there, sitting on a wall, was my beautiful Olive with Father standing beside her. When I saw them both I knew the baby was dead. The nurse had taken him to the park in his carriage and somehow he'd died in his sleep. Olive was beside herself with grief, and Father was upset that she had come out, because in his old-fashioned way he thought she should sit with the dead baby for twenty-four hours. But she didn't want to see the body at all and I didn't blame her.

As soon as we got back to our small apartment I went to look at the carriage. I took the sheet out, and then I took the pillowcase off, and there was a little trace of blood right where the baby's mouth would have been. He had obviously suffocated and thrown out some blood in his struggles. I put the pillowcase in the washing machine and hid away the baby's other personal things. We decided we'd better ask for an autopsy to see if there was something wrong with us as parents. So they came and took the baby. We never got a written report. The doctors simply said, "You have nothing to worry about. Go right ahead and have more babies."

The next day a death notice appeared in the paper and our telephone rang. It was Ben Robertson, one of the correspondents I'd met in Moscow. I said, "Hello, Ben, nice to hear your voice. We've got a tragedy here and I just can't talk now."

"I know about the tragedy. I'm here in your building."

"What do you mean?"

"I want to talk to you. Come on down."

I went downstairs and he walked me to the park and back and said just enough that I felt a little better. I didn't know Ben well, and it meant so much to me that he would do that—it was an act of singular kindness. That night he got on a Pan Am flying boat and was killed when it flipped over landing in fog in Lisbon harbor. But he had taught me a crucial lesson: if you can help a man in a period of great grief, you should go out of your way to do it.

We buried the baby at Sleepy Hollow Cemetery in Westchester County, where my father owned a plot that had been empty up to now. It was awful, piling into a car in the middle of winter and going to see that little coffin lowered into the ground. Then I took Olive away to a resort for military people near Jacksonville, Florida. It was an overnight train ride and I'd bought a bottle of Scotch. I poured Olive a drink and me a drink. Then I said, "I don't think this is going to help much with this kind of problem." She said, "I agree with you." So I poured the Scotch down the basin and we sat together and felt all our sorrow.

CHAPTER 13

I steered clear of IBM for most of the war. Dad and I saw each other a number of times each year, but never discussed the business. And yet IBM was hard to avoid. The entire military was beginning to move by IBM cards, because warfare had become so big and complicated that bookkeeping had to be done right on the battlefield. Toward the end of the war I'd land on some Pacific atoll just taken from the Japanese and find a mobile punch-card unit there, tabulating the payroll. (These were the invention of my brother Dick, who was a major in the army Ordnance Corps by the end of the war; it was his idea to put punch-card machines on army trucks for use in combat zones.) IBM cards kept track of bombing results, casualties, prisoners, displaced persons, and supplies. There was a punch-card record of every man drafted, and it followed him through induction, classification, training, and service, right up to his discharge. There were also IBM machines involved in a lot of top-secret applications. Our equipment was used to break the Japanese code before the Battle of Midway and to help in hunting down German U-boats at sea.

Making machines for the armed forces and defense suppliers would have been enough to keep IBM's factories whirring at full capacity. But IBM was also called on to make ordnance—machine guns for fighter planes, infantry carbines, bombsights, gas masks, and more than thirty other war items. To keep up with this, Dad set up a new factory in the town of Poughkeepsie and doubled the size of our Endicott plant. By the middle of the war fully two thirds of IBM's factory capacity was devoted to ordnance work.

Dad could have made tens of millions of dollars on

this business, but that didn't interest him. He was very sensitive about making money from war production, both on moral grounds and out of concern for IBM's image. He didn't want the company accused of profiteering. So he had a rule that IBM could make no more than one percent profit on munitions, and IBM's annual profit for each war year stayed the same as it had been in 1940. As far as Dad's own salary went, he had a proportion of it, representing the extra wartime business, set aside in a fund for widows and orphans of IBM men killed in action.

All the same, World War II benefited IBM a great deal by pushing us into the ranks of really big businesses. Even though profits didn't get any higher, sales *tripled*— from forty-six million dollars in 1940 to one hundred forty million in 1945. The war also showed Dad that IBM could expand fast without losing its character. With just a few experienced men from Endicott he was able to hire two thousand new people at Poughkeepsie, teach them IBM values, and get them to produce in a hurry. He was proud of this work force of "farmers, clerks, artists, and teachers," as he called them. This success increased Dad's appetite for growth. By 1944 he was saying that he had no intention of allowing IBM to shrink back down when peace came.

My father went out of his way to back up the IBM people who had joined the service. He paid each man a quarter of his usual pay while in uniform, and each Christmas, Dad would send a box of food and gifts and every once in a while a sweater or a pair of gloves. He did this partly out of patriotism and partly out of shrewdness, because he wanted those skilled people to come back. I got war pay and food packages from IBM like everyone else, and *Business Machines,* the company newspaper, seemed to find its way to me every week, no matter where I was. It was filled with news of how IBM was supporting America's war effort. There would be a picture of Dad surrounded by flags, opening yet another factory, with a band and a diva from the Metropolitan Opera on hand to help the festivities along.

I always turned down Dad's invitations to come to Endicott for celebrations. The longer I worked with General Bradley the more I thought about making the Air Force my career. When we left Russia we expected that we'd soon go back to help supervise the Siberian air transport operation. But the Russians abruptly stopped letting in Americans, and meanwhile Bradley's career took an unexpected turn. I was with him at the Pentagon just after Christmas 1942 when a call came from the White House. The general was asked to see Harry Hopkins, Roosevelt's right-hand man.

Bradley brought me with him, and we reported to the wing of the White House opposite the Oval Office, where Hopkins had a whole suite, including a place to sleep. It was my first visit to the White House, and I thought meeting Hopkins was the next best thing to seeing Roosevelt himself. By then Hopkins had such bad stomach trouble that after shaking our hands he stretched out on a chaise longue and propped his feet up on the wall. "Don't mind me," he said. "This is the only way I get comfortable."

Bradley sat in front of him and I was off to the side with a notebook. Bradley said, "This is Captain Watson, and I have him along because he takes good notes. If you don't have any objection he'll just sit here as we talk."

"Not at all. Are you any relation to Tom Watson?"

"I'm his son."

"Isn't that interesting! I know him. He's the only business friend Roosevelt has."

Then Hopkins turned to Bradley. "You may know that Admiral Standley, who is our ambassador to the Soviet Union, is leaving. . . ."

We were there about two hours, and I left with a fistful of notes. They had discussed the Soviets and, while Hopkins hadn't come right out and said it, it was pretty clear that Bradley was going to be offered the ambassadorship. The last thing Hopkins said to us was: "I'm sure the president will be in touch with you within a few days." As we drove back to the Pentagon, Bradley said, "If it's true, would you go back to Russia with me?" I took that as a great compliment and, of course, said yes.

The first four days we did nothing but wait for the call. Finally, after about two weeks, Bradley said, "What do you think?"

"I guess it isn't going to happen."

"I think you're right."

Roosevelt eventually sent Averell Harriman, after the post had been vacant for five or six months. But I sensed right away what had knocked Bradley out of the running. He had a weak spot where women were concerned, and the U.S. embassy officials in Moscow objected to his appointment. Bradley had lived in Spaso House, the ambassador's residence, while we were there. More than thirty years later, after I became ambassador, I'd sometimes go into his old room and sit quietly, thinking of my friend—how much he'd done for me and how sad it was that he'd missed out on something he really wanted.

After Bradley gave up waiting for Roosevelt's phone call, he went to Hap Arnold, the commander of the Air Force, for another assignment. Arnold named him to the new post of air inspector, which was later called inspector general. This meant Bradley was chief troubleshooter for an Air Force that now numbered more than a million men around the world. Bradley asked me to stay as his pilot and offered me a place as a technical inspector, which mainly involved going around to air bases to see that planes were safely maintained. I was happy to say yes, even though we'd be based in Washington, far from any action. Olive had been badly depressed since the loss of our baby, and I wanted to spend time with her.

For about a year and a half I flew a variety of inspection missions around the United States, always returning to Olive after a week or ten days. We rented a little house in the Virginia countryside and were able to live together for the first time. It was great coming home from a trip. I'd get my airplane going like hell and come in low right over our roof. By the time I'd landed at Bolling Field and gotten the airplane buttoned up, Olive would be driving in the gate to meet me. Later on we rented an apartment closer to town, so Olive would have people to talk to when I was away. One couple living near us was Eliot and Molly Noyes. Eliot was an imaginative fellow who ran the Air Force glider program and later became one of the world's great industrial designers. He wore such thick glasses that I was amazed to learn he flew, but I guess the Air Force overlooked it because glider pilots were hard to come by in those days.

In many ways, Olive and I were like any ordinary couple starting out, right down to the fact that we fought about money. I had no idea how rich we were, because Dad was still keeping me in the dark about my trust fund. Olive and I had what seemed to me a decent income—I worked my way up to lieutenant colonel and got about $750 a month including flight pay, plus $150 a month from the trust fund, and a little more in IBM war pay. But I have one of our account books for those years, showing what we spent on groceries, the cleaning lady who came once a week, and this and that, and at the end of each month we were always six or eight dollars in the red. I used to dread bringing up the subject with Olive. She was doing her best to run a thrifty house, and when I'd start boring in about our monthly deficit, she didn't want to talk about it. She would go into what I'd call her Mode Impossible. Nothing really matched it. It occurred to me once or twice to ask Dad for extra cash, but I never did. I knew he expected us to learn financial discipline. Fortunately the money argument came up between Olive and me only when we balanced our books, and overall we grew closer and closer. In March 1944, a little after my thirtieth birthday, our son Tom was born. We both felt very lucky to have another child.

Working at the Pentagon was ten times the education that IBM school had been. One of my duties was to investigate cases of cheating and stealing by Air Force personnel, and I learned a lot about human nature, including my own. For instance, I had no patience for the fact that if you didn't prove a case from seventeen different directions, a fellow could squeeze out on some technicality. One time I had obtained a full confession and even so the case got overturned when the defense argued that I had been abrasive and threatening. I was glad I hadn't tried to become a lawyer.

Oddly, I was much better at investigating sensitive matters, such as suspicious damage to Air Force planes or crashes in which high-ranking officers were hurt. I remember one tragic case involving an Air Force general named Uzal Ent. The fellow was a real hero who had led a daring raid on the Ploesti oil fields in Rumania. He was supposed to fly from Colorado Springs to San Antonio when his copilot got sick, and he asked the base commander for a replacement. They put in a new guy, and Ent didn't brief him very thoroughly. When they were making their takeoff run, Ent began singing to himself, nodding his head in time to the song. The new copilot thought he was calling for the landing gear up, although normally the pilot would make a gesture and say in a loud voice, "Gear up!" When he saw Ent bob his head a second time, the copilot let the gear up. They were only going seventy knots, too slow to fly. The plane went down on its belly and one of the propellers on Ent's side separated from its engine and walked up the fuselage. A propeller blade cut into Ent's back and severed his spine so that he became a paraplegic. When I took the copilot's testimony, I asked him, "If you knew the plane wasn't going to fly, why did you put the gear up?"

He was stupid. He said, "I thought the general wanted me to!"

Work on matters like these brought me into contact with Hap Arnold, General Bradley's boss. Arnold used me from time to time as his personal messenger. On one memorable occasion, he ordered me to get a bomber and offer Harry Truman a lift.

At that time Truman was a senator, in charge of the committee that supervised war procurement. He and his colleagues were playing hob with the Air Force because it wasn't doing a very good job managing airplane factories. The committee would tour a bomber plant and find planes stalled on the production line because a single part was in short supply. The next thing you'd know, Truman would be blasting the Air Force in the newspapers.

General Arnold was not happy about this and he sent me to do something about it. He told me Truman was visiting his hometown of Independence, Missouri, so I got a B-25, a two-engine medium bomber that could be flown safely by one pilot, and headed out to the Midwest. I finally tracked down Truman at a church supper. From the doorway of the meeting room I could see a lot of tables arranged in a U shape, with the senator way down at the end. It might have been wiser to wait outside, but when the commanding general of the Air Force gave me an order, I obeyed. So I squeezed in behind all those people eating peas and chicken, got up to Truman, and tapped him on the shoulder. He looked around and said, "Yes, Major?"

"Sir, I know this is no time to talk, but I have a message from General Arnold and an airplane. I wonder if I could offer you a lift somewhere?"

"Yes, that would be nice. I'm going to Chicago tomorrow. Meet me at the Independence airport at ten."

I met him there and he was very cordial, not aggressive by any means. He was wearing one of those white suits he liked so much, and a straw hat tipped down in front, and white shoes and socks—a neat, well-dressed little Midwesterner. Mrs. Truman and Margaret had come to see him off, and they couldn't have been more affable. I took them through the B-25, then he told his family good-bye and I flew him to Chicago, which was thrilling for me—I felt proud to have a U.S. senator in my plane. When we landed at Midway field I asked if I could have ten minutes of his time.

We went inside a fly-infested greasy-spoon restaurant with a soot-covered screen door and ordered coffee. Then he asked what my mission was. I said, "Sir, the Air Force is having trouble getting production to run perfectly, but it's not helpful to have the Truman Committee always making remarks about us in public. The message I bring you is, could you kind of pay attention to the other services and get back to us later?" He didn't fume or fuss.

He said, "The dope I have is that your organization is the worst of any. But tell General Arnold I have his message. And thanks very much." I carried that reply back to Washington.

The generals liked me because I got a lot done in a short time and wrote complete reports on what was accomplished. I came on pretty strong and pressed hard. Once in a while somebody who was full of pepper would say, "Now, look, for God's sake, you've only been in this Air Force for four years, and I've been in it fifteen. So don't think you can push me around!" At the Pentagon there were a lot of people I didn't get along with at first— old officers who were only interested in building bureaucratic empires. But as I associated with more and more different types, I realized that to make it, you had to get along with almost everybody. If you dislike the people you work with, you'd better not show it. I learned that to be a good leader, I had to strike a delicate balance. It involved pressing to a point beyond where most people would press, but short of where I became known as a troublemaker. If a group had been through a particularly tough period of work, I knew enough to ease up and have them all over to our apartment with their wives for a drink. I also knew that if they hadn't had much to do for a long time, they would welcome a period of intense activity.

Right after Bradley set up the air inspector's office in early 1943 he was sent off on a top-secret mission to England. The U.S. Eighth Air Force had started daylight bombing in Europe. They flew B-17s packed in tight formations so that, theoretically, the planes could protect one another with their machine guns. But they were no match for the swarms of German fighters and the losses were horrendous. Bradley's mission was to study the bombing results and determine if the daylight raids were worthwhile. He himself participated in raids over Germany and finally recommended that the daylight bombing proceed. But after he made his report he had a heart attack from having been at high altitudes for long periods without enough oxygen. He was only fifty-two but the

Air Force retired him. He took a job with a war contractor called Sperry-Gyroscope and I saw him only sporadically after that.

I soon discovered that I worked a hell of a lot harder if I liked my boss. The new general who came in, Junius Jones, was the opposite of Bradley—a terrible fuddyduddy. He immediately tried me out as his pilot and unfortunately liked the way I flew. He was a very odd ball, slow and ponderous without even a spark of humor. He constantly jingled the change in his pocket, which is why he had the nickname Jingle Willie. He was old and fumbly and would do the most unexpected things in an airplane. Flying with him was a nightmare. He'd sit in the pilot's seat and say, "What do I do now, Watson?" I had to watch him all the time.

Once, on takeoff, he tried to yank a heavily loaded plane into the air before it was moving fast enough to fly. That could easily have killed us all, and I shoved the wheel forward to hold us on the ground. Approaching a landing he'd say, "Landing gear down, Watson." And I'd point out, "We're going a hundred and eighty miles an hour, General." The wind would tear the sheet-metal fairings off the wheels if they came down when the plane was going that fast. Finally I'd call out one hundred forty, or whatever the safe speed was, and he'd say, "Gear down, Watson," as if nothing had happened. I lost count of the number of scrapes I pulled him out of. Jones got to depend on me, but he got to dislike me too. As far as my military career was concerned, this was disastrous. For two full years I got stuck as a lieutenant colonel. Jones wouldn't promote me, but he wouldn't let me go.

With Bradley I never had any doubt that what I was doing was worthwhile. But under Jones I began to feel I should have pushed for a combat assignment when I came back from Russia. This bothered me all the time I was in Washington, and I finally decided to do something about it in the middle of 1944, when I went with Jones to inspect the most famous airlift of the war. Japan had conquered Burma and most of the Chinese coast, essentially trapping Chiang Kai-shek and the Nationalist

Chinese in the country's interior. American pilots had to fly supplies for the Allies over the Himalayas, from the Assam Valley in India to Kunming in the interior of China. This was called "flying the Hump," and the route was the most dangerous imaginable. The weather was violent—horrible storms and freakish winds that could flip an airplane upside down. The airplanes themselves were unreliable at high altitudes—the engines would ice up and stop or catch fire. So many planes crashed on one stretch of ground that it was called the "aluminum trail." The planes that made it over often had to face Japanese fighters on the other side. But in spite of the dangers, the pilots would sometimes fly two round trips over the Hump in a day. If it hadn't been for their heroic efforts, the war would have been over in this part of the world, and we would have lost.

The six air stations in the Assam Valley had gravel runways and were unbelievably primitive. Only one of them dated from before the war; the rest had been scratched out of the ground after the Hump airlift started in 1942, and we saw more that were still being built. The workers were civilians—whole families drafted from tea plantations—and they had almost no construction equipment. Women made the gravel for the runways by chipping large rocks with hammers, and you'd see them carrying it in baskets on their heads to the construction site. The runways were crude and bumpy but a welcome sight to pilots. Some of these air stations were undisciplined—with sloppy quarters and high disease rates—but they were succeeding in moving thousands of tons of supplies. To keep the planes in the air, the mechanics had to provide a level of maintenance that was practically impossible in such a rough place, and they worked around the clock to do it. I saw men changing engines in 110-degree heat in the open sun, and doing major overhauls in wind and rain.

When we got to the Assam Valley, the monsoon was just beginning, but that made no difference to flight operations. Planes took off and landed for sixteen hours each day under low skies and in heavy downpours. It wasn't part of my official duties, but at the first opportunity I pushed myself onto a mission over the Hump. I'd heard so much about its terrors and difficulties that I felt I owed it to myself and the Army to find out what the pilots were up against.

The pilot I went with was a young captain named Carpenter who was taking four tons of oil to Kunming; I flew as copilot. We wore oxygen masks, heavy boots, and parachutes. We had silk maps that showed how to walk out if we got shot down, and money belts so we could trade with the natives. The route we were assigned involved a four-hour trip, two of those hours behind Japanese lines. We took off in dark and rain before dawn and cleared the high ridges flying at twenty-one thousand feet on instruments, using oxygen masks on the way up. After daybreak we could see patches of ground below, but fortunately there were enough clouds to help us hide from Japanese fighters. For the third time I thrilled at the sight of China—even though this part was held by the Japanese. I could see little isolated valleys beneath us, with every inch of ground under the most intensive cultivation, and neat clusters of thatched huts.

We landed at Kunming on a runway where coolies were constantly at work refilling holes from the Japanese bombardment. We delivered our oil, and then Carpenter took me to a very primitive restaurant at the edge of the field. A Chinese guy ran it, and when he saw us coming he said, "Eggis, eggis."

I asked Carpenter, "What the hell does that mean?"

"He means eggs." It was all the restaurant had to serve. I ate eggs and eggs and eggs—eight of them. I guess fear had made me hungry.

On the way back to India, Carpenter let me fly. I made a textbook landing when we reached Assam, and it gave me a triumphant feeling to know that I'd been over the Hump. Undeniably it could be the worst flying route in the world, yet I thought I could handle it. That night I got carried away, and enthusiastically imagined myself commanding one of the air stations in the Assam Valley, participating in the contest among stations to see which could put the most tons over the Hump each month.

After a couple of days I went back to Kunming, sought out General Claire Chennault, the commander of the Fourteenth Air Force, and asked for combat duty. Chennault was famous in the world of aviation as the founder of the American Volunteer Group, or Flying Tigers. This was a squadron of American military pilots who slipped into China to fight on the Nationalist side long before the U.S. was in the war. At that time Chennault was retired from the U.S. Army and serving as air adviser to Chiang Kai-shek; Roosevelt knew all about his activities and looked the other way. The Flying Tigers flew obsolete fighters and were heavily outnumbered, but Chennault was such a brilliant tactician that they disrupted Japanese air operations all across China and Burma. After Pearl Harbor, the Flying Tigers were absorbed into the Air Force, and Chennault went back on active duty. The squadron gradually grew into an entire air force, and by the time I arrived had even launched an air raid on Japan itself, the first since Jimmy Doolittle's daredevil bombing of Tokyo in 1942.

Chennault was ill on the day I met him. He only agreed to see me at the recommendation of Colonel Clayton Claassen, my closest friend from the Pentagon, who was now serving as chief of operations in Chennault's command. I found the general lying in his hut with a nurse by his cot. I'll never forget that face, which was scarred from a number of plane crashes and had no expression at all. He asked if I'd like to join him.

"I would very much, General Chennault."

"We need people like you. I'm going to put in a request." If that request had gone through, I might have stayed in the Air Force for life. But when old Jingle Willie got wind of it about a week later, he had other ideas. "I've had a request for you," he told me, "but I've turned it down because you're too important here."

I suppose I could have pursued it further. But in the interim I'd pushed my way onto another combat flight as an observer, and it had scared me enough to last the whole war. It was a medical evacuation flight over a new route that followed a series of mountain passes into Burma. This paralleled the so-called Ledo Road, and it was expected to become a major airlift route, lower and less dangerous to fly than the Hump. It led to a jungle airfield that had just been captured by American and Chinese troops under General "Vinegar Joe" Stilwell. He was the senior American general in this part of the world, a tactician who was supposed to train and equip the Chinese and urge them onward in the fight against Japan. In 1942 the Japanese had crushed Stilwell's army and chased him out of Burma, but now he was back on the attack. There was a major battle going on for the town of Myitkyina, around which several thousand Japanese were dug in. Stilwell had large numbers of wounded as well as men critically sick with dysentery and typhus. They all had to be taken out.

The pilot, a Lieutenant Taylor, told me he'd been convicted of selling black-market cigarettes and had been assigned to fly this route for another year as his punishment. We took off in weather that would have been considered unflyable in the States—a ceiling of three hundred feet with one-mile visibility. When he and his copilot took us up the first valley we were flying so low that, according to the elevations on the map, we were flying underground. The only reassuring thing was the uncanny way Taylor knew where we were. Every few minutes he'd tell me that a road or a hamlet was just ahead, and it would turn up exactly as he had said. But as we got into the narrowest part of the pass, we ran into solid fog. We were flying at less than a hundred feet, and I was sure the end had come. I curled up behind Taylor's seat and braced for the crash. Taylor said, "What the hell? You want to live forever?" We cleared a final ridge in heavy rain and after that the clouds were at about four hundred feet and we stayed below them. I watched a very green, lush, flat valley rushing by, and noticed a number of wrecked DC-3s that had been shot down, which was far from reassuring. Finally we started to circle, and I said, "How can you tell where the battle lines are?"

Taylor said, "Well, they keep changing. But the Japanese only have small arms to shoot at us with, so don't worry." At last we landed. We were so close to the lines that I could hear small arms fire, which made me awfully jumpy. Suddenly right behind me there was a tremendous *whoom* and I dove for cover only to see that nobody else did. I hadn't noticed that I'd been standing right next to a camouflaged 75mm cannon.

The field hospital was run by a doctor named Gordon Seagrave, a friendly, kindly man who'd spent twenty years in Burma as a missionary doctor before the war. Now he was in the U.S. Army and had just written a successful book called *Burma Surgeon.* Seagrave's hospital was cut into the side of a hill, with a crude grass roof the only protection. All around were wounded men covered with jungle mud and blood and bugs—a terrible sight and terrible smell—but somehow Seagrave kept the infection rate very low.

We had to load the stretchers ourselves, because the soldiers on the field were too demoralized to help. Those wounded were the most moving sight I'd ever seen—an emaciated blond boy with the look of a hunted animal who had lost his unit and wandered for weeks in the jungle; a huge, bearded man who was painfully wounded in the legs but kept up the morale of the others with his constant smiles and conversation; other pitifully hurt men fighting for their lives with abdominal wounds, brain injuries, jungle fever. The smell and flies in the hot cabin were overwhelming—I kept gagging and finally went forward to the flight deck out of embarrassment. That day we evacuated twenty-eight men in two trips. Seeing these men, I could understand why pilots were willing to fly through hell to give them help.

But as much as I admired the courage of men like Lieutenant Taylor, that flight was enough for me. I wasn't sorry to leave the Assam Valley behind and to head back to the Mediterranean, where the war was mostly won by now. We inspected bases in North Africa and along the Adriatic coast of Italy and then flew over to Rome. Flying across Italy just a little north of Monte

Cassino, we passed over steep, rugged terrain where the Fifth and Eighth armies had faced their toughest fighting the winter before. In that section of Italy most of the towns are on the peaks of the mountains, and every town we saw had been badly bombed. We landed outside Rome, and on the drive into the city we passed the sight of many wrecked German 88mm antiaircraft guns. Rome itself had been spared, by Allied-German agreement, and the people looked neater and the girls prettier than any I'd seen since leaving the States. We stayed at a hotel that had been taken over as an officers' rest camp and had a bath and a good dinner on an open terrace, listening to Viennese music and the yells of merrymaking soldiers on the streets.

The next day, I found myself looking up IBM—or Watson Italiana, as it was called—in the telephone book. For some reason I felt compelled to go there and see what the situation was. The office was in an excellent location right near the hotel. It looked closed, with a big sign on the door that said PROPERTY OF I.B.M., NEW YORK CITY. But the door was unlocked and I walked through a very bare showroom into the office of Giuseppe Samarughi, the manager, whom I'd met once in New York. He shook my hand warmly and then an American major who was also there said, "I'm glad you've come. Maybe you can help us out." This was Harry Ritterbush, formerly of IBM's New York office and now in charge of all the punch-card records in the Mediterranean theater. He told me he'd been trying to look after this office since the liberation of Rome. Amazingly, rents were still coming in from customers around the area, but dealing with the occupation authorities was a big headache. Like all the businesses in Rome, Watson Italiana had been taken over by the American military government, and they weren't letting Mr. Samarughi run the office the way it needed to be run.

I really had no authority to act, but Samarughi and Ritterbush seemed to expect it of me. Maybe I'd become more decisive in general, or maybe for that one instant I was ready to get back to IBM. In any case I headed straight for the military governor's office, where I gave assurances that IBM equipment was American and not alien property. I stayed there until the logjam was broken and they agreed to put Samarughi back in charge. Then I gave him responsibility for all of Italy until Milan could be liberated and the regular country head could take over. Samarughi was very grateful and, as a keepsake, presented me with a Beretta pistol. It was a neat little weapon of the type carried by Italian officers; I accepted it even though it crossed my mind that guns like it had been used to kill American boys.

General Jones didn't want to leave the Mediterranean without taking a short holiday on the island of Capri. After all the destruction we had seen, the beauty of the deep blue water and the seaside villas built amid spires of rock was almost shocking. On the beach I met an Italian marchesa who invited my colleagues and me to a party that night. We were the only Americans there. The marchesa's whole crowd struck me as depraved. There were beautiful Italian ladies accompanied by men who looked like international loafers, and I danced with a wealthy Swiss woman who told me in all seriousness that she was "sweating out the war on Capri." I left the party feeling glad to be an American serviceman.

On the way back to Washington I began to think seriously about what I would do after the war. It was clear that an Allied victory was coming, even though it would take a while. In spite of what I'd done for Mr. Samarughi, the idea of joining the ranks of my father's men didn't appeal to me. By now I'd gotten used to the satisfaction of accomplishing things on my own, and I loved the daily thrill of flying. So I decided that owning and running a small aviation company would be just about right. In August 1944, I went up to New York on leave and told Dad I wasn't coming back.

Father was very shrewd about it. I expected him to say, "Your mother and I are terribly disappointed." But rather than make a fuss, he told Fred Nichol to help me turn up opportunities in civil aviation. Nichol jumped right on it. First he wrote to Pat Patterson, the head of

United Air Lines, whom Dad knew, telling him I wanted to be a pilot and eventually to move up into management. I got a letter back from Patterson that said, "Come see me at the end of the war." Then Nichol found a young fellow named Osbourne who had invented floats for seaplanes. In those days seaplanes were very popular and Osbourne's business seemed solid. It was called the Edo Float Company, and to my surprise Dad didn't object when I talked about buying it. He wasn't applying any pressure at all. But Nichol's eagerness to find me something outside IBM made me wonder what I was passing up, which was probably the effect Dad intended.

In the spring of 1945, I was back in Washington, and asked General Bradley, who was now a vice president at Sperry-Gyroscope and visiting Washington on a business trip, to come to our apartment and have dinner with Olive and me. I waited for him at the Pentagon, and when he emerged, led him to my car and started the drive home. More than a year had gone by since his retirement and we'd only spoken a couple of times. But our conversation on the road in the twilight of that spring day is riveted in my mind, because it completely changed my life.

He said, "Tom, what are you going to do when the war is over?"

"Well, General, I've got a job lined up that I think I'm going to take. I'm going to be a pilot with United Air Lines."

I expected Bradley to say "That's a good choice," and maybe compliment me on my flying. Instead he said, "Really? I always thought you'd go back and run the IBM company."

I was stunned. I concentrated on driving for a moment or two, and then I asked the question I suppose had been buried in my mind from the time I got up from the curb as a boy and went home crying. "General Bradley," I said, "do you think I could run IBM?"

And he said, "Of course."

I kept going over and over the conversation as I mixed drinks and carried dishes back and forth at dinner. After

I took the general back to his hotel, I parked on an un-traveled road and sat behind the wheel for half an hour, trying to evaluate what he'd said. Since he had made his point in a conversation that was thoughtful on both sides, I concluded that he had indeed meant it. The next question was whether or not his opinion was important enough for me to act on it. Bradley was by no means an easy man to serve. He was a great leader, but he had his up and down moods and I hadn't always performed in an exemplary fashion for him. But in spite of this, he had high respect for my abilities. This made me think that I might be selling myself short by going to United Air Lines—or anywhere else but IBM.

I said to Olive when I got home, "General Bradley thinks I could run IBM." She was silent for so long that I said, "Olive, what do you think?"

She said, "Tom, you're a fun-loving boy and it's hard to believe you really want to do it. But when you put your mind to something I've never seen you fail."

I concluded that Bradley's words must be true. It amazed me how much I'd changed in the Air Force. My attitude had improved dramatically and my energy level had greatly increased. I'd realized that I had the force of personality to get my ideas across to others, as long as I took the time beforehand to think things through. I was sure of my ability to speak in public and write clearly. These were all strengths that had developed under Bradley. He was my bridge to self-confidence.

Twenty-four hours later my mind was made up and I started planning a trip to New York. I called my old man and said, "I'd like to come up on a workday and meet the people there, because, to be honest with you, I may be coming back to IBM if you will have me." Of course, this was something he'd been waiting for years to hear, and there was warmth and happiness in his voice as he said simply, "I'd be delighted, son."

To this day, I do not know for certain if my father was clearing the way for me. But when I went up to IBM that spring to look things over, I could see that the prospective competition for the top jobs wasn't great. IBM was booming along, but the executive office in New York was oddly empty. A lot of the old guard who'd been with Dad from the beginning had retired, and as they dropped by the wayside, he hadn't replaced them as rapidly as he might. Before the war there were some bright, hard-driving fifty-year-old managers bucking for those senior jobs. But when I got back, these hotshots were gone—they'd taken jobs elsewhere or gone into business for themselves —and unimpressive men were in their places. I never found out why—at the time I honestly thought there was something magical about it. I remember thinking, "Gee, maybe I've got a chance here."

After that I had to leave on another long inspection tour with General Jones, all over the South Pacific. By the middle of August 1945, we had gotten all the way to Sydney, Australia, and I was drowsing in my hotel room, half listening to the radio, when a British announcer said, "The Japanese have surrendered unconditionally." I ran onto the street and danced with an Australian nurse. Four years of war, five years of the Army, and now victory! The news was hard to believe but it gave me a delicious, weak-kneed feeling. By lunchtime there were eighteen people in my little room singing and dancing. The street in front of the hotel was crowded with cheering throngs and I only saw a few people who were not deliriously happy—perhaps those who had lost loved ones and knew the cost of the prize we'd won.

Within a few days we were on our way home, flying from Hawaii to San Francisco in the middle of the night. General Jones was sound asleep and I was at the controls. All told, in my five years, I'd flown about twenty-five hundred hours, fifteen hundred of them either over the sea or close to enemy territory, and finally the war was over. I remember the beauty of the full moon on the scattered cumulus clouds two thousand feet below us. As I sat listening to a Honolulu radio station playing a symphony, and in the background the singing of our engines, I thought of how Olive would have enjoyed that scene.

CHAPTER 14

The way at IBM seemed clear for me, and I never had anything in mind but to aim for the top job. But I came home from the South Pacific in September 1945 to a terrible shock. Dad had replaced Fred Nichol with a new number-two man, a smart, hard-driving executive named Charley Kirk. I'd never taken Fred Nichol very seriously. He'd started out as Dad's secretary, just like George Phillips; he was the kind of fellow to whom Dad could say, "Why don't we build a tower to the moon?" and Nichol would say, "Yes sir, I'll order the steel this afternoon." Charley Kirk was a different story. He was only forty-one, a prodigious worker, aggressive and yet very popular with the men. He came from a rough background, somewhat like Dad's, and he'd made his reputation as a supersalesman in our St. Louis office. When the war came Dad brought him to Endicott, where Kirk was in charge of the rapid and successful expansion of the plant.

I never expected to have to contend with Kirk at headquarters. In my mind he was the factory boss who belonged up in Endicott. But the anxiety of working for Dad finally took its toll on poor Nichol—in the spring of 1945 he had a nervous breakdown and after a few months he retired at age fifty-eight. When it became clear that Nichol wasn't coming back, Dad brought Kirk down from Endicott, promoted him to executive vice president, and gave him a seat on the board. This was hard for me to understand—I guess Dad still seemed so self-sufficient to me that I couldn't appreciate why he needed a number two. But one thing I later learned about managing a company is that it's like trying to run a family with a lot of children: too many things need doing. You want to get the factory going right, you want the sales to go up, you want to motivate this guy, put a better fellow in that job —you have a list on your desk and the items are all hard to accomplish. If you have a man like Kirk, you can show him your list and he'll say, "Let me handle these four things." That has a powerful appeal for a harried executive such as Dad, who by then was in his seventies. But all I could think of was that if Dad ever got sick or died, Kirk was the logical successor.

I left the Air Force at the end of 1945, and on the first business day of 1946, I reported to IBM. Dad greeted me in his office. I had on a stiff paper collar and a good dark suit. He shook my hand and gestured toward the other end of the room. "Tom," he said, "you've met Charley Kirk." Then Dad told me I was going to be Kirk's assistant. I'm sure I shook Kirk's hand and said how glad I was, but I was so surprised that I don't remember doing it. It took several days for me to sort out how I felt about this assignment. I knew it wasn't as demeaning as it might sound, because the title of "assistant" had a special meaning at IBM. Dad always preached the idea that executives and managers should see themselves not as bosses of employees but as their "assistants." And he often made promising young men assistants to the top people. So there was no stigma in being an assistant.

On the other hand, the fact that I'd be working with Kirk and not with Dad really bothered me. By the end of the following week it was clear to me that the two men had formed a tight bond. Kirk and I went up to Endicott, where Dad had ordered a week-long meeting for all of IBM's sales managers. Conferences like this were called "executive schools" at IBM, and this was the first big one since the end of the war. Kirk ran it, and Dad didn't show up until Wednesday. When he came in he sat down in the back of the assembly hall. At the podium making a presentation was one of IBM's youngest branch managers, a close friend of Kirk's from St. Louis by the name of Jim Birkenstock. I saw Dad beckon for Kirk to join him at the rear, and the two of them put their heads together and talked quietly behind their hands. Suddenly Dad said dramatically, "Mr. Kirk, that man on the platform is so impressive that he will be our new general sales manager. I am going to make the announcement right now." There was a gasp from the people who heard this, because Birkenstock had thereby leaped from a junior position to become practically everyone's boss, and with his new job went a twenty-thousand-dollar-a-year salary. So Dad made the announcement, while Kirk took Birkenstock's predecessor aside and told him he'd have to shift to another job. Dad was known for giving unexpected promotions, but this was unheard of. I took it as an indication of Kirk's great influence on my father.

I have to hand it to Kirk that from the moment we got back to New York he treated me fairly and went flat out to teach me the business. He had a large desk in his office, and he simply told me to pull up a chair alongside. "I don't have time to explain everything I do," he said, "but you'll learn if you sit here and watch." That was where I perched every day for months, and whenever Kirk went out to a meeting I'd go along. I saw practically everything he did. I learned how to make decisions, for Kirk was excellent at making them fast and making most of them right. When you have his kind of experience and feel for a business, you can make very rapid decisions, particularly where you can forecast the result. But he also knew when to not go pell-mell, for example on a matter that, if handled wrong, could hurt IBM's reputation or provoke a lawsuit. At this point Charley was handling dozens of different responsibilities—I'd never seen such a prodigious worker. Sitting by Kirk, I had as good a cross-section view of IBM's problems as I could have gotten anywhere in the company.

Even so, friendship between Kirk and me didn't seem to be in the cards. One night early on, he invited me up to his place with three or four IBMers, all friends of his. He had a room at the Ritz Towers because he still hadn't had time to move his family down from Endicott. After we sat down Kirk pulled out a bottle, tossed it on the bed, and said, "Have a drink, Tom." I said, "No, thanks." They all pulled back a bit at that, Charley especially. He knew that I'd spent a lot of time in nightclubs before the war. What he didn't know was that around the middle of 1944, I'd decided that my career would be better served if I completely gave up drinking, even social drinking. "Look," I said, "it's no reflection on any of you—it's after hours—but at the moment I don't drink a drop." That made me the odd man out. Everyone else had a drink and started talking about old times in St. Louis, and I left.

IBM's situation in those days was enough to make anybody want a drink. Like hundreds of other businesses, we had to switch as fast as possible from wartime to peacetime production. Dad had no intention of shrinking IBM back down to its prewar size—that would have meant firing his new employees, selling the new factories he was so proud of, and closing the door on some of the returning veterans to whom he felt a deep obligation. Yet two thirds of our factory space was devoted to making war matériel, and that market disappeared the day America won. So how were we supposed to keep all the employees busy and the factories full? Somehow IBM was going to have to sell *three times* as many business machines as before the war.

Dad was surely one of the most positive-thinking and optimistic businessmen who ever lived, but even he worried about this one. There is a record of a meeting in 1944 where he was already leaning on his engineers to develop new products for peacetime. "Supposing the war in Europe ends in three months," he said. "What can we go out and take orders for that we are not taking orders for now?" The engineers called off the names of machines being developed, but Dad said none of them opened up new fields. "What I have got to look for is new business," he said. "Otherwise, there is no use in talking about keeping all those people employed full time, gentlemen. It is easy to say but hard to do, and I lost a lot of sleep last night just thinking about how we are going to do it." Dad told the engineers that from then on they would have to work a lot faster. Before the war it wasn't unusual for new IBM products to take five years from conception to market. But Dad pointed out that with machine guns, something totally new to IBM, the company had gone from a standing start to full production in a matter of months. "If we can do it on the gun," he said, "we can do it on this apparatus that we know something about." He wasn't just being arbitrary—somehow he sensed correctly that, because of the war, the pace of technological change in American life had permanently accelerated.

One of the things keeping Dad awake at night must have been the memory of the year 1921, when the U.S. economy contracted after World War I and CTR almost went bankrupt. I'm sure he also had unhappy visions of the hundreds and hundreds of accounting machines on rental to the U.S. armed forces. Most of this equipment would be turned back to IBM. Defense contractors who had built up for the war and now had to cut back couldn't be counted on to keep all their machines either. So unless we could find armies of new customers, our warehouses were going to fill up with used machines earning no money, and our factories would have nothing to do.

In the face of possible calamity, Dad's impulse was always to hire more salesmen. That's just what he proposed around the time I came back from the war. He was determined that IBM should have an office in every state capital, and everybody from Kirk on down was scrambling to expand the sales network as rapidly as possible. In the midst of this we got hit unexpectedly with an avalanche of orders for our products. The postwar recession never materialized. Instead, the U.S. economy boomed because of a huge pent-up demand for consumer goods that nobody had been able to buy during the war—cars, houses, appliances, and clothing. This in turn boosted supporting industries like banking, insurance, and retailing—our big customers. All of them suddenly had rapidly growing record-keeping and accounting needs. We quickly found ourselves in a race to keep up with demand. By the time I joined, Kirk was working sixteen-hour days.

The first business trip I took with Kirk could well

have changed the course of computer-industry history, if either of us had understood what was in front of our noses. It was a gray day in March, and we went to visit the ENIAC at the University of Pennsylvania. This was one of the first computers, a giant, primitive number-cruncher for solving scientific problems. It had just gone into operation, making a big name for its inventors, Presper Eckert and John Mauchly. They broke new ground by using electronic circuits instead of electromechanical relays like the ones in our tabulating machines. Dad was very big on supporting projects like ENIAC, more for prestige and philanthropic motives than commercial ones. During the war IBM and Harvard University had built a gigantic non-electronic computer called the MARK I. It consisted pretty much of two tons of IBM tabulating machines synchronized on a single axle, like looms in a textile mill. The MARK I got a lot of attention as "Harvard's robot super-brain," and was used successfully on top-secret war problems.

Dad heard about Eckert and Mauchly late in the war, when the Navy asked IBM to supply punch-card equipment to assist in getting data in and out of the ENIAC. That gave Kirk and me an entree. But going to see ENIAC was really Kirk's idea. He was curious because there was so much publicity about ENIAC's ability to make lightning-fast calculations. Another reason he wanted to have a look was that Eckert and Mauchly were talking about filing a patent, causing our lawyers to worry that IBM would have to pay big royalties if the idea of electronic computing ever went anywhere.

I remember the ENIAC vividly. It was made up of what seemed like acres of vacuum tubes in metal racks. The air was very hot, and I asked Eckert, a trim, urbane man, why that was. He explained, "Because we are sharing this room with eighteen thousand radio tubes." They hadn't air-conditioned it. I asked what the machine was doing and Eckert said, "Computing ballistic trajectories." To show us what he meant, he sat down with a pencil and paper and drew the curve an artillery shell follows through the air. He explained that to make maximum use of a gun, you had to be able to calculate where its shell would be at every fraction of a second of its flight. This required a tremendous amount of computation, and ENIAC was doing it in a very short time—less time, in fact, than it would take an actual shell to reach its target. That impressed me. Eckert went on to tell me that computers were the wave of the future. He didn't quite call our punch-card machines dinosaurs, but he said he and Mauchly were going to take the ENIAC patents and go into business. As he talked I got the impression that they thought they were going to push IBM aside pretty quickly. I said, "It's a great idea you have, but you're going to run out of money. Building these things for customers is going to be very expensive."

The truth was that I reacted to ENIAC the way some people probably reacted to the Wright brothers' airplane: it didn't move me at all. I can't imagine why I didn't think, "Good God, that's the future of the IBM company." But frankly I couldn't see this gigantic, costly, unreliable device as a piece of business equipment. Kirk felt the same way. On the train from Philadelphia back to New York, he said, "Well, that's awfully unwieldy. We could never use anything like that." We both agreed that, even though electronics innovations like radar were attracting a lot of popular attention, this ENIAC was an interesting experiment way off on the sidelines that couldn't possibly affect us. I never stopped to think what would happen if the speed of electronic circuits could be harnessed for commercial use.

Fortunately, this myopia was only temporary. A few weeks later my father and I were wandering around IBM headquarters. Dad always liked to nose around the offices when he had spare time; that afternoon I happened to be along. In a part of the building I'd never seen before we came upon a door labeled "Patent Development." Inside was one of Dad's engineers who had a high-speed punch-card machine hooked up to a box with black metal covers. It looked like a suitcase, only it was about four feet high. I said, "What is this doing?" And the engineer told me, "Multiplying with radio tubes." The machine was tabulating a payroll, a common application for punch cards—wages times number of hours worked, less Social Security deductions, retirement, medical deductions, and so forth, and coming out to net pay for each worker. Then the engineer told me how fast the machine was working. It did its calculation in one tenth of the time it took the punch-card machine to punch out the answer and go on to the next card. The box spent nine tenths of its time waiting, because the electronics were so fast and the mechanics so slow. That impressed me as though somebody had hit me on the head with a hammer, because the multiplier looked like a relatively simple device. I left that room and said, "It's fantastic, what that thing's doing. It's multiplying and coming out with totals, and doing it all with tubes. Dad, we should put this thing on the market! Even if we only sell eight or ten, we'll be able to advertise the fact that we have the world's first commercial electronic calculator."

That is how IBM got into electronics. In September we announced the machine with a full-page ad in the *New York Times*. We called it the IBM 603 Electronic Multiplier. Technically speaking it wasn't a computer—it had no stored program and processed numbers only as they were fed in from punch cards. In fact, the 603 was mainly a gimmick—it could calculate at electronic speeds, but that was not very useful because the punch cards couldn't keep up. But in spite of this, the thing caught on. We were hoping to rent out a handful, enough to justify the expense of the ad, but big customers were anxious to get their feet wet with electronics and we sold a hundred of them. Within a year we got past the gimmick stage. We figured out how to make electronic circuits not only multiply but *divide*—a job that was almost prohibitively expensive to do mechanically. At that point electronic calculators became truly useful, and our next machine, the IBM 604, sold by the thousands.

Although Kirk and I were never friends, he impressed me in the first few months we worked together. He was not prepossessing looking—he was of average height, balding, pear shaped, with rumpled clothing and wire-rim glasses, and he was never without a cigarette. But the man was a perpetual-motion machine. In this great seething expansion of the company, I watched him organizing and hiring, promoting and moving armies of managers around. He understood manufacturing so well that when Dad wanted to praise the work of a factory manager he'd say, "That was a real Kirk job." Kirk was also extremely popular with the salesmen and the customers. He was a talented piano player, and whenever we were in Endicott people would gather around him after hours at the IBM country club. Charley would sit sideways at the keyboard, his cigarette dangling from his mouth, tapping his foot and banging out tunes for people to sing.

I learned a lot from the man. For example, Dad used to encourage people to think of IBM as family and to come to him with their problems, but Kirk warned me never to get too involved in factory workers' lives. All it took was one story to convince me he was right. He told how, when he was in charge at Endicott, he'd gotten a letter from the wife of an employee. She complained that her husband had installed his mistress right in their house. Kirk figured this wasn't right and also not very IBMly, so he called the couple in. The husband said, "It's really not like my wife says. The woman is just a friend and she was in need. I don't sleep with her." The wife said, "You certainly do! At dinner you have some kind of sleeping pill. You look back and forth and decide which one of us you want to spend the night with and then you put the pill in the other one's coffee!" That was too much for Kirk. He concluded that the less he interfered in factory personnel cases, the better. "They're a bottomless pit!" he told me. This was hardly the way Dad would have seen it, but all the same it was marvelous advice.

The turning point in my relationship with Kirk came after we'd been working together about four months. In May 1946 he had an attack of appendicitis and missed six weeks of work. I was still operating from the corner of his desk, and by then I'd seen and heard enough to begin to have a little knowledge of the business. While Kirk was out, a great many matters came to me for decision, partly because I was his assistant and partly because my name was Watson. I think people found it easier to approach me than T.J., who was always unpredictable. They'd ask questions, I'd answer, and I'd see results. Being in that position was fun—it whetted my appetite for management. I began to love the decision-making process —the feeling of responsibility and the opportunity to see later whether a decision was right or wrong. It was thrilling to be in the middle of the technology business as it picked up speed in the postwar world.

Kirk was surprised when he came back in June to find that I was right in the thick of things and a lot of decisions had been made. I wrote them all down for him, just as I had for my superiors in the Air Force, in a memo that was waiting for him when he came in: "We have done the following things in your absence for the following reasons. . . ." Dad, who'd been traveling much of the time, must have been impressed, because that month he had me elected vice president. This was no small thing —I was only thirty-two and IBM had only four other vice presidents and twelve officers in all. Dad's staff immediately put my picture on banners for one of IBM's frequent sales campaigns. Its motto was "Let's Break All Precedent for Our New Vice President," and it embarrassed the hell out of me. So when I went on the road to speak at sales offices, I started calling it the "Jump for Junior" campaign. That made everybody laugh and took some of the hot air out of the situation.

I think Kirk and I began some serious reassessment of each other then. Kirk probably started worrying what was going to happen to his job. At the beginning I don't think he'd seen me as a contender—after all, he knew my reputation from before the war. But now he realized that I could make decisions. It couldn't have helped that in October, after the 603 came out and was a success, I was elected to the board of directors. All this put Kirk in the toughest spot imaginable. He knew Dad was a hard-driving character. He knew I was the son and the apple of Dad's eye. And he knew that the more he taught me about the job, the less his chances were of coming out on top. And yet he elected to keep helping me. I think he must have figured, "The best thing I can do is to cooperate and hope that something will happen. Maybe he'll fall on his face. Or maybe if the old man drops dead, I can get to the top by talking directly to the other directors." He might have been right on that count. If Dad had died then, the board probably would have preferred to go with Kirk rather than take a risk on me.

I was still his assistant, but now I had an office of my own next to his, and a secretary. I started wondering how long I might have to work with this man. He wasn't very polished, and unlike my father he had no impulse to raise himself up culturally. It was hard for me to imagine him ever representing IBM to the outside world, which was a big part of Dad's job. I'd watched Kirk give a few speeches around New York at places like the Advertising Club, and he was so awkward that I felt embarrassed for him and IBM. The more time we spent together, the more he got on my nerves.

Part of my dislike of Kirk stemmed from competitiveness and jealousy of his relationship with my father. Kirk was not at all like Dad, and I couldn't understand why they were so close. But there was more to it than that. I didn't like the side of my father that Kirk brought out. What bothered me most was the shuffling of men and jobs. There were constant firings and transfers after the war, some of them heartrending. I thought IBM was starting to seem pretty damned ruthless in the way it moved people around. Part of this I put down to the difference between business and the military. When I was in the Air Force you had to get a couple of poor efficiency reports before they'd even transfer you. I missed that methodical way of reaching judgments about people, and I questioned whether business was really for me. But I realized that if those executive powers are used sparingly, and intelligently, a business could be the most efficient thing in the world, a heck of a lot more efficient than a government. The government has checks and balances, but a business is a dictatorship, and that is what makes it really move.

The trouble at IBM was that the firings and demotions were getting out of hand. For many years Father's normal practice had been to criticize someone he thought was not pulling his weight. He'd say, "I've just gone out to Kansas City and seen that man Blair. I don't know. Blair impressed me as being a man who smokes a lot and whose clothing is not really neat. The office didn't look too good either. I'm not sure Blair is a proper representative for IBM." Now, what he hoped was that if Blair was a good man, someone would leap to his defense and say, "Mr. Watson, you're wrong. Blair is one heck of a guy and is bringing in a lot of business." Blair might even end up with a raise as a result. That's how it had worked before the war. But when Kirk came in, so many of the old guard had resigned or retired that there were not a great many men around who would stand up to Dad. Instead, when he complained, more often than not Kirk would say, "Since you feel so strongly about Blair, I'll get on the sleeper tonight. I can be in Kansas City to handle Blair tomorrow morning and be back here the following day." "Handle" meant "fire," and that really shocked me, because providing job security had been a hallmark of Dad's management.

In the midst of the growing tension between us, Kirk unintentionally put me through one of the worst nights of my life. We were working late and went out for dinner, and we started talking about the early days of IBM, when it was still called CTR—maybe there was some company anniversary coming up and we were discussing how to celebrate. I said something about how Charles Flint had brought Dad in as president and Kirk looked at me in a funny way. He put his cigarette down and slowly said, "There's something you ought to know. When your father was hired he was only the general manager. The board wouldn't let him be president."

"What do you mean?"

"When your father was first hired, he was under a criminal indictment. The board knew he was a good executive, but they didn't want to risk having him be president unless he cleared his name."

Kirk must have seen from my face that I was shocked. He spent twenty minutes explaining this episode in my father's life that was apparently common knowledge but that I'd never heard mentioned. It had happened a couple of years before I was born. Dad and all the top management of the National Cash Register Company, including John Patterson himself, were put on trial in one of the first great antitrust cases. The charge was criminal conspiracy in restraint of trade and maintaining a monopoly. Patterson had pioneered the use of cash registers, and NCR still made almost all the cash registers in America. Patterson thought the antitrust laws of the 1890s had nothing to do with him. The market was his personal preserve, where competitors deserved to be hounded and destroyed.

The federal trust-busters set out to make an example of the Cash. It was a sensational case, because Patterson and his men used tactics that were ruthless even by turn-of-the-century standards. Dad's record in the company made him one of the most prominent figures in the case. The government claimed that in 1903 he had pretended to quit his job at the Cash so that he could set up a front operation, secretly owned by Patterson, that dealt in secondhand cash registers. The market for used machines was a particular sore spot with Patterson. He felt, in some sense, that every cash register ever built by NCR was his, and that nobody else had a right to sell NCR machines, new or used. So he put a million dollars at Dad's disposal to knock out secondhand cash register dealers nationwide. Dad would go into a city, open his own secondhand store, put pressure on the other dealers by bidding up prices for used machines, and finally buy the competitors out. For this, Kirk told me, Dad had been convicted and sentenced to a year in prison. Patterson and the others were convicted as well. But the case was appealed and no one ever served time. After a few months the conviction got thrown out on a technicality and Patterson and the others settled by signing a consent decree to clean up their business practices. Dad, who insisted all along that he was innocent, refused to sign. But by that time he had left the Cash for other reasons, and the government never sought a second trial.

This was an extremely bitter story to hear from Charley Kirk. I went straight home after the meal, and that night I couldn't sleep. In all the time I'd known my father, he had lived and done business in a manner beyond reproach. Could he have knowingly broken the law? I imagined him as a callow young man, still less than thirty years old, with humble roots and great ambition and ten years' experience in lowly jobs varying from clerking in a grocery store to selling sewing machines. I thought about how loyal he was to Patterson, and here was Patterson saying, "I trust you with a million dollars. Go do this thing—we're in the right, those machines are ours, and they shouldn't be dealt in by these secondhand guys." At that point in his life, Dad did not understand the illegality he was getting into—the antitrust laws were still quite new and he hadn't gotten much past the eighth grade. But he certainly must have seen the subterfuge. At least I now knew why my father had what I'd always considered the most irrational hatred of the Department of Justice.

I didn't blame Kirk for telling me the bad news; he was doing me a favor, and it was far better to hear it from someone who admired and sympathized with Dad. But I was gaining on Kirk in business skill, and that caused our relationship to go downhill rapidly. The more Kirk worried about his job, the more of a yes-man he became to Dad. The minute my father questioned a man's performance, Kirk would pull the trigger on the guy. It happened late in 1946 with a district manager named Harry Eilers. He was a very accomplished and popular man, and he ran the Midwestern sales district from Minneapolis. One day Dad asked Kirk whether it might not make more sense to locate district headquarters in Chicago. Kirk immediately ordered Eilers to move, and when he said that he couldn't, without probing further Kirk demoted him to running a sales office, and named a new district manager in Chicago. That burned me up, because

I knew Eilers was good. Later it came out that illness and family circumstances had kept him from accepting the transfer. But Kirk wouldn't budge and Dad backed him, so Eilers was out.

In April of 1947, I finally decided that I couldn't tolerate working with Kirk anymore. I went into Dad's office and told him I was quitting. I said, "Look, Dad. Kirk is here. I can get along with all the other people you've hired, but not Kirk. He's not my kind of guy. He's too rough. And he's only nine years older than I. If I stay I'm going to have to work for him for twenty-two years before he's old enough to retire. Then I'll run the business for eight years, and it'll be time for me to retire too. I can't look forward to that."

I was quite serious, even though I hadn't the slightest idea what I'd do next. Dad began to argue with me and I ended up storming out. I called Olive and asked if she'd drive into the city. It was probably six o'clock by the time she met me at the Waldorf. We had dinner and then went upstairs to the roof and drank champagne and danced. I told her what I'd done, and she said, "I'm sure you're going to feel sorry later." Finally, around eleven o'clock, we got in our car and drove home.

Dad really knew how to put on a show when he needed to. We got out to Greenwich around midnight. As I drove up to our house I saw Dad's car and chauffeur parked there and I said to Olive, "Oh, my God." When we walked in, Mother and Father were both in the library. The lights were turned down very low, and my poor mother was sitting way over in a corner, exhausted because it was so late. Dad was sitting hunched in a chair in the middle of the room, looking about as frail and old as he knew how. He probably had dimmed those lights intentionally to create that effect. I walked in and was ready to walk out again, but he held out his hand and said, "Tom, you just can't do this to me. You can't quit." He didn't quite come out and say, "Please don't destroy my lifelong ambition," but there was no doubt that's what he meant.

I said, "Dad, look. You're a man of the world. You can

see that even if you take out all the personalities and just call us Mr. Smith and Mr. Jones, the fact remains that I'm thirty-four and I've got to work until I'm fifty-six before I get a chance at command."

"I can see your point of view, I can see your point of view," he said. "I'll tell you what. You take Mr. Kirk to Europe. Introduce him to the managers over there, and I'll think of something."

There was a meeting of the International Chamber of Commerce scheduled in Montreux, Switzerland, in June. The organization had revived after the war, though it wasn't as influential as before. Kirk and I were both scheduled to go as U.S. delegates, and I made plans to show Charley around Europe afterward and introduce him to the managers of various countries, many of whom I'd known since childhood. I didn't know what would happen after that. I doubt Dad did either at that point. He sent us to Europe because he was playing for time. The thing keeping me calm was that I knew I was either going to get the problem fixed or leave. I'd crossed the bridge of trying to wait it out. Subconsciously, I suppose I thought my old man would "handle" Kirk.

So in May of 1947, Kirk and I set sail for Europe with our wives. The International Chamber meeting was a bore. Afterward we hooked up with Valentim Boucas, whom Dad had picked to escort us around Europe. Boucas was IBM's representative in Brazil and one of the most worldly and genial guys I ever knew. He went all the way back to my childhood, and my father greatly admired him. They'd met in the 1920s when Boucas, the son of a Rio de Janeiro harbor pilot, was struggling to get a start in the world. He had the kind of vivid personality that could project happiness to everybody in a room. He was a bit of an operator, which Dad never wanted to admit. He let Boucas have the IBM Brazil concession for almost no money, and Boucas became enormously wealthy as a result.

Boucas figured I was going to become head of IBM, and he didn't take Kirk seriously at all. The first stop on our trip was Zurich, where IBM had a fair-sized subsidiary. They gave us a dinner where there were eighty or ninety people, at a big hotel on the lake. I greeted them in French, which I spoke reasonably well, and Kirk made some remarks in English, which someone translated. Then they called on Boucas, who knew how to speak English but elected to speak in French that night because he knew Kirk couldn't understand it. Boucas immediately got my attention when I heard him say something about *le fils*. All the way through, the theme of his remarks was that the most important thing in business was the family. "Here is this fine young man," he said, "son of the *grand monsieur*." He told them how lucky they were to have me there, this man who'd been away *à la guerre* and now was back in the business, carrying on the family name. Kirk didn't know what was going on and assumed Boucas was talking about him. Every time Boucas came to a point of emphasis, everybody would clap and Kirk would smile and nod while Olive and I sank lower and lower in our chairs. Boucas wound up by declaring I was going to lead the company in the future, and that while nobody had formally announced it yet, he was committed to that end and he knew how great it would be for everybody. There was an absolute ovation. Kirk looked around and just beamed.

Our junket then took us across the Alps, along the Riviera to Marseilles, then up the Loire valley toward Paris. We had two motorcars, one of which was a lovely old Cadillac that the people at IBM France had dismantled and buried in a basement when the Germans invaded Paris. After the war they'd pulled it out and welded it back together, and it worked perfectly despite a little rust. Boucas rode with Olive and me, while Kirk and his wife rode with a secretary. It worked better that way because Kirk and I were so uncomfortable in each other's presence. In our car we had a fabulous time. Boucas charmed Olive completely. In a poor town near Milan, he told the Italians that a famous movie actress was visiting from New York. A crowd gathered around. Olive was twenty-eight and looked beautiful enough to be in the movies, and the people were all peeking in the car windows and yelling, "Give us your autograph!" Since she didn't speak Italian she didn't know what was going on until Boucas confessed what he'd done.

Finally Kirk and I almost came to blows over a side-trip I wanted to take when we reached Marseilles. An old Italian friend of Dad's, and his wife, had joined our party for a few days, and I knew that their daughter, who had just been married, was staying at a nearby resort. We were scheduled to drive to Lyons, and this resort was about forty miles in the opposite direction. So I said to Kirk, "We can just go over there and see Cecile. Her parents would like that, Olive wants to meet her, and I'd like to see her again. It won't take too long."

"Well," Kirk said, "it's an hour over and an hour back."

"Yes, and we'll only stay about half an hour."

"Well, that's five hours out of our trip."

I said, "It can't be five hours, Charley. It can only be two and a half—an hour over, a half hour there, and an hour back. Then we're back where we started."

"No, no. Because while you're doing that, the car could have been going two and a half hours in this other direction. So two and a half and two and a half is five."

I knew there was a fallacy in what he was saying but I was too damn mad to think what it was. And he hung right in there, insisting he was right. The vehemence of that silly argument is hard to describe, but I'm glad it stopped when it did. Olive pulled at my coat and I was able to shut up and get in our car.

We finally reached Lyons that evening. Late that night I was awakened by heavy knocking on our hotel room door. It was our secretary. "Come quickly, Mr. Watson," he said. "Mr. Kirk is very sick." I put on a robe and followed him. Kirk had had a massive coronary. When I got to his room he was unconscious and within an hour he was dead. The Kirks were Catholic and Mrs. Kirk said she wanted to go to Mass, so as day broke we went to the Lyons cathedral. Since there had to be an autopsy, Boucas and I stayed behind while Olive took Mrs. Kirk on to Paris where she could get her into a more comfortable hotel. Then we all brought the coffin home with us to New York.

Dad felt Kirk's death as a personal loss—Kirk was his number-two man and one of IBM's own. Probably he also felt relief that a huge problem had been solved, and I'm sure he felt guilt at that relief. I could see those emotions in the funeral he gave Kirk in Endicott. It was really something. Dad trotted out college presidents, there were a number of eulogies, and the service took over two and a half hours. For the first and last time at a great occasion Dad didn't give a speech. I later heard that during the procession out of the church, Dad was so emotional that he forced his way between two pallbearers and grabbed an edge of the coffin himself.

CHAPTER 15

I'd always looked at Charley Kirk as a barrier between my father and me. It wasn't until after Kirk's death that I realized he had also been a buffer. Undiluted T. J. Watson could be pretty hard to take. He now had the biggest and most successful one-man show in American business, with something like twenty-two thousand people working as if they were an extension of his personality. To Dad it seemed perfectly natural that his photograph should hang in everybody's office. It didn't embarrass him in the slightest when his men organized a worldwide IBM celebration on the thirty-third anniversary of his employment. The company newspaper described this as a "spontaneous tribute," even though everybody knew it took months to prepare. Dad was now in his seventies, and as he aged the songs, tributes, pictures, and adulation had gradually gotten out of hand.

Until well into the 1950s, Dad was much more famous than the company. IBM dealt with other businesses, not consumers, so it was far from a household name like Ford or Metropolitan Life. Whenever we were written up in the *Saturday Evening Post* or some other popular magazine, the spotlight was always on Dad and his ability to make tens of thousands of people march to slogans like "A salesman is a man who sells" and "There is no such thing as standing still." We were known as a personality cult. I thought this image was bad for Dad and bad for the company. But I couldn't say point-blank, "Honest to Pete, this is ridiculous." It would have caused an ungodly explosion. For anyone who questioned his way of operating, Dad had an impregnable defense: "Look at the record!" You could argue it wasn't slogans that were making the record, but he'd say, "How do you know?"

So it wasn't an easy thing to be at Dad's side during the Hundred Percent Club convention in Endicott the summer of Kirk's death. The annual Hundred Percent Club meeting had long since outgrown the Waldorf, where it was held in the late 1930s. By now we had well over a thousand men in the sales force worldwide; over eight hundred and fifty had made their quotas for 1946 and were supposed to be honored. As usual, Dad went all out for their three-day stay. He had an entire tent city put up—seven acres of tents in neat rows, including sleeping tents, mess tents, a tent where professional photographers took the men's portraits and another where bootblacks shined their shoes, tents for displaying products, and a giant big top decorated with sales slogans and banners for the meeting itself.

To keep the Hundred Percenters comfortable, all the sleeping tents had wood floors, and sidewalks had been laid down so the Hundred Percenters wouldn't get their feet muddy if it rained. Once the convention was under way, each man would wake up in the morning to find a newspaper under the flap of his tent with a complete account of the previous day's events, written and printed while he slept. Salesmen from overseas would get to their seats in the big top and find headphones through which they could hear, each in his own language, the speeches that were being made. The preparations took weeks, and Dad's convention men worked their heads off to make sure nothing went wrong. Photographers from *Life* were circulating around, taking pictures of the event for a story about Dad and IBM that was going to be called "Supersalesmen."

In many ways the Hundred Percent Club was the high point of Dad's year, and the more drama he could wring out of it, the more he liked it. He arrived in Endicott on opening morning. I met him at the train and we walked into the back of the big tent exactly twenty minutes before the band was supposed to start playing "Ever Onward," the IBM anthem. A little group of convention planners greeted us, looking both proud and nervous. Dad said, "Now, what did you fellows have in mind this morning? I'd like to go over the program. Who's going to open?"

Of course, T. J. Watson was going to open. "We allow you twenty minutes," they told him.

"That's very nice, that's all I need. What are you going to do next?"

"We have a presentation by Mr. Thomas D'Arcy Brophy, the head of the American Heritage Foundation."

"Now wait a minute, the most important person is the salesman. I want to hear from all the Hundred Percenters." I knew he was thinking of the 1930s, when each salesman would get up and speak for three minutes. Those banquets had been endlessly boring. The salesmen were great fellows but they weren't philosophical enough to write decent speeches. So I said, "Dad, this is not like the 1930s. We only had a hundred men back then and it's almost nine hundred this year."

"Well, they could each say just a line or two." Somehow he got past that issue, but then he found something else to pick at. He said, "Let me see the products. Do you have products here?" By now it was about eleven minutes until the band would strike up. He went into the display tent and pointed to the machine nearest the door. "That's a tabulating machine there. We ought to have a keypunch! The first step in any installation is the keypunch, then the cards get sorted, and then they come to the tabulating machine! But you fellows have the tabulating machine in front!"

"But Mr. Watson, we can't move it now."

"Well, let's go into that for a moment." Then they had to haggle with him about that.

"Mr. Watson, this was all planned by the Product Display Department. This tabulating machine is our best new product."

"I don't care about that! I want to have it right!"

He was having a terrific time, but it was terrible for everyone else. The real danger was that he would say, "Gentlemen, I don't care if nine hundred men are coming into this tent in three minutes. Let them wait. I want you all to come to my room. We're going to talk this out."

Fortunately it never came to that, partly because I intervened and made an appeal to his heart and his common sense. "Dad, some of these men have been up for two nights working to get these machines positioned and running where they are. We can't tear it all up now."

"Well," he said, "I guess not." A couple of minutes later the band began to play, the men filed in, and the Hundred Percent Club came off gloriously—as planned.

People expected this kind of cantankerousness from Dad. But I don't think any employer gets away with being truly arbitrary for long before his best executives quit and his workers join unions. That didn't happen to Dad because he was extremely sensitive to the needs of the people he hired. From the minute IBM started making large profits in the 1930s, he kept the company in the vanguard of humane employers. IBM offered the best benefits money could buy, which in the early days meant good pay, steady employment, a chance to get promoted, educational opportunities, clean shops, and country clubs. The New Deal and the rise of labor unions changed the public's idea of what big institutions ought to provide, and Dad responded with a broad new plan. As soon as the war ended he unveiled it step by step, in a series of addresses that were made in the most dramatic possible way.

They were modeled after Roosevelt's fireside chats. Because IBM was so big that it was impractical to gather everybody together in a single place, Dad arranged for the telephone company to put a microphone on his desk and hook it up so that he could be heard simultaneously over the public address systems of the factories in Poughkeepsie and Endicott and in several large offices. He was very good at these speeches. He'd start by saying, "The war is over and you've supported the company very loyally during the war." Then he'd review the success of the business, thank the employees for their efforts, and remind them of the benefits IBM already offered. He'd talk about intangible things that made IBM a good place to work, like the right of any man to appeal to Dad personally if he thought he was being unfairly treated. Finally he'd announce a new plan to cover sickness and accident, hospitalization, disability, or whatever. When he announced the new IBM pension plan, Dad wrapped up his speech by saying that IBM's "constant purpose" was to relieve its people of "fear for the care of themselves and their families." Roosevelt himself couldn't have said it better. Underneath all the old-fashioned folderol, the IBM of 1947 was amazingly up-to-date.

I discovered that Dad had his finger in everything at IBM. A phenomenal number of executives—at one point I counted thirty-eight or forty—reported to my father directly. All these individuals had titles, some high and some low, but such distinctions didn't matter because they all reported to him. People were constantly waiting outside his door, sometimes for as long as a week or two before they could see him. He saw the important ones, of course, but when I complained about people wasting time in his anteroom, he said, "Oh Tom, let them wait. They're well paid."

We had no organization chart because Dad didn't want people to be so focused on specific jobs that they concentrated only on those jobs. He loved to tell the story of visiting a friend from the Cash who had gone to work at an automobile company. At the man's office there were organization charts everywhere. Each employee had one over his desk, along with a small framed job description spelling out what that individual was specifically responsible for. "It was the worst thing I ever saw," Dad would say. "It was so restricting!" He wanted everybody to be interested in everything. It wasn't unusual for Dad to call a sales manager to do a factory job or a factory manager to do a sales job, and he would demand answers and opinions and judgments on any segment of the business. Obviously IBM was becoming too big for that to be entirely practical. But it was his way of stretching each man and making him think about the business as a whole.

I was fascinated by the routine he followed on ordinary business days. He never came to the office without having in mind four or five things he wanted to get done. He might have thought these things up the night before, or while he was shaving in the morning, or maybe he'd talked with somebody at dinner and a casual remark had reminded him of something. But when he hit the office, he knew what he wanted to accomplish. He'd sit down at his desk and then, for item A on his list, he would pick an executive. It wasn't necessarily the guy you'd think would get the job, but the one he felt was the right man to do it that day. Dad would buzz and the man would come in and Dad would give him the word. For some things he might call several men and then there would be a meeting. But in the course of the day he'd clear those four or five items out of his mind.

If he got everything launched before lunchtime, after lunch he'd sit in his office and call in a few more men at random. He'd think, "Well, I haven't shaken up So-and-so for a while. So I'll get him in and ask some questions about his department and in the process part his hair a little. He'll get a pat on the back if I find something good or a kick in the tail if I find something bad." In the course of a month, he'd have seen nearly every one of the thirty-eight people reporting to him. He dealt out kicks in the pants and pats on the back in about equal proportion.

Dad used to badger the financial men mercilessly. Even though our business was to sell accounting equipment, Dad didn't particularly trust numbers. He thought they could distract a businessman from the real issues at hand. Our controller in those days was a contemporary of mine named Al Williams, who soon became my best friend and eventually rose to be president of IBM. He was extremely talented, but that never stopped Dad from giving him hell. Al had a little loose-leaf book where he'd write, in very fine print, the basic figures of the business. Father would look at that book and say, only half jokingly, "This fellow Williams can't keep anything in his head. He has to go to that little book." Of course, the kinds of questions Dad asked were so arbitrary that you'd need twenty books to answer them. He'd say, "Now, Williams, how did we do last year in Peru?"

Williams would say, "I'll have to find that out. Our subsidiary in Peru is very small. I just don't know how we did."

"Never mind. Let's take a bigger company. Let's take Brazil. We do a nice business in Brazil, don't we?"

Williams would go back to his office and call together his assistants. These were old professionals who really knew the business. He'd say, "Let's add a section to my book here that will give the status of each of our foreign subsidiaries." We were operating in almost eighty countries, so that would mean several new pages, all written very small. But the next time Al and Dad met, Dad would be on a different track. "Mr. Williams, how about platinum? Do we use any platinum? I notice it is going up quite a little. You ought to have those figures!" That little notebook eventually grew to four hundred pages—it was so fat Al couldn't get it into his pocket. He always perspired easily, but in my father's office Al's palms would get so wet that he needed a handkerchief to turn the doorknob when it was time to leave.

Like Williams, some of the men on the receiving end of Dad's kicks and pats were very able executives. Dad would often be on the road or be busy with outside commitments, so that for weeks at a stretch, IBM would run itself, which is to say that the vice presidents and department heads would make the necessary decisions and do the work. Yet with the exception of Al and one or two others, it was rare for these men to speak their minds when Dad was around. The longer I worked at IBM, the more I became convinced that my father's style silenced too many people.

Dad never formally tried to teach me about business. When I spent time with him I almost always picked up something, but it would never have worked for me to pull up my chair alongside his desk as I had with Kirk, because it didn't take much to get us into a tangle. Generally I stayed in my own office on the sixteenth floor of our Madison Avenue headquarters, and if he wanted me, he'd call. His office was one floor up, on the seventeenth floor;

there was a buzzer near my desk and a stairway outside my door. Dad was totally unpredictable. When that buzzer sounded I never knew whether he was going to bring me up there and say, "Son, I want you to meet Mr. Alfred P. Sloan," or "Tom, I'm really dissatisfied with the way things are going west of the Mississippi."

His method was to give me more and more latitude in making my own decisions, and at the same time to make me fight on anything that required his approval. I'd have to go up to his office and do a sales pitch, and more often than not, we'd end up in an argument. I knew that he was trying to test me, temper me, and expose me to the thinking processes that had made him so successful. That didn't make his methods any easier to take: he would second-guess virtually anything I did. Sometimes I'd get the feeling that no detail of my work was too tiny to escape his notice. For example, when I'd first moved out of Kirk's office, a pretty secretary named Claudia Pequin was assigned to me. One evening when we were working late, Father came to the door of my office and knocked. The room was overheated and we'd been in there a while, so he must have gotten hit with a blast of perfume when I opened the door. He let several days go by—he would often let time pass for the sake of drama—and then one day he said, "You know, Tom, there is an unusual relationship between a man and his secretary. I've always had male secretaries. Now, I don't mean to suggest that you are doing anything wrong, but in the course of business you end up having to travel with your secretary, for example, and the *look* of it might be misinterpreted." By coincidence Miss Pequin left IBM to go to McGill University not long afterward. I saw to it that the next secretary assigned to me was male.

Dad was teaching me but he wasn't ready to promote me yet. He took Kirk's job and gave it to George Phillips —old George Phillips who had been my babysitter and taught me to shoot. At first I didn't mind, because Phillips, though thoroughly devoted to Dad, was no operating man, and with him in the job, the organization got used to the fact that I was probably going to move up.

But I'd have Phillips all lined up in total agreement with something I wanted to do, and then we'd go into Dad's office. If Dad didn't agree, he'd treat Phillips just the way he used to when Phillips was only his secretary: "Phillips! How could you possibly say yes to that? You know that isn't right!" Phillips would instantly reverse himself—at such moments there was no way to persuade him that Dad wasn't infallible—and I'd be back where I started.

I was in a pell-mell rush to make a success of myself, and pretty quickly I took over the role of vice president of sales, even though someone else normally performed that function. It didn't surprise anybody who knew the other fellow that I could do this. He was a nice man, but shy and weak, and he tried to conceal it by buttering up my father and being pompous. He was the first Harvard graduate IBM ever had. Dad had hired him because he was the son of one of Dad's friends in Short Hills, and he thought the man raised IBM's image so much that he eventually put him on the board. But all the other executives knew that the fellow never really pitched in.

It seemed perfectly natural for me to get involved in the sales force, because that was the area that meant most to Dad. I went on the road as Dad had always gone on the road, spending long weeks inspecting offices, calling on customers, and praising and encouraging the men. Our great expansion meant that there were hundreds of mundane problems to solve. I remember taking a trip with Phillips in the Midwest, and going to inspect the struggling little office we had in Pierre, South Dakota. This was one of the offices we'd opened after Dad decided we should be represented in every state capital. Pierre itself was a tiny place—we spent a morning shooting ring-necked pheasants in a field no more than three miles from the center of town. Dad's idea for making small offices like this succeed was to install "three-way men" who sold products from all three of our divisions: time clocks, tabulating machines, and typewriters. But the office was losing money and I saw that three-way men would never work—the products were too diverse for most salesmen to span. I complained about this to Phillips, but then decided not to make any further fuss. It was better for Dad to open a few offices he might later have to close than never to open any new ones at all.

One change I did push through was designating liaison men to serve as Mr. IBM in cities where we had multiple operations. In places like Chicago we'd have one office selling to banks, one to government agencies, one to small businesses and so on. That helped hone our sales pitches, but it made for labor problems because there was no coordination on things as basic as salaries. There would be two or three IBM offices in a building, and when typists met each other on the elevator they'd talk and find out they were making different wages in the different offices. The liaison men, usually older managers who wanted to slow down a bit, helped iron out these discrepancies.

The part of my work that I loved best was picking and choosing men. In the maelstrom of postwar activity promotions came very rapidly. We were constantly naming new branch and district managers, assistant managers, and so forth. Many of these jobs went to young men just back from the war, and the average age of IBM officials quickly dropped below forty. I was very outspoken about who should get promoted, and I never doubted my ability to make personnel decisions fast and make most of them right. I never felt too sure of my intellectual depth, but I knew I had a lot of common sense. When I found people who I thought could contribute a lot to the business, I would prod them along. I did this with a self-confidence that surprised people who knew what I'd been like before I came under General Bradley's influence. I'm sure one of those taken aback was Vin Learson, who eventually succeeded me as IBM's chairman. Vin was still just a branch manager in 1947, in charge of our Philadelphia office. But he was a man of great force with a superior record, and I was planning to promote him. Then I got a letter from a man complaining that he had rented a house from Learson, and now Learson was suing him. They were fighting over the cost of repairing damage from a broken water pipe, or some such problem. So I called

Learson in. I handed him the letter and said, "Get your sights up. You are tremendously able and you are going to the top of this business. Don't mess around with petty little things where everybody is going to know you're in a lawsuit for two thousand bucks." Learson just nodded. The lawsuit never came up again and he was put in charge of a sales district the following year.

I remember the first time I ever fought to keep a man from quitting. It was Kirk's pal Birkenstock, the one Dad had promoted over so many other men. He came to see me soon after Kirk's death, and things weren't going well for him at all. He hadn't been able to handle the job of general sales manager, and even before Kirk died he had been demoted to running a market research department called Future Demands. He knew Kirk and I had been rivals, and I'm sure he expected me to do him in. But I actually thought he had a lot going for him. He was even smarter than Kirk, more attuned to the outside world, and could think down into the depths of things. I would have told him so if he'd let me. But the minute he got into my office he made noises like, "There's nothing much left for me, I've lost my job as general sales manager, all I'm doing now is make-work. . . ."

I didn't like his tone, so I forgot about giving compliments. I said, "You must not have much confidence in yourself. So you had a big mentor, and if he had lived you'd have had an easier time. But all of a sudden, he's not there. Do you want people to think you've lost your nerve? If you're any good, you can make it with me, with T.J., with anybody, not just Kirk! Now, if you think I'm not fair-minded, you ought to quit. But otherwise you ought to stay, because this is where the opportunities are." He said, "Do you mean I can stay and not be under a cloud?"

If a man wasn't willing to stand up for himself, I didn't want to work with him, and I didn't think he should be in the company. I hated the atmosphere of adulation Dad had surrounded himself with. He had people hanging on his every word as if he were the Messiah. I thought the executives at IBM were stunted because of it: the higher a man rose, the less opportunity he had to use his common sense. From my days as a salesman I had a pretty good idea who Dad's yes-men were, and I'd pick on these guys at the slightest provocation.

I was right most of the time, but occasionally I was wrong as hell. I made a terrible mistake early in 1948, for example. Dad was after me because he thought IBM repairmen were spending too much time on what we called "inspections." This meant checking machines in the field even if they were running just fine. Today it would be known as preventive maintenance and I was for it; but Dad thought of it as "fixing things that weren't broken," and we had some pretty hot words on the subject. Dad then decided to seek the opinion of J. J. Kenney, who was in charge of sales promotion. Poor Jack Kenney didn't know the first thing about repairmen, and he was the type of guy who was so awkward with tools that he probably would have had trouble putting in a screw straight. But he'd worked around Dad a long time, and I figured Kenney would automatically agree that inspections should be cut. I was waiting for him near his office as soon as he came back from talking to Dad.

"Tell me," I said, "did the subject of inspections come up?"

When he said it had, I blew up. I accused him of yessing the old man. I was in such a state that I almost called him a coward, except that he quit first and walked out. I knew I'd gone too far—Kenney was a superior man who had started as an office boy and worked his way up, and Father would be furious if we lost him. To make matters worse, I found out later that day that Kenney hadn't yessed Dad at all. On the contrary, he'd gone into Dad's office carrying an automobile owner's manual, and used it to point out that cars needed periodic maintenance even though they were much less complicated than IBM machines, so presumably IBM machines needed it too. I really panicked. The next morning I had a man waiting for Kenney on the train platform to ask him to reconsider, and when he came into the office I went straight to him. He listened to me apologize and beg for two hours until finally he was pretty sure he'd taught me a lesson. Then he agreed to stay.

I'd have made more mistakes like this if it hadn't been for the good advice of an executive named Red LaMotte, whom I'd known from boyhood. There weren't many old-timers left who were bold enough to speak their minds but LaMotte was fearless. He was best known within IBM for having landed the massive Social Security contract in the thirties, but I thought of him as the only man who had ever done to my father what J. J. Kenney had just done to me. It happened back in the 1920s. Dad had been letting LaMotte have it for not making a sale. Finally Red said, in a rather dignified way, "Mr. Watson, I don't really think we can continue to do business together. Thanks a lot." And he went home to Gramercy Park, where he and his wife had a lovely apartment. Within a few hours Dad was there rapping at the door. Red and his wife politely took Dad's coat and his derby and sat him down, acting as though they had no idea why he'd come. With LaMotte sitting right in the room, Dad turned to his wife and said, "Lois, I've made a great mistake and I need your help. Red is one of the people I count on to move IBM ahead. He has resigned, and I'm here to apologize and make sure I'll have him back with me." Dad was too proud to say "I'm sorry" directly, but Red gracefully accepted the apology anyway. LaMotte was an able guy in his own right, but it didn't hurt that his wife was the daughter of one of IBM's directors. Of all the people at IBM, he was perhaps the only one who moved in the same social world as Dad. He came from a genteel family, rode to hounds, went to the opera, and belonged to many of the same clubs as T.J. I think Dad was always a little resentful of him. After their reconciliation they agreed that Red should run the Washington office, which enabled him and Dad to give each other a wide berth. He knew everybody at IBM, young and old, and had a humane and balanced view of character that was tremendously helpful to me.

Another of Dad's men I quickly came to count on was Al Williams. I admired him because he came from a background just as rough as Dad's. His father had been a section boss in a coal mine who got fired and blackballed during the Depression for siding with the miners. At the same time my father was becoming famous as the highest-paid executive in America, the thousand-dollar-a-day man. Al, who was in accounting school, saw that in the newspapers and thought, "Boy, they pay good money in that company. That's where I want to work." When I came back from the war he'd been at IBM five years, and everybody agreed he was outstanding. His office was right across the hall from mine. Instead of looking as if he'd come from a little mountain town in Pennsylvania, Al seemed like a graduate of Yale. I asked him how he got so smooth and he was very open with me. He said, "I found out people I admired bought their clothes at Brooks Brothers, so that's where I started buying mine. I noticed I couldn't talk easily at dinner parties, so I began to read the classics." Besides working long and hard hours, he was trying to make up for not going to college. He had his day set up so that he got up at seven, played tennis from seven-thirty to eight-thirty to stay in shape, got to work on time, did his work, went home, read great books for an hour, had dinner, listened to classical music for a while, and went to bed.

Al was so much more demanding of himself than I. I knew he'd come to IBM out of admiration for Dad, and it pleased and surprised me to find that he took me seriously as well. I was never sure that people I respected would take me seriously once they got to know me. But Al and I made a good combination. He was totally policed as a man, orderly, and a little cautious; I was innovative, highly motivated, and not cautious at all. With his CPA and his financial sense, Al made up for a big gap in my knowledge. I never had any pretensions about understanding money, and at the beginning I didn't even know the difference between debt and equity in the company accounts. But I never felt embarrassed to ask Al a question, and an answer from him was like an answer from on high. With Williams and LaMotte and a few others in those early days, I knew I'd found a team of my own.

CHAPTER 16

F ather was famous for having the longest entry in *Who's Who in America*—sixteen and a half inches, in fine print, of clubs, associations, foundations, honorary degrees, and decorations. I doubt very many people ever surpassed that; I certainly never did. Running IBM took only about half his time, and he spent the rest in public life, constantly extending his influence on behalf of world peace, IBM—and T. J. Watson. Dad was by now as prominent in reality as I'd imagined him when I was a boy, but he never stopped courting people in high places. J. Edgar Hoover, for example. I had a chance a few years ago to look at Dad's FBI file, which consists mostly of letters he exchanged with the director after the war. I had to laugh. He bombarded Hoover with compliments—for being decorated by King George, for getting an honorary degree, even for being named in 1950 "Big Brother of the Year" by a charity for boys. In his free moments Dad liked to study the newspapers and seize opportunities to fire off telegrams to prominent people, some of whom he hadn't met yet, congratulating them on something they'd done. He also liked to send copies of IBM publications in which they were mentioned. All this was pure salesmanship, of course, and Dad kept it up as long as he lived.

But most of Dad's accomplishments in public life were much more serious, and were motivated by genuine concern for the good of mankind. The United Nations was his passion. He thought it could succeed where the League of Nations and the International Chamber of Commerce had failed, and as soon as World War II ended he started campaigning again for World Peace Through World Trade. "When there is a proper flow of goods and services across borders," he said, "there will be no need for soldiers to cross them." In one of his more memorable *Think* magazine editorials he called the opening session of the UN the "first day of school" for mankind. He said, "Everyone everywhere should clearly understand that this is the most important international meeting in history."

Dad never worked in any official capacity for the UN, but for years statesmen and diplomats came to him for advice and for his terrific ability to make things happen. He was constantly hosting receptions and dinners for members of the international community, and the staff at IBM was often busy with UN affairs—everything from organizing public education programs to lining up boxes at the Met and seats at Broadway musicals for visiting dignitaries. Trygve Lie and Dag Hammarskjöld, the first two secretaries general, came to see Dad at his office at IBM, and in 1946 even Winston Churchill sought him out. They met in Florida; Dad was on vacation and Churchill was on his way to Missouri, where he made the great speech in which he said "an iron curtain has descended across the Continent."

As involved as my father had been with FDR, he shied away from the Truman White House. He and Truman had a lot in common—they both came from poor rural backgrounds and both had strong, simple philosophies about the value of hard work, honesty, and so on—but I think Dad saw Truman and his rough Missouri friends as representing a step backward for the country. Dad gave him the respect of office, but like most people never expected Truman to survive the election of 1948, and even after Truman upset Tom Dewey, Dad kept his distance. But the rest of us knew the Trumans pretty well. My sister Jane had met Margaret Truman at the end of the war, and they'd become fast friends. When Jane got married in 1949, Margaret gave her a bridal dinner and was a bridesmaid at the wedding. My brother, who was finishing his last year at Yale after coming back from the war, also was friendly with Margaret. The gossip columns made a lot of the fact that Dick escorted her to the opera in New York and spent a few weekends visiting her in Washington, but there was nothing serious behind it.

Dad was using the Truman years to build a relationship with the one American he thought was as great as Roosevelt: Dwight Eisenhower. In 1946 everybody knew that Eisenhower was dissatisfied serving as army chief of staff, and the most powerful people were competing for his attention. Financiers were offering him companies to run, and there were both Republicans and Democrats who thought he ought to be president. Nobody knew Eisenhower's political leanings—in fact, after FDR died, Eleanor Roosevelt and her children tried to get Eisenhower to run as a Democrat; and even Truman volunteered his support. But Eisenhower said no to everything. He didn't want to go into business, and said he didn't feel it was right for a career soldier to hold high public office.

Dad had been introduced to Eisenhower right after the war and the two of them really hit it off. Eisenhower liked businessmen, and his optimistic idea of America's future was very similar to Dad's. Dad also understood something about the general that a lot of people hadn't figured out yet: Eisenhower was ambitious, but his ambitions weren't of the usual sort—he was just looking for the best way to repay the great debt he felt he owed America. He'd started poor in Kansas, and he'd risen to become a great hero and the supreme commander of all the Allied forces in Europe. He wanted to spread peace and the American way of life all over the world, but he didn't know how to go about it.

That was where Dad came in. He gave Eisenhower a transition into civilian life by getting him appointed president of Columbia University. Dad was a major benefactor of Columbia and vice chairman of the board of trustees. By the end of the war Columbia's great president, Nicholas Murray Butler, was becoming very infirm. Most of the board wanted to recruit another educator to succeed him. Dad didn't object to that, but he thought that General Eisenhower would do more for Columbia's stature than any professional educator.

So Dad talked the board into letting him go to the Pentagon and offer Eisenhower the job. He told Eisenhower, "You are a great hero, and I represent a great university. We'd like you to be its president."

The general said, "You've got the wrong Eisenhower. You should talk to my brother Milton." Eisenhower's brother was head of Kansas State University at the time. Dad kept after the general for more than a year. Finally, in the spring of 1947, Eisenhower said yes. He and Dad ran Columbia together until Eisenhower left three years later to head NATO. Eisenhower took to calling Dad his "partner" at Columbia, and really went to school on him. With the help of my father and other prominent businessmen such as Phil Reed of General Electric and William Robinson of Coca-Cola and the New York *Herald Tribune,* Eisenhower got into the right clubs and onto the right committees, and learned which social invitations to accept and which to decline. Later on, when the general joined the Republican party, Dad stepped into the background because he was a loyal Democrat. But he probably did as much as anyone to get Eisenhower ready for the White House.

Even though I had no illusions about becoming Dad's equal, I wanted to be ready to represent IBM to the world. I totally believed the idea he had drilled into my head since boyhood: that what a chief executive does outside his business is just as important as what he does at his desk. So I set out to build my reputation by doing charitable work and making friends with prominent people outside the business. After the war Dad made sure that opportunities started coming my way—things that were suited to my modest ability and modest pocketbook. For instance, I had a call from Roy Larsen, the president of Time Inc., asking me to serve in the 1948 New York City United Fund drive, of which he was chairman. My first impulse was to say, "I don't live in the city, so why should I?" But I realized, "Here is an eminent man, halfway in age between my father and me. I can work with him and learn something. I can meet other important people who are involved in the drive." That's the way it worked out. Over the next few years I was invited to join the Greater New York Council of the Boy Scouts, which I eventually headed, and the United Nations Association, to promote the UN in America.

It was easy to get involved in these things because I was T. J. Watson's son, but not so easy for me actually to handle myself at those meetings. Dad thrived on being in the public eye. I'd often seen him perform at meetings and dinners in New York. He'd get up, start working the room, hit every doggone table where he knew anybody, shake every hand, and particularly—even if he was on the dais—go down to the IBM table and meet all the men and their wives. In a single evening he might meet four hundred people. I was different: I didn't like giving speeches, or attending dinners, or making chitchat at cocktail parties—and I was terribly inept at it. But even if I didn't enjoy the meetings I went to, I always came home with a notebook full of names. A good businessman needs a lot of friends. Cultivating them is a laborious process, and how well you succeed is a direct result of how much effort and thoughtfulness you bring to bear. When I was introduced to somebody new I'd often send a note saying how much I'd enjoyed meeting him; if my new acquaintance had expressed an interest in a subject that I had a good book about, I'd send along a copy of the book. People remember gestures like that for years. I kept a file on each new acquaintance so I wouldn't be handicapped by my memory. I noted his or her name, addresses, telephone numbers, spouse's name, and so on. I always made a note of where we'd met and the person's specialty or interest.

The more I circulated, the less awkward I felt and the more I learned about the fine points of sociability. Often these lessons came in unexpected ways. Once in New York I was seated next to Governor Tom Dewey at a Boy Scout luncheon. I stuck out my hand and said to him, "I'm Tom Watson Jr." He grinned and said, "You know, you're doing everyone you meet a real favor when you start a conversation that way, instead of saying 'Hello,

Governor Dewey,' and leaving me to guess who you are. Watch what happens during this lunch. Somebody will come by here and say to me, 'Hello, Tom! Mary sends her best!' I won't know who he is or who Mary is, and I'll have to sit and be the damn fool."

I thought he might be putting me on, but sure enough, pretty soon a man came up and said, "Hi, Governor! I'll bet you don't remember me!" It happened all through the lunch. I always make a point of mentioning my name to people who don't know me well.

Oddly, the community in Greenwich, Connecticut, was much harder to break into than New York. Olive and I were used to the army life we'd just left, and while military posts may be stodgy and ingrown, they have pleasant customs for making newcomers feel at home. When you arrive at a new base your neighbors drop by to make "arrival calls"—welcoming you to the post, giving you the word on the commanding officer, telling you where the best stores are, and so on. We didn't know that in Greenwich it worked exactly the opposite. You made your way into clubs through friends, if you had any, but nobody ever called on you. After a few months, Louis and Grace Walker, whom we knew vaguely from before the war, took us under their wing and we gradually started getting invitations to dinner parties and country clubs. John Bartol, an executive with American Airlines, brought me into a men's investment club, where talk about money was just an excuse for Greenwich men to get together once a month. In that club I met most of the young leaders of the town. But overall Olive and I led a fairly secluded life.

Our household at first consisted of young Tom, a new baby—a wonderful girl whom we named Jeannette after my mother—and a nurse. We all squeezed into a house that was too small on the day we bought it. After a couple of years came another beautiful baby daughter, whom we named Olive, and we moved to a bigger place, on the bank of a pond with swans. On weekends the kids and I would paddle around in a war-surplus rubber raft. For fun, I bought a used sailboat that I kept at a local yacht club—the first sailboat I ever owned. It was called *Tar Baby;* it leaked and sailed poorly but it didn't cost very much. I used it in my first tries at ocean racing.

I commuted by train into the city every day. I thought the station platform was an exciting place: there was a newspaper to buy, and my group of acquaintances slowly grew so there was often someone to say hello to. And there was always the challenge of finding the right spot on the platform so that when the train pulled in I could get a seat alone or one next to someone I knew. We all rode on fifty-trip tickets, and it cost less than a dollar to get into New York.

I started out catching an early train, to make sure I got to work by nine. But before long I figured out there was a smarter way to commute. The people on my usual train were all worker bees—young fellows on their way up who had to get to the office on time. Older, more successful businessmen generally skipped the early trains, and from time to time I'd arrange my schedule at IBM so I could ride later too. In this way I got to know some of the most influential businessmen in New York, such as Stanley Resor, who with his wife had built J. Walter Thompson into one of the world's top advertising agencies. The man I valued the most on those train rides was old George W. Davison, the retired chairman of the Central Hanover Bank, which later became Manufacturers Hanover. Father had introduced us originally, and the time I spent riding with Davison and listening to his observations was almost as valuable as the time I spent with Dad. I liked Davison from the minute we started talking. The first advice he ever gave me was on the subject of height. Davison was tall in wisdom, tall in knowledge, tall in his way of relating to the world, but physically he was only about five feet eight inches. He said, "This is not a fair world. Don't get the idea that all the good are rewarded or all the bad are punished. You can start right in with how tall you are. It's a lot easier to be a success when you're tall, because people notice you." Then he smiled and said, "On the other hand, it also helps to be smart, and I'm smart."

Davison must have heard from Dad about my tendency to blow my stack, because he was always talking about the need for self-control in business. He taught me the expression, "What you haven't said, you can say any time." That still comes back to me when I'm about to send a scathing letter that I may end up regretting. I don't always follow Davison's advice, but at least I remember it.

I always felt as if I had to be on my toes when I was around men like Davison. But Dad told me that was a good thing. He said, "Don't make friends who are comfortable to be with. Make friends who will force you to lever yourself up." Doing that broadened me, but I had to get through some awfully rough moments. One night in 1949, Davison had Olive and me to dinner at his house. There were a couple of other executives from the Central Hanover Bank with their wives, and there was a guest of honor, a Spaniard named Admiral Luis de Flores. De Flores was a dramatic fellow with a turned-up mustache who had flown in World War I and invented a number of instruments for airplanes. His latest project was more along IBM's line. He and his son had designed an electronic filing system for libraries, and the Central Hanover people had put a couple of hundred thousand dollars into it.

We had a good dinner, and then we men repaired to the library for brandy. No sooner was the door closed than Davison's colleagues really let me have it. They said de Flores was going to eat IBM up with his library system. Of course, it should have been obvious that libraries rarely have enough money to pay for fancy technology. Instead I thought, "Gee, here we have this multi-million-dollar research budget, and this Spaniard is beating us." All the same, it steamed me up that Davison should let his men gang up on me. When it was time to leave the library and rejoin the ladies, I said, "Just a minute, gentlemen. I'd like to propose a bet. If any of you would like to buy three thousand dollars' worth of de Flores's stock tomorrow, I'll be glad to buy three thousand dollars' worth of IBM stock. Then we'll wait five years. If IBM goes up more than de Flores, I'll take your stock, and if de Flores goes up more, you can have mine." Nobody wanted to bet. Within a year, de Flores was defunct, to my relief, even though I had nothing against him personally. I doubt that it was ever Davison's intention to put me through the wringer like that, but it's an illustration of what it means to have those difficult friends Dad recommended.

Surprisingly, I made my best contacts in the business community not through Dad but through old Fred Nichol, Dad's right-hand man before Charley Kirk stepped into the job. When Fred retired he had arranged for me to take his place in an organization called the American Society of Sales Executives. The ASSE was not well known but had tremendous influence on a lot of businesses, and once I realized this I started going to the meetings religiously. The membership consisted of senior men from thirty companies, chosen so that each was the sole representative of his industry. There was a steel guy and a fellow from Heinz and a drug guy and a clock guy, from the Hamilton Watch Company. There were men in real estate, life insurance, tobacco, and paint. The head of the Coca-Cola bottling company in Chattanooga belonged, and so did Pat Patterson of United Air Lines, H. W. Hoover of the vacuum cleaner company, King Woodbridge of Dictaphone, and Paul Hoffman from Studebaker, until Truman called on him to run the Marshall Plan. Twice a year these men would meet and tell all their business sins.

The format was very simple. Each meeting started with an extended presentation—a member would get up and give a history of his company. This was done on a rotation system so that each company came up every five years or so. Then we'd go alphabetically through the entire group and each man would give a fifteen- or twenty-minute report on the state of his business. I learned more about managing salesmen than a hundred business schools could have taught me—tips for hiring, ways to set up incentives, mistakes to avoid, and so on.

Many of the men were as old as Dad. I spent a lot of time listening to Al Fuller, the entrepreneur who founded the Fuller Brush Company. He told me how he'd started out driving a streetcar in Hartford. Each day by quitting time he'd have so much grime under his fingernails that he couldn't get them clean. So he and his wife started experimenting with making brushes. Finally they invented a machine that could make a brush out of the bristles of a hog, held in place by twisted wires. On that foundation, and the new concept of door-to-door selling, they built a large business and a great fortune.

The older men still ruled the roost at the ASSE but the younger generation was coming in, and I found a couple of men my own age who became lifelong friends. The first was Bob Galvin, who took Motorola from his father, the founder, when it was still a small manufacturer of car radios and made it into an electronics giant. Another friend was Charles Percy, who was then known as the boy wonder running Bell & Howell, and later became a U.S. senator. The thing I particularly loved about the ASSE was that other people saw me as distinct from my father and gave me a certain amount of respect accordingly. Everybody knew IBM was going like gangbusters, and when we talked about, say, a trend in employee benefits, somebody would always ask, "What have you done about that, Tom?" I'd sit up late into the night and shoot the bull with these men. I wanted to be able to sell IBM equipment to every business, so I tried to learn the wrinkles of each industry and the culture of each company. I'd go back to IBM full of new ideas, and never let on where my inspirations were coming from.

Once I'd been around IBM for several years, Dad decided I was ready to join the Business Advisory Council, and he set it up so that I took over his seat in 1951. This was a tremendous public compliment, his way of broadcasting to the world his great confidence in me, but to tell the truth I learned more from going to the ASSE. The Business Advisory Council was a federal advisory group that dated from the New Deal, when Daniel Roper, Roosevelt's first secretary of commerce, organized it to try to win the cooperation of top businessmen. In the 1950s there wasn't very much for the council to do, but it had become the most prestigious forum for businessmen in America and represented a tremendous concentration of power.

Dad arranged the invitation without my knowledge. At a banquet I found myself seated next to the business council chairman, John Collyer of B. F. Goodrich. He asked if I knew anything about the council and I said no. That must have seemed stupid, because later on I realized that everyone knew about the business council. But Collyer patiently explained what it was and asked if I would like to join. At least I knew enough to say I'd be flattered.

It was a great privilege to belong, but for me it could also be agony. Each year the council met a couple of times at the Homestead, a luxurious hotel in Hot Springs, Virginia. These meetings always began with a black-tie dinner, and everyone brought his wife. Olive and I were the youngest people there. We'd sit in our room wondering what time it was appropriate to go down to cocktails, and poring over a little book they gave you, trying to memorize names and faces.

I remember being put off by something I saw at the first dinner. One member was a powerful railroad man from out West, and during the cocktail hour he had a few drinks. Then, on his way into the dinner, walking across the ballroom with his little wife, he fell down flat on his face. Everybody gasped, but it turned out this was a trick he could do—arching his body slightly and turning his head so he wouldn't kill himself when he fell. He got up and everybody roared and applauded. Then he did it again, and again. He was all covered with dust from the floor. It was a shock to see such slapstick from one of America's business leaders.

The majority of the people to whom we were introduced were somewhat cool to us. They knew we were Democrats for one thing, and big business was still as overwhelmingly Republican as it had been in Roosevelt's day. Also, I wasn't the head of IBM yet, and a lot of people must have thought Dad was jumping the gun by having me there. More than once I felt so out of place that I told Olive we should go back to New York. I did that knowing I could count on her to persuade me to stay, for IBM's sake.

CHAPTER 17

My growing prominence began to get on Dad's nerves. He wanted to make me the head of IBM, but he didn't like sharing the limelight. So he was contradictory in his attitude toward me. When I wasn't around, he'd tell people that I was a world beater and that without question I was going to run the company someday. But then Dad would see me accomplish something—he'd be in the audience when I gave a speech, or he'd read in the paper that I'd joined a charity board—and he wouldn't say a word about it. When you got right down to it, Dad wasn't always so comfortable with the idea that Tom Watson Jr. was making a name for himself. This was a side of Dad I had never known was there. During all my years as an aimless boy making poor grades in school, he'd given me nothing but love and support. As a young salesman I'd gotten so much help it was embarrassing. And as I went into the business community, Dad quietly saw to it that all kinds of doors were springing open. But when it came to power, real power of the kind he held over the lives of tens of thousands of people, my father made me fight him for every scrap.

That's why I got so upset in 1948 when it looked to me as if Dad was about to hand over half of IBM to my brother. I was now a vice president, but Dick had stayed in the Army and then gone back to Yale, where he finished a bachelor's degree with a major in international relations. He'd been at IBM less than a year and was just getting started as a salesman. I definitely thought of him as my junior in the company. But Dad was an old man in a hurry. He had dreams of his two boys running IBM together, and with his seventy-fifth birthday looming, he knew there might not be time to put Dick through the same tough apprenticeship I'd had. He needed to set Dick up in a way that would allow the two of us to work together and not fight too much, because someday there would be no one around to arbitrate.

For years, before I had any successes of my own, the idea of Dick getting ahead really bothered me. Even though he was five years younger, I thought he was in many ways my superior. He'd gotten into Yale, and his grades were a hell of a lot better than mine had been in college. He was a better athlete. He had a natural command of languages and an easier way of relating to other people—he was much more gracious, a relaxed guy, very charming. He could sing and he could yodel and he was a real entertainer at parties. Seeing Dick do so well had made me feel like the black sheep. I thought people admired him because he lived up to what Dad wanted, and I didn't. But I began to resent Dick much less after my successes during the war. Now I had great ambition for myself, and also felt warmly toward him. He was my brother, and I wanted him to succeed too. My gripe was with Dad—it burned me up that he seemed to see us as total equals. I'd been at IBM three years before the war and almost three years since—they weren't all happy years but I wanted credit for them—and here was Dick, who'd been in the company eight months, being handed the world on a silver platter.

Dad's idea was to give me the U.S.A. and Dick everything else. He made a place for Dick by taking our offices and factories on six continents and forming a subsidiary company. It was called IBM World Trade, and it was the great labor of my father's old age. Looking back on it today, I'd say it was one of the most astonishing accomplishments in Dad's long career. And just as Dad wanted, Dick took it and ran it flawlessly, making it everything Dad hoped it would be. But when Dad first thought it up, I fought him harder on it than I'd ever fought before. I bucked so hard that I damn near got disowned.

Our foreign operations at the end of World War II were pretty thin. IBM had scores of offices and factories abroad—we were represented in seventy-eight countries. Unfortunately, that number was much more impressive than the profits generated. In 1939, for example, only about one eighth of IBM's profits came from abroad, and of course the percentage fell during the war. The "foreign department," as it was called, seemed pretty unimportant compared with our booming business in the U.S. But Dad thought otherwise. I can remember going to a meeting in the spring of 1946, where I watched him chew out Charley Kirk and George Phillips about the wretched state of our overseas business. He called it "nothing short of a disgrace," which wasn't really fair, because the lion's share of foreign sales always came from Europe, which was in a shambles. At the end of the meeting Dad declared that we must set up the foreign department as a separate company and make it stand on its own. But he gave no specific orders, and everyone figured he was just blowing off steam.

A couple of months later I came up with an idea that helped revive the European operation. The problem over there was not lack of demand; many of our customers had survived the war and were eager to get punch-card machines. But our offices found it almost impossible to deliver the right gear—they were crippled by shortages and by widespread import restrictions that made it impossible to bring in new machines. An inspiration came to me at home in the middle of the night. I woke up and said, "As-is machines!" The American armed forces had been turning in millions of dollars' worth of punch-card equipment that was no longer needed. We took those machines—some with the mud of the battlefield still on them—and sent them to the European factories to be refurbished. At first people thought our employees would be insulted to be given used, dirty equipment to fix. But they loved it when they saw that with a few hours' work and a new coat of paint, those machines were something they could sell.

As far as Dad's idea of setting up a world trade subsidiary was concerned, I gave it no more thought. But a year or two later, after Dick joined the company, it hit me that our international operations were reinvesting a large portion of their profits rather than turning the money over to IBM in New York. I discovered this because we needed the cash to keep growing in the U.S.—expanding a rental operation requires a lot of dollars. The then manager of the foreign department was a big, genial fellow named Joe Wilson. When I called him in to ask where the profits were going, he said Dad had ordered him to try to expand abroad as rapidly as we were doing in the U.S. I thought that was utter folly, but Dad ignored me. Before long I heard him talking again about splitting off the foreign department. He wanted it to have its own executives, its own board of directors, and much more autonomy to do the great things he expected. With an enormous leap of logic he said, "The United States has six percent of the world's population, and the rest of the world has ninety-four percent: someday the World Trade Company is going to be larger than the U.S. company."

My friend Al Williams, for one, thought this was very profound, but I thought Dad was being simplistic and naive. We had endless opportunity and little risk in the U.S., it seemed to me, while it was hard to imagine us getting anywhere abroad. Latin America, for example, seemed like a bottomless pit. Many of those countries were running their economies in such a way that for us ever to make a dollar and get it home was going to be impossible. Meanwhile, even with the success of as-is machines, our business in Europe was far from healthy. Trade was still paralyzed, the Marshall Plan was only on the drawing board, and it was unclear when we'd ever be able to start manufacturing again.

The solution my father came up with shows how resourceful he really was. He invented a way for IBM's offices in Europe to have their own free trade across international borders. Within IBM, he created a kind of common market ten years before the real one existed— and unlike the Common Market, my father's worked right from the start. Our European factories were not giant plants like Endicott or Poughkeepsie; the biggest one employed about two hundred people and the rest were more like shops. Dad made these little units dependent on one another. He came up with the simple rule that each factory had to make parts not only for the country in which it was situated, but also for export. So if you were making keypunch mechanisms in France, perhaps 60 percent of your output would be used in machines for the French market, but 40 percent had to be exported to assembly lines somewhere else—in Italy and Germany, say. By shipping those parts, you earned foreign-exchange credits—which you then could use to import parts of some other type that, for instance, a Dutch IBM plant might be making for you. Because tariff barriers were so high, we shipped finished machines only to the smaller countries where we had no plants, and few IBM machines were 100 percent manufactured in the country where they were finally assembled. This trading around allowed us to operate on a much larger scale, and far more efficiently, than any company that was bound to a single country.

Dad's second great innovation before turning World Trade over to Dick was to hire down-and-out aristocrats and use their connections to get our business rolling again. Dad had always been inclined toward highborn people, and by now he had the necessary prestige to attract them to IBM when they needed work. Even though the form of government had changed in most European countries, Dad understood that the aristocracy had selling power. Sometimes he'd find out he'd gotten a man who was dead from the neck up, but most of those he picked did very well. Baron Daubek of Rumania covered all of Eastern Europe. He had so much brass that he'd fly in behind the Iron Curtain and collect rentals from the guys who had taken our companies away. Another of our aristocrats was Baron Christian de Waldner, a French Huguenot who became known as "Mister IBM of France." He was a frail-looking but tough man who built up IBM to be one of France's largest companies. De Waldner would fight with anybody to get what he thought the company needed. He even convinced Dad that to succeed in France, IBM had to bend to local customs, going so far as to serve wine at lunch in the cafeteria.

Dad didn't advertise the fact that he was clearing the way for my brother until he took Dick around Europe with him in late 1948. It was Dad's first visit to the Continent after the war. He traveled around for several months organizing his factories and renewing old ties, and he kept Dick with him the entire time, introducing him as his "assistant." That made it pretty clear to everybody who IBM's next great internationalist was going to be.

I wish I'd thought back on my own experience of having sales pushed my way and realized how hard things must be for my brother. As the youngest in our family, he was low man on the totem pole. Not only did he have Dad over him, but he had me five years in front. To complicate things still further, there was our sister Jane, who was always Dad's favorite. So Dick grew up in a very, very tough position. Maybe because of this, Dick's relationship with Dad was different from mine. If Dad got mad at me, I'd get mad right back and we'd fight. My brother had just as strong a temper as I did, but he seemed to believe that in order to get ahead, he had to take what T.J. dished out. Knuckling under was traumatic for Dick. He had asthma, and sometimes when my father lit into him he'd get so short of breath he'd need a shot of adrenaline to bring his breathing back to normal.

I was amazed at how far Dick let Dad go. That tour they took of Europe, for example, was supposed to be my brother's honeymoon. In June of 1948 he'd married a superb girl from Syracuse, New York, named Nancy Hemingway. They were going to sail to England, and of all the pushy things, Dad asked if he and Mother could go along. I think Dad may have felt his time was running out. Dick must have had misgivings about combining his honeymoon with a business trip, but he said yes. So off they sailed, the four of them together. Even then Dad didn't let up. One night they were in Stockholm, staying at the Grand Hotel, and were scheduled to have dinner with the king of Sweden. When it was time to leave, Dad noticed that Nancy's dress wasn't floor length. He asked her, "Do you have a long dress?" and she explained nervously that she hadn't brought one along. Dad lit into her and said, "You are going to disgrace me and my family," and Nancy burst into tears. That was where Dick finally drew the line. He said, "Look, old man. You can tell me anything you want because I'm your son. But don't talk to Nancy that way. She is my wife and has nothing to do with you." That really knocked Dad back. He apologized, and they went, and Nancy dined with the king in her short dress.

Dad came back from that trip and sat down with me in October to tell me how he was going to divide up the world. World Trade—Dick's company—would build and sell machines everywhere except the United States; IBM Domestic—my side—would be confined to the continental U.S., but as the parent company it would also handle aspects of the business like financing and research and development for all of IBM. For the time being Dad was going to add the chairmanship of World Trade to his usual duties, with a senior man named Harrison Chauncey as number two and Dick as a vice president— the same rank I had! I told Dad that splitting off World Trade was the worst idea I'd ever heard. I said darkly, "If you do this, you'll live to regret it."

He looked at me with total innocence and said, "Why do you object to this so much?"

There were a lot of plausible business arguments I could have used. But the question caught me so completely off guard that the only thing that came to mind was personal: "There's no place for me to travel! I like to travel!"

That made my father smile. "Well," he said, "I'll tell you what. I'll give you Alaska, Hawaii, and Puerto Rico, and you can travel there."

I was so embarrassed that I agreed and left his office feeling totally stymied. Later that week he called me in, this time with Dick, to discuss the plan again. I started to present my business objections one at a time. Setting up World Trade would only multiply bureaucracy and expenses, I said; and I predicted that the minute World Trade was separate, it would start developing its own products, thereby wrecking IBM's manufacturing efficiency. Dick took the diplomatic course of sitting by and not saying a word, but I sensed a rising tide of impatience in Dad. The objection that finally caused him to flash was my pressing him on who should get Canada. Our business there produced a big cash flow and I hated to lose it. There was no reason for giving Canada to World Trade except that they needed the cash more than we did. It was a real weak spot in Dad's plan. I could see him bristle, and I really bored in. I said, "Anybody can see that Canada belongs with the domestic company! If World Trade can't stand on its own without Canada, then you shouldn't split it off at all."

Dad rose up and thundered, "What are you trying to do, prevent your brother from having an opportunity?" Those words killed me. They set me up against my brother, who was right there. Dad would say that kind of thing without thinking, because he always aimed to win. He used the Marquis of Queensberry rules if he had time to think about them, but when he was in a corner, it didn't matter what the rules were; he wanted to accomplish his purpose. There was really nothing more I could say. Dick and I rode down in the elevator with Dad and walked him outside to where he had a limousine waiting. He got in and rolled down the window and said, "Now remember, boys, stay together." I was devastated. Dick and I went back upstairs and I tried to paper over the rift between us by saying I hadn't meant anything personal. Having won his point, Dick was generous enough not to rub it in.

The old man went ahead and organized the IBM World Trade Company in early 1949, formally splitting it off as a wholly owned subsidiary a year later. Most of my fears turned out to be unfounded. World Trade did not drag IBM down. It capitalized on Europe's economic recovery, financed itself through its own profits and foreign borrowings, and grew as fast as the American company. Dad did not insult me by giving Dick equal rank. He made Dick a vice president, sure enough, but he also gave me the big promotion I'd been working so hard to earn. In September of 1949 I became executive vice president, the job Kirk had when he died. I didn't even lose my dreamed-of chance to travel in Europe. Since the U.S. Army stayed there in force, and its punch-card installations were the responsibility of the domestic IBM, there were ample opportunities for me to go around inspecting.

As my brother rose at World Trade, I made great efforts to stay out of his way and help in any manner I could. I bowed out of the International Chamber of Commerce, so he could take my place. I took him to a meeting of the American Society of Sales Executives and introduced him around. I avoided any discussions of European business or international affairs. Later on, when he needed executives who knew how to twist tails and produce results, I sent him some of my best men—most notably Gilbert Jones, my former executive assistant, whom Dick chose many years later as his successor as chairman of World Trade. I thought Dick was extraordinarily able, and in our off-hours we grew very close. We often took our wives and children on ski trips together, and Nancy and Olive became best friends.

None of this was enough to defuse the tension in our family. Dad remained suspicious that I was secretly out to undermine my brother, and Dick, taking his cues from Dad, played very close to the vest. He would discuss World Trade with Dad but never with me. The situation made it very difficult over the next few years for the three of us to do business. There were aspects of World Trade in which the domestic company had to be involved, since we were the parent—important matters like financing and product planning. But when Dad and Dick and I would meet to talk about IBM's future, there was constant strife. Even the smallest difference of opinion between Dick and me would cause Dad to question my motives, and this in turn led to bitter fights—always between Dad and me, with Dick sitting silently by. Usually this happened behind closed doors, but at one point I blew up at them in public. We were at the Metropolitan

Club, and Dad told me to keep my opinions on Europe to myself. I completely lost my temper, told them that one business could not have two heads, and swearing loudly at both my father and Dick, I stormed out. I don't remember the details, but I remember the outcome, because I thought it was the end of my IBM career.

I spent the night paralyzed with remorse for my outburst. The next morning Dad buzzed me up to his office. "Young man," he said, "if you fail in IBM or in life, it will be because your temper did you in." He dismissed me without letting me say a word. That was just as well, because too much was at stake. We were right on the brink of estrangement—both of us felt it—and neither of us wanted to jump over the edge. Dad came very close to firing me. Many years later, after his death, I found a note he had drafted at the time. It was written in pencil on the back of a luncheon menu, and it said:

> I gave a great deal of thought to this relationship between Dick and you and came to the decision that if the past differences were to continue, you and he must part. I am writing this as I want you to have plenty of time to look about.

Fortunately he never sent it. I'd have felt shattered, but the immediate consequence would have been to escalate the fight. I'd have gone to him and said, "You're threatening me. Let's get this out on the table right now." I was very peppery with him, and I've often wondered whether I behaved that way because of courage or because I thought I had power over him as his firstborn. I never could decide which. But Dad knew it was much more effective to let me stew in guilt. The more I thought about my outburst, the more miserable I felt.

The only way to be sure of ending one of our battles was to write. I have quite a collection of the apologies I sent him during the years after the war. Following the incident at the Metropolitan Club, I wrote him this:

Dear Dad,

I have given a great deal of thought to what you said about my temper and believe that you have put your finger on the one thing which can bring to an end a career which otherwise can be very successful. The lack of control of temper and the tendency to think last and speak first is something which has hampered me in my dealings not only with you but with my own family, my business associates and my friends. My last break at the Metropolitan Club and my swearing at you is an act which I will never forget and from which my heart will never fully recover. Family conferences with you and Dick are something that I've looked forward to all my life and for me to thoroughly ruin one of our first is something for which I owe not only you but also Dick a real apology. . . .

You mentioned . . . how you wanted to feel that I would and could take a place as a rallying point for the family as its oldest and really if I can successfully do this it will fulfill my greatest ambition. Of course, you can never have confidence in my ability to do so until I prove to you that I can control Tom Watson Jr. and think before I speak. You are a practical businessman and have built IBM on fact not promises. . . .

Believe me, I have and will continue to pay for my statement at the Met. Club but that's my fault. If you see fit to watch from now on you'll see a change that will please you. Temper will be watched and also stupid jealousy and I'll be a different and better son and brother.

> With sincere intentions & great love,
> Tom

This was one of our worst clashes, but Dad and I got into big arguments practically every month. We'd reconcile and try to cooperate, but pretty soon he'd second-guess me on a decision or I'd express an opinion on something he thought was none of my business, and we'd go at it again. In retrospect I realize what a toll these flare-ups must have taken on Dad. Another of the papers he left at his death was a meditation he wrote around his seventy-fifth birthday. From the way it reads, he is smarting from something I said. I've obviously accused him of driving able executives out of IBM so he can surround himself with yes-men. He feels depressed and haunted by the names of those who have died, or quit, or been fired. He thinks Dick and I are anxious for him to leave—something he's fiercely determined not to do.

Nobody should have the right to challenge my knowledge of IBM due to my 35 years experience. Think what I could have done with the guidance of someone of experience.

I will give all I have got to leaving IBM with enough people in the Executive end who believe in me. Joe Rogers, Fred Nichol and Charlie Kirk, Titus & Ogsbury all helped me—the latter 2 thought my policies were not good & they brought great damage to us. That is why I had to let out two vice-presidents. That was the hardest job I ever did in my whole work in IBM—but I had to do it.

The reason I'm sticking on the job & working is because the leading industrialists and bankers of the world seem to be unanimous that I have accomplished something worthwhile in building a sound business & in establishing certain policies which have proven to be beneficial to all of the employees of IBM & last but not least to the public we serve & the stockholders who entrust us with their investment. The moral to this is: It has always been my hope & ambition that my two sons would be ambitious & determined to prepare themselves to carry on the IBM Company & put the name of Watson far above its present standing in the industrial, social & economic world & as a result they will each have a greater opportunity to be of service to their family, relatives & worthwhile institutions and deserving people everywhere.

I am equally proud of both my sons and I'm also proud of what they have accomplished in the short time of their respective service with the company and I know that both my sons realize that experience is the greatest teacher.

I'm glad I never saw the note at the time. I'd have felt guilty as hell, and probably I'd have gotten mad, because Dad made it sound as if our apprenticeships were never going to end. I'd have started fighting all over again.

It didn't occur to me then, but I suspect that my sister Jane was behind some of these disputes. Jane had Dad's ear, and at that stage in our lives, she and I didn't get along very well. She'd have seen the World Trade issue in terms of rivalry because she was so competitive herself. If you had to pick who was the strongest and hardest driving of T. J. Watson's children, it would be a toss-up between Jane and me. She was a handsome woman, tall and dark haired, and she'd already made a name for herself in Washington and New York social circles. She had Dad's ability to get to know and charm the top people, but it was going to take another twenty years before she and I learned to get along.

Dad's feelings for Jane were complicated. I could never see what he wanted for her, and maybe he didn't know himself. It probably never crossed his mind that she might have a career, even though women executives were not unheard of at that point, and IBM actually had a woman vice president in charge of our field force for systems service. But Dad didn't seem to want Jane to get married, either. She stayed single until she was thirty-three years old, and to me it seemed as if she'd come close to wrecking her life for Dad. She'd had several suitors, but he'd driven them away. It wasn't until after the war that Jane found an acceptable man. His name was John Irwin II, and he was tall, attractive, and probably the best dancer I ever saw. Jack never drank, never smoked, but boy could he dance. He'd been president of his class at Princeton all four years and captain of the track team. His war record was outstanding too—he served on General MacArthur's staff, rose very rapidly, and was discharged a full colonel, one rank higher than mine. He was starting a promising career as a lawyer and diplomat.

Once Jane got married I had hopes that we might become tolerant of one another. She and Jack and Olive and I had some good times skiing together in Vermont and going to Margaret Truman's parties at the White House. But any success I had at IBM seemed to burn Jane up. I finally saw just how competitive she felt toward me during a visit to her house in the spring of 1950. There were pictures and trophies of Jack everywhere— Jack as an oarsman, Jack as a track star, Jack as this, Jack as that. Jane knew I was a little envious of Jack because every opportunity I had missed in my youth he had hit on the head. She saw me looking at mementos of his war career and said, "Tom, did you know that Jack was a *full* colonel?" She was needling me because I hadn't made it to that grade. I completely lost my temper. "Yeah, of course I know he was a full colonel. But I was the one flying airplanes all over the world!"

There were always certain things Dad could say that would tick me off in ten seconds. After this episode, telling me to be nice to Jane was one of them, and holding Jack up as an example was another. Jack and I got along fine, but Dad was never convinced I meant him well. He'd say, "I don't know why you object to your brother-in-law. He is a very thoughtful fellow. He thinks very carefully before he speaks." His implication was clear: Jack had the discipline and self-control that I lacked. I'd rise to the bait every time.

There were times in those early years when Dad and I really got along—generally when he relaxed his grip enough to let me run parts of IBM as I knew I could. As executive vice president, I was now IBM's number-two man, practically speaking, even though Dad had arranged things, perhaps wisely, to keep George Phillips as a buffer between us. He did this by shuffling titles, promoting Phillips to president and kicking himself upstairs to the new position of chairman.

In my new job I was responsible for a great deal more than our sales operation. I was supposed to oversee all of IBM's manufacturing, which meant that I had to find a way quickly to become somebody in the eyes of more than nine thousand factory workers. They were tremendously loyal to Dad, they'd been loyal to Kirk, but they barely knew me. Dad saw that this could be a problem, and six months after I got promoted, he called me to his office and handed me an envelope. "Here's your opportunity to endear yourself to the factory people," he said. "Why don't you talk to them?"

It was an anonymous letter complaining about the working conditions in one of our plants. It said, "We have fifty people working in a building that was designed to be a warehouse. It isn't properly heated and there's only one toilet. It is a disgrace to have IBM people working this way." I left the next day, and when I reached the factory, I found that conditions were exactly as described. Somebody had decided May was a warm enough month for the furnace to be overhauled. They'd torn it to pieces, and then a cold snap hit, so everybody was miserable. I did what I thought Dad would have done. I got temporary heaters put in within ninety minutes of my arrival. Within two hours I had men cutting foundations for new toilets in the back. Then I called all the workers together. I took a stepladder and climbed up on it and said, "I want to read you this letter. Unhappily it's unsigned, because I would like to give a raise and a promotion to the man who wrote it. I wish he'd had enough confidence in me to sign his name. But he's absolutely right. Those men with jackhammers are putting in eight more toilets and we're going to permanently improve the building's heat." It was a happy way for me to begin my duties in manufacturing, and word of what I'd done spread through all our plants.

Dad was pleased when I got back to New York and

told him of my performance on the stepladder. It showed I was learning. What may have pleased him even more was that IBM was beginning to make money from some of my earlier decisions. For example, thanks to a personnel change I'd made the year after Charley Kirk died, our typewriter division was about to earn its first profit. Ever since Dad had bought the Electro-Matic Typewriter Company in 1933, we'd been trying to sell American business on the virtues of electric typewriters. Dad thought they were a sure bet, because they were fast and neat and enabled the women in the office to type without knocking their manicures to pieces. But the machines were several times more expensive than ordinary typewriters, and after the war they still hadn't caught on. Our annual typewriter sales were only eleven million dollars, and we'd lost money in the business every year. So in early 1947 I told Norman Collister, the division chief, "I'd rather sell this operation outright than keep bleeding forever." I was sharp with him, but he came back at me just as strongly.

"We're still getting our feet under us."

"It's pretty hard for me to convince myself of that because we've been at it for thirteen years," I said. "We have a big distribution system, a trained sales force, and there's been no lack of money for development. If we were going to make it, we should have made it by now."

"I can't really talk to you about this, Tom," he said. "You just don't understand the typewriter business."

That was as good as telling me that we had to accept losing money all the time. So I went to Dad and said, "You can't go on with that guy. The only way he can run the business is in the red. Let's get somebody else in." I had in mind H. Wisner Miller, a man I had known since before the war. Wiz was a few years older than I, and I admired him because he'd had to fight real adversity. He came from a prominent family and he'd been a Princeton freshman in 1929 when the stock market crashed. His father lost everything and Wiz had to quit school. The only job he could find at first was selling vacuum cleaners door-to-door in the Bronx. One of IBM's directors knew him and introduced him to Dad, who hired him to sell typewriters because he liked Miller's spirit.

Choosing Wiz to run the typewriter division had been a big gamble. Dad went along with me, even though it meant jumping Miller from a fairly low position over men Dad knew a lot better. But Wiz had exactly the sales approach necessary to sell those machines. The IBM method for selling punch-card systems was much too analytical for electric typewriters. You couldn't overcomplicate it. What Wiz brought was zip and enthusiasm and leadership. I loved to watch him inspire his men at sales conventions. He'd have a typewriter onstage under a spotlight, all by itself. Wiz would walk up in his blue serge suit, look at it, and extend a finger to flick away an imaginary speck of dust. Then he'd step back and say, "A magnificent machine. I hate to see even a speck of dust on that machine. It's so beautiful." He taught his salesmen to use this blarney on the secretaries, and started making the typewriters in different colors like red and tan. He even made a white typewriter that my father presented to Pope Pius XII. A lot of systems men called Miller corny and simplistic, but he was one of IBM's great sales leaders. In 1949 the machines caught on and for years after that the division grew at a 30 percent annual rate. My first important personnel move had been a great success.

CHAPTER 18

T he newspapers in the late 1940s were full of talk about laboratory computers with funny names like BINAC, SEAC, MANIAC, and JOHNNIAC. Scientific conferences on computing and electronics were jammed. IBM had no plans to build such machines, but we kept hearing of projects at American and English universities, big-name companies like Raytheon and RCA, and some tiny start-ups whose names nobody recognized. All of the new machines were cumbersome and enormously expensive, none was intended to be sold commercially, and for quite a while the ENIAC, the celebrated University of Pennsylvania machine that Charley Kirk and I went to see, was the only computer that actually worked. But this didn't stop people from speculating what the "giant electronic brain" was going to mean for mankind.

Of course, calculating devices had been around since even before the Chinese abacus was invented. And there were a few giant calculators, such as the MARK I machine IBM built for Harvard during the war, that could do a wide variety of mathematical jobs. But they did it, in essence, by counting on their fingers. Their inner workings were electromechanical, like those of an ordinary tabulating machine. When ENIAC was unveiled it created a huge stir because it was fundamentally different. It had no moving parts, except for the electrons flying at close to the speed of light inside its vacuum tubes. All these circuits really did was add one and one, but that's all they needed to do. The most complicated problems of science and business often break down into simple steps of arithmetic and logic such as adding, subtracting, comparing, and making lists. But to amount to anything, these steps have to be repeated millions of times, and until the computer, no machine was fast enough. The quickest relay mechanism in our punch-card machines could only do four additions per second. Even the primitive electronic circuits of the ENIAC could do five thousand.

This boost in speed promised to change the lives of everyone who worked with numbers—I heard one engineer compare it to the difference between having one dollar and one million dollars. A *Time* magazine writer who was at ENIAC's debut wrote that its "nimble electrons" opened a whole new frontier. Until then there were known principles in science and engineering that no one used because they required too much figuring. Aircraft designers, for example, knew perfectly well how to predict wind resistance theoretically. But it was so much trouble to do the calculations that they used the hit-or-miss method of making scale models and testing them in expensive wind tunnels instead. So when ENIAC appeared, people had visions of computers helping to break the sound barrier, predict the weather, unlock the secrets of genetics, and design weapons even more terrifying than the A-bomb.

My father initially thought the electronic computer would have no impact on the way IBM did business, because to him punch-card machines and giant computers belonged in totally separate realms. A computer revolution might sweep across the scientific world, but in the accounting room the punch card was going to stay on top. Dad was like the king who sees a revolution going on in the country next door to his own, yet is astounded when his own subjects get restless. He didn't realize that an old era had ended and a new era had begun. IBM was in the classic position of the company that gets tunnel vision because of its success. In that same period the movie industry was about to miss out on television because it thought it was the movie industry instead of the entertainment industry. The railroad industry was about to miss out on trucking and air freight because it thought it was in trains instead of transportation. Our business was data processing and not just punch cards—but nobody at IBM was smart enough to figure that out yet.

I don't mean to say that Dad totally ignored the challenge that computers posed. He believed that no one could beat IBM when it came to building giant calculators for science, which is all he thought the new computers were, and he set out to prove it. In the spring of 1947, when I was still only a vice president and spending most of my time overseeing the sales force, he called in the engineers who had worked on the MARK I machine for Harvard. Dad told them he wanted a new "super calculator" that would be the "best, fastest, biggest—better than the Harvard machine, certainly better than ENIAC." They could use vacuum tubes if that would make the machine work better, but he wanted it finished in eight months.

Dad had his engineers pretty intimidated, and they didn't dare ask for more time. Instead they went flat out. They put all their other projects aside, worked virtually around the clock for the rest of 1947, spent almost a million dollars—and built a machine that worked. It was called the Selective Sequence Electronic Calculator, or SSEC, and it was a weird gigantic hybrid of electronic and mechanical parts, half modern computer and half punchcard machine. In was 120 feet long, with 12,500 tubes and 21,400 mechanical relays. It could do the equivalent of ten years of paper-and-pencil work in an hour. In some ways the machine was extremely innovative: it earned a spot in computer industry history as the first big calculator ever to run on software. This made it much more practical than the ENIAC: you could switch the SSEC to a new problem just by feeding instructions into its memory, whereas programming the ENIAC involved manually resetting hundreds of switches on its consoles. Yet because of its mechanical innards, the SSEC was a technological dinosaur—it was inherently slower than the all-electronic ENIAC, and speed was the thing users craved.

Trying to make sure the SSEC would get as much public attention as the ENIAC, Dad had it installed in our showroom on the ground floor of IBM headquarters in

Manhattan, in full view of the sidewalk. Passersby on Fifty-seventh Street could look in the window and watch the SSEC work. It was an amazing sight to come upon in the middle of the city—three long walls filled with electrical consoles and panels, all studded with dials, switches, meters, and little neon indicator lights that flashed whenever calculations were going on. Hundreds of people stopped to watch it every day, and for years it was the image that popped into people's minds when they heard the word "computer." When Hollywood started to put computers in science fiction movies, they looked just like the SSEC—even though it didn't exactly qualify as a computer. Dad dedicated the machine "to the use of science throughout the world" and ran it on a nonprofit basis. Anybody with a problem of "pure science" could use it for free; for anybody else—such as an oil company needing to do a statistical analysis of a drilling field—there was an hourly charge of three hundred dollars that covered the machine's operating costs.

The great missionary for the SSEC was an influential Columbia University astronomer named Wallace Eckert. In the late 1920s Eckert (who was not related to Presper Eckert, the ENIAC inventor) pioneered the use of punch cards in solving scientific problems. He was a small, retiring man, easy to underestimate. But he played a major behind-the-scenes role in the fight against German submarines during World War II, by calculating naval almanacs of unprecedented detail. These navigation tables enabled convoys under attack in the North Atlantic to determine their positions quickly and precisely and radio for help. Eckert became the first scientist with a Ph.D. on the IBM payroll. After the war my father hired him as director of pure science and set him up with a research lab next to the Columbia campus. His work gave many scientists their first glimpse of the possibilities of machine computation and brought large numbers of people to the SSEC.

Dad really thought that the SSEC was the calculator to end all calculators. And in a way, that was true. It was like a vintage car I once owned, the Stanley Steamer—

quite remarkably advanced for what it was, but not the technology to carry the day. The SSEC marked the end of an era at IBM. It was the last great achievement of a talented group of inventors who had spent their lives working for Dad. They'd designed the punch-card machines on which IBM built its success, and now they'd produced one of the most advanced machines ever. But even though they reached the threshold of the computer age, few of them stepped across. The SSEC was built in splendid isolation. Its design was kept secret, so that in spite of its success, it did little to change IBM's image in the technical community. The new generation of electronics engineers continued to think of us as a stodgy company that was wedded to punch cards and the past.

My father was highly skeptical when ENIAC's inventors, Eckert and Mauchly, quit the University of Pennsylvania and went into competition with IBM, setting up their own company in a Philadelphia storefront. But before long it was clear that they were good salesmen as well as brilliant engineers. They named their new machine the Universal Automatic Computer, or UNIVAC, and claimed it was going to be useful in both the laboratory *and* the accounting office. The first UNIVAC wasn't due to be ready for years, but with nothing more than a paper description Eckert and Mauchly won financial backing from two of our ten biggest customers—the Census Bureau and Prudential Insurance—and at least one other insurer besides. When Dad found out about that, his skepticism turned into fury.

On the Wednesday before Labor Day of 1947, I walked into his office to find him ripping up Frank Hamilton, one of our senior engineers. There was a secretary present who took down the scene verbatim. Father started in by saying, "Now, I understand these fellows who built the ENIAC machine are being backed by insurance companies to build something for them. Why don't we build a machine to meet their specifications?"

"I think we intend to do something on that," Hamilton said. He was acting a little sullen, because my father was forgetting that he and the other engineers had been working day and night trying to get the supercalculator built. Meanwhile Dad was getting madder and madder.

"We can't *think* and *intend* when insurance companies are backing this outfit to build machines! We can't afford just to think about and intend to! This business wasn't built that way! What is the quickest way to go ahead and build a machine to meet their specifications in the very shortest possible time?"

"The best plan is to survey the specs and see what they want."

"We know their specifications and we have already lost three months on it. If we can't build it, let's drop out. If we can do it, let's do it at a price those other fellows can't meet. If we can't build a machine and give it to them on a better basis than anybody else, then we are not entitled to the business. *It's an indictment against IBM to have these two fellows backed by those insurance companies!*"

Hamilton finally realized how angry Dad was. He started yessing to save his life. "There is no question that we can do it," he said. "Not a bit of doubt about it."

I knew what was upsetting Dad the most about the UNIVAC design. He felt it was an insult to our main selling proposition: the IBM card itself. Eckert and Mauchly were saying that punch cards were not appropriate for use with modern electronic equipment. Instead, the UNIVAC was going to store data on the new medium of magnetic tape—the same stuff being used in the early tape recorders of the day. This method was still largely unproven, but it was called for in almost all the new computer designs. Eckert and Mauchly explained to customers that magnetic tape had big advantages over punch cards. First, it was fast—it could pump data into and out of a large-scale computer at a rate more closely matched to the speed of the electronic circuits. Second, it was compact. A single reel the size of a dinner plate could hold the policy records of an entire insurance district, which normally required around ten thousand punch cards stretching several yards.

I doubt that Frank Hamilton had much time off that Labor Day. The following Tuesday he appeared, looking haggard, at a meeting convened by Dad in the big walnut-paneled boardroom next to his office. All of IBM's officers were there, along with the company expert on insurance industry accounting. Hamilton presented an ambitious plan for a machine to go up against UNIVAC. It would use tape in combination with punch cards, and would cost $750,000 to build. People gasped. From a punch-card standpoint, this was a staggering amount. Our average installation in those days cost about $20,000 to manufacture and rented for about $800 a month; by that yardstick, the rent on a $750,000 computer would have to be $30,000 a month!

Dad complimented Hamilton on his hard work and then picked the plan to pieces. It was obvious that he didn't like Hamilton's machine because it resembled the UNIVAC. Having built his career on punch cards, Dad distrusted magnetic tape instinctively. On a punch card, you had a piece of information that was permanent. You could see it and hold it in your hand. Even the enormous files the insurance companies kept could always be sampled and hand-checked by clerks. But with magnetic tape, your data were stored invisibly on a medium *that was designed to be erased and reused.* Imagining himself in the customer's shoes, Dad said, "Why, you might be going ahead and thinking you are storing information on that magnetic tape and when you try to get it off, you might find you have nothing there!" Frank Hamilton's design died on the table while Dad told the marketing men to call on Prudential and persuade them that the UNIVAC idea was not sound.

At that point I wasn't sure that building computers like the UNIVAC—or abandoning punch cards for magnetic tape—would ever make business sense. The new computers were clumsy, extremely expensive, and involved so much exotic and unproven technology that there was a real chance they might never be dependable enough for business use. I shared many of Dad's misgivings, but I was compelled by the tremendous speed of electronic circuits. Customers were snapping up our little 603 Electronic Multiplier, which Dad had put on the market at my urging. Compared with the UNIVAC, it was a tiny mouse of a machine, designed to fit in with ordinary punch-card equipment and renting for only $350 a month. But it was a success—my first at IBM—and I thought it might be a sign of things to come. We had a small team of electronics engineers in Poughkeepsie working on an improved version called the 604, but I started getting concerned that we might not be doing enough. I suppose on some level I was thinking that I was only thirty-three years old, and that a decade or two down the road IBM might run out of string.

In 1948 I got even more nervous. My friend Red La-Motte sent up a letter from the Washington office saying he'd assigned a man to attend engineering conferences around the country. By that man's count, there were no fewer than nineteen significant computer projects under way—most of them involving magnetic tape. Red said this made him wonder, "Inasmuch as IBM is the leader in the field of calculating equipment, does it not seem reasonable that it too should be kept abreast of all developments by active participation in this field?"

I started getting warnings from customers as well, that the punch card was headed out the window. Jim Madden, a vice president of Metropolitan Life and a friend of Dad's, invited me downtown to his office. "Tom," he said, "you're going to lose your business with us because we already have three floors of this building filled with punch cards and it's getting worse. We just can't afford to pay for that kind of storage space. And I'm told we can put our records on magnetic tape." Roy Larsen, the president of Time Inc., said much the same thing. I was working for him in the New York Hospital Fund drive, and his company was one of our big accounts. He explained that the success of *Time* and *Life* magazines depended on their getting to millions of readers each week while the news was still hot. Time Inc. was using IBM equipment to handle the mailing lists and address labels, but each subscription required three punch cards, and with the lists growing by thousands of new subscribers each month, the machines were barely keeping up. "We have a whole building full of your gear," Larsen told me. "We're swamped. If you can't promise us something new, we're going to have to start moving some other way."

I didn't think it would be prudent to run to Dad with the idea that punch cards were dying. He'd have thrown me out of his office. Instead I used a systematic approach that I knew would make sense to the old man. In 1949 I organized a task force of eighteen of our best systems experts to study whether we should add magnetic tape to our product line. With Dad it was almost a religion that ideas for improving the product line should come from customers. Of course, customers weren't always asking for the same thing—some wanted the machines to be faster, some wanted them to print more neatly and handle more carbon copies, some wanted them to be less noisy—and if you panicked and did everything they suggested, you'd go broke. You needed to sort out what improvements made sense and would really pay. The task force studied the magnetic tape issue for three months. When they came back, their answer was that punch cards were the best thing in the world for accounting jobs, and that magnetic tape had no place in IBM. I tried again, bringing in top salesmen and describing what magnetic tapes could do, but they all ended up saying no, it's better to use punch cards. They gave me nothing I could take to Dad.

I was beginning to learn that the majority, even the majority of top performers, are never the ones to ask when you need to make a move. You've got to feel what's going on in the world and then make the move yourself. It's purely visceral. I didn't trust myself enough yet to insist, but I knew in my gut that we had to get into computers and magnetic tape. To my great surprise, this was echoed by one man at headquarters who kept prodding me to act: Kirk's old crony Birkenstock. Talking him out of quitting after Kirk died was one of the best moves I ever made, because Birkenstock did more to put

IBM into the computer business than any other man. After his demotion from general sales manager, he'd been sidelined in a little department called Future Demands. Its job was to help fine-tune the product line by keeping track of customer requests. It took Birkenstock only a few months to transform Future Demands into a watchdog of IBM's future. He was no engineer himself, but he had a natural understanding of technical matters and an ability to articulate them.

Birkenstock was constantly telling me that the punch card was doomed, and so were we unless we woke up. Customers wanted more speed, and we were reaching the limit of how fast our machines could go. When we made our punches punch faster, they wore out quicker; when we pushed our high-speed sorter up from six hundred cards a minute to eight hundred, the cards themselves started getting ripped to shreds. He was constantly goading me, calling my attention to all the activity in electronics, and asking if I really wanted to miss out. This was nerve-wracking to listen to all the time because I didn't know how I'd convince my father. But I knew I'd be a fool to close my ears.

Not long afterward I reached the conclusion that the smart way to protect our future would be to hire electronics engineers—large numbers of electronics engineers. Whether we ended up trying to commercialize computers and magnetic tape or not, IBM needed to understand what was going on; the field of electronics was advancing so fast, on so many fronts, that I thought a small group would never keep up. We needed a critical mass. But this was before Dad made me executive vice president, and nobody in his research and development operation would listen to me. IBM's main laboratory, on North Street in Endicott, was a very peculiar place. Between three hundred and four hundred people worked there, but the whole thing was built around seven senior engineers whom Dad called his "inventors." They were mostly self-taught and they'd been with T.J. for decades. Even though there was a laboratory manager and a vice president of engineering, these inventors reported directly to Dad. He was really the chief engineer. When he had an idea for a product, he'd call in one or two of these old birds and describe what he wanted it to do. Then the inventors would go back and try to "put it in metal" as they used to say. Each one had his own workshop and assistants, and Dad liked to make two or more of these teams compete when he had a technical problem that absolutely had to be solved. "Nobody is smart enough to determine such things in advance," he used to tell me. It was an expensive but very effective way to develop products, and later on I used it myself.

Unfortunately, none of Dad's inventors understood electronics. The man who designed the SSEC, for example, didn't know how to hook up vacuum tubes, and he literally had to go out and hire young engineers two and three years out of school to do the job. The inventors had been so successful for so long that they were set in their ways, and they pooh-poohed my concern about our lack of electronics expertise. The vice president in charge of engineering became a real thorn in my side. He was a Princeton graduate with a degree in electrical engineering who had been with us since 1930. He was extremely creative in his way, and had been a great success at promoting the use of IBM equipment in the world of scientific computation. It turned out that punch-card machines were useful on small scientific problems, and one of our punch-card machines was so popular among scientists that it was called the "poor man's ENIAC." The trouble with this vice president was that he was more engineer than executive: although he was interested in electronics, he never really understood that pursuing it adequately would require a fundamental change in direction for IBM.

The only electronics experts we had on staff worked far outside the company mainstream. Their lab was in Poughkeepsie, in an old country mansion overlooking the Hudson, and they had to share it with engineers from our typewriter plant nearby. Most of the electronics men had wartime experience on things like radar. Their boss, Ralph Palmer, had worked on top-secret electronic circuit projects for what later became the National Security Agency. In 1947 and 1948 the main project at Poughkeepsie was improving my pet machine, the 603. The group had also started to experiment with UNIVAC-style computing and magnetic tape, but when Palmer asked for manpower and funding to expand this effort, the vice president of engineering told him no. He thought such work would merely soak up resources that the main lab in Endicott could use for improving our punch-card line. The boys at Endicott had high hopes for a number of projects. They had a new line of machines in the works that could use giant punch cards. These were twice the size of ordinary cards, could hold much more information, and were being counted on to help keep customers like Time Inc. loyal.

IBM had so much built-in resistance to exploring electronic computing that we might have been better off simply buying out Eckert and Mauchly. Ironically, we were offered the chance to do just that. In 1949 their principal backer got killed in a plane crash and before long the two inventors ran out of money and came to Dad. I was in his office for their visit. I was curious about Mauchly, whom I'd never met. He turned out to be a lanky character who dressed sloppily and liked to flout convention. Eckert, by contrast, was very neat. When they came in, Mauchly slumped down on the couch and put his feet up on the coffee table—damned if he was going to show any respect for my father. Eckert started describing what they'd accomplished. But Dad had already guessed the reason for their visit, and our lawyers had told him that buying their company was out of the question. UNIVAC was one of the few competitors we had, and antitrust law said we couldn't take them over. So Dad told Eckert, "I shouldn't allow you to go on too far. We cannot make any kind of arrangement with you, and it would be unfair to let you think we could. Legally we've been told we can't do it." Eckert understood perfectly. He leaped to his feet and said, "All the same, thanks very much for your time." Mauchly never said a word; he slouched out the door after an erect Eckert. A couple of months later came an announcement that they'd been bought out by Jim Rand. Remington Rand, our old rival in punch cards, was now getting ready to fill orders for six UNIVACs.

It was the success of the 604 Electronic Calculator that convinced me that electronics was going to grow much faster than anyone had anticipated. Like its predecessor the 603, this machine was designed to fit into an ordinary punch-card installation—right down to its clumsy, Victorian-looking black metal case. But there was nothing old-fashioned underneath that shell. Palmer and his men had produced an amazingly elegant design that made it easy to cope with vacuum tubes, which were constantly burning out or otherwise going haywire. They mounted each tube and its supporting circuits in a standard plug-in unit that could be mass-produced at very low cost. That way, every tube could be thoroughly tested before it ever went into a machine; if it went bad while the machine was in use, it could be easily replaced. The design also made it simple for us to increase production when customers started snapping up the 604.

When we first brought it out in mid-1948, we expected to sell a few hundred over the machine's lifetime. But by the end of 1949 we'd already installed almost three hundred and demand clearly was going into the thousands. The 604 rented for $550 a month, about the same as a sophisticated electromechanical tabulator, but it could handle division and other jobs that were almost prohibitively expensive to do mechanically.

But Palmer's operation was an anomaly. I did a complete review of all our development projects once I became executive vice president in 1949, and decided that IBM was still in the Dark Ages. I finally told Dad we needed something different. By then I was terribly frustrated, so I criticized his organization in Endicott in the roughest possible way. I said to him, "All you've got up there is a bunch of monkey-wrench engineers. Don't you see? The time for hacking machines out of metal is gone. Now you're getting into a field where you have to use oscilloscopes and understand the theory of electron streams and scanning beams inside the tubes. You've got to do theoretical things, you've got to do them with able people, with different backgrounds from the people we now have. You've got to hire engineering graduates—a lot of them.''

I was attacking a source of the old man's pride. He was always telling people that IBM had the greatest engineering department in the world and that he put all his faith in engineering. But he didn't answer me directly. Instead he buzzed his secretary and asked for the vice president of engineering to be sent down. He came about two minutes later and Dad said to him, "My son tells me that we don't have any kind of research organization. Is that true?"

The vice president thought awhile. He was slow in the way he gave his answer; he wasn't being glib. He said, "We have the finest research organization in the world." That was the end of him as far as I was concerned. All businessmen get asked a question like that sometime in their lives. They either answer it with courage and get fired or promoted, or they answer like a patsy. He'd just made a major mistake, because Dad wasn't going to live very long and I was never going to want the vice president around me again. If I knew we lacked the organization we needed, he should have known it too. He knew research and he knew engineering and he ought to have been able to see enough of the future to understand we were in a bad spot. I think he was afraid to push Dad very hard; maybe he sensed that Dad didn't want him to. But there are a lot of ways he could have hedged it. He could have said, "Mr. Watson, you're both right. We have a superior engineering department for what we've built until now. But we're going to have to move into vacuum tubes and electronic circuits and we've got almost nobody who knows about them."

I don't know how long Dad and I would have stayed at an impasse on engineering if it hadn't been for Al Williams. At that point he was still in finance, and he did a study comparing IBM's research-and-development spending with that of RCA, General Electric, and other successful companies. It showed us falling behind. On average, the others were spending three percent of revenue—three dollars out of every hundred dollars in sales flowing back into R and D. We were spending about two dollars and a quarter.

Williams took these figures to Dad. "Mr. Watson," he said, "I don't know if you're aware of it or not, but we are slipping back on research." Dad was totally noncommittal. But the next day he called a meeting of the executives and said, "Now, gentlemen, I've been thinking about our efforts in research, and we're not putting enough into that. I want you to go out and build this up. Now Mr. Williams—Mr. Moneybags over there—may complain to you about the cost. But don't let him stop you. I want you to build this research up."

Williams had acted without my knowledge, but I was delighted. Dad knew full well that this meant a major expansion in electronics. I looked across the room at the vice president of engineering and started thinking about who we had to replace him. Palmer wasn't the right choice to manage the expansion—putting the leader of the Poughkeepsie mavericks in charge would be an unnecessary insult to Dad's inventors in Endicott. Besides, Palmer was simply too important in the lab. It took me several days to settle on my choice: Wally McDowell, the head of the Endicott lab. McDowell had some vague connection to Dad because his father was a doctor in the town of Corning, about forty miles from where Dad grew up. But he was also an MIT graduate—one of the few we had at that stage—and while he had come to work at IBM in the same year as the vice president of engineering and had the respect of the old guard, he struck me as more farsighted. Even though he had no experience with hiring electronics engineers, I thought he could do it well.

There was no formal procedure for getting McDowell promoted or the other man removed; I just waited for the right moment to ask Dad. It came in May 1950, when we were in Endicott for the Hundred Percent Club convention. There was a company field day, and Dad and I went down to the IBM country club to watch the sports. I spotted McDowell near the tennis courts and said to my father, "We've really got to move in expanding our research program, Dad. I think we ought to start with Wally. We don't have anybody else. He's got a degree from MIT, that's something, and I don't think the man we've got in the job has the energy and he doesn't really see the need."

Dad had apparently thought it through and decided for himself that a change was necessary. He said, "That's a good idea. Why don't you go over and talk to him?"

I walked around the tennis court, got hold of McDowell, and asked him if he'd move down to New York and hire engineers in quantity. "What do you mean by 'quantity'?" he said. "A few dozen? I could do that from up here."

"No, I mean at least a few hundred and perhaps a few thousand."

Wally was surprised, but he agreed and we made him director of engineering. His predecessor stayed on as a vice president; ironically, having the burden of responsibility taken away seemed to free him up, and he became a strong and effective advocate of electronics research, particularly in the area of transistors. McDowell, meanwhile, got on with the hiring. It wasn't easy to attract top electronics people at first because we didn't have anything in place. We couldn't say, "Come see what we have." Our pitch was more like, "Come hear what we're gonna do." But we hired plenty because I told McDowell to take any man who had even a reasonable chance of being good. I didn't give a damn where they came from. So he gathered all sorts in his net—Americans and Europeans and Egyptians and Indians. Some of the ones from very different cultures did badly—we had a higher percentage of successes with the British and Americans. But until we had a critical mass, that didn't matter. The problems in electronic computing were so diverse and so vast that we couldn't do anything without enough people on the job. Once we had them, we could sort them out. Thanks to McDowell's efforts, we grew from five hundred engineers and technicians to well over four thousand in the space of six years.

Our veteran sales executives and planners watched this wave of immigration with extreme skepticism. These were tough marketing men, the core of IBM, and with punch-card machines selling like hotcakes, it made no sense to them that we should be scrambling into electronics. They had nicknames for the new MIT types we were bringing in. They called them "double domes" and "long hairs." But Dad let us do our thing, although I later found out he was watching very closely indeed. When Wally McDowell first moved down to New York, a messenger would show up at his desk each morning at 11:30 with two box lunches. At 11:35, Dad would come in, sit down, unwrap a sandwich, and start asking Wally questions. I never knew about it at the time, but that went on almost every day for months.

We finally started producing computers after the outbreak of the Korean War. That was in June 1950, while Father was in Europe, busy setting up World Trade. He cabled President Truman, putting the resources of IBM at the government's disposal and naming me as the man to contact. I assigned Birkenstock to go to Washington and find out what we could do. I knew he would volunteer IBM to build a computer for the war effort, and I thought that was fine. It seemed to me that if we could build a couple of one-of-a-kind machines under government contracts, we'd have a way of getting our feet wet. Birkenstock spent the fall of 1950 knocking on doors at the Pentagon and traveling around visiting government labs and defense contractors to ask about their computing needs. With him he took Cuthbert Hurd, a mathematician who had joined us in 1949 from the Atomic Energy Commission's laboratory at Oak Ridge. Hurd knew all about scientific computing—in fact, he had helped spearhead the drive to get punch-card machines into engineering laboratories and workshops.

They looked into a lot of defense-related fields—atomic energy, guided missiles, cryptanalysis, weather forecasting, war games, and so on. What they found was that engineers and scientists were desperate for computing power. There was a terrible sense of urgency in America in those days because of Korea. Only five years had gone by since the end of World War II, but we had thoroughly demobilized—our soldiers were back in civilian life, our fleets were in mothballs, our tanks and bombers had been scrapped. When Korea tied up the only standing army we had, people worried that Russia would take advantage and attack in Europe or some other part of the world. So in the fall of 1950 there was a frantic rush to remobilize and rearm. As Birkenstock and Hurd traveled around, the situation in Korea kept getting worse—in November the Chinese launched a bloody attack that drove our army out of North Korea and down into the bottom one third of the peninsula.

In the context of those grim days, Birkenstock and Hurd came up with a plan much bolder than I expected. They said we should build a general-purpose scientific computer to work in *all* the defense applications they'd studied. "Probably it won't solve a hundred percent of anybody's problems, but it will solve ninety percent of them," Hurd told me. He thought we could find customers for as many as thirty machines.

This idea was radical on two counts. It was radical technically because, all told, there were probably only a dozen computers in existence, and with the exception of Eckert and Mauchly, most designers were still thinking in terms of one-of-a-kind machines. And it was radical financially because Birkenstock and Hurd wanted us to pay for the design ourselves. Birkenstock pointed out that if we accepted taxpayer money, we'd have to turn over so much information to the government that we'd never have a solid patent position.

"How much is this going to cost?" I said.

"For the design and a prototype, three million dollars," he said. "For the whole program, three or four times that."

What he was talking about was by far the most expensive project in IBM history: ten times the size of Dad's

SSEC. I asked to hear more about the machine and shortly after New Year's Day 1951 we held a meeting in my office. Williams and I were the only nontechnical men there. Hurd, Palmer, and Birkenstock put their briefcases on the table and took out diagrams of the new computer —a confusing bunch of black boxes connected by lines. After years of pushing, I'd finally come to the moment of truth. We had the money, and I knew I could justify the project to Dad and the other executives simply by saying it was vital to the war effort. I didn't want to ask the advice of our sales or market research people, because they'd howl the minute they saw what we wanted to do. And it was not a decision that I could discuss in any detail with Dad—I only had a rudimentary understanding myself and would never be able to answer the questions he was sure to raise. So I was on my own. I had a roomful of talented technical men who were enthusiastic and wanted to try, but it was a three-million-dollar gamble—a sum as big as IBM's entire research budget two years before. So I said to Birkenstock, "Let's go ahead. But I'd like you to do me a favor. Take these plans, clean them up, and you and Hurd go out and see whether we can get any orders for this machine." Meanwhile, to ward off skeptics from the sales staff, we gave our new computer a patriotic name: the Defense Calculator.

Before Birkenstock and Hurd could leave on their selling trip we had to decide what the computer was going to cost customers. Nobody at IBM knew how to put a price on a computer. So Palmer and his men figured out how much we'd have to pay for the vacuum tubes, boosted that by 50 percent, and came out with a rental rate of eight thousand dollars a month. Then Birkenstock and Hurd went around to all the defense laboratories they'd visited before and made a sales pitch that emphasized the new things the Defense Calculator would make possible. Customers jumped at the idea; in less than two months, we found eleven takers for the Defense Calculator and ten more prospective ones. With orders in hand, Williams and I presented the project to Dad, who approved it without a single question.

Many people had the impression that my father and I never agreed on the subject of electronics. There was that single instance when he called the vice president of engineering in, but oddly, except for that, electronics was the only major issue on which we didn't fight. I like to think that if I hadn't been around to push, Dad would have eventually put IBM into electronics anyway, because he loved calculating speed. Before the Defense Calculator ever came up, Dad visited a laboratory he'd endowed at Columbia University where researchers were experimenting with high-speed circuits. He stopped off at my office when he came back and I could see how excited he was. He said, "You ought to go up there and see that. I don't know what it was, but the fellow was doing it two hundred thousand times a second!" But as things worked out, I think Dad decided the electronics opportunity should be mine, and the Defense Calculator was the first big risk he let me take as an executive.

Once the project got under way, the idea of putting out an electronic computer captured my imagination more than I thought business ever could. I thought of the Defense Calculator project as being similar to what the Wright brothers had done. They wanted to fly, and there were dozens of obstacles that stood in their way. They had the problem of power, and the problem of how to make a wing that would lift, and the problem of how to control the wing. They had the problem of how to take off. They had to build efficient propellers, and when they tried to model them on boat propellers, they found out that was no good; there was no comparison between water and air. Each of these problems was a discrete and different issue, and if they'd failed at any of them they'd never have flown. And yet those two men, along with one assistant from their bicycle shop, solved every one of those problems in the space of about seven years.

The problems we faced were just as complicated, though we had hundreds more men and much more money to work with. We were moving away from the punch card, a relatively slow medium that we understood very well, to something a hundred times faster that we didn't understand. We were trying to develop logic circuits, memory circuits, tape-handling devices, recording heads, card-to-tape data transfer techniques, and, in conjunction with other manufacturers, vacuum tubes and tapes themselves. Palmer's laboratory overflowed the old mansion and into another building, a onetime pickle factory that stood on our land along the Hudson River. We made that our lab for vacuum tube and circuit research, while all the magnetic tape work was done in the original house. We were essentially learning a whole new trade.

To me it was wonderful and amazing. You only had to visit Poughkeepsie to get a sense of the fundamental change taking place in engineering. Our laboratory back in Endicott had always felt to me like a stuffy museum—a place where ideas were scarce and had to be jealously guarded and preserved. But Poughkeepsie was wide open —the ideas seemed as abundant as air, and you had the impression of a limitless future. The old Endicott inventors worked in isolation from one another; in Poughkeepsie everybody believed that collaboration was the only way to move a complicated electronics project along. There was tremendous imagination and inventiveness everywhere you looked. I remember walking into the mansion one day and finding a Hoover vacuum cleaner rigged to the base of one of the magnetic tape machines. I asked the engineer, James Weidenhammer, what he was doing. He told me he had an idea for using suction to keep slack tape from getting tangled. It was a very clever concept, and to this day all high-speed tape drives are patterned after it.

The further the Defense Calculator progressed, the more the rest of IBM got involved. The project won some important allies, including Red LaMotte, who by now had become vice president of sales, and Vin Learson, who was sales manager of the punch-card division. I kept waiting for Dad to second-guess me on the machine, but he never did. Instead, Dad publicly blessed the project when it reached its halfway mark. He announced to shareholders at the annual meeting in April 1952 that IBM was building an electronic machine, "twenty-five times faster than the SSEC," that was going to be rented and serviced along with our regular products. He gave it a number, the IBM 701, just like our other products, instead of calling it the TOMMIAC or some such, which I was grateful for. I'm sure he must have had his doubts. In March he had come up to Poughkeepsie with the whole board of directors to see the Defense Calculator prototype. One of the engineers presenting the machine got carried away and said that the future belonged to electronic computing. I was later told that Dad looked upset at the emphasis being given to computers. But he never mentioned it to me. A year earlier he'd have said, "Hasn't anyone told that young man that *this company*'s future is still in IBM cards?" I think he was making a conscious effort to let me and my machine have our day.

CHAPTER 19

D ad was in his mid-seventies and slowing down. He started coming to work later and later in the morning, and after lunch he'd take a nap for an hour or two on the couch in the anteroom next to his office, where he kept a blanket to put over himself. The secretaries kept this secret, because Dad liked to project an image of absolute vigor. When he appeared in public, he was the consummate actor: even if he didn't feel well he'd pull himself up and stride like a man thirty years younger. Sometimes he actually seemed to draw energy from working. We'd be at a conference and he'd tell me he was dead tired and going to lie down. But on his way to the elevator he'd run into somebody he hadn't seen in a long time and they'd start discussing business. Dad would talk for twenty minutes on his feet and apparently be completely refreshed by it.

But I knew he wasn't as strong as before and I started being protective of him. When we traveled on a train together, I'd always go check on him if I woke up in the middle of the night. I remember once, on a trip from Indiana to Washington, I looked in on him and he wasn't there. So I put on my clothes and started searching. I found him walking through the train fully dressed in a business suit and tie. I said, "Are you all right, Dad?"

"Yes. I had a peculiar feeling, so I thought I'd take a walk. But I'm all right."

Probably he'd woken up and thought he was going to die. I now know that is a feeling all old people sometimes have—you wake up with a start and wonder if your time has come. He just needed to walk it off.

In 1950 I went with him to a dinner one night and he made a poor speech. The Masons were giving him an award at the Biltmore Hotel and all he did in preparation was scribble a few ideas. He thought he could just wing it, but at age seventy-six, you can't. I watched him fumbling with his notes and felt embarrassed for him. Afterward he asked me, "How was it?"

I said, "It was fine, Dad. But, you know, giving speeches takes too much out of you. You really shouldn't be doing it very much." I told him that he was of a stature in business where he could limit himself to making two or three minutes of observations instead of a full address. After that I did what I could to keep him from getting in a bind in public. When it came time for our next annual meeting, I got it across to him that if there was going to be flak in the form of questions from professional gadflies, I ought to take it. Dad was perfectly agreeable: he realized he was a little less able. In private he still wanted very much to be boss, but each year he let me run a little more of the annual meeting.

I never thought to myself, "When is this old gink going to quit?" I remember at one point George Phillips said, "You know, Tom, your father is seventy-seven. He's past the age when most people drop from heart attacks and cancer. If those things were going to get him, they'd have gotten him by now. He may end up living quite a while." I thought, "Gee, wouldn't that be great?" I had no feeling of "Oh, God, if he hangs on that long I'll die." Most of the time my life was enriched by him, because I could now give my aging father some help and be appreciated for it. Only when things between us got especially rough would I go home to Olive and say, "I wish Dad would get the hell out." Mainly I wanted him there. I later had a good friend on the IBM board, Maersk Moller, who had to operate under almost the same conditions with his old man. His father had founded one of the world's great shipping companies, A. P. Moller, Inc., of Copenhagen, Denmark, and Maersk was supposed to succeed him. Old Mr. Moller was about ninety, and he'd go into the hospital because he was getting weaker and weaker. But then he'd jump up out of bed, come down to the office, and countermand all the orders Maersk had given. Maersk's wife once told me that if Mr. Moller had lived another few years, Maersk would have been the one in the hospital instead. But Maersk tolerated it because he had the same dogged devotion to his old man as I did to mine.

I wish that my relationship with Dad had been such that I could have gone into his office, put my feet up, and shared thoughts with him about the future of IBM. By about 1950 I thought I'd learned the business. I understood what we were doing, had the confidence of Williams and the other young men, and knew where I wanted IBM to go. But Dad wasn't finished with me yet. I was still only executive vice president, and he made it pretty clear that if I wanted more responsibility I was going to have to keep fighting him for it every step of the way. Once when I complained of his rough treatment Dad growled, "I don't have a lot of time to teach you and I'm doing it the only way I know how." He was determined not to stop until he had tested me, tempered me, and forged me in his image.

Dad and I would usually meet toward the end of the day, after I had been working tremendously hard. He'd only really get going around five o'clock at night, which was the time I'd want to catch my train to Greenwich. But the buzzer would buzz and there I'd be, fagged, and Dad would say, "I'm going to send Farwell to Kalamazoo," which would be exactly the opposite of what we'd agreed on the day before.

I'd say, "Dad, you know, we really talked that through and we decided it wasn't a very good thing to send Farwell to Kalamazoo."

"Well, I've thought about it further and I've changed my mind."

"But I already told Farwell that—"

"You shouldn't have done that!" he'd say, and we'd be off to the races.

Our worst fights were not at the office, where outsiders might hear, but at my parents' townhouse on East Seventy-fifth Street. If I had a late dinner in the city, or early meetings scheduled for the next day, I'd sometimes stay overnight with them rather than commute home to Greenwich. I'd sleep in the same bedroom that I had before the war. Looking back now, I'm not sure why I kept doing that. To my father, that opulent house represented everything he had ever aspired to in life; for me it just brought back memories of the unhappy years I lived there as an IBM salesman.

Often my parents would still be out at some social event, but I had a key and I'd let myself in. In her frugal way, Mother kept no nighttime help, and all the lights would be off except for a dim ten-watt bulb in the foyer. So I'd turn some lights on. There was a winding staircase of beautiful marble, and along the walls were large oil paintings of the kind Dad loved—dark landscapes with tired cows. The second floor had a tremendous living room with paneled walls, big armchairs with maroon upholstery, and of course Persian rugs. Every inch of table space was covered with family pictures and photographs of world leaders inscribed to Dad. Pictures of FDR and Churchill had the place of honor on the mantel.

My room was one more flight up. It was comfortable but spare; it looked like an ordinary guest room. I'd go straight to bed, and by the time Mother and Dad came home from their dinner party, I'd be asleep. Dad would wake me up under the guise of saying good night. He'd sit down on the chair by the bed, ask how I was, and after a few pleasantries he'd say, "By the way, son, I just want to cover that matter of the Western sales region once more."

It never made any difference that this might be something I'd worked on over a long period and just gotten resolved. "I'm not at all satisfied with the way it's being handled," he'd say, and there would go the whole wall that I'd laboriously put up brick by brick by brick, right down in my face. I loved the old boy and he knew it, but I didn't have the energy or time to rebuild walls he mashed down. I'd come out of a deep sleep and be in the middle of a battle in no time.

The best strategy would have been to let him blow himself out. Maybe if it had been 9:00 A.M. and I'd just come back from a week's vacation, I'd have been able to say, "Let me take another look at it." But usually I would come back at him hard, and we'd be in one hellacious fight. He'd get livid. His jowls would shake. All the old family tensions would come boiling out, and I'd let him have it with everything I had.

My mother would hear our enraged voices— "Now let me tell you something!" "Don't talk like that to me!" It would be 1:30 in the morning, and finally she'd get up from bed. I can remember her standing in the doorway in her nightdress, with her hair unbrushed because she'd been asleep. She never took sides. She'd say, "Can't you boys just go to sleep?"

It would frequently end in tears. Then Dad and I would hug—and go to bed frustrated. We'd swear we'd never do it again, and within two or three weeks there would be another moment of difference which would escalate into another white-hot argument. It amazes me that two people could torture each other to the degree Dad and I did and not call it quits. I remember once we had an awful battle in my office and I ran out of the room. Down the corridor was the office of a distant cousin of Dad's named Charley Love. I made it as far as Charley Love's door, threw myself on his divan, and sobbed, while Charley sat there at his desk. It must have been a shock, but he was a sensitive guy and asked what was the matter.

"Charley, did you have terrible fights with your father when you were growing up?"

He said, "Of course." It was very reassuring.

Dad was constantly trying to change me, and I was trying to change him. I wanted an easy old-shoe pal and he couldn't be that. He'd have liked me to be more pliant and defy him less. Each of us wanted something that the other couldn't give. Mother did what she could to calm things down; sometimes she'd talk to me privately about it. She'd say, "I'm enough younger than your father to know he is difficult. I also know that you have to say yes to him on almost everything. But you've got to remember, he's a very old man. It's probably not good for him to get worked up and blue in the face. You'd feel terrible if anything happened to him while you were having one of those big battles. I don't know how they get started or what you can do to slow him down, but please do as much as you can. Try to moderate it."

In truth there wasn't much I could do, which is why those fights were so deeply disturbing. They were savage, primal, and unstoppable. My father loved me and wanted me to thrive; I loved him and wanted to see him live his life without trauma, without embarrassment, without strain to his health. But while I always tried to live up to his expectations, he was never satisfied, because no son can ever totally please his father. And when he criticized me I found it impossible to hold back my rage.

By that time I had very little doubt about my ability to manage IBM. I was much more concerned about whether I'd be able to manage Dad. Most of our business differences stemmed from the fact that I had a better feel than he did for IBM's increasing size. Our business was exploding. When I came back from the war, it was $140 million a year, and by 1952 it had more than doubled. Dad was constantly torn between the huge numbers we were beginning to deal with and the way he had managed the little cash-register company when his boss Mr. Patterson was away. He'd call me to his office and say, "You and Al Williams are really mismanaging the sales operation." I'd ask what he meant, and he'd say that the only way to keep track of the business was for branch and district managers to read the call reports. A call report was the write-up a salesman would hand in after meeting with a prospect. Dad had read all of the call reports when he was a regional manager at the Cash. So I'd have to explain that he was asking the impossible: our salesmen were averaging four calls a day, and in a bigger office we had forty salesmen; in a sales district there would be close to four thousand reports a day. If a manager read them, he wouldn't have time for anything else. "This is a big company now, with big-company problems!" I kept telling Dad.

For the same reason he didn't want to borrow money. We were building factories and churning out rental machines that paid us back only after several years. So the business required an awful lot of financing. Dad liked the idea of growth, but he hated debt. Having lived through several depressions, he felt you should always have enough liquid assets to pay any debt that was called. In 1950 we owed eighty-five million dollars—not a lot considering we only had to pay 2.5 percent interest and we could offset it with the steady income from our rental business. But Dad harped on that debt in meetings. "I cannot get that eighty-five-million-dollar debt out of my mind," he said. "It is there all the time. It's something which cannot be laughed off. Every one of us must think about it all the time."

Dad's idea for financing IBM's growth was to plow profits back into the business. That was not easy to do, because he also believed in paying substantial dividends to IBM's shareholders. For years Dad relied on smart accounting to get around this dilemma. Instead of paying dividends in actual money, he paid in stock, so that if you held one hundred shares, you might get another five shares at the end of the year. Meanwhile Dad would have his accountants put the newly minted stock on IBM's balance sheet not at its market value, which was something like $200 a share, but at a nominal value of only five dollars. That way it only took a small fraction of the profits to balance it out.

This was a neat maneuver, and our earnings were growing so fast that the stockholder was at no risk, but it made authorities at the New York Stock Exchange nervous. There was nothing to stop a badly managed company unlike IBM from using new shares to disguise the fact that it lacked the profits to pay a dividend. So Emil Schram, the head of the stock exchange, started a crackdown. He made a rule that stock issued as a dividend had to be accounted for at its full market value.

Dad never accepted that. Every spring, when the time came to declare the annual dividend, he'd hitch up his belt and say, "Well, I've got to go down to Wall Street and straighten out Emil Schram on this silly accounting business." Around 1949 he took me with him. "If you'd like to come along, all right," he said, "but keep your mouth shut."

When we got down there he said, "Now, Emil, I want to show you the record of the business for the last year." Schram was a big hefty guy and he'd try to stand up to Dad, but for some reason Dad could always snow him. Schram would say, "I don't see how I can keep letting you do this. I'll have to let other companies do it."

"My company is not like other companies! Just look at our record!"

Finally Schram would let him have his way for another year. In 1951, Schram retired and the stock exchange got a new chief named Keith Funston, the former president of Trinity College in Hartford, Connecticut. Funston knew me slightly from a business luncheon the year before, and he called me up and said, "My people have told me about your father and his stock dividend. I've really gone into this, spent several hours on it, and we cannot let your father do it anymore. So please prevent him from coming down here. I'd hate to start out in New York by having a fight with one of the most respected businessmen in town."

I told Dad, who said, "That's preposterous! Preposterous!" For once I played it fairly cleverly by not saying anything. I went back to him a second time on it, and a third. Finally he said, "All right, you go down and make the best deal you can." After that he was always poormouthing Keith Funston. He'd say, "You know that fellow Funston. He's not quite right. He doesn't understand finance." But I liked Funston for his grit, and after Dad died I asked him to join the IBM board.

We needed to borrow because even if Dad had succeeded in putting every penny of profit back into the business, it wouldn't have been enough. Everybody at IBM knew it. If T.J. had been more tolerant of debt, things would have gone very smoothly. But instead I had Williams and LaMotte and everybody else coming to me and saying, "Look here, your father doesn't want to borrow any more and we need the money."

Nobody wanted to tackle him, so I had to. I'd go to him and Dad would say, "The only reason we need to borrow is that you men are spending in a very careless way." I had a devil of a time until finally I hit upon the perfect argument. I'd say, "All right, Dad, we don't have to borrow. But we'll have to stop hiring salesmen because we've got all the orders we can fill right now."

That would just kill him, because he'd been a salesman himself, and because he believed salesmen meant growth. He'd say, "Let me see those numbers again." Then he'd order his secretary to make an appointment for us to go see the Prudential and borrow more.

The toughest issue Father and I ever faced was antitrust. The Truman administration was pretty hard on big business, with the Justice Department winning antimonopoly cases left and right. It broke Alcoa's hold on the aluminum market in 1945, and then a few years later forced the United Shoe Machinery Corporation to diversify and to tolerate competition from foreign manufacturers. We knew that sooner or later the government would come after us. Our equipment was in the accounting department of virtually every major American company, and the government knew all about us because we were in every federal agency too. We charged premium rents for a premium service, and our growth and profits were astounding—year after year we were making about twenty-seven cents, pre-tax, on every dollar of revenue. Yet, as lucrative as the business was, we'd attracted very little competition, and we still held about 90 percent of the market for punch-card machines. To the Justice Department, all of this was proof that IBM was a monopoly. Right after the war they began investigating us and snooping around. Sometimes the investigation seemed to die down, but then we'd report another record year, or the Antitrust Division would win some other big case, and they'd be after us again.

Dad did not approach this problem in a good frame of

mind. The terrible trauma of getting sentenced to jail for antitrust violations when he was at the Cash never really passed for Dad. Thirty-five years had gone by, but it was like a raw wound to his self-respect. He swore we would fight "to the bitter end." Most entrepreneurs would sympathize with his point of view. IBM was a success not because we drove other people out of business, but because we had good products, superior salesmen, a lot of satisfied customers—including the federal government—and because we kept our energy concentrated on punch cards. Dad didn't see how any of this could be bad. What was the law against building a great business? And if it wasn't illegal, why was IBM being hounded? The thing Dad could never accept about monopoly law is that you don't have to *do* anything wrong to *be* in the wrong. The Department of Justice was coming after us entirely because they didn't think there was enough competition in our market.

Dad was sure of his ground. He took out full-page newspaper ads praising the free-enterprise system, and he told the government that we would cooperate fully because we had nothing to hide. He turned over thousands of pages of documents, and spent many hours in meetings with government lawyers, patiently explaining his business philosophy and IBM's business practices. Once in a while the Justice Department would do something that drove him wild—such as the time they sent in agents posing as anti-espionage experts and went through our foreign-trade records. But Dad fully expected that the government would eventually see the light. Not only did he want them to desist—he wanted a full public exoneration of IBM. He told us executives in a meeting once: "If they are willing to acknowledge that we have not violated the laws, the very best thing they can do would be to make a statement to that effect, including a reference to our fair policy of giving good service to our users, and raises in pay and other benefits to our employees. . . . A statement of this kind would prove to the public that the Department of Justice, when it knows the facts, stands for justice."

But the investigation ground on and finally Dad asked for an appointment with Attorney General Tom Clark. Dad thought we might persuade him to call off the attack before the thing went to court. Like many monopoly cases, this one really came down to how you defined the market, and Dad gave me the job of presenting our definition. For the attorney general's benefit I put up a big diagram that represented the accounting world as a pyramid.

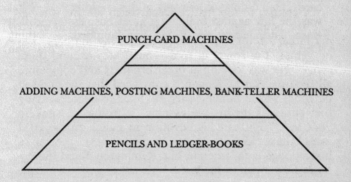

PUNCH-CARD MACHINES

ADDING MACHINES, POSTING MACHINES, BANK-TELLER MACHINES

PENCILS AND LEDGER-BOOKS

The point was simple. If you defined the market as the entire world of business calculations, then we had lots of competition, and the huge bulk of the business belonged to the makers of ordinary pencils and paper. By comparison, IBM was very small. I gave a few government statistics to drive home our point: a congressional committee had estimated IBM was doing only about 16 percent of the accounting work in the U.S.; according to Commerce Department figures, we constituted only nine percent of the total man-hours of production workers in the "office and store machines" industry. Our own estimate—straight out of Dad's head—was that IBM only did about two percent of all the numerical calculations in American business. "We aren't a monopoly," I told the attorney general. "In fact, we've barely scratched the surface."

Dad pointed out that he'd turned down any number of

chances to buy out the competition in other parts of the office-equipment pyramid. Over the years people had tried to sell him the patents for all sorts of machines. He'd had the chance to acquire Underwood Typewriter, Eckert-Mauchly Computer, and other companies. After John H. Patterson's death in 1922, National Cash Register's investment bankers proposed that Dad merge IBM with the Cash and run them both. Dad turned all of this down, and he told the attorney general that proved he was no monopolist.

Of course, to the Justice Department all this was beside the point. But it shows something important about my father's thinking. As he once told my mother, "I'm no genius. I'm smart in spots—but I stay around those spots." He was looking at other products and companies all the time, yet he remained convinced that the greatest potential was in punch cards. He liked to quote a saying that summed up his philosophy: "Shoemaker, stick to your last." Without his devotion to punch cards, IBM would have lost its focus; it might have become a hodgepodge conglomerate like Remington Rand. Sometimes Dad stuck to his last a little too closely—we came close to missing the computer business, for example, and in 1941, Dad turned down the chance to buy the patents for xerography. The inventor Chester Carlson came over from Queens and offered them to Dad before founding the company that eventually became Xerox. That was the biggest opportunity my old man ever missed.

The attorney general was not persuaded by our pyramid, and I couldn't blame him because I wasn't convinced myself. Probably the only person in the room who fully believed our argument was Dad. That's because he was the only one with the vision to see that pyramid as one big, open market. He really thought punch-card accounting had potential that far-reaching. He would have told you that accounting machines would someday take business away from the pencil—just as personal computers do today. But Tom Clark didn't see it that way. He listened, and then he simply said, "We think punch-card machines are a separate industry." Of course, we did monopolize there.

If Dad had been reasonable on the subject, we could have settled the matter then. The Justice Department thought we needed competition, but they weren't asking for anything drastic, like breaking IBM up. They thought it would be sufficient if we simply loosened our hold on the market—by granting licenses to other people to manufacture under some of our patents, and by putting up our machines for sale as well as rental. The natural forces of competition would then do the rest. This would mean some complicated changes in our business, but I didn't think it would hurt us as badly as fighting the case in court might. Since the 1930s the government had won 90 percent of its antitrust cases, and if we fought and lost, the court might well take the company apart. But when I proposed to Dad that we settle the case, he was adamant. To him a settlement was the same as an admission of guilt.

Our lawyers only made matters worse. The partners in IBM's usual law firm knew we ought to settle—they were the ones who initially convinced me of it—but they were not as aggressive with Dad as I thought they should have been. It was very hard to tell my father he was wrong. He was so exercised by antitrust that he'd latch onto anybody who agreed with his position. He hired an additional lawyer in Washington, named Joseph Keenan, to help negotiate with the Justice Department. Keenan was a retired federal judge, but he was a wormy guy, a fixer. He told Dad, "These things can always be handled, Mr. Watson," and sent a fantastic bill. But the investigation kept marching ahead. Around 1950, to my great relief, Dad brought in a third lawyer. This was Judge Robert Patterson, who had been Truman's first secretary of war and was a great man. The minute Patterson came in, he told Father there was no fixing this kind of case, and that Keenan had to go.

Dad put Patterson on our board, and I had high hopes that he would be able to make Dad see the light. While Dad was in Europe in 1950, Patterson went over to spend time with him and I asked him if he'd talk to Dad about settling the case. He spent half the summer with Dad. But I didn't hear anything, and when Patterson finally came back, I took him to lunch. "Well, did you get Dad to come around?" I said.

"I'll tell you the honest-to-God truth," he said. "I didn't."

I was indignant. "Are you kidding? You were over there six weeks! What did you do?"

"Tom," he said, "it's pretty doggone hard to sway your father when he doesn't want to be swayed." I understood that, but I'd been hoping Patterson could wash that particular piece of dirty laundry for me. Maybe Patterson could eventually have gotten him to change his mind, but he never had the chance. The Justice Department filed its suit against IBM on January 21, 1952. The following day, Patterson died in a plane crash.

Dad and I were so addicted to fighting that we even managed to make a struggle out of my promotion to president of IBM. By 1950, Al Williams and I were essentially running the company day-to-day, with Dad tuning in and out to check on us or make a major decision while spending most of his time working out the kinks in World Trade. George Phillips was still in between us and my father, and the arrangement still wasn't working well. Williams and I would get all set to do something. We'd tell Phillips and he'd say to go ahead. But then he'd talk to Dad, who'd say, "That's the most ridiculous thing I ever heard!" And old Phillips would reef his sails and turn round and round. I never really blamed Phillips; he was totally loyal to Dad, and everybody needs a few people like that. But by the spring of 1951, as I was pressing to get the Defense Calculator under way, it happened once too often. I don't remember what the issue was, but I stormed into Dad's office. "God damn it!" I said. "You've got your secretary as the president of this company. He'll agree to something I want to do, then talk to you, and reverse himself!" My father sent me out to the anteroom where he took his naps. Then he called Phillips in. Some mumbo-jumbo went on in there, and then he called me back in. They both turned toward me and Dad said, "We've decided to make you president." I'd expected to keep fighting, and Dad could see he'd knocked me speechless. "What's the matter?" he said. "Don't you want the job?"

I wanted to feel that he considered my succession to the presidency a major victory of his life, along with his winning of my mother and the record he had made at IBM over so many years. Instead he did it as though it were a way to prevent another argument. I felt crushed. Dad seemed alienated too, and left on a business trip without saying another word to me or even writing a note. Instead he had Phillips send a letter confirming our conversation. All the same, Dad went through with the promotion, setting things up so that I would take over as president in January 1952. Meanwhile Phillips got a raise and a promotion to the new job of vice chairman—where Dad continued to use him as a buffer. I had more autonomy than before, but I still had to go through Phillips on important matters of finance and the like, and Dad still used him to second-guess me.

On the day before my official promotion, hoping that becoming president would somehow make my relationship with Dad smoother and happier, I wrote a letter to thank him and to try to set a new tone.

Dear Dad,

I am deeply grateful that you are doing what you are doing tomorrow. I love my work and the company but in addition, I believe that through this move your life can be made far far pleasanter. You are and always will be Mr. IBM to all of us and the advice and counsel you have given me has been responsible for 90 percent of my present qualifications. I would hope that you would be willing to remain as IBM's chief executive for years to come giving Mr. Phillips and me your ideas on the policies and top decisions of the company and perhaps leaving some of the dirty details to us.

I share your belief that this company can continue to grow rapidly. My incentive is great—salary—stock, etc but without either, I would still love my job as long as I had a living because IBM is your company and I am your son. . . .

I have always looked to the day of my promotion to President of IBM as a day of complete fulfillment for me. Of course I will be happy but I will not have the sense of fulfillment I want until I see in your face and your eyes that my work and accomplishments are making you happy. No son ever believed more deeply in a father than I believe in you.

With love,
Tom

As it turned out, the next six months were sheer utter hell. IBM had just passed the quarter-billion-dollar-a-year mark, and there was too much to do, too many decisions to be made. I was working frantically, calling on important customers, pushing into electronics, and trying to stop the antitrust case before it did any real damage. I was also spending a lot of time outside IBM on the Boy Scouts and a whole range of other public service jobs. My new position included a lot of ceremonial responsibilities—giving speeches at conventions and visiting offices all over the country to hold "family dinners," as Dad called them, with the people who worked there.

Administrative duties tied up too much of my time. For example, the wages of everybody in the company had to be raised, partly because of inflation and partly because Dad was aware that labor unions were winning big pay increases in other industries. Any other company would have simply announced a general raise from headquarters. But that was not Dad's way. He thought declaring a general pay increase would undermine the relationships of individual workers and their managers, and give unions an opening by making employees receptive to the idea of collective bargaining. So every raise at IBM had to be presented as an *individual merit increase,* awarded to each employee by his boss. Instead of telling a department of twenty people that they were all getting a raise, their manager had to have twenty separate interviews. He'd tell each person the same thing: "You've done a good job, here's your raise." When we gave a general increase, tens of thousands of these interviews had to be coordinated all over the company, and business would just about grind to a halt. The employees knew full well what we were doing, of course—it was one of the times when IBM probably reminded some of them of the rituals of life in the army.

The frustrations of working with Dad made me pretty demanding of other people. When I went out to inspect a sales office, I was not by any means a benevolent patsy passing through and saying everything was rosy. Instead I'd be smarting from all the anger inside me, and I'd pass a bit of it along. But usually only a bit. I knew that I was likely to see the people at a given office only once every two or three years. So I held myself back, for the practical reason that if I made them too sore, the hard feelings would just stay out there and fester and hurt the business. I often ended up carrying my frustration home with me, where my wife and children would bear the brunt. By now Olive and I had Tom, Jeannette, Olive, and Cindy, ranging in ages from eight down to two. Olive would spend the entire day working with them and she'd have them all shined up and ready to greet me when I came home. I'd come in the door and say, "That child's sock isn't pulled up. That child's hair isn't combed. What are these boxes doing here in the hall? They should have been mailed." It was the same demanding IBM attitude, and it was very hard on them all.

I don't think my father realized how far he was pushing me. There were times when I wondered if I was going to have a nervous breakdown. That summer one of the managers in our typewriter division died in California. He was a fairly senior guy, married to a woman who had a vindictive personality. For some reason she had the idea that he had been unfairly treated by IBM, and when he died she told somebody she was going to sue the company because his heart had failed from lifting heavy typewriters. When I heard that, I thought it would be important to show some respect by being at his funeral. In those days that meant a nine-hour flight on a propeller-driven airliner called a Constellation. Just as I was leaving for the airport, Dad called me in and we had a terrible argument. Finally I said, "I can't talk to you anymore. I have an airplane to catch." And I walked out.

Dad went down and got in his limousine and somehow beat me to the airport. Wiz Miller, the head of the typewriter division, was traveling with me, and when we got to La Guardia field and started walking out to the airplane on the tarmac, I saw my father. He was a very old man then, seventy-eight, and I remember him painfully making his way out from the shadows under the terminal building where his car was parked. I thought he was playing his age for all it was worth. He slowly came up to me across that tarmac, and with a lot of people standing around watching this curious scene, he reached out his gnarled hand and took my arm. I completely lost my temper. "God damn you, old man! Can't you ever leave me alone?" I said. I didn't strike him, but I ripped my arm away with great vigor, turned my back, and went up into the plane.

That flight was the longest nine hours I ever spent in my life. I was beside myself, terrified that he'd be dead before I could talk to him again, and that I was going to have to live the rest of my life with the knowledge that I'd cursed my father. When we landed I couldn't wait to get to a phone to tell him how sorry I was.

That fight passed, like all our other fights, but it shook me up badly. I think it was the first time I ever really understood that my father might die. On some level I started to realize I could no longer afford to act like an adolescent. I took my family on vacation that fall; even though I'd been president for less than a year, we all needed the time off. We spent a quiet two weeks in a wood frame house on Fishers Island off the Connecticut coast. I played with my son and daughters and thought a lot about Dad. Then I took another week sailing down the eastern seaboard with Williams and Learson and some of the other executives I'd come to count on. That gave me even more time to sort things out. Finally, on a train trip a few days after we docked, I took out a yellow pad and wrote down the affection and tenderness I felt for the old man.

Dear Dad,

I've been thinking about this letter ever since I started for the Chesapeake. On that sail down with the IBM boys I began to think of our 38 years together. My main theme seemed to be to realize again and again how very wonderful, fair, and understanding you have always been to me. I have always realized this but it becomes more clear when I have a son of my own to work with. I only hope that he may think of me when he's grown the way I think of you. Of course, I hope he won't argue and defy me as often as I have you because I know how painful that can be to a father.

I so well remember the problems I gave you in the Short Hills School when you were on that board and I returned to the school when I was at Carteret and got in a mud fight that was reported to the board. You were patient—I am afraid I wouldn't have been.

Then I've thought of your constant problem with me and my marks and your ability never to lose your temper about my schoolwork.

I remember so well the morning you and I started out from Camden with the avowed purpose of finding a college which would accept me. I'm so glad Brown did. Then the flying problem and all the way through our relationship—no forbidding—just reasoning. I pray that I may do it the same way with Tom.

I'm disappointed that I haven't been a better son in countless ways. You and Mother have always set me such a sterling example but I'm still pitching and I always *wanted* to make you both proud.

Every detail of our moments together flood in on me and have for the past three weeks like a pleasant cloud. We've had our battles and I soberly believe that in 90 cases out of 100 you were right and in the other ten a better son would have held his tongue.

I've written you a dozen times, Dad, and said that I would do better, but somehow I've felt different ever since I went south. I want so to have you satisfied.

What I'm trying to say is that I love and respect you deeply and want to have a chance to try again to show you. The company is your shadow and health and I hope that I can help keep it that way. I want your direction and advice in the business as I have never wanted it before and would like to spend most of my time with you while you are in, if we can work it out.

This letter probably isn't conveying what I feel in my heart but I wanted to try anyway.

What I mean essentially is that no one could have done a better or more sympathetic job of being parents than you and Mother and now I'm going to try harder than ever to make you proud.

Love,
Tom

I am very glad I wrote that letter, because I think it was the happiest moment I ever gave my father.

Dear Tom

After reading your letter my heart is so filled with joy I cannot think of anything else, so I am going home and let Mother read it and we will have a quiet and happy time filled with kindest thoughts and prayers for your happiness and usefulness to your family and the Watson clan as a whole and I know we can help you and you can help us.

I just can't write any more today, but you can imagine and realize what is in my heart and will fill Mother's heart as soon as I reach home. May God

bless and keep you and help me to be a better father
to you and Olive.

                    With a heart filled with love,
                    Dad

The letter didn't end our fighting, but some of the
bitterness went out of it on both sides.

CHAPTER 20

One day in the early 1950s I stopped off in Washington to change planes and Red LaMotte, who was then in charge of our Washington office, came to see me at the airport. "Tommy," he said in his casual way, "the guys at Remington Rand have one of those UNIVAC machines at the Census Bureau now, and soon they'll have another. People are excited about it. They've shoved a couple of our tabulators off to the side to make room." I knew all about the UNIVAC, of course, but the Census Bureau was where punch-card machines got their start back in the 1880s, and it had always been IBM's backyard. I thought, "My God, here we are trying to build Defense Calculators, while UNIVAC is smart enough to start taking all the civilian business away!" I was terrified.

I came back to New York in the late afternoon and called a meeting that stretched long into the night. There wasn't a single solitary soul in IBM who grasped even a hundredth of the potential the computer had. We couldn't visualize it. But the one thing we could understand was that we were losing business. Some of our engineers already had a fledgling effort under way to design a computer for commercial applications. We decided to turn this into a major push to counter UNIVAC. Two and a half years later this product would finally come out as the IBM 702, but the name it had while it was still in the lab was the Tape Processing Machine. It was obvious to everyone that we were finally making major strides away from my father's beloved punch cards.

Now we had two major computer projects running side by side. We had teams of engineers working three shifts, around the clock, and every Monday morning I'd ignore all my other responsibilities until I'd spent a few hours with the project managers and pressed them on how we were doing. People at IBM invented the term "panic mode" to describe the way we worked: there were moments when I thought we were all on board the *Titanic*. One morning in 1952 McDowell came to me with a new analysis of what the Defense Calculator was going to cost. "You're not going to like this," he said. It turned out that the price we'd been quoting to customers was too low—by half. The machine we thought would cost $8,000 a month was actually going to cost somewhere between $12,000 and $18,000. We had no choice but to go around and let the customers know. To my total amazement, we managed to hang on to as many orders as we'd started with. That was when I felt a real *Eureka!* Clearly we'd tapped a new and powerful source of demand. Customers wanted computers so badly that we could double the price and still not drive people away.

We knew UNIVAC was years ahead of us. Worse still, Remington Rand seemed to be making all the right moves. On election night 1952, as Dwight Eisenhower was beating Adlai Stevenson, a UNIVAC appeared on CBS. The network had agreed to use the computer for projecting election results. So millions of people were introduced to the UNIVAC by Edward R. Murrow, Eric Sevareid, and Walter Cronkite, who called it "that marvelous electronic brain." It performed flawlessly—so well that the people running it didn't believe what it told them. All the pre-election polls had predicted a close race, but on the basis of a tiny fraction of the returns, the UNIVAC said Eisenhower was going to win by a substantial margin. That made the Remington Rand people so nervous that they disconnected a part of the UNIVAC's memory to bring its prediction in line with the polls. But the machine was right, and at the end of the evening an engineer came on screen and sheepishly admitted what he'd done. Remington Rand's machine became so famous that when our first computer came out, we found it being referred to as "IBM's UNIVAC."

The Defense Calculator, or the IBM 701 as it was

officially called, came off the production line in December 1952. In some ways it was different from any computer that had ever been built. We'd thought of it as a product, not a laboratory device, right from the start. So in spite of its enormous complexity we built it in the factory, not the engineering lab. It also looked different from other computers because we'd designed it to be easy to ship and install. Other machines consisted of oversize racks and panels that were to be delivered in pieces and painstakingly assembled in the customer's office. The UNIVAC had a main cabinet about the size of a small truck. But the 701 was made up of separate modules, each roughly the size of a large refrigerator, that could fit onto ordinary freight elevators. Our engineers could uncrate the units, cable them together, and have them doing useful work in three days. Any other machine took a minimum of a week.

Dad wanted to launch the 701 with all the usual IBM fanfare, in part because we needed to divert attention from UNIVAC. So we shipped the first 701 to New York, installed it on the ground floor of headquarters, and got ready for a big dedication. To make room for the new machine we dismantled the SSEC—Dad's giant calculator-to-end-all-calculators was only five years old but already obsolete, thanks to the rapid progress of electronics. The ceremony was held in April, and one hundred fifty of the top scientists and leaders of American business showed up, including William Shockley, the inventor of the transistor, John von Neumann, the great computer theorist, General David Sarnoff, the head of RCA, and the heads of AT&T and General Electric. The guest of honor was J. Robert Oppenheimer, the brilliant physicist who led the scientific team that built the first atom bomb. He gave a speech calling the 701 "a tribute to the mind's high splendor," and in our press releases we bragged that the 701 would "shatter the time barrier confronting technicians working on vital defense projects."

Our visitors were impressed with the new computer, and newspapers all over the country picked up the story. But the noisiest reaction came from the big customers who had been pushing us for years to start building computers. Now that we'd delivered the 701 for scientific use, they wanted us to announce the computer we were designing for businesses. "Stop fiddling around," said my Time Inc. friend Roy Larsen. "Show us what you've got so we can decide whether to buy a UNIVAC." Even at this late date some of our punch-card executives were still insisting that computers would never be economical, but the fact that we had customers waiting helped me to override their objections. We announced the IBM 702 in September, and in the space of eight months we had orders for fifty of them.

Meanwhile I turned my attention to the most important sale of my career. In the 1930s Dad had been able to boost IBM into the top echelon of corporations by supplying punch-card machines for Social Security and the New Deal. There were no such massive social programs under Truman or Eisenhower for us to tap into. It was the cold war that helped IBM make itself the king of the computer business. After the Russians exploded their first atom bomb in 1949, the Air Force decided that America needed a sophisticated air defense system. They also decided this should incorporate computers—a very bold idea for the time, because computers were still little more than experiments. The government gave a contract to MIT, and some of the country's best engineers there drew up plans for a vast computer-and-radar network which was supposed to blanket the United States, operate around the clock, and calculate the location, course, and speed of any incoming bomber. The military name for this system was Semi-Automatic Ground Environment, or SAGE. Air defense until then consisted of a few scattered radar stations, where observers did calculations on slide rules and then plotted flight paths by hand. The faster airplanes became, the harder they were to track. An air defense commander might get redundant messages from two or three different radar operators who each thought he had spotted something. The idea of SAGE was to avoid confusion. The commander could use it to monitor his entire region and transmit orders to his interceptors and antiaircraft batteries.

The MIT engineer responsible for procuring the SAGE computers was Jay Forrester, an austere man about my age who was driven by a belief that computers could be made to do more than anyone thought. In the summer of 1952 he was traveling around the industry visiting the five companies in the running—RCA, Raytheon, Remington Rand, Sylvania, and IBM—and everybody was pulling out the stops. RCA and Sylvania trotted him through their huge vacuum tube factories that were supplying everyone in the industry. Remington Rand showed off the UNIVAC and brought in as their spokesman the famous general, Leslie Groves. During the war Groves had been the boss of the Manhattan Project, which built the atom bomb.

I tried not to worry about Groves or the other competitors; I just let IBM speak for itself. I took Forrester to see our plants and introduced him to our most gifted people. He was under extreme pressure to get the system into production as soon as possible, and I think what impressed him was the fact that we were already building computers in a factory. We won a small contract for the first stage of the project, to build prototype computers in conjunction with MIT.

To make SAGE possible the computers had to work in a way computers had never worked before. In those days computing was typically done in what was called batch mode. This meant that you would collect your data first, feed it into the machine second, then sit back for a little while until the answer came out. You could think of the batch processor as a high diver at a circus—each performance involves a lengthy drum roll in preparation, a very fast dive, and then a splash. But the SAGE system was supposed to keep track of a large air defense picture that was changing every instant. That meant it had to take a constant stream of new radar information and digest it continually in what is called "real time." So a SAGE computer was more like a juggler who has to keep a half dozen balls in the air, constantly throwing aside old balls as his assistants toss him new ones from every direction. As if real-time computing were not enough of a technical challenge, the Air Force also wanted the system to be absolutely reliable. In those days it was considered an accomplishment if someone could build a computer that would work a full eight-hour day without failing. But SAGE was supposed to operate flawlessly around the clock, year in and year out.

When Russia exploded its first hydrogen bomb in the summer of 1953, the need to finish SAGE became even more urgent. We took many of our top engineers off our other computers and put them to work with Forrester and his men. A year after we started we had seven hundred people on the SAGE project, and it took only fourteen months to design and build a prototype that would do the job. It was a monster of a machine, far larger than any computer that had ever been produced. The Air Force called it the AN/FSQ-7—or Q7 for short—and it had fifty thousand vacuum tubes and dozens of cabinets spread out across a large warehouse. It was so big that even though electricity in wires travels at close to the speed of light, signals sometimes took too long to get from one part of the computer to another.

Although we'd built a successful prototype, we weren't guaranteed the next stage of the project. The lion's share of SAGE—the contract to manufacture and service the dozens of computers that would make up the actual system—was still up for grabs. I thought it was absolutely essential to IBM's future that we win it. The company that built those computers was going to be way ahead of the game, because it would learn the secrets of mass production. We had the inside track because we'd built the prototype, but there were times in our dealings with MIT when I thought we'd blown it.

Forrester was a genius at computer hardware, but he didn't appreciate how hard it is to set up a reliable production process. He thought we were handling the project all wrong. His idea of management was what he called the "man-on-the-white-horse principle." The man on the white horse was Napoleon; Forrester thought ev-

ery engineering project needed a dictator, which was not
the way our manufacturing men liked to work. His constant criticism made them angry and stubborn, and I was
worried he'd shift SAGE somewhere else. I worked harder
to win that contract than I worked for any other sale in
my life. I was constantly making trips up to MIT. Forrester hemmed and hawed, but I finally told him that if
he promised me the production assignment, I would
build him a factory without waiting for a contract. "Give
me your handshake, and we'll start on the plant this
week," I said. I knew he was afraid that he might have to
wait a long time for the paperwork from the Air Force.
So he told me to go ahead.

Within a couple of years we had thousands of people
working on SAGE and those big Q7s were in operation all
over the continent. We built forty-eight in all. You'd
sometimes see a SAGE center if you were driving in a
remote place. They were huge windowless concrete buildings, each covering an entire acre and housing two machines. The control room in these places was a big room
lit with an eerie blue light. The watch commander would
sit in front of a giant map of his entire area. On that
board, the computer would plot in yellow the movement
of all the airplanes in the sky, along with symbols to show
whether they were friends or foes. If there was an at-
tacker, the commander simply had to point to its blip
with a device called a "light gun" and SAGE would automatically radio information about its position to intercep-
tor planes and antiaircraft batteries. The system even had
the reliability that the Air Force wanted. We'd solved
that problem by having the Q7s work in tandem, taking
turns. One machine would juggle the radar while its twin
was being serviced or standing by. By that method the
average SAGE center was able to stay on alert over 97
percent of the time.

SAGE was celebrated as one of the great technical
achievements of its day. But although the system worked
fine, the arms race made it obsolete before it was even
finished. It could guard against attacks by bombers, but
not missiles, so when the Russians launched Sputnik in

1958, SAGE became passé. I remember I was sitting in a hotel dining room in Bremen when word of Sputnik came. A waiter who knew I was American walked up and said "Where is your Sputnik? Where is your Sputnik?" We got scared all over again, because we'd left ourselves vulnerable to an attack from space. But in fairness to Jay Forrester and all the military men who decided to build SAGE, none of us ever questioned its suitability at the time it was designed. And it gave IBM the giant boost I was after. Until the late '50s, SAGE accounted for almost half our total computer sales. We made very little money on the project, in keeping with the policy against war profiteering laid down by Dad. But it enabled us to build highly automated factories ahead of anybody else, and to train thousands of new workers in electronics.

Even though IBM was supplying a large proportion of the Defense Department's electronic brains, I was never much of a cold warrior. Like most things conceived in a panic, the air defense system only *seemed* to make sense. We built it because the Russians had the bomb and we were afraid they might fly over here and destroy New York. It amazes me that nobody ever thought to ask why they'd want to do that. Our State Department probably could have told us that the Russians would never attack because they knew we could retaliate against their cities. And in reality they didn't have any airplanes that could make the flight. So SAGE was a costly fantasy, the SDI of its day. Before long we found ourselves vastly overarmed, faced with the danger of mutual annihilation.

But at that point the country was in a terrible state of paranoia because of the Red scare. Senator Joe McCarthy was holding hearings and claiming to find Communists in every crack in the wall. There was a moment when I truly thought IBM was going to lose its shot at defense work because of the kind of window blinds I had in my office. Window blinds in those days were almost all horizontal—ordinary venetian blinds. But vertical blinds had just been developed, and some had been ordered for me. An IBM engineer was in my office one day for a meeting and he was interested in getting the same kind of blinds for his office, so he drew a little diagram of how they were attached on axles to the floor and the ceiling. He put that little piece of paper in his shirt pocket and forgot about it. A few days later the man who did the engineer's laundry was checking the shirt before putting it in the washer, and he found that little slip of paper—just a diagram with no explanation. McCarthy had so spooked this country that everybody thought everybody else was a Red. So the laundry man sent the paper to McCarthy, and pretty soon Senate investigators came and said to the engineer, "We've identified this as the plan for a radar antenna, and we want to hear about it. We want to be perfectly fair. But we know it is a radar antenna and the shirt it was found in belongs to you."

The guy said, "Oh, for Chrissake, those are the blinds in Watson's office!"

So they asked to see me. When they came to my office they explained what the engineer had told them and I said, "Well, those blinds are right here." I showed them how the blinds worked. They looked them over very carefully and then left. I thought that I had contained it, but I wasn't sure, and I was scared. We were working on SAGE, and it would have been a hell of a way to lose our security clearance.

The McCarthy years were a formative period for me. I was only beginning to run the business and I had no idea how forcefully I ought to speak out. My reaction to McCarthy was like that of many other concerned citizens: at the beginning I felt it was possible that he might be onto something, but gradually this gave way to outrage and dismay at his bullying and lies. At one point I took a week off to go skiing in Switzerland and sat in my bedroom reading a story in the *International Herald Tribune* about accusations McCarthy was making against the top people in government. I thought to myself, "How can we let him go on like this? He is making the United States of America look like Salem of the witch trials." For the first time in my life, I felt embarrassed for my country, and I told this to Dad when I got back to New York. He shared my disgust for McCarthy, but counseled restraint. "These things usually work themselves out," he said. It was both a great strength and great weakness of Dad's that his optimism prevented him from making negative public statements about anything. In this case, I wasn't sure he was right. He had set a powerful example for me years before by taking an early, vocal stand in favor of Roosevelt and the New Deal.

Shortly after that I was invited to a lunch at Lehman Brothers, a Wall Street investment bank that in those days was all powerful. There were some very important men present and we all sat around a large round table. Bobby Lehman, the head of the firm, talked about McCarthy. He said, "The man is uncouth and I don't like his approach. But none of us can argue with the idea of rooting Communism out of our government." Then he asked me what my view was. I said, "I don't happen to agree with Senator McCarthy. I think he is doing more harm than good. I don't believe that the highest councils of our government are riddled with Communists. I think it's undesirable that a few army clerks are Communists, but it's not terribly important." It was a very conservative crowd. Of the twenty-odd people present, I was the only one who took that position. That didn't bother me. What bothered me was that the following week I got letters from several people who had been there, and they all had a similar message: "I didn't want to commit myself in public, but I certainly agreed with everything you said."

The businessman whose response to McCarthy I admired most was Walter H. Wheeler Jr. He was the head of Pitney-Bowes, a very successful manufacturing company in Connecticut. "Tiny" Wheeler was well over six feet tall and weighed about 230 pounds. He was really irate over a two-million-dollar lawsuit McCarthy filed against Senator William Benton of Connecticut. Benton had given a speech calling McCarthy a liar and saying his witch-hunt tactics were tearing America apart. McCarthy sued him for libel and slander and helped defeat Benton when he tried to get reelected. Then McCarthy withdrew the complaint just before the case went to court; he said his lawyers had advised him he could not prove damages because they could find no one who believed Mr. Benton's statement. Tiny Wheeler had no connection to that case, but he sent McCarthy a telegram that said, "Your lawyer could not have looked very hard. I would be glad to testify for you that I believe what Senator Benton has said about you, and am sure there are many millions of others in this country who would be happy to do likewise. Walter H. Wheeler, Pitney-Bowes Incorporated." Wheeler gave copies of the telegram to the newspapers, and it appeared in the *New York Times* the following morning. It was one of the most courageous moves I ever saw a businessman make—which sounds peculiar today, but for that brief period McCarthy's power was awesome. I called Wheeler up, went and visited him, and from then on, Walter Wheeler was one of my business heroes.

I saw a graphic illustration of how not to behave when I went to Washington to watch Army Secretary Bob Stevens testify in the hearings McCarthy held on the army. Stevens was a friend of Dad's and had been head of the great textile firm J. P. Stevens, which his family owned. He was no match for McCarthy. Stevens was trying to play the Marquis of Queensberry rules with McCarthy, trying to treat him like a senator. He said, "I certainly want to help you, sir." And the more he cooperated, the more trouble he got into. I thought, "He must have gone to too many boarding schools. He's not getting down in the gutter with this guy. The only way to fight a guttersnipe is in the gutter." Most of the people I knew were eating and breathing those army hearings, the final sessions of which were on TV. It was the first time TV played a role in a great national debate. Stevens's lawyer, a brilliant strategist, hired a Boston attorney named Joseph Nye Welch to represent the army. He was the man who said to McCarthy, with millions of people watching, "Have you no sense of decency, sir, at long last?" That one sentence was the beginning of McCarthy's downfall.

By then I'd decided that McCarthy was a symptom of

a real weakness in America that I wanted to tackle publicly, even if it meant taking a negative position that would be unlike Dad. I was asked to speak later that year in Fort Wayne, Indiana, to a large gathering of salesmen from various industries. My host was Ernie Gallmeyer, head of the Wayne Pump Company. Ernie knew me from the American Society of Sales Executives and thought of me as a bright young businessman. That is a very conservative area of America even today, and back then it was the heart of McCarthy country. I thought it was an ideal forum for an anti-McCarthy speech. "Many of you may not agree with me. That's good!" I said. The point I made was that in an atmosphere of open discussion, McCarthy would never have gotten as far as he had. I told them that as American salesmen, who made their living by talking, they had a patriotic obligation to promote the thoughtful debate of public issues.

> We as salesmen have an added duty beyond selling our products. We ought to put our salesmanship behind the American way of life—and not let evil or unjustified suspicions frighten Americans. We have the duty of helping to form an honest, fair-minded public opinion in this country. . . . Uncontrolled suspicion is like a plague. It would wreck America. So if this uncontrolled suspicion starts rolling around America again, we must fight it. That will be a time that calls for cool heads and persuasive salesmanship.

When I finished there was modest applause—very modest. Even though many prominent people were critical of McCarthy by this time, and even though my speech had been relatively mild, Ernie Gallmeyer was in shock and tried to get me out of the hall before anybody could talk to me. To judge from Ernie's reaction, what I said was so distasteful to the people in Fort Wayne that he felt his reputation had been damaged. Unfortunately this was before the days of flying home after a meeting, so I had to spend an awkward night at his house. I guess I had thought I could win all of them over. But the feeling of being treated like an outsider was so disturbing to me that I said to Olive when I got home, "It was as though I had gotten a frightful disease." Later I talked to my father about it. He said, "Tom, I was always an outsider too, because I spoke for the poor, and higher taxes, and better social programs." He read my speech and didn't object in the least. "These are things that need to be brought out. I'm glad you're saying them. And I'm glad to see you take public positions, even though they're minority positions."

After a while I stopped feeling embarrassed when other businessmen dismissed me as a liberal nut. I felt as Dad did. The country had given him an awful lot, and it was in the process of giving me an awful lot. I had a very profitable company. I was young and vigorous and willing to say what I believed. Being able to make liberal speeches is a luxury for a businessman. The whole picture would have been different if IBM's profit margins had been lower. People wouldn't have been as interested in having me speak, and I would never have been so outspoken. When I made a public appearance I always had the huge IBM engine behind me blowing a whistle that signaled, "Look at this company. This kid is running it. Don't take him lightly, because he knows what he's doing." If I'd been president of a coal company instead, making, say, six percent a year in profits instead of 23 percent, I could never have gotten public attention for my views.

CHAPTER 21

I n 1955 my picture was on the cover of *Time*. Dad
had never been honored that way, and I felt both
proud and embarrassed. I was running IBM practically on my own now, but obviously a lot of the
credit belonged to him. The *Time* story is a perfect example of that. The magazine had a reporter named Virginia
Bennett assigned to find out about automation in America. In those days Remington Rand had its headquarters
near ours in Manhattan, and she went to interview them
because of the UNIVAC. Fortunately for us, they weren't
very forthcoming that day, and Miss Bennett didn't get
the interview she needed. She was walking back to her
office, somewhat discouraged, when she happened to pass
IBM. She saw the Defense Calculator in the window and
must have thought, "These people are in the computer
business too, so I'll stop and give it a whirl."

That was where Dad had his effect. He was an absolute stickler on how the public should be greeted at the
door, and we always had skilled receptionists in the
lobby. Dad chose these women himself. He would talk to
them about the importance of relating well to the public,
and tell them that if a stranger looked important, he or
she should be given VIP treatment. One of these experienced receptionists was on duty when Miss Bennett
walked in and said she was a reporter from *Time* with an
idea for a story. The receptionist knew enough to say,
"Well, the head of this company is Mr. Watson. He isn't
in the building today, but his son Tom is the president
and you certainly can see him." Ten minutes later Virginia Bennett was sitting in my office hearing about
IBM's electronic marvels.

The editors at *Time* had a theory that there was a

second industrial revolution under way because of electronics, and they liked the way IBM fit this theme. Before long they had reporters interviewing all our top people. They sent a man to see Dad on vacation in Palm Beach, and another correspondent came to one of our sales conventions in Chicago. I spent three days there in a hotel room with him, telling him my life story. Then they took pictures of our computers, our factories, and my family. When it came out, the cover showed a portrait of me, and behind my back was a gray computer holding a mechanical finger to its lips while reaching out to push its own control buttons. The headline was:

IBM'S THOMAS J. WATSON JR.
CLINK. CLANK. THINK.

It was the best publicity any executive could ever hope for. For millions of readers, *Time* equated our products with the advance of civilization. "The prospects for mankind are truly dazzling," the story said. "Automation of industry will mean new reaches of leisure, new wealth, new dignity for the laboring man." While Dad kept himself pretty far removed from the computer projects, leaving them to Williams and me, this was the message he had always been interested in putting across. Decades before computers even existed, he had seen that potential in punch-card machines.

The article included a small picture of Dad and told how he had built IBM. Still, I knew I'd feel slighted if I were in his shoes and it were my son getting top billing. That put a damper on my excitement. When I found out I was probably going to be on the cover, I felt obliged to try to cushion the blow to Dad's ego by sending a letter to him and Mother. "Whatever they say about me is a reflection on you both if it's favorable," I wrote. "There would be no IBM for me to be president of had it not been for your initiative and courage, Dad. This I know, and this I have told *Time*. While I hope I have in me what it takes to do a good job now, I know I don't have what you had in building the company." It was a sincere but clumsy attempt to reassure him, though I doubt it made him feel any less upstaged. He didn't talk to me about the article at all. He never said, "Great going!" and I never brought it up.

By the mid-'50s "computer" was becoming a magic word as popular as vitamins. Top executives rightly believed that the companies of the future were going to be computer run. Board chairmen would say, "We've got to get a computer!" Everybody wanted one, even though precisely how to use the machines was still a mystery. It became the conventional wisdom that management ran a bigger risk by waiting to computerize than by taking the plunge.

If Remington Rand had put their money and hearts behind the UNIVAC right at the start, maybe they'd have been in *Time* magazine instead of us. But nobody at the top of the company had a vision of what computers might mean. Jim Rand was more of a conglomerateur. While Dad was saying "Shoemaker, stick to your last," Rand's company was selling everything including office equipment, electric shavers, autopilots, and farm machines. Rand wouldn't even let Eckert and Mauchly use his punch-card salesmen to market computers—he said it would cost too much. Instead things were set up so that if a new UNIVAC displaced Remington Rand punch-card equipment, the punch-card salesman lost commissions.

At IBM there was never any question—we put the whole weight of our sales force behind our computers as soon as they were announced. At first our salesmen knew almost nothing about them, of course, so we made sure that senior executives and the engineers who did know were available to help them sell. Months before the machines were ready for delivery we hired dozens of graduate mathematicians and physicists and engineers to help customers decide how they might use the computers when the machines arrived. To spread knowledge of the new field, we held seminars in Poughkeepsie for our customers and salesmen both.

In the history of IBM, technological innovation often wasn't the thing that made us successful. Unhappily there were many times when we came in second. But technology turned out to be less important than sales and distribution methods. Starting with UNIVAC, we consistently outsold people who had better technology because we knew how to put the story before the customer, how to install the machines successfully, and how to hang on to customers once we had them. The secret of our sales approach was the same thing that made Dad so successful in punch cards: systems knowledge. That was where IBM had its monopoly. No competitors ever paid enough attention to it, not even the people at Remington Rand, who should have known better because they were in the punch-card business too.

By the spring of 1954, IBM and UNIVAC were running a close horse race. In terms of computers actually installed, Remington Rand still had the lead by about twenty to fifteen. But our salesmen, racing far ahead of our factories and engineers, had piled up enough orders for us to outdistance Remington Rand four times over. All we had to do now was deliver. Our bestseller was the new computer we'd announced for accounting applications, the 702. We had orders for fifty of these, which we were getting ready to build in a three-year production run starting that fall. The program was on schedule, but so much was riding on the 702 that everybody involved was extremely jumpy. Even Dad felt the tension and worried that other companies were going to steal the business away. "At the rate we are going we will never fill those orders," he would scold.

Bringing out the 702 on time meant that all of IBM's departments—product planning, engineering, manufacturing, sales—had to cooperate. I didn't assume this would happen automatically—the project was complicated, and there were a lot of punch-card men who would be just as happy to see computers disappear. We could easily trip ourselves up, and I decided we needed somebody in charge of making sure that didn't happen. I chose Vin Learson, who had emerged as one of IBM's best operating executives. He was six feet six inches tall, and his mere presence in a room was enough to get people's attention. The job turned out to be one of the most important assignments in IBM history.

By summer our engineers realized, to their horror, that the 702 was probably not the great UNIVAC-beater we thought. One big problem was the machine's memory. The type of storage circuitry we were using worked faster than the circuitry in the UNIVAC, but it also "forgot" bits of data more often. We could make the 702 perform reliably enough that delivering it to customers wouldn't hurt IBM's reputation, but only by providing laboratory-trained teams of specialists to babysit the machines. Our engineers and production managers weren't sure how to proceed.

Learson turned this quandary into a triumph. His first move was to order a crash redesign of the machine. He took what we'd learned working for the Air Force on SAGE and used it to skip a grade, so to speak, in computer development. The MIT engineers on SAGE had achieved a historic breakthrough in memory technology that involved storing data on arrays of tiny doughnut-shaped magnets called "cores." Core memory was ultra-reliable, and our engineers had been planning to incorporate it in the next generation of IBM's computers, about three years down the road. But Vin told them to jump on it right away. He drove the engineers at such a ferocious pace that in less than six months we'd revamped our entire computer line with core memory. Meanwhile Vin decided that we'd go ahead and manufacture the relatively unreliable 702s, but just for a year as a stopgap. As soon as the newer design could be produced, we'd switch our customers to those and either upgrade or replace the old machines.

In a little over a year we started delivering those redesigned computers. They made the UNIVAC obsolete and we soon left Remington Rand in the dust. By the time the presidential elections rolled around in 1956, we had eighty-seven machines in operation and one hundred ninety on order, against forty-one in operation and forty on order for all other computer-makers. Eisenhower beat Stevenson again, but this time the computers you saw on TV were IBM machines.

Whenever we had superior technology to complement our systems knowledge, our business skyrocketed. That happened when we started delivering a small computer called the 650, in 1954. It was far less powerful than the Defense Calculator, but much cheaper. Competitors like Underwood Typewriter and National Cash Register were racing to build small computers that could be used by ordinary businesses, but the 650 outperformed them all. Over the next several years it enabled us to bring thousands of punch-card customers into the computer age. The 650 rented for about four thousand dollars a month, and was the perfect choice for companies eager to try computing because we designed it to work along with ordinary punch-card equipment. Yet it could do accounting jobs that were beyond punch cards. For example, life insurance companies used to spend a lot of money calculating premium bills. Depending on age, sex, and other factors, each life insurance customer was supposed to be charged at a different rate, and typically this calculation was done by hand. Clerks would look up the rates in tables and work out the amount due on adding machines. But with the 650, the companies could load their actuarial tables into its memory and the computer did the work. Its ability to handle these bread-and-butter applications made the 650 hot. While our giant, million-dollar 700 series machines got the publicity, the 650 became computing's Model T.

We played a large role in creating new professions such as programming and systems engineering. As it finally became obvious that we were giving birth to a whole new industry, we discovered that the world wasn't entirely ready for our machines. It was as though we had the airplanes, but no one to fly them and no place to land. Our customers often complained that the most difficult thing about having a computer was hiring somebody who could run it. They'd ask for help, we couldn't provide all those technicians ourselves, and there was not a single university with a computer curriculum. Sometimes we even found ourselves in a position where we had to hold back from taking a customer's order. So I went up to MIT in 1955 and urged them to start training computer scientists. We made a gift of a large computer and the money to run it, and they shared that machine with ten other schools in the Northeast. For the 650, we adapted a very aggressive college discount program that existed for our punch-card machines: you could get 40 percent off for setting up a course in either business data processing or scientific computing, and 60 percent off for setting up courses in both. I put these education policies near the top of the list of IBM's key moves, because within five years there was a whole new generation of computer scientists who made it possible for the market to boom.

Wherever I traveled during those years I tried to recruit top people for IBM's research and development side. The engineers who were hardest to attract were those graduating from Stanford and Caltech and the University of California—the smart ones never wanted to leave the West Coast sun to come East. So, very early on, we decided to put a laboratory out in San Jose, and I bought a building that had been intended for a supermarket. The man we sent to manage the new lab was Reynold Johnson, one of Dad's self-taught inventors from Endicott. He had started out as a high school teacher in Minnesota and he came to IBM in the 1930s proposing a machine that could automatically read and grade multiple-choice tests for schools. Some executives told him the idea was impractical, but Dad overruled them, put Johnson on the payroll, and let him build his machine. IBM made several million dollars on test scoring equipment, and the method is still used on college admission tests today.

Johnson was delighted at the thought of escaping from the rivalries and pressures of Endicott and directing his own lab. He moved to California, hired three dozen young engineers, and in less than three years presented IBM with an invention that was truly spectacular: the computer disk. It stores data in the form of tiny magnetized spots on its surface, and one problem Johnson faced was how to lay down a coating on the disk that was uniform enough to permit this. I remember the day I saw him demonstrate his solution. He stood in front of a spinning aluminum disk with some magnetic coating in a paper cup, and began pouring it slowly, like a milkshake, onto the disk's center. When the stuff spread out to near the edge, he stopped pouring, and he had a magnetic disk. The machine he invented, which we called the RAMAC, incorporated fifty of those disks stacked like records in a jukebox, except that they all were spinning at once. A little arm would move in and out among the disks, extending a recording head over the disk surfaces to pick up the data that were needed. The descendants of Rey Johnson's disks are the main data storage devices in virtually every computer system today, from very large mainframes down to ordinary PCs, and they revolutionized the computer's usefulness. Computer tapes like those used with the Defense Calculator don't work well in applications where a computer has to look up a particular piece of information—to check a customer's bank balance, say, or tell how many seats are still available on a particular airline flight. Without Rey Johnson's disks those applications never would have been practical. To see why, you only need to imagine a music lover who has a collection of both records and tape cassettes. If he wants to play a favorite song on a tape, he has to wait while the tape deck fast-forwards to the proper spot; but with a record, he can move the phonograph needle directly to the right track and hear the music instantly. A computer equipped with a disk homes in on data in much the same way, and the RAMAC made it possible to retrieve information two hundred times as fast as with magnetic tape.

While we were proud of our computers, proud of our disks, and proud of our tape drives, I didn't fool myself into thinking that IBM had much genuine scientific prowess. We were a maker of electromechanical equipment trying to go into a very sophisticated field with almost no background. Because of this I kept working to increase the flow of technical information into IBM. When we first started building computers, for example, we arranged for John von Neumann, the eminent Princeton University computer theorist, to give seminars to our men at Poughkeepsie. Von Neumann was one of the atom bomb pioneers and he practically defined the modern notion of software; I didn't understand his work, but I knew how important he was. From then on we kept a steady stream of experts coming in, and we frequently sent our engineers out to university courses as well.

But it was soon obvious that this wasn't enough, and we began searching for a senior scientist to come and organize a program of pure research within IBM. Wally McDowell, our chief of engineering, spent the better part of 1955 scouring the country for candidates. I took about a month and went around interviewing them, even though I was somewhat in the dark because I didn't know the scientific community that well. Finally I settled on a candidate who had done an impressive job at building up the school of engineering at a major university. But before I presented my choice to IBM's board, I attended a meeting at MIT and mentioned his name in a chat with Jim Killian, MIT's president. Killian looked horrified. He said, "Oh, no, he wouldn't be appropriate at all for that job."

"Why not?" I asked. I felt my ears burning because I had apparently done something stupid and didn't know what it was. Killian was evasive about his reasons, so finally I said, "Look, we want a distinguished scientist. Until a minute ago I thought I'd found one. But if you know of someone better than this fellow, tell me!" What I didn't understand then, and Killian did, was that American science was dominated by a coterie of men who had worked together during the war. These were people like Leo Szilard and the team that had built the atom bomb, and Isidor Rabi and the team that pioneered radar. The qualifications of the man I'd found were superb, Killian said, but that made no difference. Unless I hired someone from this circle, IBM might spend large sums and still end up with a lab that was merely second rate, because we'd have trouble attracting other top people.

"So who should I call?" I asked, and Killian said promptly, "Emanuel Piore." He was one of them. I'd never heard of him, but Killian filled me in: until the year before Piore had been chief scientist at the Office of Naval Research, and he had played a major role in funding cold-war military work at universities. Now he'd left the government and was working for a New York defense contractor. I tracked Piore down that night by phone and went to see him the next day. He seemed familiar, and it turned out that his uncle was Michael Romanoff, the self-proclaimed Russian prince who founded Romanoff's restaurant in Hollywood. The prince had been a celebrity during my nightclubbing phase. Manny looked exactly like him, a tweedy man with bushy eyebrows, shaggy, unkempt hair, a dark complexion, and a perpetual slouch. He smoked a pipe, had a sort of mumbling demeanor, and tended not to look you square in the eye. All the same I found him very appealing and on the strength of Killian's recommendation I hired him.

Now that the matter was settled, I wondered if I'd picked the right guy. I didn't know what to make of Manny's odd, self-effacing manner. But a couple of months later I took him to Zurich to introduce him at the laboratory we had there. Manny was mumbling at the dinner they gave us, and a Swiss scientist who was pretty arrogant decided he must be a pushover. So he criticized him, in a nasty tone of voice, for not setting sufficiently precise research standards and goals for IBM. Piore came back at him like a lion. "I'll take that and I'll answer it," he said, and gave a detailed five-point response. Then he said, "Is there any facet of this you'd like explained further? I came here tonight to make sure we understand each other. I thought we'd keep things pleasant, but I'm willing to take it right down to the bare knuckles if that's what you want." The other guy didn't breathe another word. I thought, "I've got a winner here. Killian was right."

Piore gave a jolt to some of our product-development

engineers as well. They were like sprinters encountering their first marathon runner, and were amazed to see IBM start funding experiments in exotic fields that seemed unlikely to bear fruit for decades, if ever—like superconductors and artificial intelligence. What the engineers thought of as basic research Piore often dismissed as mere long-term product development, and what he called research was so far removed from what the engineers were doing that they saw no reason for it at all. At Piore's urging we doubled the percentage of our revenues devoted to research and development, and much of the additional spending was earmarked for pure science.

With all this creative ferment, IBM's potential seemed unlimited as long as we avoided horrible mistakes—a feat much harder than I first assumed. One day near the end of my first year as president, Al Williams came into my office with a very long face. Al was treasurer at that point and he'd just added up the financial results for 1952. "Boy, you've got a problem," he said. Sales that year were up by 25 percent—and profits were barely up at all. I was flabbergasted. Without knowing it, we had allowed our costs to eat up the profits from over sixty million dollars of new business. It was too late to do anything about it. The money—about seventeen million dollars—was gone. Even worse was the way this had happened: we'd spent more than we expected because IBM had no budget. Williams and I had been trying to run this major corporation out of our vest pockets, the way Dad always had. That might have worked before the war, when IBM was a forty-million-dollar company, but by then we were almost ten times that large.

That night Al and I stayed late, figuring out how to break the news to stockholders without hurting the price of the stock. Our best bet, we decided, was a straightforward explanation of how the funds had been spent: on activities very necessary to IBM's growth, such as developing new products, expanding the engineering force, and hiring and training new salesmen. The following morning I was waiting for Dad when he came to the office. "I'm embarrassed to have to tell you this," I said as I showed him the numbers. "I got trapped by a lack of financial controls." It was no surprise to Dad that we'd overspent—he'd been warning us all along, but he was letting us run things for ourselves, and we'd thought he was out of touch with the scale of the business. Dad became calm and grave as he sometimes did when confronted with a major problem, listened to the public statement I proposed, and said simply, "I think the shareholders will accept that." He was right—the price of IBM stock held steady when we released the figures. All the same, I walked into the annual meeting that year filled with dread. Any minute I expected a stockholder to say, "I have a question for the younger Mr. Watson. Is this the kind of performance that we can expect from you as president?" Luckily nobody asked, but I felt shaken, as I have a few times after doing something stupid in an airplane and surviving by sheer chance.

Generally I need to be hit on the head only once to learn a lesson—a trait I've come to think of as absolutely essential in business. Al and I set things up so that we would never be surprised again: we put budgets in all the departments, appointed the toughest-minded guy we could find as budget director, and had him report to me. From then on I always knew in June approximately where we were going to be financially on December 31.

In spite of the mistakes we made, I couldn't have run IBM without Al. He was my alter ego. He had the ability to be analytical while I was intuitive and to make sure everything was tightened up and done right while I was out in front setting the pace for the business. Without him my success would not have been possible and without me he wouldn't have had as much success as he did. Our friendship was one of the few I had at IBM that extended outside of business hours. I would seek him out just for the pleasure of his company, and Olive loved him too. He and his wife Pat wanted to learn to sail, so Olive and I went down to their house once a month for twelve months and taught them the basics. One visit we worked on charts—how to plot courses, with all the variations and deviations; another day I tied the basic knots, tacked them onto a board, and took it to him. I made diagrams of how a boat works in the wind, how the forces of wind and drag and momentum act on the hull.

The funny thing about Al was that he was terribly modest and didn't like to promote himself, and yet if I gave him an opportunity, he always took it. I introduced him to the business community by nominating him as treasurer of the New York Boy Scouts; from there he was invited to join the board of a small bank; and eventually he ended up a director of the First National City Bank and Mobil and General Motors. I looked after his career within IBM as well, telling him he could never get promoted out of the financial department until he'd trained people to take his place. "You've got nothing but clerks in there," I said. That was overstating it, because Al had two excellent men, Barney Wiegard and Herb Hansford, who were the cornerstones of the finance department but had to do practically everything themselves. Before I knew it Al had punch cards shooting all over and had identified everyone at IBM across the country who had been to business school. He brought the top young men to New York, and within a year not only had he gotten the finance department to run itself, but in the process he'd singled out some real leaders, including Dick Bullen, who emerged as the best organizational architect IBM ever had, and a future chairman, Frank Cary.

Those were confused years at IBM. Even if Dad had been ten years younger and kept control of the operation himself, he couldn't have made his one-man style of management work for very much longer. Important problems were taking too long to filter through to the top, and we had unmade decisions piling up in every corner. With notable exceptions like Learson, most IBM executives were so used to dancing at the end of Dad's string that they didn't dare think for themselves—in spite of our much publicized company motto. Just before I became president I saw a secret project with the Xerox Corporation ruined because of this. The idea was to couple their technology with our tabulating machines for printing at high speeds. It was a modest project but it interested me because I thought it might lead to an alliance between Xerox and IBM. Instead, their engineers and ours butted heads and by the time I heard there was any problem, the project had collapsed. That's what was maddening about highly centralized power in a growing company.

My first step in breaking that pattern was to surround myself with top-notch people, so that not every decision had to wait for the boss. To find even a half dozen executives who were qualified I had to dip into IBM's second and third ranks. That shows how big a vacuum there was at the top: I'd inherited eight vice presidents from Dad, but apart from Williams and LaMotte, only two had minds of their own, and both of those were manufacturing specialists who were indispensable at the Endicott and Poughkeepsie plants. So Al and I set up an inner circle with men like Birkenstock, who by now was in charge of our patent department; McDowell, our chief engineer; Miller, who ran the typewriter business; Jack Bricker, the director of personnel; and Learson.

I was able to push enough responsibility onto these men so that we began to make great strides. We got launched in the computer business, made good on our Korean War commitments, and expanded our punch-card sales by another 50 percent without having IBM disintegrate. But during the year I was busy landing the SAGE contract, our decision-making process bogged down again. I still had fifteen top officials reporting to me, counting the old guard and the new men I'd brought up, and I was shocked to find myself making people cool their heels outside my office just like Dad. Given the pace of change in our business, I didn't think I could afford to do that.

So I took another step away from Dad's vest-pocket management style. I told him I wanted to make executive vice presidents of LaMotte and Williams and have all the other executives report to them. LaMotte would oversee IBM's sales and R and D, while Williams would cover manufacturing and finance. This would speed up my work, because the only problems that would come to me would be those that Al and Red couldn't handle themselves. I'd picked them because they complemented each other. Al was the best of the new guard, and I wanted him there to help me navigate IBM through the sweeping changes I could foresee. Red, on the other hand, was almost sixty years old and stood for continuity in the business. When it came to motivating and managing people, he could extract enormous amounts of work without ever seeming tough, like an unintimidating version of Dad. I thought of him almost as my uncle, and it was easier to take criticism from him than from anyone else.

The idea of delegating so much power was totally antithetical to Dad's personality, and for weeks he fought my plan to promote Williams and LaMotte. Once we'd been through all the rational arguments, he finally even tried getting Mother involved. I think on some level he must have been worried that I was throwing my patrimony away. I was at his house one weekend, and with Mother there in the living room, Dad started attacking my choice of men. It was pretty easy to ignore him when he called LaMotte careless—I knew Red irritated Dad because of his upper-class background and because he didn't necessarily jump to attention when Dad came into a room. But what shocked me was the way he went after Williams, telling me point-blank that Al couldn't be trusted. "Watch your flanks," he said darkly. "Everybody is for you until they see an opportunity to be against you."

I didn't know what to make of this and I would have lashed out, but Mother spoke up. She explained in her neutral way that Dad remembered losing his job at the cash register company through the treachery of Mr. Deeds. Her eyes locked on mine, and I realized she was trying to remind me that I was dealing with an eighty-year-old man. All the anger went out of me. I turned back to my father and said, "Dad, Al Williams is my best friend. If I'm wrong about the guy, then I deserve to lose my shirt." Dad piped down after that, and when I went to present the promotions to the board, he and I walked into the meeting together.

•   •   •

IBM's growth was hard even for me to comprehend. It was 1955 and we were about to break the half-billion-dollar mark in sales. The bulk of our business came from punch-card machines and computers, but even our side-lines were becoming bigger than all of IBM had been before the war. We had a factory complex just outside Endicott making bombsights for the Air Force under contracts carried over from the Korean War; we had our electric typewriter business; we had a set of plants that did nothing but manufacture hundreds of millions of punch cards. Altogether IBM was expanding at close to 20 percent a year—and the billion-dollar mark was only a few years away.

If I was scared when I first became president I was doubly scared now. IBM had already reached a size at which I felt it might be prudent to slow to a more sedate rate of growth that I was sure we could finance and manage. That summer I asked Al Williams to clear a couple of days on his calendar so that we could sit down and discuss the company's future. He agreed that it was a good time to think about reining in IBM. The problem was that this failed to take the computer into account. Demand for those products was accelerating, and it seemed clear that the market wasn't going to wait. If IBM didn't grab the business, somebody else would, and we would never have this kind of opportunity again. Like every one of my father's employees, Williams and I had been trained to think of even a single order lost as a disaster. So we decided to push IBM as rapidly as the market would permit—even though this would mean growing on a scale unprecedented in American business.

We knew that as we neared the top of the Fortune 500, IBM would have to be totally transformed. Every entrepreneurial company, if it succeeds, must eventually face the transition to professional management. In our case, Dad had been so good at his job that this maturing process was long overdue. As big as IBM now was, it had almost none of the things that corporations count on to keep small problems from ballooning into big ones—such as a clear chain of command, large-scale decentralization, a planning process, or formal business policies. Our way of getting things done consisted mostly of wisdom carried in a few people's heads. If we kept growing and tried to run a billion-dollar business that haphazardly, IBM would probably not survive. It would explode like a supernova and end up a dwarf.

So Al and I began talking about how to organize IBM more scientifically. I remember the first thing we did was to break Dad's taboo against organization charts. We got big sheets of paper, spread them out on a table, and put down all the segments of IBM the way they ran under Dad. In the early days the old man would have fired anybody he found doing this. We were absolutely amazed at the result. There were about thirty-eight or forty boxes, every one of them reporting to T. J. Watson. Then we did another chart that showed IBM under me and Williams and LaMotte. It was pretty much the same old chaos, except that we had divided Dad's job into three.

Finally we drew a new chart showing how a reorganized IBM might look. I wanted the people at headquarters free to concentrate on computers and punch-card machines. So we made our other operations—military products, typewriters, punch cards, and time clocks—into autonomous divisions, each with its own sales force, financial people, research, and its own general manager who would make the decisions and have the successes and the headaches. This was the beginning of a process of reorganization that went on for all the years I ran IBM.

Once Al and I were happy with our charts, I locked them up in a cabinet in my office. Later that week I named my assistant Dick Bullen as director of organization, to map further changes. Meanwhile I explained our idea for new divisions to Dad. He approved this plan without any of the fuss he put up over Williams and LaMotte, but I don't think the reorganization made him very comfortable. At one point he told a newspaper reporter that, looking at the new decentralized IBM, he'd be more interested in working as a divisional sales manager than as chairman of the board.

•   •   •

The new structure we created left plenty of room for World Trade to operate separately from the rest of IBM. My brother Dick's side of the business was becoming a great success. Because of Europe's economic revival and Dad's genius for coping with trade barriers, World Trade was growing just as fast as IBM Domestic; it passed one hundred million dollars in sales in 1954. Dad ran it, and Dick had worked his way up to where Dad made him president that summer. Right around then World Trade also moved out of IBM's headquarters on Madison Avenue to offices across the street from the new United Nations building.

Dick was thriving in his job: he knew French, learned Italian, German, and Spanish, traveled incessantly, and managed that complicated business extraordinarily well. When he became president World Trade was already operating in seventy-nine countries, with full-blown national subsidiaries in thirty-six and branch offices and sales agencies in the rest. There was no other company in the world like it. Of the sixteen thousand employees working under Dick, only two hundred were Americans, and almost all of them stayed in New York. Dad had the philosophy that Germans ought to sell to Germans, Frenchmen ought to sell to Frenchmen, and so on, so each major office was completely managed and staffed by citizens of that country.

I had conflicting feelings about my brother moving up, and it is hard for me to know the truth behind those feelings even today. Like most chief executives, I felt the desire to be totally dominant in the company I was running. But I also loved my brother and knew that Dad wanted us to manage IBM in tandem. By this time Dad was more active on Dick's side of the business than mine —no doubt partly because he was trying to stay out of my hair. But I also suspected he was acting out of competitiveness, turning to World Trade as if to say, "I'll show you, young Tom. You don't want to listen to me, so I'm going into business with your brother." Whether he felt that way or not, there were strong business reasons for him to concentrate on World Trade. He wanted IBM to be a global force, and World Trade was the part of the company that needed the most work. Dad had been driving at this goal since he was forty, and the fact that he was now eighty only made him more impatient. As I look back, I can imagine how rough that must have been on Dick. But at the time I was jealous of the closeness he and Dad built up from working together day by day. It came out on one occasion, when Dad had some sort of cerebral spasm. He was in a Guaranty Trust Company board meeting and started to say something, but he couldn't get the words out. That sort of episode isn't uncommon in old people. It can be a prelude to a stroke but Dad didn't have one. When he recovered his power of speech after a few minutes, he went out to a telephone, called Dick, and asked him to come and pick him up. I felt that as a real blow. I kept wondering, "Why didn't he call me?" I thought maybe he had tried and I hadn't been there. But I went and checked my secretary's telephone log, and no call had come.

Dad was extremely proud of Dick, and Dick was very close-mouthed about the details of his operation. There was nothing I could do but stay out of their way. Here I was, trying to keep IBM running with reasonable consistency in the face of vast growth, traveling constantly, dealing with tremendous numbers of people, and yet having to walk on specially marked paths when it came to business abroad. Dad wanted World Trade to be as independent as possible, but, as anybody could see, it could never be completely independent. The two sides had to be coordinated and issues routinely came up, such as whether World Trade would manufacture a new machine itself or simply get it from our U.S. plants. I couldn't even get financial information about that side of our business. At one point I sent Dad an exasperated note:

I couldn't be more behind your plan of operating the World Trade Co. as an independent subsidiary. I will defend this concept & operation as long as I am in the IBM Co. because I realize the soundness of a separate team for foreign operations. Nevertheless a minimum of financial data about World Trade results is vital in order that our financial department can reply intelligently to outside queries about our company. Whenever this matter comes under discussion between [domestic] IBM people & yourself, it appears that you feel we are trying to usurp power from World Trade. Nothing could be further from our minds. On the other hand, if you cannot believe this & have peace of mind, the only thing to do is change the IBM team to suit yourself.

I don't recall whether he finally released the information we were after, but the fundamental dispute never got resolved. Dad remained convinced that I was out to trip my brother up. I told him over and over that he was wrong, and that I hoped Dick would head IBM after me someday. I told my brother that his success was mine and mine was his. I believed these things, but as I look back I see a competitiveness in my attitude toward Dick that Dad was aware of and I wasn't. It helps explain why in his old age he was working so hard to give my brother a sphere of his own.

Dad must have felt as if IBM wasn't entirely his anymore—but I didn't feel as if it was mine, either. Often I'd wonder whether I was having any real impact on the company at all. It's an odd thing, inheriting a one-man show from your father. When I traveled as president, groups of IBM people would often come to greet me at the airport, partly out of curiosity but mainly because that's what they'd always done for Dad. It brought back scenes from my boyhood—large IBM crowds waiting for our family on train platforms or as we docked at Liverpool harbor. Dad thrived on that sort of attention, but it embarrassed me, so I told people not to do it.

Part of my job was to inspect the local IBM office wherever I happened to be, and I only had to walk into one of these places to be reminded who IBM still belonged to. It was full of the old-fashioned practices and traditions that Dad had started. We still had our songs

and banners and slogans, our company newspapers, our
codes of behavior and dress, and a photograph of Dad in
every room. Some of these customs were starting to moderate on their own. Most branch managers had stopped
making the salesmen sing in the morning before going
out to call on customers, for example. I wanted to get rid
of the hoopla that seemed ridiculous for a mature corporation. But there was a limit to what I could do. Many of
these practices were just as dear to the people who
worked in those places as they were to Dad, and I didn't
want to offend them. Still, I needed something that would
signal that I was running IBM now, and that times had
changed. We were a computer company, not a punch-
card company; we were firmly in the 1950s, not the
1920s; we were leaders in a new field that would shape
the future.

I decided I could put my stamp on IBM through modern design. Dad had always paid close attention to IBM's
appearance. It was a key to his success: he understood
earlier than most American businessmen how important
it is to project a corporate image. Right at the beginning,
when the company was just hanging by its fingernails, he
improved the way its people and products and offices
looked and gave the company an aura of solidity that
raised morale and won customers. I figured that what
had worked for him would work for me. The computers
we were building were the very epitome of modern technology—on the inside. But on the outside they were
about as exciting as a collection of filing cabinets. Meanwhile everything else about IBM looked obsolete. I
wanted to make IBM's products, offices, buildings, brochures, and everything the public saw of our company
exciting and modern.

The inspiration for the design program came to me
during a stroll I took down Fifth Avenue in the early
1950s. I found myself attracted to a shop that had typewriters on sidewalk stands for passersby to try. The machines were done in different colors and had sleek
designs. I went inside and saw modern furniture and
bright colors that all worked together and gave the shop

a lively feel. The name over the door was Olivetti. A few months later an old family friend, the general manager of IBM Holland, mailed me a thick envelope in which I found two bundles of brochures and photographs. A small note explained that the first was a collection of Olivetti advertisements and sales literature, as well as photographs of their headquarters, plants, sales offices, employee housing, and products. The second bundle was of similar material from IBM. My Dutch friend suggested that all I had to do was to lay these out on the floor in two columns and I'd see IBM had to improve. I tried it and he was right: the Olivetti material was filled with color and excitement and fit together like a beautiful picture puzzle. Ours looked like directions on how to make bicarbonate of soda.

I carried that envelope with me to a conference for IBM executives in late 1954. It was at an old resort in the Poconos that my father liked. I knocked on the door of Dad's suite during a quiet hour and said, "Can I show you something?" I laid the materials out for him on a large table. "I think we can do even better than these people if we just get our designers to raise their sights a little," I said. I didn't press the point because Dad had personally approved every single product and building in the IBM brochures. He looked at the Olivetti things and the IBM things and said quietly, "I see what you mean. What do you intend to do?"

I told him I wanted to hire the best young industrial designer I knew. His name was Eliot Noyes, and I had first met him during the war when he'd been head of the Air Force glider program. I'd run across him again years later, when he designed a good-looking new typewriter for IBM. Eliot was a compact guy with thick glasses who seemed extremely unassertive and easygoing, but he had strong ideas about what did and didn't belong in a product's design. Basically, he believed that machines should look like what they are, not be dressed up in phony streamlining or frills. The same principle extended to architecture, in which Eliot was also trained.

The first project I put him on was the ground floor of

IBM's World Headquarters. Eliot came to New York and we looked at it together. The place was a terrible eyesore and projected a split personality. If you looked in the window on the Fifty-seventh Street side of the building, you saw the Defense Calculator—a set of drab gray cabinets in a large room with dark carpets and yellow drapes. But if you walked around the corner onto Madison Avenue and went in the main lobby, you found yourself back in the 1920s. Dad had it decorated to suit his taste, and it was like the first-class salon on an ocean liner. It had the Oriental rugs he loved and black marble pillars trimmed with gold leaf. Lining the walls were punch-card machines and time clocks on display, cordoned off by velvet ropes hooked to burnished brass posts.

Our IBM would look dramatically different. The new 702 was scheduled to be installed in the lobby the following summer; we decided that we'd use its unveiling to make a splash. We covered the windows on the street and closed off the lobby behind the receptionist with beaverboard. It stayed like that all spring while we got the place ready. Dad had given his approval in theory, but once he was barred from his beloved lobby he became terribly uneasy. He'd walk into the building every morning and look at that beaverboard barrier. Then he'd say to me, "Why can't I get in there?" If I'd let him, he probably would have vetoed the whole project.

The new Data Processing Center was modern, spare, and very dramatic. Eliot made the floor completely white. He made the walls a vivid red. He put up understated signs that read "IBM 702" in silver on the red wall. It was a beautiful presentation for anybody who was interested in modern design. The product made the statement, not the surroundings.

Before we opened the lobby to the public we asked Father down to see it. He had a whole coterie of guys following him with notebooks as he walked through. He looked at the 702, which was done in the standard gray finish trimmed with chrome, set against the red wall as a background. Dad kept looking at the wall, then back at the computer, then back at the wall. Finally I said, "Dad, what do you think of it?"

"I like it," he said. "I like it a lot. I particularly like that wall. That wall is painted. If any of you fellows should ever decide that you don't like it, you can change it overnight." This compliment, while left-handed, was good enough for me. I kept the wall the way it was. We opened the doors the next day to a hundred reporters and photographers, and the day after that the heads of forty railroads from all over America came at our invitation to spend a morning learning about the new computer. The Data Processing Center generated enormous excitement. Like the SSEC and the 701 that had preceded it in the window, the 702 was actually a working machine. Customers who wanted to rent computer time would simply bring their data in, and we kept the computer running around the clock. If you went by on Madison Avenue in the middle of the night you would see it behind the big plate-glass windows, tended by well-dressed technicians in its brightly lit room.

Working with Noyes was quite an education. He came from an old Boston family and had a real streak of Yankee independence. When I offered him a big job as director of all of IBM's architectural and industrial design, he turned me down flat. "I'll work with you, not for you," he said. "The only way I can do this job right is to have full access to top management." So we made an arrangement whereby he pledged a major part of his time to IBM, and I named him consultant director of design. The next thing he straightened me out on was my idea of giving IBM a recognizable style. I wanted the factories, products, and sales offices all done in such a way that a person could look at any of them and say instantly, "That's IBM!" But Noyes said this would be self-defeating. If we tried to fix a single, uniform corporate image, it would eventually become tired and dated. Instead, he suggested that IBM's theme be simply the best in modern design. Whenever we needed something built or decorated, we would commission the best architects, designers, and artists, and give them a relatively free hand to explore new ideas in their own styles. As it turned out, Noyes was a fantastic judge of talent, and the people he found for us were as great a contribution as the award-winning products and buildings he designed himself.

We needed architects in particular, because we were just about to begin the greatest factory expansion in IBM history. By 1955 our factories in both Endicott and Poughkeepsie were overflowing with almost ten thousand employees each. In the nearby communities of Owego and Kingston we were building huge satellite plants to house ten thousand more workers for our military work. Still, we needed more manufacturing, and I didn't want it all in these places. We were already in danger of turning them into company towns and driving other employers out. So we began a great movement west.

Dad had extended our business across America by incessant traveling in trains and cars, but he liked to stay close to his factories, and for that reason he kept them near New York. But I was a pilot, and I'm sure that the Midwest and California seemed much less distant to me than they did to T.J. We decided to build major plants in Rochester, Minnesota, which is the home of the Mayo Clinic, and San Jose. We envisioned each place to be another Endicott—an IBM center complete with a factory and a school and an engineering lab; only the design would be different.

Eero Saarinen was the architect Eliot chose for Rochester. It was the first great test of his idea that we should hire top people, because Saarinen was already famous and quite expensive. He designed us a complex of connecting buildings laid out in a checkerboard pattern around gardens and courtyards. It was both beautiful and practical, and got attention in all the architecture magazines. That was pleasing, but what really sold me was the fact that the plant was completed on time and under budget. To me this proved that hiring a good architect is good business.

The San Jose plant got us into the magazines too. The architect there was a Californian named John Bolles. He designed a set of low-slung H-shaped buildings in the new "campus" style. They were set around a plaza with reflecting pools, a footbridge, and modern sculptures. Bright colored metal panels fastened to the walls made the place lively, and the employees could sit on the terrace and eat lunch with a view of the mountains in the distance.

That plant has a small place in history as the first computer factory in the San Jose area. I remember going out to buy the land, a 180-acre walnut grove. I had told our real estate manager, "We have to build quickly or we'll be in tough shape." He met me at the airport and said, "We can take possession any time we want. But it'll cost you an extra eight hundred thousand dollars if we do it in the next five months."

"What!" I said. "Why is that?"

"Because that's what the walnut crop is worth."

I was trying not to get us financially overextended so I decided to wait until the farmer harvested his walnuts. Then we put up our plant. There were a few other companies around, mainly defense contractors like Lockheed, and we were planting the seeds of what later became Silicon Valley.

CHAPTER 22

My father knew that he was vulnerable to criticism for staying on the job as long as he had. He had set IBM's retirement age at sixty-five, and yet here he was, more than eighty years old, still taking his salary and a percentage of the profits, pulling in over a thousand dollars a day. He made a point of never bringing up his age or his health, and although he was less and less active each year, no shareholder ever challenged him on whether he was still earning his pay, because the record spoke for itself. My friend Robert Galvin of Motorola had a philosophy about this. He told me, "The founder of a business has the right to stay on until he dies. He can take all sorts of privileges and enjoy all sorts of perquisites. But those who succeed him, whether they belong to his family or not, do not have the same right." Galvin had been thinking about the question because he was in the process of taking over Motorola from his own father, and I used him as my guide. Whether having Dad around was good or bad for me I can't really judge. At times it was quite difficult to refrain from saying, "For God's sake, Dad, I'm running this thing now," because I felt terribly frustrated. But on the other hand, as long as he was still chief executive I never had to bear full responsibility. I discussed my important decisions with him and always felt him there as a backstop.

Toward the end of his life Dad would disappear from the office for weeks at a time. He loved to take long, practically aimless trips around the United States. Dad always felt best when he was on the move. He'd get Mother and his chauffeur and some suitcases and drive as far as Chicago, or they'd start from San Francisco and

drive eastward, visiting IBM offices all along the way and
every night sitting down to a "family dinner" with the
local group from IBM. Dad always spoke at these gatherings, saying how grateful he was to Mother and remi-
niscing about how the two of them had traveled together
more than a million miles. "We've never really been away
from home, because we've always been right in the IBM
family," he'd say. Mother would sit by his side smiling
sweetly, and she'd sometimes tug on his coattail if he
went on too long. She never said more than a simple
thank you herself.

I never knew what to expect when Dad went off on a
trip. One of the eccentricities that made him difficult was
his conviction that he could pick talent just by looking at
a man. At every dinner he went to there would be a
receiving line and he and Mother would stand there while
Dad shook hands with everybody—even if there were five
hundred people. There would always be a secretary
standing opposite, unobtrusively, with a notebook. When
Dad met a man he thought looked like a fine, square-cut
fellow, he'd nod slightly, and the secretary would seek
the man out. "Mr. Watson would like to have your name,
your position, and where you live," he'd say. Dad would
often send the man to us in New York. This worked more
often than not, but when it didn't it was a headache both
for the man and for me.

During his travels Dad would sometimes send a memo
expressing his worry about the expenses IBM was running up in the field; sometimes he'd visit a customer and
get embroiled in trying to help a local office close a sale.
One episode started when he paid a call on the executives
of a Miami bank. Over lunch they mentioned they were
thinking of replacing one or two IBM machines with specialized banking equipment made by somebody else. This
was a routine sales problem being handled by our local
office. But the prospect of IBM's losing a rental to a competitor upset Dad a lot. He sent me an urgent three-page
single-spaced letter and pointed out, "this has caused me
to put forth greater efforts in connection with one particular machine application than I have ever done before in

all my years with the company." Happily, I was able to tell Dad that we were about to announce new banking equipment that would do exactly what the customer wanted, and the account was saved.

Digging into local situations is something every good executive does on occasion, but I didn't like to see my father get so upset. I would drop everything until I could reassure him, but eventually I ran out of patience. Early in 1955 a woman wrote Mother a letter saying her husband had been fired unjustly from IBM. The man was a low-level manager I'll call Smith, who had been caught doing something wrong and had been fired. Mother was upset, and showed the letter to Dad, who became so angry about the apparent injustice that he felt ill and had to go to bed.

It seemed to me there was much more at issue than our handling of one employee. My parents were worried that with Dad less active, IBM's management was losing the concern for the individual he had tried to build into it. I was convinced that wasn't so, and sat down to explain on paper to both of them the role I wanted Dad to play. It was the longest letter I ever sent them—twelve pages—and I poured into it everything I thought about IBM, our prospects and problems, and my accomplishments as president. I wanted to convince him, once and for all, to spare himself and leave the running of the business to me.

All of the thoughts which you, Dad, have expressed to me . . . about the possibilities of things not going well in IBM—the fact that we must watch expenses—the fact that if the business starts slipping, it's hard to stop—these are all facts which I knew about before you mentioned them. In truth, they are possibilities which I go to bed with every night. If they should come about my reputation as a businessman is vanished—my reputation as a successful son is finished. No wonder I think about them frequently. I have got to make good.

There are literally hundreds of incidents

throughout the year like the Smith situation. That Mrs. Smith saw fit to write you, Mother, is unfortunate. But before she did, the matter had been fairly & well settled. Therefore I don't believe we should panic or be rushed into decisions because of a dishonest man who has been fired. I would tend to discount his threats and allegations. Let's suppose though that Mrs. Smith had not written you & let's suppose we handled the matter as we did. Isn't it vital that we be capable as a team of handling these matters well because you both can't know of all of them nor can I. If the present team . . . isn't operating to your satisfaction, I believe you should make adjustments until you have a group in which you have complete faith—a group who can give you peace of mind about the IBM Co.

Nothing would please me more or help me more than to have your advice on every matter which comes to my attention—much of the time, I'm somewhat in the dark. . . . [But] I don't share your fears about IBM. I believe the company is as strong as it has ever been—with as competent a management as ever, and as well run as ever! This is because you have trained me to think along the lines you think and because you have permitted me to pick a team of the strongest men in the business.

If I am right in my beliefs about IBM, then it ought to be possible for the builder of this great business to drop around and chat with us about our really important problems: Our Department of Justice case—how much of our capital investment should go into electronics—how we should improve the Time division—how we can find and upgrade more executive possibilities from the field. This rather than getting involved in criticizing . . . our operations as in the Smith matter or the general administration of the company.

Can you not by looking at our annual Report . . . convince yourself that we are not doing too bad a job? Can you not take some pride in the fact that the job is being done by T. J. Watson trained men? Can you not find some personal satisfaction and peace of mind in watching this wonderful business enterprise which you have built, grow on to greater heights & move forward on all fronts with a continuing fine profit directed by your team?

Love to you both,
Tom

As I look back, much of this was beside the point, an example of my own desire to have total command. Because on the big issues affecting IBM's future, Dad already was deferring to me, serving more as mentor than as boss. He had pretty much stopped fighting with me, but it took me a while to notice. He'd gotten over his aversion to debt, for example, and with his permission Williams and I increased IBM's borrowing at a rate roughly equal to our growth. We ended up owing the Prudential well over a third of a billion dollars, all of which was amply covered by the profits rolling in from new equipment built by our expanded factories. Dad also let me make dramatic improvements in IBM's pension and benefit plans. The changes were in line with his idea after the war of relieving IBM people of "fear for the care of themselves and their families," but they went far beyond what he had envisioned. The pensions he'd put in were advanced for their day, but the most any employee could retire on was $3,300 a year, depending solely on the number of years he or she had worked for the company. Under the new, alternative formula, which was more in keeping with the times, we took salary as well as service into account, and a retiree could collect as much as $25,000 a year. IBM also became one of the first companies in America to offer major medical insurance.

But the concession that surprised me the most was Dad's letting me persuade him to give stock options for the first time. He was always conservative about anything having to do with IBM's stock. Although he never owned more than about five percent of IBM—which includes stock he put in family trusts or gave to other family members, as well as his personal holdings—Dad always operated as though the company belonged to him. In earlier years the very mention of selling more stock would sometimes send him into a rage. Dad never issued any options and didn't believe in them, but he urged IBM employees and everyone else he met to invest in the stock. Some of the men who made sandwiches behind the counter at Halper's drugstore next door to our headquarters, where I had coffee as a young salesman before the war, ended up with fortunes. But in spite of the dim view he took of options, Dad stopped objecting as soon as I told him they had become accepted practice and that we couldn't hang on to our best executives without them. The options we gave were liberal, about five times the employee's salary, so that executives making $70,000 got $350,000 in options that were probably worth seven million dollars eventually. In the first two rounds more than fifty people got them, and each one ended up a wealthy man.

The only issue we still fought about was antitrust. After the government lawsuit was filed in 1952, IBM spent the last year of Truman's administration and the first couple of years of Eisenhower's in negotiations with the Justice Department. I was determined to settle the suit before it went to trial. Periodically our lawyers would have me come to the federal courthouse in Manhattan and sit at a long table with the Justice Department lawyers and the judge. He was a short, raspy voiced man named David Edelstein, only a few years older than I. This was the biggest antitrust case he'd ever had and he was determined to do an exemplary job. But he never had much to say to me, and neither did the prosecutors, and I always thought those meetings accomplished very little. Whether there were legal reasons they couldn't talk, or whether they just thought I was stupid and not worth their time, I could never tell. I always had the impression that they were more comfortable talking to our lawyers.

Dad knew we were negotiating, but in some part of his mind he was still adamantly opposed to signing a consent decree. One day he showed up at IBM earlier than usual while I was getting ready to go to the courthouse. He was sitting at his desk, riffling through his mail to see what was interesting and what he had to do in the way of chores, and he must have thought, "Tom! I can see Tom!" So at about nine o'clock the frightful little buzzer he had in my office rang. My appointment downtown was for nine-thirty. But I never ignored that buzzer, so I went up the stairs to his office.

"Good morning, son!" he said. "Sit down." I sat down and waited for a minute while he kept reading his mail.

"Say, Dad, I have an appointment."

"What's that?"

"I have an appointment. I've got to go downtown."

"That's interesting. Why don't you bring me up to date? What are you going downtown for?"

"It's on this antitrust matter. I'm going down to talk to the judge."

He instantly went into a rage. "You're totally incompetent to do that! You have no background! What do you mean, you're going down to talk to the judge?"

So I said, "Now, look, Dad. I've been talking to the judge every week down there—you've known all about it —and we're going to talk some more today."

"Now, young man, I've been mixed up in antitrust all my life. I know all about antitrust. I know about those people down at the Justice Department. It's awfully easy to say the wrong thing down there."

I was forty-one years old, but he really bloodied the walls with me. I said, "Dad, I'm going to be ten minutes late if I leave right now. So you either tell me you want me to go, and I'll leave, or tell me you don't and I'll call and cancel."

He said, "No, you go. But don't you make any decisions!"

There was a car waiting for me downstairs and I went and got in. I was so upset that I was shaking. I got to the courthouse and sat down at that long table. I didn't say very much to anybody because I was so tense. Then into the back of the room came Dad's personal secretary. I thought, "Oh, God, Dad's had a stroke and died." But the secretary simply passed me a little slip of paper torn out of a "THINK" notebook. It said

> 100%
> Confidence
> Appreciation
> Admiration
> Love
> Dad

It was my father's way of telling me, "I realize I shouldn't be throwing you around at your age."

The relief was so great that my eyes filled with tears. The judge said, "I take it you've had some bad news."

"No," I said, "as a matter of fact, it's rather good news. It's just emotional news."

Eventually Dad let me persuade him that the prudent thing to do was sign the consent decree. Our lawyers signed on behalf of IBM in January 1956. Settling that case was one of the best moves we ever made, because it cleared the way for IBM to keep expanding at top speed. With Dad the consent decree was always a sore spot and we never discussed it again. But there was no longer any doubt for either of us that I was running the show.

In retrospect I think Dad may have felt relieved to have our long struggle at an end. I wish I'd noticed it at the time, because it would have made me go easier on him. One thing I kept trying to persuade him to do was ease up on IBM's liquor ban, even though I knew he'd cared passionately about that issue his whole life. I said, "Dad, we hold these IBM dinners, and the people come half an hour or forty-five minutes ahead of time, and they have to drink orange juice. It's an awkward time. Maybe we should have white wine during that period."

"You can't temporize with that!" he said. "You start with white wine and the next thing you know . . ."

"Look," I said, "let's be realistic. What are people doing now? They come to a banquet and one in every ten of them takes a room in the hotel. He puts a nice array of booze up there and everybody goes and fortifies himself before the party. That's not so great, either."

Dad seemed determined not to budge. But the following week there was a large meeting of IBM engineers and scientists in Florida, and both he and I were scheduled to go. I'd been traveling and arrived a bit late. When I walked into the banquet hall I thought I detected a slightly louder tone than usual. They showed me to the head table and I was bending over to kiss Dad when I saw that they had wine! In ice buckets, and not just beside his table but all the tables. I got McDowell, the chief of engineering, off to the side and said, "Wally, what in hell is this?"

"Your father called me twenty minutes before the dinner and said 'Why don't we have wine for everybody?' So I ordered wine."

When I made a speech I said, "This is a precedent-breaking dinner." There was a roar of laughter. But later on I got Dad in his suite and asked him why he had done it.

He said, "You made such a point about having wine. You're young, you understand these things, and I'd hate to be an old fuddy-dud. So I changed it!" Of course, he knew that news of that dinner would travel to every corner of IBM instantly, and it was going to take me weeks to put any rhyme or reason back into our liquor policy. I was amazed. It was the first time Dad had shown the mischievous side of his personality in maybe twenty-five years. Now that I was becoming the boss, he was playing a prank by acting like my yes-man.

Three months later, in May 1956, Dad formally passed the job of chief executive on to me. He made the gesture spontaneously and with a great sense of dignity, which meant a lot to me because it was the first promotion I ever got from him without a fight. After the board voted its approval I went to a bank and bought a stack of five-dollar gold pieces. I handed them out to the directors over lunch, and gave a speech about Dad's years being the golden years of IBM. Then came a press conference, and the *New York Times* picture the next morning of Dad and me shaking hands. He made a point of telling the newspapers, "I am not retiring. I simply want to spend more time with IBM World Trade Corporation." Within a week Dad made a similar move with Dick, promoting him to chief executive of World Trade.

I somehow had it in my head that Dad would stay around indefinitely, that he'd be by my side as a kind of consultant, just as he had become during the past year. But his health had begun to fail. He'd had an uneasy time that winter in Florida. He couldn't eat right because of his stomach ulcers. For as long as I could remember, Dad had trouble with his stomach. He was constantly suffering from indigestion and taking bicarbonate of soda. As a boy I used to listen to him let out tremendous belches behind closed doors and then go on about his business. Sometimes he had trouble with bleeding as well, but never any pain. The idea that he had ulcers was intolerable to him, because in his old-fashioned way of looking at things, the only people who got stomach ulcers were people who drank. He forgot that for twenty-five years he'd smoked cigars one after another, and he never accepted the idea that ulcers can be brought on by stress.

Dad's doctor was named Arthur Antenucci. He was a great diagnostician whose patients included the Duke of Windsor. After he looked at X rays of Dad's stomach he told me, "Your father's stomach looks like the battlefield of the Marne." The tension of Dad's career had pretty much pulled him apart inside. Antenucci said that the buildup of scar tissue was so bad that the exit to Dad's stomach was gradually closing up. That was why he couldn't eat. A simple operation would have remedied it, but Dad chose not to have it done. He hated the idea of going under the knife as much as he hated the idea of flying in an airplane. He'd never had an operation, not even to fix the painful hernias he'd had for half his life. He just kept putting on his truss every morning and never complained. Antenucci warned Dad that the scar tissue problem could kill him if it turned into a total blockage, and for a while Dad agreed to get his stomach fixed. But then he changed his mind. He and Mother were at the dinner table one night and Dad said, "I don't think I'm going through with that operation."

"But Tom," she said, "you told Dr. Antenucci you would."

"That's true," said my father. "But you know, as he was leaving the room, I could just see him sharpening his knives."

Without the surgery his digestion began to fail, and my father slowly but surely starved. Over the course of a year he lost twenty or thirty pounds, and by the spring of 1956 he looked very frail. The only thing he'd let Antenucci do was give him blood transfusions. For the last several months of his life, Dad would go down to Roosevelt Hospital about every three weeks and get new blood. It would pep him up for a while, but then he'd hit a period of exhaustion until the next transfusion.

It's strange to me that a man as powerful as Dad should have been so superstitious. But he was totally lucid when he decided against surgery, and none of us felt we had a right to intrude. The old man had bursts of amazing vigor right up to the end. I will never forget the last time I saw him before an IBM audience. It was at a sales meeting in Washington that March. There were perhaps five hundred people assembled in a large hotel auditorium. Father got there late. The man running the meeting spotted him in the back of the room and said, "I see that we have the honor of Mr. Watson's presence. Mr. Watson, won't you come up and take the floor?" Dad was a wispy old man of eighty-two and he started carefully down the inclined aisle toward the stage. The men jumped to their feet and were clapping and shouting. The more they clapped and the farther he got down the aisle, the more erect he became. He stood up straighter and straighter and walked faster and faster until he finally got to the steps leading up to the stage. He went up them with such a surge of energy that he seemed to take them two at a time. The thrill of salesmen's accolades was so great that Dad shed about thirty years on the way down that aisle. He grabbed the podium and made a very stirring speech, punching his fist into his hand and telling the men how they must take advantage of the great opportunities before us, and how IBM was going on forever.

I think that by the time he turned the company over to me, he must have felt the hand of death on his shoulder. Perhaps that was the only thing that could have made him decide to step down. But I also think he willed his death by refusing medical treatment. If Dick and I hadn't been ready, if he'd still felt IBM depended entirely on him, maybe he'd have risked surgery and survived a few years more. But he could see that I was running the business well, and he could see Dick gaining more and more recognition abroad. I suppose he thought, "It has been a good life. I guess it's about the time." Within a month it was obvious that he was going to die. It was a sweltering June in New York, and Dad stayed up at his country house in New Canaan. The 1956 election campaign was on, and he took a lot of pleasure in watching it on television and laughing at the way politicians repeat themselves. He was totally lucid, not in any pain, but he had no strength left because of his inability to eat. He got more blood transfusions, which would briefly perk him up, but then he'd slip back.

I visited him early in the month before going up to Newport, Rhode Island, to get ready for the Newport-to-Bermuda yacht race. I had a good crew picked out and had my boat all set to go. Dad had been a little ill when I left, but seemed steady enough. The race was to start the next day. But my mother phoned, and I took the call at the end of the dock. She said, "Tom, I just want to tell you, I don't think you ought to go. I can't tell you why, because your father's not terribly ill, but you shouldn't." I went back to my boat, designated the senior guy as captain, and said, "You take the boat to Bermuda."

When I got back to New Canaan, Dad was still perfectly lucid. He said, "Oh, son, that's too bad, you shouldn't have to interrupt your race."

"I just wanted to be around," I said.

My brother and sisters were also at the house. Dad

was lying in bed and had each of us in for a long visit. One of us would go in and talk, and then Mother would say, "Why don't you let him rest a little." After a time the next would go in. Dad knew he was going to die, but he never said, "This is how I want you to take care of your mother," or anything like that. Instead he was just renewing his contact with each of his children. I had a long, pleasant conversation with him that seemed to cover everything under the sun. He talked about the confidence he had built up in me over the ten years we had worked together, and how he knew that the company was going to move ahead rapidly in the right direction and become much, much bigger. Then somehow we got onto the subject of antique furniture. He said, "If you ever see a piece of furniture you like, buy it, even if you don't think you can afford it. Because if you don't buy it, you'll wish for the rest of your life that you had."

Dad had a chance to talk to all of us. But the next day he lost consciousness. It was a Sunday, and we had a doctor come out to the house. He said Dad was suffering from heart failure and got an ambulance to drive him to New York. Meanwhile I called Antenucci, who had a house on Shelter Island. I was piqued at him, because in those days I didn't understand, as I do now, that many doctors set aside time when they're going to work—when they'll go out in the middle of the night or do anything else that's necessary—and other times when they're going to rest. Antenucci was in a rest period. He arranged a room for Dad at Roosevelt Hospital and had an assistant greet him at the door, but he didn't come in until the next day.

It was too late to operate for the stomach blockage that was causing Dad's problem. Antenucci told me, "Your father is going to die." Dad had regained consciousness, but he began drifting in and out of it. We'd go in to see him and sometimes he'd recognize us and sometimes he wouldn't. I remember his stomach got swollen; you could see it through the sheets. Telegrams and messages began pouring in from all over the world. President Eisenhower tried to call, and when he found out Dad couldn't talk, he sent a message. It said something like, "You have had a terrific life, but you have many more things to give, so get well soon." I went in and read it to Dad several times and he seemed to hear it.

Antenucci was doing things that upset me, putting tubes into Dad and so on. Dad obviously was unhappy about it because he made noises to indicate he didn't like it. So I said, "For God's sake, the man is dying. Let him die in peace. There's no chance of him surviving, is there?"

"No," Antenucci said, "but we doctors still have to do what we can."

"Well, you know, I've talked to my mother and the other children. We think you ought to try to keep him comfortable but not stick things in him anymore." So they stopped.

A couple of days went by. From time to time each of us would go to the church up the street and say a prayer, but not with any idea that Dad would live. It was a joyous and very sad time. This old gentleman had, in a variety of ways, commanded tremendous love and respect from all five of us. I can't characterize anybody's grief but my own, but I felt as if a very big piece of my life was being pulled away. He was the foundation on which I had been standing for forty-two years. I had an awful hollow feeling about the future, how it would be without this man I had fought with so. Underneath it all, nobody ever had a greater influence on anyone else than T. J. Watson had on me.

I'll never forget the moment of his death. All our lives we build up a tremendous desire to live. Jumping away from cars, running out of burning buildings. That instinct has been passed along in the human race for millions of years. I had never seen this will to live demonstrated the way I did now. Here he lay, head somewhat up, the room brightly lit, eyes closed, no oxygen mask, Mother and all of us present. He'd take a deep breath. Then there'd be nothing. Then he'd take another deep breath. Each breath during those last few minutes seemed to come harder than the last. The period between breaths became longer. Finally he took a long breath, sort of a shuddering breath, and it went out. As though to say, That's it, all the cares of the world have departed. And he never breathed again.

We sat there a few moments. Mother started to cry. I guess we were all crying. The nurse came, and then the doctor, who felt his pulse and said he was dead.

I think I went back to my office with my brother to check on the funeral arrangements. Dick and I had agreed that the greatest tribute we could give him was to make the funeral as well run as any IBM meeting during his life. We had already made the plan and conferred with other IBMers. First, telegrams went out to every IBM location and all of Dad's friends. We shut all the plants, all over the world, and had the flags lowered to half mast. Any employee who wanted to come to New York for the funeral was given time off to do so, although we didn't offer to do it at company expense because they'd have taken it as a signal that they were all expected to come. We had crape-edged tributes to Dad put up in the lobby windows at headquarters, and Dad's obituary in the *Times* ran four columns long and quoted a statement from President Eisenhower that said, "In the passing of Thomas J. Watson, the nation has lost a truly fine American—an industrialist who was first of all a great citizen and a great humanitarian. I have lost a good friend, whose counsel was always marked by a deep-seated concern for people."

Dad wanted a funeral that was old-fashioned and formal—an open coffin with friends coming by, and then a great service at Brick Presbyterian Church on Park Avenue, where his old friend Paul Austin Wolfe was the minister. Dick and I arranged all that. We dressed in our dark clothes and went into that chapel, just Dick and I, to spend a few minutes at the open coffin. The first people to turn up were Spyros Skouras Sr. and Bernard Gimbel, both great businessmen and rough tough guys. Gimbel had built his department store and made it famous, and Skouras had started out by organizing a chain of movie theaters in St. Louis and rose to become head of Twentieth Century-Fox. He'd been very kind to Dad toward the end of his life, sending him a sound movie projector and then every month or two a movie Dad wanted to see. The two of them came in and said, "Don't be upset about his death, boys. You feel a great vacuum now, but think of what he did with his life. Look at that face and remember where it came from. Think of the farm, think of the Cash Register company." Their words meant a lot to me because they were self-made men and they knew Dad's history. There were hundreds of people more—the UN secretary general and diplomats and heads of businesses and plain people who worked at IBM.

When the time came, we closed up the coffin and went over to the church. His funeral was on the first day of summer, a hot New York day with a steady rain. Brick Church was filled to overflowing. There were people standing in the vestibule and more were seated in an auxiliary chapel and still more in the basement. We had special sound systems set up for them all to hear what Dr. Wolfe had to say. He gave a powerful eulogy about the determination and great simplicity that enabled Dad to succeed, and about his devotion to people. Then the service was over and only the family went out to Sleepy Hollow Cemetery to bury Dad. He had bought a plot there during the war, when Olive and I lost our first baby, and now we buried my father next to our son. In his eulogy, Dr. Wolfe had quoted something from the Bible for Dick's and my benefit: "Now the days of David drew nigh that he should die; and he charged Solomon his son, saying, I go the way of all the earth: be thou strong therefore, and shew thyself a man." But I didn't feel like King Solomon at that graveyard, burying my father; I felt shattered.

I took Olive and two of our daughters down to Bermuda. We stayed at a beach club and rented motorcycles so that we could really get to know the island. After a couple of nights the shock of Dad's death finally hit me, and I had a horrible allergic reaction, similar to what Dick had had for years. My throat swelled up and I couldn't breathe. Olive had to get a doctor in a hurry. He

gave me a shot of adrenaline, which kept me from chok-
ing to death. But I had terrible rashes that just wouldn't
go away. When I got back to New York I went to see
Antenucci, who told me I was having a psychosomatic
reaction to grief.

I was worried about how my mother would adjust to
Dad's death. Right away she'd told my brother and me,
"I'm not going to be able to live without your father."
But after the funeral some of her strength began to show
through. I asked her, "What do you want to do, Mom?
What's your plan?"

She said, "I want to sell that house." She hated their
Manhattan townhouse. It was palatial, and from her
point of view it was a huge headache. She ran it for Dad
and ran it well, but housekeeping and entertaining on a
grand scale never really interested her. Dick and I put the
place on the market and within four hours it sold at the
asking price. I called Mother and said the house had been
sold. That worried her. She said, "It must be a signal
from your father. What do you think it means?"

"Mother, it's affirmative, not negative. The buyer
didn't haggle about anything."

That was a big load off my mind. She had plenty of
time before she had to get out, and my sisters took her to
Spain and Ireland as a diversion. I visited her for six days
in Ireland and found her in remarkably good spirits. She
was staying near Ashford Castle in a lovely part of the
country, and she'd rented an old-fashioned high-back
Bentley with a chauffeur, a very articulate Irishman
whom she got along with well. As always Mother wanted
to see everything and learn local history, so each day
they'd sally forth into the countryside. She was particularly taken with the beautiful ten-foot stone walls that
surround some of the buildings built by the British, and
she pointed them out for me to admire. The chauffeur
said, "You have to remember, Ma'am, that during the
famine a man would work a full day for a bowl of soup
and that is how these fences got built." My own grandfather had fled from that famine, and Mother said less
about the stonework after that.

When I came back to New York, I tried going to the office. But I found myself too upset to work. Everything about IBM reminded me of Dad. I'd spent four years rearranging the place so I could run it instead of him, but that made no difference. I decided the only medicine strong enough to make me forget all this would be to spend time with my own son. I decided to take him away for a week, and I picked Alaska because I thought it would be thrilling for Tom. I wanted to give him something to remember—I wanted to take him to the edge of civilization and show him glaciers and mountains and the Bering Strait, where I'd come across from Russia in a Soviet cargo plane when his mother and I had only been married a year.

Before I left one of our directors came to see me. He was Gilbert Scribner, the senior partner in a Chicago real estate company, and a man of influence. Scribner was head of our compensation committee, and he said to me, "What do you want to be paid?"

It hadn't occurred to me that we would have such a discussion. I expected to be paid what my old man was paid. I said, "Well, Gilbert, equal pay for equal work. I want precisely what my father got, with the same profit sharing."

He said, "Your father started this business from nothing! He had to go out and call on banks! He had to really do things!"

This made me furious. I said, "Dad has been less active in recent years and we are sustaining growth here of sixteen percent. I take it that's what you directors want to have continue?" He said he would have to go back to the committee.

It was a very tough position to be put in with Dad just dead. But I thought that to start in by being a patsy would make it impossible for me to manage the board. It never even occurred to me that my position was the slightest bit unreasonable. I was affronted that the question had even been raised, and I left for Alaska without waiting to see what the board would decide.

Tom was at summer camp up in Maine. I got a plane

and a copilot from IBM, splitting the cost with the company because I was planning on visiting our Alaska offices. We picked up Tom and his friend John Gaston at the Bar Harbor airport and headed west. This was a grueling trip to make in a small plane—we had a twin-engine Beechcraft that cruised very slowly, at about 160 miles an hour. It took us two days and about twenty-one hours of flight time to reach Canada's west coast. I was concentrating on Tom and his friend and the details of flying. Apart from that, my mind was a blank. I never thought about Dad for the entire week we spent in Alaska. But my sense of helplessness and grief seeped through in a hundred ways as I saw how people had to struggle to get along in that wild place. The argument I'd had with Gilbert Scribner also gnawed at me, and I kept calling Al Williams whenever I could find a phone.

The first place we stopped was Queen Charlotte Island, off the Canadian coast. I wanted to show Tom everything I could, and that island had a big lumber operation. We stayed in a little shack hotel run by the lumber company. For the first time in my life I saw how a living tree is trimmed and used as a derrick to lift and pile its neighbors as they are cut. Then we flew up the coast, got some fuel, and took the plane down low over the water in Glacier Bay. I didn't know if I'd ever get an opportunity to sail up that way, but we simulated it in the airplane. It was a beautiful day, with the sun coming off the glaciers and mountains, and the water was full of jagged ice. We stayed in Juneau and the next morning we went out and saw bears scooping salmon out of a nearby river. I remember it was a hot summer day, and as I watched the bears sitting on their tails in that cool water, I thought it probably felt nice. But there was something melancholy about the fish. The guide told us that when salmon come up the rivers to spawn, they're so old they're actually falling apart. They're decaying as they swim. They get up there somehow, lay their eggs, and die.

I couldn't have picked a better companion for this trip than Tom, who had inherited Olive's mildness and her gift for sympathy. Though he was only twelve years old and we didn't directly discuss Dad's death, he sensed the crisis I was going through, and having him there was a tremendous consolation. He was fascinated by wildlife, and took remarkable pictures of a moose during one of the side trips I arranged for him and his friend while I flew north to visit our sales office in Fairbanks.

The Fairbanks airport had a display of mammoth tusks, all thousands of years old, that had been dug out of the tundra. The local IBM manager came out to meet me, and he brought along a salesman who'd made quite a good record up there. The wall of the air terminal had a map showing part of Russia. I was so proud of the fact that I'd been there that I guess I started bragging about my war experiences and how we'd been stranded after nearly crashing our plane. I pointed to the map and said, "I stayed right over there! In Yakutsk!"

"My, my, isn't that interesting," the salesman answered in a very sarcastic way. Like some of the other IBM people I met in Alaska, this fellow had grit. I didn't get mad at him because I was glad to have the hint. I thought, "I'd better slow down. I'm sounding like a loudmouth."

We had a meeting that night at a restaurant on a lake. I remember being impressed because almost every house on the lake had a seaplane moored in front of it. It was the main means of transportation in this part of Alaska. At the meeting were maybe fifteen IBMers, mainly from railroad and defense installations, and some of them had brought their wives. The restaurant had only one room and a section had been curtained off for us. Everything went fine until it came time for my speech. I was just standing up when a floor show began on the other side of the curtain. It was a song-and-dance man, cracking jokes and making the audience laugh. I looked at the local manager and said, "I'd better wait till that guy sits down."

"No," he said. "All these people are busy. Some of them have children waiting at home. I think you should just go ahead." He was as tough with me as the salesman had been.

I wanted to say, "God, I can't do that." But it was one of those things you have to live with. I made my speech damn short, but I shouted that entertainer down, or at least spoke loud enough so that on our side of the curtain I made myself heard. Somehow Alaska was so far out of the loop that the fact that I was chief executive of a major corporation didn't seem so impressive—to anybody, including me. I found that was kind of a relief.

I went back and retrieved the boys, and then we flew across the Divide, a spine of mountains that cuts diagonally across the state. We needed fuel and stopped at a tiny airstrip, where I pulled the airplane up to a general store. They ran a hose out from the porch and filled the plane with gas. It struck me that this was the remotest place I'd been since Siberia. I wanted to go all the way up to Point Barrow, the northernmost town in the United States. But the Air Force was building the Distant Early Warning radar line, and the airport there was already full. We had to turn back at Kotzebue on the Bering Strait, just above the Arctic Circle. I was able to get the airplane high enough so that we could see the Soviet islands of Little Diomede and Big Diomede, not far from Anadyr, the last place I'd stopped in Siberia during the war. I told Tom all about it.

We flew back to Nome, two hundred miles to the south, and spent two nights at a hotel with a restaurant called the Bering Sea Café. I got to know the young man who ran it. He and his wife ate dinner with us the first night, and he asked the boys if they'd ever read Jack London stories about the Yukon. Tom said yes, and the hotelkeeper said, "How'd you like to go panning for gold?"

Tom's eyes got big as saucers. "Oh gosh," he said. "Great! But what'll we do it with?" The hotelkeeper peeled five bucks off a wad of cash and said, "Go down the street and bang on the door of the hardware store. Tell him I sent you down for a gold pan." Tom and the other boy made a beeline to the store and got a gold pan.

The next day the hotelkeeper took us way out in the country. We saw ptarmigans, which are a beautiful species of grouse that lives in cold climates. They're unusual because they have feathers on their legs, right down to their claws. Finally we got to a place where a man and his wife were working a claim using pressurized water and a sluice. As we drove up their little valley, we must have passed hundreds of thousands of dollars' worth of abandoned tractors, trailers, water pumps, cars, and trucks. We found the guy and his wife sitting on a couple of boxes with an open loaf of bread and some peanut butter between them. We talked a bit and I asked how their operation was going.

"We make a living out of it," he told me.

I said, "You know, when people think of gold mining, they think of something pretty big."

"Well," he said, "we've gone through a lot of stuff. You probably passed some of it coming in. We're doing well enough now, and we have one decent truck. We can go down to Seattle for the winter."

He was still evading my real question. "No," I said, "I mean, have you made any money?" They really hadn't. They were still hoping to hit that big nugget. Meanwhile Tom and his friend found gold in the stream—tiny flecks of it. We took a piece of Scotch tape and taped them to a card so we could see them. When we drove away I was thinking of the futility of the life this man and his wife had, eating their way up this bank, taking a little gold out, buying a truck, bringing the truck back, wearing it out, letting it rot, finding a little more gold, buying another truck, and so on.

By the end of seven days we were all exhausted. We spent the last night in a hotel in Anchorage, and I found Tom's friend John crying in his bed. The boy was homesick. I felt frustrated and helpless. I couldn't bring the boy's mother to him—he had no father, his mother was a widow—and I couldn't get him to his mother, so the situation was just impossible. The next day we left for home. We flew straight—from Anchorage to New York in twenty-two hours. I don't know how the copilot and I stood it. We flew home so rapidly that Tom and John had fresh trout to take to their mothers. We'd bought a mess of fish in Anchorage just before leaving.

The compensation committee finally met in September, after I was back in New York. They agreed I should be paid the same as Dad. Soon afterward, Gil Scribner came and said, "I suppose you are going to want my resignation."

"Not at all," I said.

"Ever since your father put me on this board—"

I said, "Gilbert, look. My father didn't put you on the board; *I* put you on the board. Everything that happens around here gets attributed to my father. But I met you on the Mutual Life Insurance board and admired you greatly, and you were very kind to me even though I was a newcomer. When Dad asked me to suggest someone as a director from Chicago, I gave him your name." My telling him this healed the rift between us, and Scribner remained a valued board member for many years.

CHAPTER 23

F ear of failure became the most powerful force in
my life. I think anybody who gets a job like mine,
unless he's stupid, must be a little bit afraid.
There is such a long way to fall. Yet the fear I felt
when I went back to IBM took me totally by surprise.
Before Dad died I was running the business and even
chafing at not getting full credit because he was around. I
didn't realize how much I still needed him emotionally. I
remember standing in the corridor outside my office soon
after I came back from Alaska, looking dumbly up the
stairs that led to his. Except for Dick's operation at
World Trade, the weight of IBM was now all on me; if
Dad hadn't died I could have been chief executive for
years and never felt so burdened.

I decided it would be foolish to act as though I could
totally take his place. Rather than move into his big,
wood-paneled suite, I kept my own office downstairs and
ran IBM from there—later we turned his office into a
library. I retired his title of chairman, keeping the one he
had given me: president. There was the problem of what
to do with his seat on the board; I solved that by asking
Mother to join. She had been at Dad's side for so long
that many IBM people felt a personal loyalty toward her
that I didn't want to lose.

The worst thing that can happen when a leader dies is
for his followers to lose their inspiration and carry on like
robots. I moved as fast as I could to prevent that. So
before the year was out I called the top one hundred or so
executives to a conference at Williamsburg, Virginia, and
distributed power and responsibility even more broadly
than before. In three days we transformed IBM so com-

pletely that almost nobody left that meeting with the same job he had when he arrived.

I picked Williamsburg because it is a historic place and this meeting was meant to be a kind of constitutional convention for the new IBM. Almost everybody came knowing a few details of what we were about to do, and you could feel the anticipation and excitement in that rented conference room. After the tumultuous events that had already taken place that year—the settling of our antitrust case, my promotion to chief executive, and Dad's death—everybody felt that this was the takeoff point. It was the first major meeting IBM had ever held without Dad present, and we knew how far we'd come from the days of his Hundred Percent Club meetings with their circus tents and banners and songs. Of the old guard, George Phillips was the only one at Williamsburg, and he was scheduled to retire the following month. There were a lot of young men and one young woman. My age and experience were typical of the people present —I was forty-two and I'd been in management barely a decade.

What we created was not so much a reorganization as the first top-to-bottom *organization* IBM ever had. It was largely the work of Dick Bullen, the young MBA I'd named as organizational architect the previous year. Under his plan we took the product divisions that we'd already established, tightened them up so that each executive had clearly defined tasks, and then turned the units loose to operate with considerable flexibility. These were IBM's arms and legs, so to speak. At the head of the corporation, to oversee plans and major decisions, we set up a six-man corporate management committee that consisted of me, Williams, LaMotte, my brother, Miller, and Learson. I gave each man responsibility for a major piece of IBM, while leaving myself free to roam across the whole company. Finally we superimposed a corporate staff that included experts in such areas as finance, manufacturing, personnel, and communications. Their task was to work as a kind of nervous system and keep our adolescent company from tripping all over itself, as had happened a few months earlier when we had two divisions unwittingly bidding against each other on the same tract of land for a factory.

By the mid-'50s just about every big corporation had adopted this so-called staff-and-line structure. It was modeled on military organizations going back to the Prussian army in Napoleonic times. In this sort of arrangement, line managers are like field commanders—their duties are to hit production targets, beat sales quotas, and capture market share. Meanwhile the staff is the equivalent of generals' aides—they give advice to their superiors, transmit policy from headquarters to the organization, handle the intricacies of planning and coordination, and check to make sure that the divisions attack the right objectives. Du Pont and General Motors began applying this system to business as early as the 1920s, but to the IBMers at Williamsburg in 1956 it was a revolution. Everybody in that conference room had been trained under my father in exactly the same way—we'd all started out as salesmen and we'd all been molded as line managers. The phrase you heard about a successful IBM executive was, "He knows how to get the donkey over the hill." We all knew how to get the donkey over the hill. But when it came to thinking about *which* hill, or whether it might be wiser to go down and around a hill rather than up and over, we tended to be as stupid as donkeys ourselves. When the meeting convened I gave a little speech saying that times had changed: "We've been a company of doers. Now we must learn to call on staff and rely on their ability to think out answers to many of our complex problems."

We then created the staff right before their eyes. There were dozens of slots to be filled, and since IBM had very few specialists on the payroll, we "made" our experts simply by naming people to the jobs. Williams and I had rejected the idea of recruiting outsiders, except in highly specialized fields such as law and science. We'd spent years weeding out Dad's yes-men and replacing them with fierce, strong-willed decision makers. If we'd hired a bunch of professors or consultants to come in and play staff against these people, the newcomers would have been eaten alive. Instead I put IBM's best executives in the new jobs, starting with Al as chief of staff. It was a huge sacrifice to move him outside the chain of command —and for Al it meant swapping a position in which he had twenty-five thousand people working for him to one in which he was boss of only eleven hundred. But by shifting our stars into the staff we enabled it to command the respect of the divisions, and that was the key to making the whole thing work.

The great strength of the Williamsburg plan was that it provided our executives with the clearest possible goals. Each operating man was judged strictly on his unit's results, and each staff man on his effort toward making IBM the world leader in his specialty. So on every operating proposal we had financial men demanding to know how it would improve profits, public relations men fighting to make sure it enhanced IBM's image, and manufacturing men insisting that we maintain the highest productivity in our plants and quality in our products. When the conference came to an end after a couple of days of workshops, there was no doubt that IBM had been totally transformed. To underline that fact we ran a special issue of the company newspaper featuring the first organization chart IBM ever had. Oddly, I had no feeling at all that we were going against Dad. I didn't think he'd have been alarmed by anything we did. If I could have asked him, "How do you want this thing run?" his answer would probably have been "I don't know, son. It was getting so big when I left that I could hardly understand it. Do whatever you think is right." That was the mandate I thought I had. Not a day went by when I didn't think about the old boy, but the only thing I really worried about was lousing the business up.

My friend Al never worked harder in his life than he did whipping IBM's new staff into shape. He had to take men of action and turn them into men of thought. There were thirteen people reporting directly to him, and he was working sixteen hours a day, six or seven days a week. The first thing he did was try to teach them to

write. A good staff report is supposed to be intelligible
and direct. It should lay out a problem concisely and end
with a clear recommendation, so that all top management
has to do is read it and say, "Go ahead" or "Don't." Al
told the staff, "You have to pay attention to this written
stuff. Remember you're going to hand it to a senior manager and he has to understand it. If he approves your
recommendation he's going to hand the report to somebody else to carry it out, and that person has to understand it too." This advice didn't take. After six months
the reports were still so chaotic and obtuse that Al got
desperate. He called the staff together and showed them a
manila folder. "Every time one of you hands me a sloppy
report," he said, "I'm going to take a folder like this and
put your report in the left-hand pocket. Then I'm going
to rewrite it the way you should have done it in the first
place, and put that in the right-hand pocket. Then I'm
going to circulate the folder to each man in this room."
After that, if somebody did a lousy job, his twelve associates saw it. The quality of the written work went up dramatically.

Al constantly had to arbitrate disputes between the
staff and the line. A typical headache was that when any
of the staff men spotted something wrong in a division,
he'd revert to being a man of action and fire off a blister-
ing memo dictating what ought to be done. This would
cause the division executives to howl that the staff was
trying to interfere. The staff also developed the bad habit
of dragging their feet on projects they didn't like. Al must
have lectured his men a hundred times: "Quit acting like
bureaucrats. You've got to facilitate things, not block
things."

In the months leading up to Williamsburg, Al and
Dick Bullen had spent many hours discussing how to
transform the natural tension between the staff and the
line into energy that would move IBM forward rather
than friction that would slow us down. The organizational solution they finally came up with was as simple
and brilliant as the transistor—a check-and-balance
scheme that eventually became famous as the IBM sys-

tem of contention management. Not only did it make staff versus line conflicts acceptable; it actually encouraged them. In this system, no operating plan at IBM was final without a staff man's concurrence. And if he signed, his job was just as much at stake as the executive's who made the plan. When an executive and a staff man couldn't agree, the problem automatically would get kicked upstairs. They'd have to come in and air their differences before the corporate management committee, which did not suffer indecisiveness gladly. This was enough to make our executives hammer out all but the thorniest problems among themselves, while it forced major problems to surface quickly for top management to see.

With so much contention built in, why did the new system work? For one thing, every IBM employee had job security, dating back to the days when Dad had refused to fire people during the Depression. If a man proved ineffectual at his new assignment, he wasn't going to be put out on the street; instead we'd reassign him to a level where he could perform well. In doing this we would sometimes strip a man of a fair amount of dignity, but we would then make a great effort to rebuild his self-respect. We also abided by the IBM custom of promotion from within. As inexperienced as our executives might be in their new jobs, they had all come up from the bottom and knew what IBM stood for as well as they knew their own names.

Money was another reason the contention system worked. On one occasion I was ranting in a management committee meeting about something—I hope something worthwhile—and a rather sarcastic and outspoken fellow from my office named Tom Buckley leaned over to Spike Beitzel, later a senior vice president, and asked, "Do you know why they all take this bunk from him?" Beitzel, who was anxious not to attract my attention just then, shrugged. Buckley said, "Because they're all getting filthy rich!"

I went out of my way to reward the people IBM counted on most. Not only were there lucrative stock options for those near the top, but before 1956 was over I met with the board and quietly set up a unique incentive plan. It involved my father's pay, which now of course was my pay. He'd always taken a salary plus a percentage of the profits, and when he died, I'd made a great point of fighting to keep that arrangement intact for myself. But after Williamsburg, it no longer fit. If anyone had a right to a percentage of the profits, it wasn't Watson but the Watson team. My cut of IBM's profits that year was one fourth of one percent after dividends, or $298,000. I split it with Williams and LaMotte, letting them apportion the money in a way they decided was fair, and it worked out so that my own pay was only two thirds of what it would have been. In subsequent years we took the same money and distributed it even more broadly, to the thirteen top men. This arrangement had a powerful symbolic effect, because it proved that the one-man show was over.

From then on I managed IBM with a team of fifteen or twenty senior executives. Some of these men were my friends, but I never hesitated to promote people I didn't like. The comfortable assistant, the nice guy you like to go on fishing trips with, is a great pitfall in management. Instead I was always looking for sharp, scratchy, harsh, almost unpleasant guys who could see and tell me about things as they really were. If you can get enough of those around you, and have patience enough to hear them out, there is no limit to where you can go. My most important contribution to the company was my ability to pick strong and intelligent men for these slots and then hold the team together by persuasion, by apologies, by speeches, by discipline, by chats with their wives, by thoughtfulness when they were sick or involved in accidents, and by using every tool at my command to make each man think I was a decent guy. I knew I couldn't match all of them intellectually, but I thought that if I used fully every capability that I had, I could stay even with them.

I was pretty harsh and scratchy myself. I wanted all the executives of IBM to feel the urgency I felt; whatever they did, it was never enough. I was a volatile leader, perhaps even more volatile than Dad, and I justified this by telling myself that I was never harder on any of my men than he had been on me. Only gradually did I learn the virtue of restraint. We had an executive in those days named Dave Moore, a ruddy-faced, two-fisted guy I'd known growing up. Our families had been friendly. Like his father before him, Dave was manager of our International Time Recording division, which mainly sold factory time clocks and went all the way back to the company's origin. Up through the 1930s it had been one of IBM's strongest units. But after the war, when the idea of looser, more flexible factory management came along, the time clock became a symbol of the sweatshop. Not only was this bad for IBM's image, but a lot of companies simply quit using them. The division became stagnant and its profits fell because there were a lot of time clock makers and they were all competing for a smaller and smaller pie.

Moore did his best to turn the situation around, but year after year the results were poor. Finally Williams and I decided Moore had to be replaced. We promised him an equivalent job at the same salary, but Dave was stunned. He sought out his immediate boss, Red La-Motte, and said, "Well, I've made a success of the time division, haven't I?" Of course, if it had been a success we wouldn't have taken him out of the job, but Red equivocated, being a gentle man. When I heard of their conversation I should have just let the thing ride. But I always lost my temper when an IBM man refused to face a problem squarely. I called Moore in and said, "I don't know how the hell you can say things like that, Dave. Let's be realistic. The time equipment business is going nowhere. How can you call that a success? You can say you did as well as you could under the circumstances. But did you make money? Did your division move ahead? No, you were not a success." He left the meeting and my words festered in him. After a few months he quit, sold all his IBM stock, and took a civilian job in the Air Force. I've always regretted driving Moore out—especially since, in retrospect, it's clear he had an impossible job. His successor couldn't turn the business around either, and eventually the unit was sold.

Gradually I learned to control myself better. But it would have been a fatal mistake to expect perfect harmony at IBM. You can't run a business well simply by announcing, "Tomorrow we're going to do A and Friday we're going to do B and next year we're going to do C." The best way to motivate people is to pit them against one another, and I was constantly looking for ways to stir up internal competition. This led me, a few years after Williamsburg, to one of my most controversial decisions. In spite of all our efforts at decentralization, the Data Processing Division, which was responsible for all our computers and punch-card machines, was just too big. It was in danger of becoming clumsy and bureaucratic. So I assigned a task force to figure out a way to break it into manageable parts. They came back to me after a month and said, "It's impossible. It's all one business. There's no way to divide it."

"All right," I said. "I'll do it for you. All products that rent for over ten thousand dollars a month will belong to one division, and all products under ten thousand dollars will belong to another division." I picked ten thousand dollars because that was our average rental price, and it made the two camps roughly equal, with about thirty thousand employees each. But apart from that, it was a very awkward split. It essentially broke our computer business into competing halves. The corporate staff had a terrible time figuring out how to divvy up our laboratories, factories, and sales force between the two new units.

I didn't think we were smart enough to manage IBM any other way. From then on we didn't have to depend on the brilliance of top management to decide what needed to be changed; when you have separate units competing against one another, to a large extent they discipline themselves. The new arrangement put the hot breath of competition into every division executive's ear and we could gauge IBM's efficiency by comparing one division with the other. I could go to the head of the Data

Systems Division and instead of saying, "Gee, are you sure your overhead cost is reasonable?" I could say, "How come the overhead in the General Products Division is lower than yours?" Or: "Why does it take you four years to develop a computer while it only takes General Products two years to develop a roughly comparable machine?" Much of the time it wasn't even necessary to ask. Procter & Gamble was doing something like this with consumer products—they'd develop two or three brands of detergent and let them compete against each other in the grocery stores—and of course General Motors sold several different lines of cars. But it was radical thinking to apply internal conflict to the degree IBM did. A lot of people told me it would never work, but it was one of the secrets of how we got as big as we did.

The Williamsburg organization came none too soon, because IBM's growth was *accelerating*. The business grew faster in the two years after Dad's death than ever in its history, except the wartime expansion of 1943. Once we won the numbers race against Remington Rand, the psychology of the market swung completely in our favor. Even though computers were the most complicated and expensive business tools anyone had ever seen, customers were deciding they couldn't be without them. They picked IBM because of our reputation for both machines and service. We had the salesmen and technicians who knew how to provide systems that worked, scores of experts who could unravel tough programming problems, and a huge library of computer programs we offered to customers at no charge. Getting a computer was a major investment that required approval by the board of directors in most companies, and for the executive in charge of picking the right machine, IBM became known as the safe choice. As *Fortune* magazine put it at the time, "Boards of directors may know little about machinery, but they know about IBM."

Although we were having success after success, I worried about whether we could hang on to the advantage we'd gained. RCA was coming into the industry, and I thought they were going to be terribly tough. On the other hand, Al Williams always believed the most serious competition would come from General Electric, which around that time landed a huge contract to computerize the retail banking operations of Bank of America. GE is a smart company, well organized, and when they take hold of something like jet engines or even dishwashers, they really do it thoroughly. In the mid-1950s RCA was half again as big as we were and GE was five times our size. If either company had decided to hire away some of our best people and commit large amounts of money to this thing, they would have wiped us off the map.

Shortly after Dad died, while we were still planning for Williamsburg, I was summoned over to RCA to see General David Sarnoff. RCA had been experimenting with computers since the 1940s and had just delivered a giant machine called BIZMAC to the U.S. tank arsenal in Detroit, where it was used to keep track of inventories. Some RCA executives believed computers would be as important to their company's future as color televisions. It was hard for me not to feel awe standing in front of the father of American radio and television. The general was a short man, but he sat either on a high chair or on a platform and he looked very big to me. He had a long cigar that he pulled at sporadically as he spoke.

Although I had met him socially, this was a different General Sarnoff. He said he wanted licenses under our computer patents and he thought we were reluctant to make them available, even though we were required to do so under our new consent decree. He told me that the expertise that produced RCA's TV sets could also be used for computers and that he intended to capitalize on that. I didn't let my feeling of awe stop me from pointing out that computers were a highly specialized market, more dependent on sales and systems expertise than hardware. I said that while we would license him any patents he wanted, I thought he would have a difficult time in the computer business.

Meanwhile one of the people helping us get ready for Williamsburg was a management consultant named John

L. Burns. I knew Burns casually—a big, heavyset Harvard Ph.D. who had started his career during the Depression as a laborer in a steel mill and had risen to senior partner in the consulting firm of Booz Allen & Hamilton. When I'd asked him to work with IBM, Burns had explained he was a top consultant to RCA and would have to get their permission. Then he accepted and worked quite intimately with us until Williamsburg. Not more than three months after the conference, Burns telephoned and said that Sarnoff was offering to make him president of RCA. He asked if I had any objection. I said, "I most certainly do, John!" because we had entrusted him with detailed knowledge of our organization and methods and plans. Nevertheless he took the job.

The threat posed by Burns would have been much more grave had I not paid attention to some advice I got from Al Williams. Al had telephoned one day to tell me that Booz Allen's team was asking for an explanation of IBM's pricing practices. "Sure," I said. "It's like your doctor, you have to tell them everything." But Williams insisted it was unwise to give them the data. I was irritated because I thought highly of Burns, but I always made a point of listening to Al. So I said, "All right, if you feel that strongly don't tell them." The pricing practices had been built up since the early days of IBM. Behind the price of each rental product we had our own cost of marketing, cost of servicing, and rate of planned obsolescence—all carefully kept secrets. In Burns's hands this knowledge would have enabled RCA to aim where IBM's product line was weakest and avoid attacking where we were strong and could cut prices to fend off competitors.

We tried to make sure that for well-financed rivals like GE and RCA, the computer business seemed too risky a bet. We did this by making ourselves tremendously sensitive to toeholds. The feeling among our sales force was that if a General Electric could get five percent, it could get 100 percent. If a salesman lost a customer without having first alerted management that the account was in jeopardy, he was subject to discipline. IBM salesmen had two types of call reports to fill out. The first were routine; the second were named special account reports and came in two colors. Pink ones were for situations where IBM was bidding against somebody else to win a new customer; yellow slips represented sick accounts, where a customer was dissatisfied. These reports were compiled and exhaustively analyzed by geographical location, by customer type, and by product type. Coupled with other research, the special account reports enabled us to assess accurately how the competition was doing.

Any inroad made by a competitor like RCA was worrisome. In an industry exploding like ours, it was one of my unwavering convictions that gaining and holding market position was crucial. Any deviation from this goal in an attempt to maximize short-term profits would, over the long term, reduce the total amount of our profit. By the same token, to try to pick and choose a limited number of areas in which to be strong was a foolish and dangerous course. If we were to do that, we would limit the scale of our business, making it easier for competitors across the board.

I believed that the only way for IBM to win was to move, move, move all the time. As the computer industry grew, we had to grow with it, no matter how fast that growth might be. I never varied from the managerial rule that the worst possible thing we could do would be to lie dead in the water with any problem. Solve it, solve it quickly, solve it right or wrong. If you solved it wrong, it would come back and slap you in the face and then you could solve it right. Lying dead in the water and doing nothing is a comfortable alternative because it is without immediate risk, but it is an absolutely fatal way to manage a business. So I never hesitated to intervene if I saw the company getting bogged down. A few months after Williamsburg we were having a dreadful time moving over to transistors. The transistor was obviously the wave of the future in electronics: it was faster than the vacuum tube, generated less heat, and had great potential for miniaturization. Nobody was selling transistorized computers yet, but a great many companies were racing to perfect them, including RCA, Honeywell, Control Data, NCR, and Philco. We too were experimenting with transistorized computers and calculators in our Poughkeepsie lab. Early transistors were unreliable—they were sensitive to heat, moisture, and vibration—but by 1956 Ralph Palmer and the people he directed at Poughkeepsie had done enough testing to be sure those limitations could be overcome.

The big remaining hurdle was cost. Transistors were selling for about $2.50 apiece and it seemed impossible to design a computer using them that would ever make any money. But Birkenstock, as usual the one to goad me in technology, pointed out that by moving aggressively we could make this difficulty disappear. The leading supplier of transistors in those days was Texas Instruments in Dallas. Not many people had ever heard of them, but they'd stolen a march on big vacuum tube makers like GE and Sylvania by learning to mass-manufacture transistors first. Pat Haggerty, their factory chief and later president, understood the unique economics of the transistor game better than anybody else. When Texas Instruments first went into the business, transistors were costing up to sixteen dollars each and one of their few practical applications was in hearing aids. Haggerty figured that by getting the price down to about $2.50, the company could open up a mass market in portable radios. They gambled two million dollars on a circuit design and production process to meet this goal, and in 1956 the transistor radio was born. It became a hit with consumers and put Texas Instruments on top.

We thought similar magic might work for IBM. By designing computers on the assumption that the cost of transistors could be pushed down still further, to perhaps $1.50, we could set prices that would attract customers and still let us make a profit. Birkenstock flew to Dallas to ask Texas Instruments to help. They agreed to build a factory with high-volume production lines that would cut the cost of transistors so dramatically that they'd be cheaper than the high-grade vacuum tubes we were now depending on. In turn we promised to use the lion's share of the millions of transistors the new plant would produce.

That's where we almost bogged down. This bold plan gave us an incentive to transistorize all our products, computers and punch-card machines alike, because the more transistors we used, the cheaper they'd be. While the idea of transistorization delighted the computer engineers at Poughkeepsie, it raised a storm of protest from the punch-card designers up in Endicott. They had barely learned to handle electrons in a tube, and this new invention shocked them. I would go up to the lab and say, "Why not transistors?" hoping they'd take the hint. But for months every new design they sent down to New York was full of tubes. Finally I issued a memorandum that said, "After October 1, we will design no more machines using vacuum tubes. Signed, Tom Watson Jr." The Endicott people were awfully mad and said, "What does he know about it?" But I got a hundred of those little transistor radios Texas Instruments was making and carried a few along whenever I went to Endicott. Each time I heard an engineer say that transistors were undependable, I would pull a radio out of my bag and challenge him to wear it out.

On Wall Street, IBM was a darling stock. Brokers in those days used to tout promising new companies as "the next IBM." The value of the stock had multiplied fivefold just since I'd become president; and if your family had been fortunate enough to invest $2,750 in a hundred shares during the year that my *father* took over the business, by 1957 that stake would have grown to $2.5 million. A big event on Wall Street that year was our first stock sale. Father had always rejected the idea of selling new shares, but it finally came down to a question of common sense. We'd borrowed as much as you could borrow—we owed the Prudential well over $300 million, which made us the biggest debtor in American business. Yet at the rate we were building factories and rental equipment, we were going to need more capital—a lot of it. Al Williams calculated that we could easily make use of $200 million. So I called our man at Morgan Stanley, Buck Ewing. Up to that moment he was probably the most underemployed investment banker of any major corporation. Buck and I had flown together in World War II, and after the war Morgan Stanley had assigned him to the IBM account. The first time Buck had called to ask if IBM needed capital, I told him, "I don't think my father is ready for this," but I introduced him to Dad all the same. They chatted very briefly. After Buck left, Dad said, "That man is not using his head. The last thing we want to do is sell stock." The head of Morgan Stanley was Perry Hall, whom Dad knew from the Short Hills Episcopal church. Hall was sharp; he had listened to Dad's views on selling new stock once and had never raised the issue again. Buck, on the other hand, called on us each year, and it finally got to the point where Dad, who admired persistence, would give him five minutes and talk in a friendly way.

So when Williams and I decided to go ahead, it seemed reasonable to call Buck. He came rushing up instantly, brought a whole team in, and the thing got done. Morgan Stanley's name appeared at the head of the list of underwriters, which was quite a coup because $200 million was the second-largest stock sale in Wall Street history. (The largest had been a $328 million offering by General Motors in 1955.)

We hit the billion-dollar mark at the end of 1957, my first full year as chief executive. Selling a billion dollars' worth of anything in those days was like supersonic flight —there weren't many organizations that had achieved it. Only thirty-six American industrial companies—such as Procter & Gamble, Boeing, and Standard Oil—were bigger than IBM, and almost all of them depended on us for computers. It no longer took Watson optimism to say we were a significant factor in the U.S. economy. I allowed myself a small celebration. We had been wanting to upgrade our corporate airplanes, so we bought a Convair, a twin-engine fifty-passenger airliner that we fitted out with bunks and a meeting area. We used it to fly customers to sales demonstrations, not for junkets, but all the same it is heady stuff for a fellow of forty-three to buy a million-dollar airplane like that.

I was terribly proud of the start I'd made. I didn't like it when people compared me to my father, but I felt that if I could keep my record going for perhaps another ten years, I'd be able to count myself in the same league as Dad. So it came as a real slap in the face when one member of my family decided to hedge her bet on my making it. The second year after Dad died, my sister Jane sold a million dollars' worth of IBM stock—about one third of her total holding. This was a real vote of no confidence, the first time *any* Watson had ever sold IBM stock, and it cut me so deeply that I went down to her house in Washington.

"Of course it is your right to sell whenever you want," I told her, "but why did you do it?" Jane was awfully surprised that I knew about the sale, because she didn't understand corporations well enough to realize that a million-dollar sale is reported to the chief executive. But getting an answer out of her was exactly like having a discussion with the old man. Sometimes when you tried to pin him down, my father would give a totally ridiculous answer. If you said, "Dad, you picked up my bags and left me at the station!" his answer might be, "Oh, I thought you wanted to walk home!" That's the kind of impossible response I got from Jane: "I didn't think you'd be interested!"

"How can you possibly think that? I've been running this business and you've been a beneficiary of it. But you've never given the slightest hint that you think this record is worth tipping a hat to."

"Oh, Tom. You know I think that."

"So then why are you selling your stock?"

"Because I have to protect my family's future."

In retrospect, I can see Jane was probably following the advice of some financial counselor who convinced her it was prudent to diversify her holdings. But at the time her selling of the stock really knocked me back, and it was the end of warm feelings between us for a number of years.

CHAPTER 24

M anagement is no science; it is much too human a process ever to qualify. Since we built such sophisticated business machines, people tended to think of IBM as a model of order and logic —a totally streamlined organization in which we developed plans rationally and carried them out with utter precision. I never thought for a minute that was really the case. While the 1950s was a boom time for such fields as organizational engineering and systems analysis, that was not the kind of leadership the people of IBM expected, or the job for which I'd been trained. Dad had taught me that a good businessman has to be an actor. You have to make a show of getting angry a lot more often than you really lose your temper; you have to look more worried than you really are when trying to stimulate someone to tackle a problem. Dad was a master at hamming it up in this way, and I patterned my actions after him whenever I got the chance.

As IBM became huge and decentralized, the challenge was to find ways of maintaining personal contact with the people of the company, and to motivate other top executives to follow my example. One July an airliner carrying a number of IBM employees turned over taking off from Rochester, New York, in a thunderstorm. Seven people died in the crash, including one IBMer, and eight or nine others from our group were hospitalized. I was at an IBM conference in Vermont when word of the accident came, and I checked quickly to make sure the chiefs of the divisions involved had gone to Rochester to help. But one executive was still in his Westchester office. I got him on the phone and said, "Are you going to go up there and go from bed to bed, or will I?"

"Jeez, Tom, I never thought of it." He'd been in the business a long time, and I asked how he could possibly have forgotten the example Dad had set after the Port Jervis train wreck in 1939—getting out of bed in the middle of the night and driving to the hospital to see the IBM families involved. "I'm giving you fair warning," I said. "You're supposed to run your division as if it were your own company, but if you're not in Rochester by the end of today, I'm going myself."

"I'll call you from the hospital," he said, and he did about four hours later.

Like Dad, I went to dozens of "family dinners" for IBM employees each year, and paying visits to local offices was standard procedure for me on any business trip. I kept a whole squad of secretaries busy doing things in the same way Dad would have—making sure every letter I received was acknowledged within forty-eight hours, sending flowers to the hospitalized wife of an employee, and making thousands of other small gestures of thoughtfulness. Dad often answered his own phone himself, and so did I whenever I could. If the caller was a customer it was a delightful surprise to reach Watson directly; and if the caller was an IBMer it set a powerful example for him to treat his own callers with equal consideration. Probably an efficiency expert would have condemned these practices as a gargantuan waste of time for a chief executive. But in a service-oriented business like ours, these seemingly minor details of courtesy and style were too important to let slide. If the head man stops taking a proprietary interest in them, pretty soon everybody else stops caring too.

I'd succeeded in changing so much about IBM—the way we were organized, the technology we sold, the actual look of the company—but the hardest task of all was what Williams and I called riding the runaway horse: keeping IBM coherent as it multiplied in size. Eventually I was able to distill into a simple set of precepts the philosophy Dad had followed in managing the business for forty years:

Give full consideration to the individual employee.

Spend a lot of time making customers happy.

Go the last mile to do a thing right.

I thought that to survive and succeed, we had to be willing to change everything about IBM except these basic beliefs. Dad had always conveyed his way of thinking to employees by personal visits, speechmaking, and the sheer force of his personality. Everyone understood his values so well that apart from the old slogans like "A manager is an assistant to his men," he never got around to codifying them. I felt compelled to change that because IBM was now many times larger than when he was in his prime, and because we were hiring thousands of people every year and large numbers of relatively inexperienced IBMers were being promoted into management jobs.

The most important thing for these young managers to learn was not the professional or technical dimension of their work, but the proper way to treat the people who reported to them. Dad called this day-to-day contact the "man-manager relationship," and it was as essential to IBM as the family is to society. We depended on this relationship to help safeguard respect for the individual no matter how highly structured the rest of the business became. As long as workers and supervisors understood each other, unions were superfluous at IBM, but if we let that bond erode, sooner or later the business was sure to become a battleground.

Our training methods at that stage were still surprisingly primitive. We had our sales school and machine school, but nothing to teach a person about how to be someone's boss. A branch manager would call a salesman in and say, "You're promoted to assistant manager. Be careful with people, don't swear, and wear a white shirt." Around the time of the Williamsburg conference I took one of our most gifted sales managers, Tom Clemmons, and put him in charge of executive development. He started a program that was taught at the Sleepy Hollow Country Club. At first he was using cases straight from the Harvard Business School. I took him aside one day and said, in my usual undiplomatic way, that if our company was really going to be unique, we had to teach something unique.

He said, "I thought you wanted them educated to be good managers!"

"You don't understand," I said. "I want them to be educated in *IBM* management: communications, supreme sales and service efforts, going to a guy's house if his wife is ill and seeing if you can help out, making post-death calls." You couldn't read that in anybody else's manual. They were the practices we'd built up over the years, and new IBM managers had to know them in addition to the technology. So Clemmons changed direction, and the training system became so good that eventually we made a rule that people could not manage anything in IBM unless they had been to management school. The courses lasted from two to six weeks, and I made sure that I or another top executive visited each group of trainees that went through, because it was crucial for them to see who they were working for.

I never thought the proper place for a senior executive was sitting behind a bare desk looking at the ceiling, dreaming up great deeds for the future, and drawing new lines on the organization chart. I spent the equivalent of at least one day per week on employee complaints or walking through plants, talking to salesmen, and chatting with customers. I asked what was right and, more important, what was wrong. You don't hear things that are bad about your company unless you ask. It is easy to hear good tidings, but you have to scratch to get the bad news. Working in this way, I uncovered shoddy and seamy things in IBM that we were able to fix before they became very serious.

In 1964, for example, one of our branch managers staged a burlesque show at a sales conference in the Midwest. The skit was too vulgar to believe—about an Indian village, starring the manager himself as the chief and some scantily clad models as squaws. They even had live chickens running around on the stage. At the end of the skit the manager disappeared with one of these models into a tepee, and as he turned to go into the tent, the audience saw a sign on his back that said something like "Branch Manager: I do all things for all people." Then he and the girl pulled the tepee flap closed behind them. There were families present, and somebody who witnessed the show wrote me a letter saying, "Is this what you call IBM dignity?" So I started a big inquiry. The manager in question was a top performer, one of IBM's best men, but it was our policy to run a clean show, and I said he should be fired. His bosses tried everything to keep him, and even tried hiding him from me by transferring him to the West Coast. But finally he left the company because everybody knew that whenever his name came up I was going to raise hell.

Anytime I intervened in a matter of personnel policy, or spotted something I didn't like at a branch office or plant, I'd write it down in the "THINK" notebook I carried in my pocket. Often I'd use it as raw material for a type of memorandum called a Management Briefing that was sent to every manager right down to the foremen on the factory floor. I put as much energy into writing those memos as Dad put into his editorials in *Think* magazine. When you are coping with a business full of new managers you learn to take nothing for granted. For example, one of my memos was a primer on how to hold a meeting without wasting time. (My advice was to keep it as small as possible, short, and to the point.)

I wrote nearly a hundred of those memos, trying to teach how to handle everyday problems in an IBM way. For example, there was the issue of employee transfers. Being transferred was a standard part of white-collar life in the 1950s, but when people started joking that IBM stood for "I've Been Moved," I realized our transfers must be getting out of hand. We looked into how we moved people around, and found that many transfers were being made solely for the convenience of IBM without regard for the employee whose family was being uprooted. That violated one of the basic tenets of IBM philosophy—consideration for the individual. So I wrote to our managers that no one should be offered a transfer without a substantial increase in pay and responsibility, and the number of transfers dropped right away. Another case typical of the time was the employee who got fired for refusing to shave off his beard; his manager told him his appearance did not fit in with the decor or with IBM's corporate image. Many of the scientists and mathematicians we were hiring off the campuses were bringing their beards and informal wardrobes with them. I wanted IBM people to be well groomed, but I thought informality was fine in the research labs. So I insisted that we offer the man his job back, and sent out a briefing explaining that IBM's corporate design program applied to products, buildings, and decor, but not people.

Of course it's true a conservative appearance had always been the custom at IBM. A whole folklore grew up about IBM conformity—the white shirts and dark suits. But there was a reason for it. In one way or another we were all salesmen in IBM, individually and collectively, and nothing distracts from a sale like an outlandish appearance. Conservative dress made sense as a marketing tool, just like a plant tour, an education program for customers, or a reputation for excellence. It showed we took our work seriously.

The quality I looked for in a manager, and valued above practically everything else, was common sense. Dad put less emphasis on it—maybe because he had so much of it himself and what he mainly needed from employees was enthusiasm. But now that we were a huge corporation doing business with thousands of smaller companies, too much zeal could cause harm. For instance, we had a contractor who sold us milk for the company cafeteria in Poughkeepsie. The local IBM controller was trying to save some money, and he threatened to take this guy's contract away unless he dropped his price. There's a level below which you can't sell milk without going broke, and we had that guy almost at that level. He finally wrote to me and said, "You are using your economic power here to kill me." I went to Pough-keepsie and talked to the controller and found out it was true, and I got terribly mad that any IBM employee could be that dumb.

We had a similar problem with a customer in Providence, a small businessman who was using IBM equipment to send out his bills. His business was struggling, and he refused to pay for the installation, saying he wasn't happy with the way it worked. The way our local office handled this defied all logic. They should have either satisfied the man or taken the machines out, but instead they began billing him in arrears and finally took him to court. I didn't hear about this until the trial was ready to start, and the stupidity of what we'd done drove me wild. If anybody had used his head, he'd have fore-seen what the customer's lawyer would say to the jury: "Here is this colossus, making hundreds of millions of dollars a year, bullying this little guy who hasn't paid because their machines won't work." That was not how I wanted IBM to look. I said "Settle!" and we ended up having to give him a couple of million dollars.

I could set up all the guidelines in the world to try to avoid such situations, but I sometimes found that temper was the best way to get a management lesson across. In the fall of 1956 I learned of two young men who came to IBM headquarters to apply for jobs, got snubbed, and left with the impression it was because they were Jewish. One of them sent me a complaint, and after checking I found out that they hadn't even been granted an interview. Instead somebody had labeled them "Obviously not the IBM type." The more I thought about this, the angrier I felt, because IBM had a clear rule against discrimination in hiring. I'd written that rule myself in 1953 during the early stages of the civil rights movement. I brought the job applicant's letter with me to the Williamsburg conference and interrupted the proceedings to read it out loud. "How do you expect me to represent IBM to the world outside when this sort of thing goes on inside?" I hollered to the executives gathered there. Then, I'm told, I pointed at Jack Bricker, our brand-new personnel chief who was sitting in one of the front rows, and ordered him to clean up the matter and discipline whoever had mishandled it. It was theatrical but I made a crucial point: I didn't want there to be any difference between what IBM said and what IBM did.

As time passed, I became increasingly intolerant of executives or managers who broke rules of integrity. A business is a sort of dictatorship. The antitrust laws tell you what you can do, and you don't need anyone to tell you that you shouldn't be a thief, but within those boundaries the top man has wide discretion. He can give unfair bonuses, he can suggest policies that are not right, he can run airplanes to golf resorts. I never criticized my contemporaries publicly, but there are a lot of things that IBM did differently from other businesses during my watch. I thought that the head of a business had responsibilities almost like the head of a government, without a supreme court and without checks and balances, except those that the marketplace and the annual report impose on his operation. One of the worst mistakes he can make is to apply a double standard to managers and employees. If a manager does something unethical, he should be fired just as surely as a factory worker. This is the wholesome use of the boss's power.

When we first decentralized IBM, I simply assumed that all of our executives would apply the same high standards of conduct automatically. It took me a number of years to realize that a chief executive has to spot-check decisions made by his subordinates. On one occasion some managers in one of our plants started a chain letter involving U.S. savings bonds. The idea was that one manager would write to five other managers, and each of those would write to five more, who would each send some bonds back to the first guy and write to five more, and so on. Pretty soon they ran out of managers and got down to employees. It ended up that the employees felt pressure to join the chain letter and pay off the managers. I got a complaint about this and brought it to the attention of the head of the division. I expected him to say, at a minimum, "We've got to fire a couple of guys. I'll handle it." Instead he simply said, "Well, it was a mistake." I couldn't convince him to fire anybody. Now, you could admire him for defending his team, but I think there is a time when integrity should take the rudder from team loyalty. All the same, I didn't pursue the matter any further, and my failure to act came back to haunt me.

A couple of years later in that same division, a manager fired a low-level employee who had been stealing engineering diagrams and selling them to a competitor. Firing him would have been fine, except that the manager handled it in a brutal way. The employee in question had one thing in his life that he was proud of—his commission in the U.S. Army Reserve, where he held the rank of major. Instead of simply going to the man's house and telling him, "You swiped the drawings and we're going to fire you," the manager picked a week when the fellow was in military camp to lower the boom. Somehow the military authorities got involved as well and the man was stripped of his commission. The humiliation caused him to become insanely angry, and for the next few years he devoted himself to making me uncomfortable. He sent pictures of Tom Watson Jr. behind bars to his senators and his congressman and to every justice of the Supreme Court. And he kept harking back to that chain letter, because he knew we had tolerated the men responsible for it. Eventually he simmered down, but the incident really taught me a lesson. After that I simply fired managers when they broke rules of integrity. I did it in perhaps a dozen cases, including a couple involving senior executives. I had to overrule a lot of people each time, who would argue that we should merely demote the man, or transfer him, or that the business would fall apart without him. But the company was invariably better off for the decision and the example.

I knew exactly the attitude I wanted to cultivate in ordinary IBM employees: I wanted them to feel a proprietary interest, and to have some knowledge of each other's problems and goals. I also wanted them to feel that they had access to top management and that no one was so far down the chain of command that he couldn't be kept aware of where the business was heading. As the hierarchy grew to include five, six, and seven layers of command, this became a huge challenge. I was constantly looking for ways to maintain what I called a small-company attitude. One of the surprising things we learned was that to overcome the problems of change, we had to increase communication within IBM far out of proportion to our growth rate. We used a variety of channels for listening to our employees, including surveys, suggestion programs, and even a question-and-answer program—called "Speak Up!"—that incorporated bureaucratic procedures to shield the identity of the questioner from top management.

Our most unusual method for shortening the distance between the salesman or factory man and top management was the Open Door, a practice of Dad's that traced back to the early 1920s. This was primarily a system of justice, but it also gave me a measure of IBM's health that I could not have gotten any other way. Disgruntled employees at IBM were first expected to take up their gripes with their managers. But if they got no satisfaction, they had the right to come directly to me. Nine out of ten such cases involved matters that should have been resolved further down, or where lower management had already made the right decision—but I listened anyway. I learned an awful lot about the problems of the working man, and I gained a visceral sense about IBM that enabled me to hear a complaint and say, "Something's wrong *here.*"

On at least one occasion, a single protest led to a substantial change in the way we did business. A machinist who was about to be fired from the Poughkeepsie plant came to see me. He said, "They're not treating people fairly. I'm making more pieces than anyone in that shop, and I get the lowest pay."

"I don't see how that can be true," I told him. But I called the plant manager and told him what the man had said.

"Well, you know, he is a very uncooperative employee.

He doesn't belong to the IBM club, he doesn't participate in outside activities, and sometimes he doesn't even dress neatly when he comes to work."

That wasn't the question I was asking. I called the man's foreman and said, "Does he make more pieces and get less pay?"

"He doesn't reflect well on the company. He has a couple of wrecked cars in the yard in front of his house, and he doesn't take care of his children."

The machinist was up against what I called the IBM Protective Association, where local managers close ranks to cover up rough treatment of employees who may be totally blameless. Finally the managers admitted that the man was telling the truth. We gave him a raise, disciplined the managers involved, and then we went through every one of our U.S. plants and tied pay to productivity. This caused quite a commotion, because putting in a system that rewarded the best producers meant partly undoing my father's decision twenty years earlier to abolish piecework.

Many employees did not want to take a complaint all the way to me, but the very existence of the Open Door was a morale builder. It made them feel free to approach a personnel manager or the man running the plant when they had a problem. As IBM grew, we tried to take care of more and more Open Door cases at the division-chief level, with only charges of serious mismanagement that might reflect unfavorably on IBM coming to my office. But even so my office handled two or three hundred cases each year, with each case typically taking several days to resolve. The bulk of this work fell to my administrative assistants, who were chosen from among our most promising young managers. This was the best apprenticeship an IBM executive could have, because it tested his or her ability to handle highly sensitive matters, and required full comprehension of the company philosophy. Periodically I'd see complainants myself, so that word would get around that the head man was indeed available.

My father had always felt a direct connection with the working man, because with his humble roots he had known hard times, hard work, and unemployment. As a result, he tried to blur the distinction between white-collar and blue-collar workers. Not only did he provide secure jobs and good pay for the people in our plants, but the fact that for many years IBM's pensions were based solely on length of service, not salary or position, stood my father in good stead. During the period in the 1930s and 1940s when there was a lot of labor unrest in America, organizers were hitting pretty hard at the lush retirement plans some companies offered their executives. I don't think his primary motive was to keep the unions out, but that was one effect.

While the factories had always been more closely associated with Dad than with me, I looked for a way to extend Dad's philosophy even further. In 1957 Jack Bricker, the personnel director, came back to me with a radical proposal: that we abolish the hourly wage and shift all of our employees onto salaries. This would eliminate the last difference between factory and office work and put all of our people on an equal status. It was a daring plan, affecting about twenty thousand of our sixty thousand U.S. employees, and Bricker had the details so well worked out that all I had to do was approve it.

In January 1958, I announced this change in a nationwide telephone broadcast to the factories. Although the shift to salaries came off well, a number of our managers predicted that many workers would take advantage of the policy and skip work whenever they felt like it. The joke went around that on the first day of hunting season no one would show up for work at our Rochester, Minnesota, plant. As far as I know, we were the first major industrial company to put its whole population on salary. It was a small contribution to U.S. labor history, due solely to Jack Bricker, and I was very proud of it. A few months later, at a meeting in Washington, Walter Reuther, the great United Auto Workers leader, couldn't resist needling me. "What are you trying to do?" he said. "Make us look bad?"

I considered taking even more radical steps to increase IBM's commitment to its employees. When I talked to my wife at night, I would speak of various ways of sharing our success more broadly. Those at the top were doing fantastically well on stock options—despite the fact that Williams and I stopped taking options in 1958, after Williams said, "We don't want to look like pigs." While IBM's workers were making good money, they couldn't look forward to the rich capital gains that executives with options had. In my own case, for example, I had stock options worth about five times my salary, or close to $2 million. From that investment I knew that I was going to make tens of millions of dollars if IBM kept doing as well as it always had. I asked myself, "How much more am I worth to IBM than that guy down at the bottom of the pay scale? Twice as much? Sure. Ten times as much? Maybe. Twenty times as much? Probably not." I became more and more puzzled at the idea of rewarding executives at a rate wholly different from the people down the line.

So I began to think about ways of sharing the fruits of IBM's success. My first idea was to distribute the company profits right down to the office boy. When I mentioned this to Williams, he was horrified. "That would put us out of business!" he said. He showed how, if we reckoned what our stock options would likely be worth and averaged them out over our careers, they probably tripled our annual pay. "If we turned around and tripled the whole payroll," he said, "we'd be giving away the entire profit. Nothing would be left for the shareholders." That made me think even harder.

I began asking myself whether our present form of capitalism is the best way to support American democracy in the long term. It didn't seem that way to me. I thought that the model corporation of the future should be largely owned by the people who work for it, not by banks or mutual funds or shareholders who might have inherited the stock from their parents and done nothing to earn it. Entrepreneurs and capitalists would always have a key place—if you risk your money by putting it behind Henry Ford you certainly ought to be able to enjoy the fruits of your investment. But there is enormous strength in proprietorship—people develop strong attachments to the things they own, especially if they can influence whether those things succeed or fail—and it seemed imprudent to let the ownership of a business rest with people and institutions that are not directly involved. Remedying this situation would have to be an evolutionary process, but as I imagined it, gradually, over two or three generations, a business would, by law, shift into the hands of employees.

Though I never found a practical way to achieve it on a meaningful scale, I began looking for ways to increase employee ownership of IBM. In 1958 we established a stock purchase plan, whereby any employee could allot up to ten percent of his salary and acquire IBM shares at 85 percent of their market value. This was a step beyond what my father had been willing to do. Even though he encouraged employees to buy the stock, he stopped short of setting up a formal program because he didn't want those who couldn't afford losses to take undue risks. He never forgot his own close scrape with creditors when the bottom dropped out of the stock, in the 1930s.

If everybody in IBM had started buying stock when the purchase plan started, and held on to it, the company would belong to the employees by now, and there would be IBM millionaires by the thousand. But that is not how it worked out. Instead, many people bought the stock, but very few stayed with it. Most people would get a 25 percent increase in their investment and sell out. We also found that the plan hurt morale whenever the stock value declined. I did everything I could to encourage them to hold on, short of personally touting the stock—every year, for example, we published figures showing how wealthy people became by owning IBM over a long period. But people never used the plan to the extent I envisioned.

Did this mean the average guy on the factory line was stupid? I don't think so. I figured their reluctance to stay with the stock was mainly due to economic circumstances. Most likely a man was selling out because he'd rather have the mortgage on his house reduced than keep his money at risk in the stock. If you looked at the median IBM salary, although it was above the national average, it didn't leave much latitude for fiddling around with investment risks. We decided we could do the best for our employees by developing benefits such as major medical coverage, scholarships and college-tuition loans, and matching grants for charities and schools. I wanted IBM to be recognized as one of the most generous employers in America.

CHAPTER 25

During the late 1950s I had a very popular family. *Life* came to Greenwich and did a photo essay about us. A little while later *Sports Illustrated* put us on the cover. "Skiing Family: The Tom Watsons" it said, and the picture showed Olive and me and four of our kids fooling around in a snowy Vermont scene. If *People* magazine had existed, I suppose we might have been in that as well. We seemed to have everything: my success, Olive's beauty, and by this time six bright, energetic kids. However, life behind the scenes wasn't always so ideal. We had the usual stresses and strains that anyone in a large family could understand. But the main problem was my temper.

If my disposition had been easier, I might have had a brilliant career as a father, because I did a lot of imaginative things for my children. My great shortcoming, unfortunately, was that I did not understand how to change pace when I left the office. That is the toughest thing for any manager to learn. All day long I faced a parade of people asking for decisions—whether to worry about a competitor's new product, how to resolve an ambiguity in IBM's personnel policy, what to do about a manager paralyzed with grief over the loss of a spouse. Through all of it would be the telephone ringing—more people with more problems. The decisions themselves were never that hard to make; what was hard was the cumulative effect of being the man on the spot day after day after day. Try as I might, it was never possible to delegate enough.

By the time I got home, there would be nothing left of me. I'd walk in and find the usual disorder of a large household—one of the kids had shot a BB gun at a passing car, or two of them were fighting, or somebody had bad grades. These things would strike me as crises that needed to be resolved right away, and yet I had no energy to bring to bear. I'd feel a desperate wish for somebody else to step in and make the decisions so I didn't have to. That's when I'd blow up. The kids would scatter like quail and Olive would catch the brunt of my frustration. In fact she was a wonderful mother, patient and sympathetic. I suppose I wanted her to be as strict a disciplinarian as my own mother had been with me, even though this was foreign to Olive's nature. It took me years to grasp the fundamental difference between running a company and heading a family. IBM was like driving a car: when I came to a corner, I could steer around it very nicely, and off the car would go down a new road. I hit bumps here and there, but generally the car went where I wanted. With my family, this wasn't the case. The family was more like a car with two steering wheels, or multiple steering wheels, and only one of them belonged to me. I kept trying to exercise more control than I had.

When I saw I could not bend my wife and children to my will, I'd feel totally thwarted and boxed in. Those were the blackest moments of my adult life. An argument with Olive and the kids would sometimes make me so morose that the only thing I could do was hole up. I'd lock myself in my dressing room and Olive would stand on the other side of the door and try to get me to come out. Finally she'd reach the end of her rope. She'd call my brother and say, "Can't you come cheer Tom up?" Dick would come down from New Canaan. He always knew how to make my responsibilities seem lighter and draw me back into the world.

My hot temper also backfired when I did community work. For several years I was president of the board of trustees at the Greenwich Country Day School, where we sent our children. I worked hard at this job, and I think that the people who served with me would have said, "Watson is a man under enormous pressure, but he is creative and never misses a meeting." My downfall came one summer when the local newspaper carried a police report that one of our teachers had solicited a vagrant for a homosexual encounter. The community was in an uproar, and the headmaster, who should have handled the matter, had just left for vacation with his wife. When someone tracked him down by phone, he suggested that the matter be turned over to the assistant headmaster. Instead, I did what I would have done at IBM. I organized a task force of influential board members, investigated the incident, and discharged the teacher with a sum of money from the board to help pay for psychiatric treatment. That should have been the end of it. But I was so angry with the headmaster for not having dealt with the problem himself that when he got back, I bawled him out. He really blew his top. It dawned on me too late that I shouldn't alienate the man: he was a capable administrator and more essential than I to the running of the school. Our dispute spilled over to the board, which rejected my effort to make amends by donating money for one of the headmaster's pet projects. Finally I resigned as president, but not before almost coming to blows in the middle of a meeting with a fellow board member, a prominent banker. He accused me of being self-serving, and I grabbed his arm, whirled him around to face me, and was ready to hit him when I heard somebody in the background say, "Don't be a damn fool." That outburst damaged my reputation to such a degree that I was never invited to join another Greenwich board.

My temper tantrums at home usually didn't last very long, and my father had taught me never to let the sun set on a family argument. As I cooled off I'd see the error of my ways and come back to put my arms around Olive and apologize for my inexcusable behavior. When my highhandedness and volatile temper caused hard feelings in our house, it was her patience and understanding that actually kept the family together. She had an ability to love in a perfectly natural and deep way, and she often showed me more kindness than I deserved.

Like all parents, Olive and I were trying to improve on the way in which we'd been raised. I thought my father had never taken enough time for his private life. He was always Mr. IBM, and when he wasn't working, he was somewhere else in the public arena, advancing his own reputation and the company's. I never wanted IBM to monopolize my time the way it monopolized his, and I was young and vigorous enough to do the sort of active things with my kids that Dad never did with me. I saved almost all my weekends to take them skiing or camping or sailing, and I did everything I could to give them a sense of fun and adventure.

Olive had only one brother growing up, and always imagined how nice having a large family must be. In the late 1930s she'd been able to observe one big clan closely: the Kennedys. Although Joseph Kennedy was ambassador to England then, the family was still not widely known. Just by chance Olive became friends with Jack and two of his sisters in school, and she began spending time during the summers at their Hyannis Port house. Sunday dinner in our own house was modeled to an extent after theirs. Olive would organize the meal by naming a subject for discussion—it could be anything from horses to the country of Japan—but there was one subject, and you had to do research if you expected to hold your own. In the Kennedy household, the topics had always been serious—politics, current affairs, international news. The ambassador presided, and something he did at one such meal made a lasting impression on my wife. The conversation that day was about a public figure and young Teddy—who was then only about five—raised his hand and said, "And he has curly hair!" All of his siblings began to laugh at him but Mr. Kennedy roared, "Be still!" Then he looked down the table to Teddy and said, "You are a very observant young man." He had a way of giving confidence to all his children, and that is what Olive wanted to provide to ours.

Our house in Greenwich had fifteen rooms spilling over with kids, pets, and friends. It was decorated with dozens of odd things I'd picked up all over the world, such as a hat collection from Asia and Latin America and a miniature paupau outrigger from the Pacific. Behind the house there was a rolling lawn and some big trees where I strung up a big war-surplus cargo net for the kids to climb on. We had a tiny Messerschmitt car for play rides, and somewhere I'd gotten hold of a sailing dinghy that collapsed into a couple of suitcases. We used it for voyages on nearby rivers and across the little lake at the edge of our property.

The year our family appeared in *Life* magazine, my son was thirteen, just starting at boarding school. He was a sturdy, serious fellow and his sisters often complained that he was trying to lord it over them; he and I liked camping together and spent many hours on rifle practice in the garden. Jeannette was eleven, a little dreamy sometimes and very taken with Elvis Presley, but already a wonderful storyteller with a merry sense of humor that reminded me of my mother's. Olive was two years younger than Jeannette, but much more assertive and extroverted. While all the other kids called me Dad, Olive liked to call me Tom just to get a rise out of me. Cindy, who was seven, patterned herself after Olive and was absolutely fearless, and Susan, four, was a sweet little girl attached to her dolls. Finally there was Helen, our one-year-old. She was a beautiful child but I didn't have much sense of her yet—I was never any good at playing with babies.

We concentrated on sports the whole family could do. We built a tennis court with the idea that everybody could learn together. We all had bikes, and on weekends we'd go on family rides, sometimes to the embarrassment of our teenagers. The center of our winter activity was our ski lodge in Vermont. Olive and I had been going to Vermont to ski ever since the blind date on which we met, and when IBM hit the billion-dollar mark, we built a house there. From the standpoint of family finances this decision seemed as momentous and risky as any I made at work. Skiing was still fairly uncommon then. There was only one other ski house near where we built our lodge, about six miles outside Stowe at the foot of Mount Mansfield. The chair lift on that mountain was the first in New England; it ran the chairs up single file and on busy weekends you were lucky if you waited only forty-five minutes to take your turn. The house itself had great vaulted ceilings and a wall of glass looking out on the snowy woods. It slept twenty people, with two bedrooms for couples and dormitories for boys and girls. We filled the place with souvenirs from our Alpine and Scandinavian trips, and on the floor we had carpeting that could be rolled back to bare linoleum for dancing. Near the fireplace hung an ordinary-looking painting of a snowy mountainside that symbolized what Vermont meant to me. The painting had hung originally in the banquet hall of the IBM country club at Endicott, where Dad held endless testimonial dinners. It always reminded me of a particular bend in one of the ski trails at Stowe. I'd get through those Endicott dinners by fixing my eyes on it and thinking, "In two more days I'll be there."

We'd make the seven-hour drive to Stowe almost every weekend. Some of our family's happiest times were in that house—I still recall pulling into the driveway with a station wagon full of lovely little kids clamoring to get out and show their friends where to sleep. The lodge was an exciting place for unsuspecting guests because we were constantly playing jokes on each other—rubber snakes hidden in the bedclothes, cups of water balanced on top of doors. Olive and I made the kids bring their homework, but most often they'd drop their book bags near the front door on the way in and not touch them again until the weekend was over. That was partly my fault—I kept them so active that they didn't have time to read. I'd roust the kids out each morning at seven o'clock by turning on the dormitory lights and playing yodeling music full blast. We'd feed them, then turn them loose on the slopes, and no one was allowed back into the house until the lift closed around four.

We intentionally kept things Spartan on those ski trips. There was no way for our kids not to know they were surrounded by increasing wealth, but we didn't want them growing up coddled and spoiled. The cleaning and cooking were all done by Olive and me. Fixing food is something I love, going back to the days when I earned a cooking merit badge in the Boy Scouts under my mother's appreciative eye. I had the whole kitchen organized

with labels on all the drawers and cabinets, so that whoever was helping me could put the stuff away correctly.
Olive invented a clever way to organize the dormitories.
She found out that there were six standard colors of
towel available, so she had the six beds in each dormitory
painted those same colors. Each bed had its own matching towels hanging at the end, and in the bathrooms there
were cabinets color-coded the same way. So there were
no arguments about keeping the dormitories neat. Meanwhile I tried to pass along my mother's sense of thrift.
My daughter Jeannette tells the story of how I was constantly badgering people to turn out lights when leaving a
room. This campaign failed, and finally one morning I
waited until they'd all gone out, unscrewed the light
bulbs that they'd left burning, and hid them. When the
kids came back at sunset, none of them could turn on
their lights.

Building a ski lodge was a pretty ambitious undertaking, but I had even grander ideas when we looked for a
summer house. I wanted a place where we could land an
airplane and anchor the sailboat I had for ocean racing—
and that we could afford while the kids were still young,
without waiting for IBM to grow even larger. Olive and I
did our prospecting from a small rented airplane. We flew
both coasts of Long Island, then Block Island, Martha's
Vineyard, Nantucket, and Cape Cod. Pretty soon we
were halfway up the coast of Maine, near Camden, where
Dad had a summer house when I was a boy. Finally we
found an interesting place on North Haven Island, several miles out from Camden in Penobscot Bay. The land
for sale was called Oak Hill Farm—a beautiful and rugged half-mile-long peninsula with rocky beaches, groves
of spruce, bare fields cropped short by generations of
sheep, and at the highest point, a few lonely oaks that
gave the place its name. The only building was a ram-
bling old farmhouse with falling-down chimneys, but
there was a good cove and sufficient level ground for an
airstrip.

There is nothing more beautiful than summer on the
coast of Maine, when everything blooms during the short

intermission from nine months of cold and fog. That magical place became the center of our summers, and visitors came in a constant stream—aviators, yachtsmen, kids' friends from school. The house had been vacant for twenty years when we bought it; the previous owner had been planning to bulldoze it and build a proper mansion on the highest hilltop of the farm. But Olive and I decided the existing building would suit us fine once the chimneys and roof were fixed. It actually consisted of a barn and two farmhouses that had been put together fifty years before. The houses had plenty of small, snug rooms, and the barn was a large recreation space. One year we invited the entire island for a square dance there, and the dance became a summer tradition.

We cut roads and vistas through the spruce groves; we brought horses and ponies and donkeys to ride. I got the idea that we should turn loose a lot of animals on the land, safe animals that would be fun to have around. So I talked to Dillon Ripley, the head of the Smithsonian, to get the names of harmless species. Llamas were right at the head of the list, so we got a pair of llamas. Then some fallow deer, which are yellowish brown and extremely skittish, and pheasant and woodcocks and wild turkeys. I almost got some buffalo after learning that there were two buffalo farms in Maine. I called the first guy and told him I was interested in getting some as pets and he said, "Pets! These are vicious animals! If you catch them in the wrong mood they'll attack you." I thanked him and called the second buffalo farmer, who was more of a salesman. He said they were as gentle as bunnies. "We feed them right out of our kitchen door," he told me. Both were willing to sell me buffalo but I decided to take the first guy's advice. Instead I bought a pair of reindeer and some mouflon sheep, which are domesticated but look like Rocky Mountain sheep, with long curved horns.

I saw Oak Hill as the place where no project was too whimsical to pursue. I loved to drive the kids up and down the hills in an old Model T, like the one I bought on the sly when I was only twelve. The kids named the roads with family phrases, such as "It's Hard But It's

Fair Way" and "Come On, Daddy Road." At one point we had a bright red amphibious automobile—the kids would invite their friends to a picnic and then amaze them by having me drive them across the water to a small island about two hundred yards offshore. On some projects I really got carried away. On a hill by the water is a Chinese junk. I bought it on a trip to Hong Kong and had it transported to Maine. But it turned out to be dreadfully hard to sail and the kids didn't like it, so we hauled it out of the water and put it up on blocks as an ornament. On top of another hill is a fifty-foot totem pole, the handiwork of an itinerant Native American who called himself Chief Kickpou. I ran across him in Canada one year, and although I was never clear what tribe he came from, I thought he was a charming man. He talked me into letting him bring his assistants and carve a totem pole for us. After a while it seemed lonely on its hilltop, so on a trip to Colorado I found life-size bronze statues of Plains Indian squaws grinding maize, and set those up in the tall weeds near the base. I thought of Chief Kickpou's totem pole as a monument to fast-talking salesmen everywhere.

Olive and I took our kids traveling whenever we could. Travel makes a tremendous impression on children, and I thought it was one of the most important things we could provide. Here I patterned myself after Dad—I remembered his taking us on automobile caravans in the early days, to places like Niagara Falls and Washington. Olive and I never hesitated to pluck a child out of school if it looked as if a trip might do him or her good. Cindy went with me on several business trips, and Jeannette still talks about the time we decided she seemed droopy and took her to Paris for a week.

Every couple of years I'd break away from IBM and take my family on a major journey. I put as much work and thought into those trips as I did into major business moves. For months beforehand the kids would see me making up long checklists, poring over maps on the dining room table, and studying books about the places we were going to see. The first thing I did was introduce the kids to America. I rented an IBM airplane and flew them myself from White Plains to California and back with many stops. I went down low over the grain fields so they could see how flat it was; I took them over the center of the Rockies. When we stopped in Las Vegas for fuel, they all ran into the depot and started playing the slot machines until the owner came out to tell me they were too young to gamble. Olive was the best possible partner on these adventures. She was a good sport about the inconveniences and quite intrepid when things went wrong. There was the afternoon I decided to show the family the Grand Canyon. The plane was bouncing around because of air turbulence and the younger children got sick. Jeannette still remembers the scene of me at the controls, pointing out the beautiful scenes zooming by, and Olive in the back of the plane holding airsickness bags for two children at once. She was a real trouper.

I'd use every tool at hand—imagination, money, Dad's old connections—to make these trips memorable for the kids. Our first big international journey was in the summer of 1958, when I left IBM for six weeks and took the family across Sweden in a boat, sailing the Goeta Canal and up and down the Baltic. Sailing gives me almost as much pleasure as flying, and our boat was a new fifty-four-foot yawl that I'd commissioned from the famous Bremen yacht makers Abeking & Rasmussen. We picked up the boat at the shipyard, and christened her *Palawan,* after a beautiful island in the Philippines that I visited during the war. The conventional wisdom in yachting is that you can't have a comfortable family boat that is also a good racer, but to a degree the *Palawan* was both. The next year I sailed her to my first major yachting victory in a New York Yacht Club race around Long Island.

Olive and I worked hard to organize everything on the boat, down to the food lists and duty schedules. We'd both been to Sweden before, but none of the kids knew what to expect. *Palawan* quickly turned into a floating picture of life with children, and we'd be seen pulling into ports with kids' laundry hung out to dry along the railings of our elegant new yacht. The towns we visited were very safe, so Olive and I let the kids take the bicycles we'd brought along and explore by themselves. Even little Susan, who was only four, struck out on her own— Olive would tell her we needed milk and she'd take a small pail and march to the nearest store. One thing that surprised the kids was Sweden's sensuality. The Swedes love to take off their clothes when the sun shines, and the sight of people swimming nude amazed our four proper daughters, not to mention my son. The joke on the boat was that the two Toms were always racing each other for the binoculars.

The only piece of IBM equipment we had on board *Palawan* was a dictation machine—the typewriter division was making them by then—and we used it to keep a log of our trip. Each family member was responsible for one day of the week. I made a game of it, holding the microphone up to the little ones and asking questions. I also took hundreds of pictures, and when we got back those went into a scrapbook with typed-up excerpts from the dictation tapes as a caption under each one.

The trip was such a success that we later made equally ambitious journeys to Israel, Greece, and Japan. But these travels were also a good example of how my tendency to be dictatorial undermined my effectiveness as a father. I would go to enormous trouble to plan a trip, but then defeat my own purpose by failing to sell the idea to the kids. Instead of asking if they wanted to go, I simply ordered them to do it. In retrospect it seems to me it would have been so easy to build up slowly to an idea, by saying something like, "You know, there is a canal that runs across Sweden." And then, the next day, "Gee, I wonder what it would be like to be on that canal . . ." until the kids got excited and clamored to go. But instead I'd announce, "I've booked seats on TWA this June and here's what we're going to do."

The one place on earth where I felt free to forget I was head of anything and just have fun was Europe. For two weeks each winter, Olive and I would take time off and go skiing in the Alps without the kids. We'd travel in a group of perhaps ten friends. My favorite resort towns were Kitzbühel and Davos—Kitzbühel especially, because of the beautiful zither music played there, which I love. We'd ski all day, and at night there were parties in the small restaurants in the villages and sometimes on the top of an alp. It cost almost nothing to get the cog railroad to run a single car loaded with friends up the mountain for the evening. The music would play, the sweet Austrian wine would flow, and we'd go back down the mountain afterward filled with romance and with beautiful old alpine dances still ringing in our ears.

Europe was the province of IBM World Trade, of course, my brother's territory and not mine, but I had occasion once or twice each year to go there on business all the same. Dick and I always found time to break away, and this led to some of the best moments we ever had together. One evening in the late '50s he and I flew into Berlin with Wiz Miller. We had an appointment the next morning to see Willy Brandt, the prominent Social Democrat who was then mayor of the city and later chancellor of West Germany. Nightclubs, of course, were Berlin's great attraction, and none of us felt like staying in our hotel studying our notes for the meeting, so we went out on the town. We saw a couple of unusual cabaret shows and ended up in a famous nightclub in which each table had a number prominently displayed, and a telephone. The idea was that if you saw a girl you liked across the room, you could call and introduce yourself. Dick and Wiz and I had a fantastic time watching this scene and we managed to stay out almost until dawn without doing anything scandalous. But the next morning was very confused. None of us remembered to leave a call at the desk, and when I woke up we had less than half an hour before we were supposed to meet with Brandt. I'd never seen three people put on white shirts so fast. We raced across town in a taxi, quarreling about whose fault it was that we'd overslept. The meeting with the mayor came off well, so no harm was done to Watson family honor. But I kept wondering what Dad would have thought.

CHAPTER 26

In the middle of 1959, I heard on the radio that Nikita Khrushchev was coming to visit the United States. I thought of a surefire way to make IBM stand out: we could give him a tour of one of our factories. Before sending an invitation I called the State Department to make sure I wasn't violating diplomatic protocol. An official who was helping to plan Khrushchev's stay got on the phone. "We'd like to invite the premier to visit IBM," I told him. "Does the State Department have any problem with that?"

He said, "No problem, but he won't come."

I sent a wire directly to Khrushchev at the Kremlin. It said, "I'd like very much to show you an advanced electronics plant. We have such plants in Poughkeepsie, New York and San Jose, California. We can make your visit as brief as you like, but we recommend that if you want to get a feel for the product and the people who make it, you come in the morning and stay for lunch."

I heard nothing for several weeks. We pulled some strings but never expected it to work. Then Gav Cullen, the head of the San Jose plant, called me and said, "What are you trying to do to me?"

"What do you mean?"

"I've got two Soviet lieutenant generals here who want to check out the plant!" That was how I learned Khrushchev had said yes.

I'd been to Moscow myself only a month before. There was a brief thaw in the cold war that year, and Eisenhower and Khrushchev were trying to promote understanding between our two peoples. The United States put on a big exhibition of consumer products and technology at Sokolniki Park in Moscow. IBM had a RAMAC machine on display, performing feats of electronic memory, and in the course of six weeks, two and a half million Russians crowded in to see it and other evidence of American prosperity. One of the exhibits was a model home featuring all the latest appliances, where Khrushchev and Vice President Richard Nixon had their famous Kitchen Debate. The issue was whether the U.S. was trying to fool Russians by displaying gadgets that no ordinary American could afford.

In spite of all the tension between our two countries I found it an amazing experience to walk the streets of Moscow, which I hadn't seen since the war, and to stay once again in the National Hotel overlooking Red Square. It had been pretty much off limits to Westerners for years, but by some miracle the Russians assigned me the Lenin suite—where Lenin himself had lived after returning from exile in 1917. It was like a national shrine, but to me it was very familiar—it had been our crew quarters on the Bradley mission, and many a night in 1942 I'd played poker there.

IBM spent weeks getting ready for Khrushchev. He had visits planned to a Hollywood studio, a college, and a farm, but it turned out the John Deere Corporation and IBM were the only major companies that hosted him. The business community held back partly on ideological grounds, but also out of fear. So many people had been criticized for trying to improve relations with the Russians that business leaders were afraid to extend themselves. The only other businessman Khrushchev was scheduled to visit was Roswell Garst, an Iowa entrepreneur who was selling the Russians seed corn.

The first thing I did was to go down to the United Nations and hire an interpreter. Several days before Khrushchev arrived, I went out to San Jose and set up shop in a hotel. I foresaw all sorts of potential problems and incidents I wanted to avoid. For example, IBM had led American industry in hiring refugees after Khrushchev crushed the Hungarian Revolution. I realized that some of our employees must hate him, and I wanted to make sure there was no provocation from our side. So I posted a notice on the factory bulletin boards that said, "My invitation to Premier Khrushchev is not an endorsement of his regime. I think the interests of the United States will be advanced by his visit. Anybody who objects to his presence can have two days off with pay." I figured offering only one day wasn't enough to get potential troublemakers to leave. About twenty employees took me up on the offer.

The computer demonstration we planned for Khrushchev was pretty dramatic. We had the RAMAC programmed to work like an electronic history book. You could ask it in any of ten languages for the major events of any year from 4 B.C. to the present. Of course, some years were not as eventful as others, but we had something for each year. If you said A.D. 30, for example, the machine would type out "Salome asked for and received the head of John the Baptist." And, more to the point, if you said 1917 it would reply "The Russian Revolution." This demonstration was dear to my heart because I'd thought it up myself. The fellow we picked to put the RAMAC through its paces was a tough Polish immigrant from our Los Angeles office who spoke fluent Russian. He called himself Eddie Corwin, but I knew him from sales school in 1937, when he was still Eddie Sochaczewski. When Hitler invaded Poland, Eddie fought in the Polish cavalry, got captured in the first week of fighting, and made it through six years in a Nazi POW camp. A couple of days before Khrushchev came I was in the plant going over the schedule and I asked Eddie, "How long will your demonstration take?"

"About fifteen minutes, including questions."

"But we have twenty minutes allotted to this. What about the other five?"

He looked me right in the eye and said, "I'm going to talk about the plight of Polish exiles in the Soviet Union."

I said, "Eddie, you know you can't do that."

"It's very important to me."

"Khrushchev is going to be our guest. Unless I have

your word of honor you won't do it, I can't let you give the demonstration."

He looked aside, scowled, and finally agreed, so I kept him in the program.

Khrushchev started out on the East Coast and went on to Los Angeles. I followed all the TV and newspaper reports and wondered what I was getting us into. He traded insults with the press corps in Washington, was rude to Eleanor Roosevelt at her home, and almost caused an international incident when the mayor of Los Angeles told him that he couldn't go to Disneyland because of the security risk. According to the papers Khrushchev pounded on a banquet table and said, "Why not? Do you have rocket-launching pads there? Is there an epidemic of cholera or something? Have gangsters taken hold of the place? The situation is inconceivable! I cannot find words to explain this to my people!" I began to worry that he'd use IBM as a platform for denouncing the American way of life. Day and night I imagined situations in which Khrushchev would say something insulting and I'd have to find the proper diplomatic response. But after Los Angeles there was an amazing shift of tone. Somehow he and the Americans warmed to one another. Khrushchev's message stayed the same, but suddenly his manner changed: he was all smiles. He checked into a San Francisco hotel and a huge crowd cheered when he came to the window and waved. The next morning, on the way to see us, he caused bedlam by making a spur-of-the-moment visit to a San Francisco supermarket, and then stopped off unannounced at a hiring hall for the longshoremen's union.

Finally it was our turn. His motorcade pulled in just before lunch and there was the premier, a funny little round man in a rumpled tan suit. He had on a bright white longshoreman's cap that he'd just swapped his own hat for at the hiring hall. His official escort was Henry Cabot Lodge, the U.S. ambassador to the United Nations, whom I knew slightly. With them were dozens of officials from both sides and a crush of newsmen. Olive and I came forward to say hello to him—Mrs. Khru-

shchev had stayed in San Francisco to do some shopping
—and we escorted him into the plant.

Khrushchev loved to eat, and what broke the ice was
the fact that we'd arranged things so that lunch came
first. Earlier that week I'd carefully instructed the caterer
who ran our cafeteria, "We want to show Khrushchev a
typical day at the plant. No special arrangements. Serve
an average lunch." The caterer stuck to the usual menu,
but somehow he produced the damnedest cafeteria meal
I'd ever seen—beautiful California salads and an array of
cold meats that would have graced the Waldorf. I gave
Khrushchev a tray, took one for myself, and we went
through the self-service line. The practice there was to
restrict the quantity you could take from the buffet by
using plates and bowls that were pretty small. That didn't
stop Khrushchev. As we went along I noticed he was
heaping his bowl with more and more food. I was determined not to smile because there were photographers all
around and I thought it would make a horribly embarrassing picture, me laughing at him. But Khrushchev
must have been reading my mind. He got his bowl piled
three or four inches high and then glanced up at me and
gave a pert little smile, which caused me to burst out
laughing. Of course the *New York Times* clicked it and we
made the paper the following day.

Lunch seemed to put the premier in a happy mood.
"You are well versed in psychology," he said to me. "You
started off our acquaintance by taking me to this dining
room." His interpreter, Viktor Sukhodrev, was so much
better than the guy I'd brought in from the United Nations that the UN guy couldn't get a word in edgewise. I
didn't mind because it was obvious that Sukhodrev was
giving faithful translations. Later on, when we toured the
plant, Khrushchev said, "We have plants like this in the
Soviet Union." Then he looked a little puzzled and said,
half to himself, "We *must* have plants like this in the
Soviet Union." Why Sukhodrev didn't leave that one un-
translated I never knew.

Khrushchev was constantly putting his hands on people. In the brief time he spent walking through the plant

he managed to make a personal impression on every employee there. My father was the only other man I ever knew who could affect a large crowd that way. We had the entire tour precisely scheduled and choreographed, but Khrushchev broke away in the middle of the factory floor and went up to a couple of workers. "What type of work do you do?" he asked each man. "What is your salary? How much do you spend for groceries? Is this a typical wage here?" The Russians had launched a successful moon probe called Lunik, and Khrushchev started pinning Lunik medals on people. After he went by you would see the workers pulling those medals off and looking at them. Some of them put their medals back on, and some of them said, "That s.o.b.," and pitched them in the ashcan.

We stepped up in front of microphones and Khrushchev thanked us for the warm welcome we'd given him. Then he made what were widely reported as the most amicable remarks of his U.S. stay, saying that Russia wanted to be friends with the American people and the American government, and that he drew no line of distinction between the two. There was only one insinuation in his speech that I didn't like. He said, "Whenever we meet with businessmen, we have no conflicts with each another. But often when I meet, for instance, with trade union leaders or some politicians, it turns out that matters are not so smooth." I thought this was a veiled insult to Eisenhower, who had just put him through three days of tough talks at Camp David on the subject of Berlin. Much as I wanted to be a good host, I couldn't let that ride. So after he finished I said, "Ladies and gentlemen, the chairman attributed to me a peaceful tone, but this tone was set by President Eisenhower, not me." To my great relief, Khrushchev didn't pursue the matter further, so there was no sequel in the IBM cafeteria to Nixon's Kitchen Debate.

I was intrigued at the thought of becoming a prominent figure on the national scene. Not that I was looking for a political career—I wasn't, at least not then—but I

wanted to be known as a citizen who could come to
Washington and do a job for the government just as
successfully as I ran IBM. Government service was
an opportunity to go beyond what my father had accomplished. Although he'd been close to Roosevelt and
helped organize the Business Advisory Council, Dad was
generally so busy with IBM and the International Chamber of Commerce that he restricted his government activity to ceremonial jobs. I, on the other hand, liked the
prospect of getting actively involved and going to Washington regularly, and I wasn't bothered by another consideration that may have held Dad back. When a
businessman, even a very successful businessman at the
peak of his career, steps out of his company and takes on
a task for the government, he gives up much of his power
and becomes a novice all over again. That would have
had no appeal to Dad, who above everything else loved to
rule the roost at IBM. But I was still quite a young man,
and didn't mind being seen as an amateur as long as I
could learn.

As one of the few liberals in the business community
in the late '50s, I was often surprised by the amount of
controversy I stirred up—and I enjoyed it. Two months
after Khrushchev's visit, for example, I gave a speech to
the National Association of Manufacturers at the Waldorf and shocked them with a call for higher taxes. I
pointed out that more money was probably essential if we
expected to stay ahead of the Soviets.

> We must realize that some sacrifice is necessary. We
> can't do all the things necessary for the United
> States to do—in this country and abroad—and still
> proceed on the "business as usual" basis. One of
> our first sacrifices must be a willingness to accept
> higher taxes, if necessary, in order to accomplish
> our purpose of keeping America ahead of the world
> on all counts.

I had arranged to leave right after the speech without
ever going back into the audience. I stepped down from

the podium, went out the back door, into a waiting car, and was off on a trip to Europe immediately. It wasn't until later that I found out what an uproar my speech caused. The next morning there were front-page stories in the *Times* and *Herald Tribune:*

N.A.M. Tax Stand Hit by Watson
Assails "Business as Usual" View

The president of the organization even called a press conference where he claimed that I'd meant the opposite of what I'd said. The official National Association of Manufacturers position, of course, was that Congress should indeed try to increase federal revenues—by spurring the economy with lower taxes.

I was trying to set an example for all our managers. It hadn't been so many years since the McCarthy hearings, and I urged them to participate in the democratic process. "Your rank at IBM gives you a platform in the community," I'd tell them. "Stand on it and try to influence the country for good as you see it." This was the twilight of the Eisenhower era, and prominent people from America's universities and businesses and labor unions were beginning to think about the future in an exciting new way. In his last year in office, Eisenhower put together a Commission on National Goals under Henry Wriston, the president emeritus of Brown University. Eisenhower gave it a huge job: to chart a direction for the United States in the 1960s in critical areas such as civil rights, foreign policy, unemployment, and urban decay. Over a hundred people participated, from George Meany of the AFL-CIO to Crawford Greenewalt, the head of Du Pont. I played a role as the head of a panel on technological change. It consisted of Walter Reuther, the United Auto Workers leader, George Shultz, then a young economics professor, Charles Percy, then still president of Bell & Howell, and IBM's own Manny Piore.

Even though the members of the commission were Eisenhower appointees, what they produced was practically a map for Kennedy's New Frontier. They reached a bipartisan consensus on dozens of issues, ranging from national support of the arts to the use of federal power, if necessary, to enforce voting rights. When the final report came out a few days after Kennedy got elected, I remember CBS commentator Howard K. Smith saying, "If there were not abundant evidence Senator Kennedy has been fully occupied with other things lately, one would swear he wrote the document."

Kennedy's victory transformed my status in the business world in the same way that Roosevelt transformed Dad's. Before Kennedy, most businessmen saw me as a character on the liberal fringe, and more or less tolerated my opinions because of IBM's success. Now all of a sudden I had a chance to become a much bigger fish. The Business Advisory Council, for instance, advanced me from oblivion to the office of vice chairman, and I soon found myself trying to be a peacemaker between big business and the White House.

The Kennedy family had first come into my life years before, on a train platform in Switzerland in 1952. Olive and I were changing trains on our way to Davos, and noticed a large pile of expensive-looking baggage. Olive checked the tags and said "The Kennedys!" Then Jean and Pat Kennedy ran up and gave her a big embrace. They were on their way to Davos too, and we saw a lot of them for a week. We went out together at night and they were full of fun. When the week ended they had to hustle home to give tea parties for Jack, who was running for the Senate for the first time.

Various Kennedys began to come to Stowe frequently. They didn't stay at our house, but it was often a gathering place in the evenings. Pat would show up with my close friend Bill MacDougall, the Pan Am pilot she was dating at the time, and Bobby and Ethel would bring a carload of kids. We could seat maybe twenty-five kids in the lodge, up and down the stairs and across a catwalk on one side of the room, and we'd show movies. Their kids were all full of beans but nice. When we had a party the Kennedys loved the same foolish funny games we did.

I didn't meet Jack Kennedy until 1958, when we ran into each other on the air shuttle to Washington. I introduced myself and we chatted about his family and mine. Over the years I'd heard Jack praised so much by my wife and his sisters that I felt some resistance to him, but any reservations I had evaporated very fast when I saw him debate Nixon on television. After the second debate I was sure he was going to win the election. I wrote him a letter that said, "I am for you." One of his aides called to ask if I would declare my support to the press. Since I was chairman of a corporation that did a lot of business with both Democrats and Republicans, I said no. But I told the Kennedy people I'd make no secret of who I was voting for and if they wanted to spread the word, they could. I worked hard for Kennedy's election by making gifts, writing letters, and personally trying to drum up support. He was so unpopular in the corporate world that the business people who learned what I was doing thought I had lost my mind. Before election day, Olive and I went to a meeting of the Business Advisory Council and found it difficult even to engage anyone in conversation, they were so put out.

I was delighted when he won, and got a little carried away in my enthusiasm when I addressed the Hundred Percent Club that winter. "I had to hold my tongue prior to the election," I told our salesmen, "but now that Kennedy is president of all the people, I'm free to speak. I think you will agree that we should congratulate ourselves, because we have elected a terrific president." This remark produced dozens of complaints from young Hundred Percenters, who invited me to keep my political views to myself. Somehow I'd lost sight of a basic fact of human nature. If a fellow starts out poor, works his way through college, and quickly makes a lot of money, he turns ultra-conservative. A bright young IBM salesman could earn twenty-five thousand dollars a year within five years of starting out—big money in those days. I was fooling myself to think I was head of a corporation of liberals. I realized that if I wanted to be in politics, I might as well quit, and if I wanted to be chairman of IBM, I had to button my lip. There was never any question about where I stood politically, but I didn't make any more public statements about it.

Olive and I started getting invitations to the White House as though we lived next door. Some of the social occasions we went to were historic—I remember the dinner where Pablo Casals performed. It was his first formal recital in the United States since the Spanish civil war. Olive and I also were invited to private dinner dances at the White House, including one for Kennedy's brother-in-law Steve Smith where the dancing went on until 5:00 A.M. My wife was seated on the president's right that night, which alone was sufficient to make the evening a permanent part of our family's lore.

During the Kennedy years I had my chance to learn my way around Washington. I worked on a half dozen of his committees and commissions, including the Advisory Committee on Labor-Management Policy and the steering committee for the Peace Corps. I was pleased and proud to serve the president in any way I could, but I didn't delude myself that I was playing that important a role, or that I was a real political animal. Mainly I was a witness.

Most big businessmen opposed Kennedy, of course. He hadn't even been in the White House six months when the Business Council broke off its formal relationship with the government. I got involved in that fight, which destroyed an arrangement that had existed since Roosevelt. The Council consisted of sixty-five of the most powerful businessmen in America. Its official purpose was to advise the Secretary of Commerce on economic issues, but its real usefulness had been in times of crisis. When America joined World War II, for example, the Business Council had the War Production Board staffed within a matter of days. In peacetime there wasn't that much for the Business Council to do, and it became more of an old boys' club.

Kennedy's secretary of commerce was Luther Hodges,

the former governor of North Carolina, a genial liberal twenty years older than the president. When he was first appointed, everybody figured Hodges would appeal to both businessmen and Congress, but underneath that charming exterior was a real stubborn old coot. Hodges decided big business and the government had gotten too cozy under Eisenhower, and that he was going to put a stop to it. He told the Business Council chairman that he didn't think the organization was truly representative of American business. That shocked everybody. Then he forbade us to hold closed-door sessions with federal officials and demanded that representatives from small business be made members. Before long a lot of ill will was building up.

I was by no means entirely in love with the Business Council. Members would go to those meetings at Hot Springs with a list of five deals they wanted to discuss. There would be golf games all afternoon, a perfect forum for cooking up business deals. And when it came to questions of government, they all thought alike: they were against any federal control. But in spite of all this I thought it was foolish to destroy an organization that was so important in emergencies, and I couldn't see why Hodges would want to alienate the business community when he was supposed to speak for it.

With the Berlin Wall crisis developing in 1961, I'm sure Luther Hodges was far from the most pressing problem on the president's mind. All the same, I went to see Kennedy when the Business Council started talking about ending its affiliation with the Commerce Department. "I don't think it's particularly detrimental to you," I said. "But you might want to take an active hand rather than just let it happen." Kennedy called in Ralph Dungan, one of his special assistants, and said, "I had no idea this thing had gone so far. Get into it with Tom and get it stopped." Dungan tried in every way to get Hodges to change his position, but he wouldn't. So on July 6 the Business Council called a press conference and divorced itself from the government.

The only thing the Business Council ever did for Kennedy was to supply volunteers for his foreign aid program. I organized the recruiting effort, which was nicknamed Operation Tycoon. The United States was giving away a great deal of money abroad in those days, and Kennedy wanted business people manning the foreign aid posts. The idea was to get fifty companies to provide their best young vice presidents and managers for a year's service abroad—a kind of executive Peace Corps. I used the Business Council to do the job, lining up four chief executives as regional vice chairmen, including Carter Burgess of AMF and Steve Bechtel Sr. They recruited some very talented men, and then we had to wrestle with State Department bureaucrats who were insisting that, to avoid conflicts of interest, the volunteers had to resign from their corporate jobs before they could go. But the spirit of the times was so compelling that thirty-five people agreed, at some risk to their careers. I remember that the younger brother of Bob Ingersoll, head of Borg-Warner, went to the Philippines; Bill Lawless of IBM, who had been Al Williams's assistant, went to Zaire, and another fellow from IBM named Stan McElroy managed the whole operation for me.

The contrast was enormous between the Business Council and the new committee on labor management policy, which I also worked on. The latter had all the excitement of the Kennedy era and pretty much took over the Business Council's advisory job. It consisted of nineteen leaders from business, labor, and education—people like Henry Ford II and Joseph Block, George Meany and Walter Reuther—and Kennedy himself came to the meetings. I really felt I was walking with giants, and was amazed at the amount of unanimity we were able to achieve. The president asked us to tackle the issue of joblessness, which was an enormous problem because a recession had pushed the unemployment rate to its highest level since the 1930s. On top of that, everybody was worrying about the baby boom—how to provide jobs for the children we'd all had.

My specialty on this panel was the relationship between unemployment and automation. At IBM we'd always taken a fairly hard line on that issue—after all, we sold punch-card machines on the basis of how many clerks they'd replace. Dad justified this by pointing out that modern technology improves industrial productivity, which in turn boosts the economy, creates jobs, and raises the standard of living for everyone. But now I became conscious of the workers who get put on the street in the process. What first woke me up was a 1960 television documentary by Edward R. Murrow. I appeared in it to explain the IBM point of view, but it was the show's opening scene that became indelibly imprinted on my mind. Murrow started with the meat packers. In his clear and forceful way, he laid out the background, and then he interviewed an unemployed man who was just sitting on his stoop. The fellow had worked in a slaughterhouse but his skill had been replaced by a machine. He was only forty-five or fifty, but there was nothing he could reapply himself to, and the disintegration of his morale came through on the screen. I was stunned by the tragedy of an able man sitting there saying he wanted to work but couldn't get a job because the whole industry had changed.

Walter Reuther had a tremendous influence on me. Lots of people called Reuther a Communist because he and his brother had worked in a Soviet automobile factory in the early 1930s. He was anything but a Communist; I believe he was one of America's great men and that his death in a plane crash in 1970 was a tragedy for the country. When it came to my education, Reuther picked up where Murrow had left off. He made me understand that if Buick decides to close an obsolete plant in Detroit, then builds a modern new plant in the South, five thousand people are still thrown out of work; the new jobs in Tennessee don't mean very much to those workers in Detroit. Conservatives would probably argue that that's part of the free-enterprise system, and that those families are just the chaff that gets ground out while the mill is working beautifully. But I don't think that's right, and the labor management committee studied the methods Europeans use to protect jobs. We talked at length with the

Swedes, in particular. They have cooperative programs involving industry, labor, and government to recruit workers from sections of the country where unemployment is high, retrain them, and move them to areas where they are needed. Kennedy was willing to explore any idea for inspiring a similar kind of cooperation in the United States.

That committee was my first inkling that I eventually might be able to accomplish something significant in government. The labor leaders liked me for my liberal views; the businessmen had respect for my success; and the academics saw me as someone receptive to new ideas. But I was still only a neophyte, and during the first year I learned that I would have to do a lot more homework if I wanted to be taken seriously in Washington. There was an ongoing debate in the committee about how to protect the average American worker from unemployment. Conservatives, taking the usual line, wanted to cut business taxes in order to stimulate the economy and produce more jobs; liberals wanted innovative federal programs such as job insurance. I asked an IBM economist to write a paper reflecting my views and, after talking to me, he rapidly produced a very liberal piece. That was where I went wrong, because instead of carefully reading the draft, I impetuously sent it to all the members of the committee. Labor was delighted and management appalled—what my memo proposed was essentially a return to the New Deal. Henry Ford's chief financial officer wrote a scathing response that denounced my work as spurious and without merit, and although I thought he was being too harsh, I had to admit that what I'd presented was half-baked.

Some of us on the committee hoped that if labor and management worked together, America would develop ways to run its economy as rationally as the Swedes ran theirs. Maybe we'd have moved in that direction if Kennedy had survived. But less than a year after he was shot, the United Auto Workers went on strike against General Motors, and the settlement they reached went against the national interest. To get the auto workers back on the job,

GM gave them a fat contract, including a pay raise far in excess of the anti-inflation guidelines set by the administration. That was another lesson to me. I saw that even when a major union and a major corporation agree, it's not necessarily for the best. Only the power of the federal government can protect the common good.

On the day Kennedy died, I was at lunch with a number of businessmen in New York. Bill Paley, the head of CBS, was called out of the room. He came back and whispered to the host, who rose and said, "The president has just been shot in Dallas. He is seriously injured and may not survive." We all got up to beat a sober retreat to our offices. I was sitting next to Mac McDonnell, the head of McDonnell Aircraft, who said, "Well, the next thing on my agenda this afternoon is an appointment with you."

I said, "Mr. Mac, I'd forgotten that. Let's see if we can't figure out a time to meet in a week or two."

"No, no, I'm prepared to talk right now!"

I was too shattered to object. I thought, "What the hell, he wants to talk, so we'll talk." I took him up to my office. He was offering to buy our service bureau, a part of IBM that maintained its own computer centers and sold time on the machines to customers. I talked with him in a vague way. In twenty minutes he was through, and I went home. No sooner had I gotten there—the Kennedys were always well organized—than we got a call from one of Bobby's staff confirming that the president was dead and saying that funeral arrangements were being made. That evening I got out some paper and wrote a letter to Lyndon Johnson. I knew him only from White House functions, but I wanted to tell him I recognized what an awful thing had happened to him and how difficult it was to cope with:

Dear Mr. President,
    As you embark on the free world's most difficult and trying job, I want to wish you the great success that I know will be yours.

It has been my great privilege to know you over the past two and a half years, and that relationship has given me profound respect for your abilities and admiration for your tact and diplomacy. The United States is fortunate to have you as its new President and the Free World to have you as its leader, particularly during these difficult days of challenge.

Please don't hesitate to call on me if I can be of help. I am with you every step of the way.

Sincerely,
Tom Watson Jr.

I arranged for this to be hand-delivered to the gate of the White House the following morning. I knew a letter like that, even if it is just a small thing, can mean a great deal to the man who is on the spot. Around noon came another call, one of the Kennedy staff asking Olive and me to come to view the body with the senators and the Supreme Court. Everybody remembers particular scenes from those days of mourning. The one that sticks in my mind is Bobby Kennedy standing at a turn in the White House stairs near the East Room, consoling people who had just walked past his brother's bier. It was a sympathetic gesture that nobody expected from a man under that kind of strain. Bobby shook my hand and held Olive in a long embrace, and both of them were crying.

Johnson took over, and a number of people told me that he'd shown them my letter. He carried it in his pocket for weeks. I guess it was important to him because it proved he was getting the support even of Kennedy loyalists. But it also expressed the way I felt about him. Because of differences in our personalities, I didn't think I could work for Johnson—he later asked me to be his secretary of commerce and I turned him down—yet I knew he would try to push through much of the legislation that Kennedy had initiated, and I wanted to support him in any way I could.

CHAPTER 27

I had a ritual I used to follow on the anniversary of my father's death. I would spend a quiet evening taking stock of what IBM had accomplished in his absence, and then say to Olive, "That's another year I've made it alone." The last time I did this was on the fifth anniversary, in 1961. By then IBM was two and a half times as big as when Dad left it—over two billion dollars a year in sales, counting the results of World Trade—and the value of our stock had quintupled. Of the six thousand computers in operation in the United States when 1961 began, well over four thousand were ours, and the rental revenues from computers had grown until they were about to surpass the revenues from Dad's beloved punch-card machines.

For those five years I hadn't let anybody share the spotlight with me. Inside and outside the company I wanted to establish that Tom Watson Jr. meant IBM, and I guarded my power carefully. But in 1961, I decided to make room for Al Williams by moving myself up to chairman, remaining chief executive, and making him president. The years had deepened our friendship to the point where I couldn't imagine ever being alienated from Al, despite the fact that I was still bothered by Dad's long-ago warning. In early 1962 someone from IBM brought a draft of our annual report for me to sign while I was in Washington for a meeting, and I saw that Al's signature was already on it. I hadn't told him to sign the annual report, and what I'd had in mind was for him to serve a full year as president before he did. After all, Dad had made me wait three years when I became president in the early '50s. I saw Al's action as a possible challenge to my power, and I didn't want to let it pass for fear that it might snowball. In retrospect I wonder if it was really his doing at all: probably one of the people preparing the annual report had put in Al's name, not realizing the sensitivity of the matter. But I called Al and said, "Look here. Your signature is on this annual report."

"Well, I'm president. It ought to be there."

"That's for me to decide. I'm sure I'll agree at some point. But it's one of those things that's very personal."

That made Al mad. "I don't think there's anything to decide at all!"

We'd had many business disagreements over the years, but this was the first time I felt we were seriously at odds. So I said, "Fine. If you want to pursue this, assemble the board of directors for a meeting at five-thirty this afternoon. I'll come back to New York and see you there."

Al was quiet and then said, "Let me have fifteen minutes to think about this." A little later he called back and said, "Tom, it isn't worth fighting about. I'll sign the annual report when you think it's right."

That was the end of it. Al knew how to pick his fights, and he understood I could beat him in a boardroom showdown. I had him sign the annual report with me the following year, and we became even closer.

I would gladly have run IBM in tandem with Williams until it was time for us both to retire. But I wasn't that lucky. Al was four years older than I, and he'd made it clear all along that he was going to retire early, when he reached fifty-five. "I've worked hard all my life, and I want to have time to enjoy what I've earned," he said. I didn't entirely believe he'd go through with it, but I knew that, come 1966, I had to be ready to name another president.

The most obvious candidate was my brother. Although Dad had never said so explicitly, I had always understood it was his wish that Dick should run IBM after me. He was five years my junior, so if I brought him in to succeed Al as president, and then stepped aside myself at a reasonable age, he'd have five or ten years at the top. Dick was in total command of IBM World Trade and had built it into a phenomenal success. By 1960 it had become a $350 million-a-year business—bigger than IBM Domestic when I took over as president—and he was making it grow at *double* the domestic rate. Thanks to his hard work and Dad's foresight, we were one of the few American companies in a position to cash in on the European economic miracle. Between 1959 and 1962, Williams and I provided Dick with tens of millions of dollars of extra capital to finance World Trade's growth. Al used to chuckle about the impact this would eventually have on our U.S. competitors: "They're fighting us so hard here that they're not even thinking about overseas. Wait until they find out how thoroughly World Trade has gotten itself entrenched."

Just as Dad envisioned, my brother's charm and skill as a diplomat served IBM well abroad. Dick was a merry fellow who made friends effortlessly. He far outshone me in ease and grace, and unlike me was comfortable rubbing elbows with the leaders of governments or other businesses. Capitalizing on his linguistic ability, he made his way smoothly and rapidly in the centers of commerce of South America and the Far East. There were no heads of major countries in Europe whom Dick didn't know, and Willy Brandt, the mayor of West Berlin, had become a particularly good friend. Within the business Dick had the deft touch it takes to run a widely dispersed operation like World Trade. He set high standards, chose good people as country managers, and gave World Trade the flexibility it needed to bend to the customs of the ninety countries it was in. Yet Dick didn't hesitate to buck traditions that ran contrary to good business sense. IBM stood out among European companies, for example, by being willing to promote talented young executives over the heads of their elders. Dick was also not afraid to fight when a government made unreasonable demands. Around 1957 Japan gave an ultimatum to foreign companies doing business on its soil: either sell a 50 percent interest in their operations to Japanese investors or get out. Every American company in Japan capitulated except for Texas Instruments and IBM World Trade. My brother told me, "The Japanese need the data-processing industry too much to make us leave." After years of jawboning, the government finally agreed to let our subsidiary alone. As a result we were always a major force in the Japanese computer market.

To some degree Dick and I had outgrown our rivalry after Dad's death. At Williamsburg I made him a member of the Corporate Management Committee, which was IBM's ruling council. Later, when Mother had her seventy-fifth birthday and retired from the board of directors, I asked Dick to take her place. I still followed the practice of not meddling in Dick's business—when he asked me to join the World Trade board I declined because I didn't want to breathe down his neck—but the organizational split between our two companies, which had been quite useful at first, now seemed more like a formality.

Outside of work, Dick and I had never been closer, and we spent a great deal of time with Mother now that she was slowing down. Dick built her a summer house on his property in New Canaan, and for a couple of months each year he and I lived there with her while our wives and children spent the summer in Maine. Those were warm, funny times. Mother and Dick were particularly close—he was her youngest child and he'd taken her on long trips including one to Australia to look up a long-lost branch of the Watson family. I never traveled with her, but she confided in me in a way she never had while Dad was alive, sharing her worries about this or that member of the family. What meant the most to me was that she thought I was doing a superior job running IBM. She'd say, "If your father was alive, how proud he'd be." She and Dick and I would chat every morning over breakfast and then Dick and I would drive to work together on the tree-lined back roads of Westchester County to Armonk, where IBM had recently moved its headquarters. Mother had always loved to drive, and as a surprise Dick and I bought her a Jaguar convertible. She drove it around with the top down until she was eighty and could hardly see. Anybody in New Canaan, when they saw that Jaguar coming, would get behind a tree.

Now that we'd reached a point where it was natural to set up the IBM succession, Al Williams pushed me to make the first move. "We've got to get Dick over from World Trade," he said. Our plan was to groom my brother just as Dad had groomed me, and we figured he would need a couple of years in a big job on the domestic side to establish his authority. Then he'd be ready to take Al's place, and eventually mine. I talked to my brother about it in 1963. "You're doing great at World Trade," I said. "Dad always predicted it would be bigger than the main company and maybe he had a point. But as far as I'm concerned, you're also the number-one candidate for this top job. So tell me what you'd prefer. Do you want to stay with World Trade and be the great internationalist? Or do you want to get in the running to be chief executive?"

I thought I was being scrupulously fair, but in hindsight it was the worst business and family mistake I ever made. I should never have forced my brother into a horse race with other executives for the top job, and it would have been better for everybody if he'd said, "I'll make no such choice. You decide whether you want me to succeed you, and when you're ready to make an offer, I'll consider it." Instead, Dick asked what I had in mind for him. I told him I'd bring him in at the level of senior vice president, and that meanwhile he would keep the title of chairman of IBM World Trade, although somebody else would actually run that business. He said, "I'd like to think about it overnight." When you offer a career opportunity to a man who has ambition, he'll always take the job. Dick came back the next day and said, "If there's a chance of my running this company, I want to try."

While all this was going on, we'd been getting ready to announce a new family of computers that was radically different from anything that had ever been built. This new line was named System/360—after the 360 degrees in a circle—because we intended it to encompass every need of every user in the business and the scientific worlds. *Fortune* magazine christened this project "IBM's

$5,000,000,000 Gamble" and billed it as "the most crucial and portentous—as well as perhaps the riskiest—business judgment of recent times." Building this new line meant putting IBM through tremendous upheavals. Careers were made and broken, and the mistakes we made along the way changed a lot of lives, including Dick's and my own. The expense of the project was indeed staggering. We spent three quarters of a billion dollars just on engineering. Then we invested another four and a half billion on factories, equipment, and the rental machines themselves. We hired more than sixty thousand new employees and opened five major new plants. It was the biggest privately financed commercial project ever undertaken. The writer at *Fortune* pointed out that it was substantially larger than the World War II effort that produced the atom bomb.

The need for System/360 emerged from an odd set of circumstances. In the early 1960s computing was finally coming into its own. Some of the wonders that people had confidently predicted right after the war—such as automated weather forecasting—had failed to materialize, but the machines had been put to use every place else, from the monthly mailing of electric bills to the space race. Computers were beginning to revolutionize everyday life. For example, American Airlines was about to unveil its SABRE reservation system, linking ticket agents all over the United States to a master computer in Westchester County, and making it possible for customers to book airline seats without having to put up with the traditional overnight wait for confirmation. We could imagine much broader horizons ahead. One idea that appealed to me was placing computer terminals in America's classrooms to help raise the standard of education. Meanwhile visionaries began talking about the day when computer power would be delivered to homes just like telephone service and electricity.

Paradoxically, there also was a feeling in the early '60s that IBM had reached a plateau. We were still expanding, but less quickly than before—in the year Kennedy beat Nixon, for example, we only grew nine percent. As we

My first meeting with Charley Kirk, Dad's right-hand man in Endicott, 1944. Charley wanted to take me on a tour of the IBM plant, but as we shook hands for this picture, I heard a hissing noise—the nose wheel of my plane was losing air. I took off in a hurry, since I had no orders to land at Endicott in the first place.
(IBM Archive)

In the late '40s, thousands of copies of this photograph by Yousuf Karsh were displayed around IBM. (IBM Archive)

My father always loved to be among his men—this was the Hundred Percent Club in 1947, in front of the big top. (Lisa Larsen, Life *magazine © Time Inc.)*

Each year Dad put up a tent city in Endicott to house salesmen at the Hundred Percent Club convention. (IBM Archive)

The Selective Sequence Electronic Calculator was intended to prove that IBM could build the world's fastest calculator: Dad's answer to the coming of the computer age. Dad had it installed in the lobby of IBM headquarters in New York, where scientists could come in and use it for free. (IBM Archive)

The 702 was IBM's first computer for business users. When we unveiled it in the lobby of headquarters in 1955, set off by a white floor and a bold red wall, it marked a major evolution in our product line—and a revolution in corporate style. (IBM Archive)

Two years after we delivered our first computers, electronic automation became big news.

(Time magazine, © 1955 Time Inc. Reprinted by permission.)

We did everything we could to keep IBM in the public eye. We supplied early TV quiz shows with punch-card machines, and provided a computer nicknamed Emmy for the Katharine Hepburn and Spencer Tracy film Desk Set. *(20th Century Fox)*

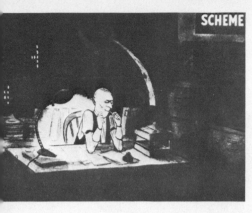

Cartoonists in the 1950s loved to poke fun at IBM's corporate culture. We loved the free advertising. (IBM Archive)

Edward R. Murrow featured an IBM computer on his show See It Now *in 1957.* (IBM Archive)

Olive and I with our children in Greenwich, late 1956: Jeannette, Lucinda, Tom, Helen, Susan, and Olive.

Saying good-bye at the station in 1955. When Dad got very old, he and Mother spent weeks at a time attending IBM dinners and visiting sales offices across the United States. (IBM Archive)

*Dad was eighty-two,
and I was forty-two,
when he finally gave
me control of IBM in
1956.*
(IBM Archive)

*The fall of 1956, after
Dad died, was the
loneliest time of my life.*
(Erich Hartmann/Magnum)

I felt great pressure to keep IBM moving fast. Here I'm lecturing executives about a product delay at our Poughkeepsie plant in 1957, IBM's first billion-dollar year. (John Loengard, Life *magazine © Time Inc.*)

I liked to fly the corporate plane— here a DC-3—on business trips. It was relaxing—for me, if not the other executives on board. (John Loengard, Life *magazine © Time Inc.*)

Khrushchev at our San Jose plant. He was the only man I ever met besides Dad who could walk into a room crowded with hundreds of people and charm everyone there. (Wide World Photos)

IBM lost its stodgy image and became a leader in corporate architecture during the postwar boom. At top, IBM's Endicott lab, built in the 1930s; at right, the Thomas J. Watson Research Center in Yorktown Heights, New York, designed by Eero Saarinen and dedicated in 1961. (IBM Archive)

Instead of adopting a single corporate look that could become dated, we hired top industrial designers and let them explore their own ideas. IBM Selectric, by Eliot Noyes; IBM logos, by Paul Rand. (IBM Archive)

IBM IBM IBM IBM IBM IBM

Mother, Dick, and I at a 1961 family reunion near Cody, Wyoming. Much to her surprise, she blossomed in the years after Dad's death.

My happiest years at IBM were the early 1960s, after Al Williams became president. (IBM Archive)

At the height of the System/360 crisis in late 1965. Vin Learson, my brother Dick, Al Williams, and I were trying to avert what would have been the worst disaster in IBM history. (IBM Archive)

System/360 prompted most businesses to adopt IBM computers as a standard. Soon after deliveries began, Vin Learson, the father of the new line, succeeded Al Williams as president. (Marvin Koner)

Off the coast of Greenland near Godhavn, summer 1974.

Aboard Palawan *off Sweden in summer, 1958. This is the way my children would see me when they came up on deck.*

As U.S. Ambassador to Moscow I usually walked to work, leaving the embassy limousine at home. The city was colder and lonelier than I remembered it. (AP/Wide World Photos)

When the Soviets invaded Afghanistan in late 1979, I was called back to Washington to confer with President Carter and Secretary of State Vance. I'd been ambassador barely two months. (The Jimmy Carter Library)

*This World War I Sopwith Pup nearly killed me in 1989. I was
flying alone, fifteen hundred feet above the wooded Maine
countryside, when a wire came loose and the engine went dead. The
only possible spot for an emergency landing was this small field.*
(Michael McGuire/Courier-Gazette)

reached the two-billion-dollars-a-year mark people began to speculate that we'd gotten so big that naturally our growth rate had to fall. But given the bright prospects for computing, that seemed illogical, and I thought it was probably our own fault that we were slowing down. The two separate computer divisions I'd created were competing with each other fiercely, just as I'd hoped, but one unhappy side effect was that our product line became wildly disorganized. By September 1960, we had eight computers in our sales catalog, plus a number of older, vacuum-tube machines. The internal architecture of each of these computers was quite different, so different software and different peripheral equipment, such as printers and disk drives, had to be used with each machine. If a customer's business grew and he wanted to shift from a small computer to a large one, he had to get all new everything and rewrite all his programs, often at great expense.

The man whose job it was to spur IBM's growth rate was Vin Learson, who at this point was vice president and group executive in charge of our manufacturing and development divisions. He thought the obvious answer was to simplify the product line, and he asked the technical people to try. But at first this request had very little effect because the engineers of each division were wedded to their own machines. The amazing thing about Vin, apart from the tremendous force of his personality, was his cleverness as a manager. He saw that it was time to break down the rivalry between the two divisions, and he did it by applying a management technique called "abrasive interaction." This meant forcing people to swap sides: taking the top engineer from the small-computer division and making him boss of the best development team in the large-computer division. A lot of people thought this made about as much sense as electing Khrushchev president, but after interacting abrasively for some months those engineers earned one another's respect, just as Vin anticipated. Slowly they worked their way around to the idea of building a single computer line that would span the entire market. Vin made this group of engineers the core of a much larger committee called SPREAD—an acronym for systems programming, research, engineering, and development—whose charter was to map out a new product strategy. The SPREAD committee met for a couple of months late in 1961, and when it was slow producing a report, Vin got impatient. Two weeks before Christmas he sent them to a motel in Connecticut with orders not to come back until they'd agreed. That was how the plan for System/360 was born —in the form of an eighty-page report delivered on December 28.

During the year of the SPREAD report I was busy on presidential committees in Washington and followed the technical debates within the computer divisions only from a distance. But by the middle of 1962 enough had gone wrong that I was spending a lot more time at the office. The stock market that May had its biggest drop since 1929, and IBM stock got hammered along with the rest, losing about one third of its value—its first major decline in thirty years. That alone would have been enough to reel me in, and with the 360 on the way, I began to get a hollow feeling in the pit of my stomach about the risks we faced. IBM had always succeeded by making bold moves, but the System/360 plan was dramatic even by our standards.

Vin was the father of the new line of machines. His intention was to make all other computers obsolete—including the thousands of machines on which we were then collecting rent—and to replace them with a completely new family of processors, ranging from little machines renting for $2,500 per month to high-performance giants renting for more than $115,000 per month. The machines would all embody a revolutionary new feature called compatibility, which meant that, despite their great variation in size, they'd be able to use the same software and hook up to the same disk drives, printers, and other peripherals. Once customers shifted to System/360, they'd be able to expand their installations simply by mixing and matching components from our sales catalog. That was good for them, and the benefit for IBM was equally compelling—once a customer entered the circle of 360 users, we knew we could keep him there for a very long time.

From the beginning we faced two risks, either of which alone was enough to keep us awake nights. First there was the task of coordinating the hardware and software design work for the new line. We had engineering teams all over America and Europe working simultaneously on six new processors and dozens of new peripherals—disk drives, tape drives, printers, magnetic and optical character readers, communications equipment, and terminals—but in the end all this hardware would have to plug together. The software was a bigger hurdle still. In order for System/360 to have a consistent personality, hundreds of programmers had to write millions of lines of computer code. Nobody had ever tackled that complex a programming job, and the engineers were under great pressure to get it done.

Our other source of worry was that we were trying for the first time to manufacture our own electronic parts. The electronics industry, after having progressed very fast during the 1950s from the vacuum tube to the transistor, was on the verge of another transformation. The wave of the future was integrated circuits—computer chips that incorporate transistors, resistors, diodes, and so on, all in a single tiny unit. Nobody was using integrated circuits in computers yet, but the System/360 design called for a lot of them. Al Williams argued that even though we'd relied on suppliers to provide the earlier generations of components, we had to manufacture these ourselves. "Whole computers are going to shrink down onto these devices," he said. "When that happens, do you think we'll want to be buying them from outsiders? If we're going to stay in the computer business, we'd better learn how to make these things ourselves." I agreed, but I'll never forget how expensive it was to build our first integrated circuit factory. Ordinary plants in those days cost about forty dollars per square foot. In the integrated circuit plant, which had to be kept dust-free and looked more like a surgical ward than a factory floor, the cost was over one hundred fifty dollars. I could hardly believe the bills that were coming through, and I wasn't the only one who was shocked. The board gave me a terrible time about the costs. "Are you really sure you need all this?" they'd say. "Have you gotten competitive bids? We don't want these factories to be luxurious."

Our original intent was to announce the first machines in April 1964 and gradually phase out the old product line by unveiling the rest over eighteen months. Unfortunately we'd miscalculated how much time we had, and the flaws in our existing product line caught up with us a year or two sooner than we'd anticipated. By spring 1963 the old computers were obsolete. We did a technical study showing that while the 360s were going to be better than the latest computers from RCA, Burroughs, Honeywell, Univac, and General Electric, all those competitive machines were superior to our existing line. A number of them offered two to three times the performance of our computers for the same price. Our salesmen were hamstrung—since System/360 had not yet been announced, and none of them even knew what we were planning, they had nothing to tell customers. By the middle of 1963, sales offices were sending in panicky reports that they could no longer hold the line against the competition. Even though demand for computers increased by well over 15 percent that year, IBM grew only seven percent, our lowest growth since the war.

The only solution was to get System/360 out the door fast, and a number of executives argued that we ought to launch the whole thing at once. This would surely make a tremendous splash in the market. Customers would see how they'd be able to grow with the product line, so we could persuade them to wait for the 360s to be produced instead of jumping to competitors. But there were big disadvantages. For one thing, although the new computers were nearly ready, not all of them had gone through the rigorous testing we required. A bigger danger was that once we started accepting orders, our factory network would be under tremendous strain to deliver every item in an enormously complicated new product line. There wasn't going to be much room for error.

It was the biggest, riskiest decision I ever made, and I agonized about it for weeks, but deep down I believed there was nothing IBM couldn't do. And so on April 7, 1964—almost exactly fifty years after my father first came to work at IBM—we staged a product announcement that would have made him proud. To attract maximum publicity, we held press conferences in sixty-three U.S. cities and fourteen foreign countries, while tens of thousands of guests all over the world showed up for customer briefings. A chartered train carried two hundred reporters in New York from Grand Central Terminal to Poughkeepsie, where the main announcement was made. I presented the 360 as "the most important product announcement in company history," and the visitors were shown into a large display hall where six new computers and forty-four new peripherals stretched before their eyes.

Within IBM there was a great feeling of celebration because a new era was opening up. But when I looked at those new products, I didn't feel as confident as I'd have liked. Not all of the equipment on display was real; some units were just mock-ups made of wood. We explained this to our guests, so there was no deception. But it was a dangerous cutting of corners—not the way I think business ought to be done—and an uncomfortable reminder to me of how far we had to go before we could call the program a success.

Williams and I felt that the 360 announcement was the appropriate moment to bring Dick into the IBM mainstream. Until then Vin had been in sole command of the project; now we set Dick up as his peer and divided responsibility between them. Dick was in charge of the engineering and manufacturing side of the business, and Vin was in charge of the sales force. In hindsight I think Vin deeply resented this change, and with reason—the 360 was his product line, and here we were telling him to go out and sell it while we brought my brother in to finish Vin's job. But to Al and me at the time it seemed natural to divide responsibility between the two men. Although Dick had never launched a major product, he had presided over World Trade's complicated factory system in Europe. And we needed Vin, with his enormous drive and years of selling experience, out there twisting the tails of our salesmen. Once the assignments were made, Williams and I felt so satisfied with IBM's course that we announced we would step back from the day-to-day operation of the company. We set up something called the Corporate Operations Board, with Vin and Dick as co-chairmen, and made it their responsibility to run the show.

I honestly thought I'd given Vin the tougher job. The engineering and manufacturing side of the company had tremendous momentum on this project by then, while the sales force was starting from scratch. Not only did they have to turn the tide against our competition, but there was danger that the 360 would alienate a lot of customers. Those used to their current machines were almost sure to balk at the idea of rewriting their software to work with the new line. Vin's people had to convince customers to make those conversions, while competitors' salesmen flocked around, saying, "Don't convert. Come to us. Convert to us." I was so afraid of losing customers that I called Dick and Vin into my office and lectured them sternly. I told Vin, "If the sales force needs new features or extra software to move those machines, I want you to shout loud and clear and we will produce them for you." I told Dick, "Be responsive to the sales side of the business."

But my anxiety was misplaced. We got immense numbers of orders—far more than expected—and even more kept pouring in. Everybody felt euphoric at first, but then the 360 program seemed to get more complicated every month. Competitors found gaps in the new line and started winning away influential customers, so we had to add two new computers to the six we'd already unveiled. We announced an ultra-fast scientific machine to fight off Control Data, and a smaller, special-purpose processor to fight off General Electric. Each new machine required a major diversion of engineering talent. Meanwhile, the effort to write basic software for the 360 line bogged down alarmingly. The more the software was delayed, the more programmers we assigned; by 1966 we had two thousand people working on it, and the cost of developing the software was beginning to exceed the cost of the hardware. We learned the hard way one of the great secrets of computer engineering: throwing people at a software project is not the way to speed it up. A piece of software is a unified thing; if you try to break up the job of writing it among too many people, it takes more time to coordinate them than the division of labor saves. Or as Fred Brooks, the droll engineering genius from North Carolina who led the project, once wrote, "the bearing of a child takes nine months, no matter how many women are assigned."

There was no way to hide our struggle from customers who were ordering the machines, so I spoke to a conference of IBM users about it: "A few months ago IBM's software budget for 1966 was going to be forty million dollars. I asked Vin Learson last night before I left what he thought it would be, and he said, 'Fifty million.' This afternoon I met Watts Humphrey, who is in charge of programming production, in the hall here and said, 'Is this figure about right? Can I use it?' He said, 'It's going to be sixty million.' You can see that if I keep asking questions we won't pay a dividend this year." I was only half joking. By the time the 360 software was finally delivered, years late, we'd sunk a half-billion dollars into it alone, making it the single largest cost in the System/360 program, and the single largest expenditure in company history.

Six months after the 360 announcement, the complications of the project were alarming enough that I began holding Monday morning meetings in my office, just as in the days of the Defense Calculator. I disbanded Vin and Dick's Corporate Operations Board and replaced it with a new Management Review Committee composed of five men: Al, my brother, me, Vin, and Dick Bullen, our organizational expert, who by now was a vice president and group executive. We made shifts like that all the time at the top of IBM, but this one didn't sit well with my brother or Vin. They knew that I had given them the business to run, and now I was taking back the reins.

Every Monday we'd get together and there would be serious problems on the table. It was not a happy group. Vin and Dick weren't getting along, and there was also tension between Dick and me. For the first time in our lives he was reporting to me on a day-to-day basis, and those meetings of the Management Review Committee were fierce. That committee, which had existed in various incarnations since just before the Williamsburg conference in 1956, had always been where I evaluated top executives and determined whether they were pulling their weight. Since the success of the corporation was directly related to how this group performed, I judged them harshly and it was easy to find a man wanting, even if his performance in lower jobs had been superior. It was the crucible.

I went after my brother in the same way I'd have gone after anybody else in that position. I remember one episode at the 1964 World's Fair. Dick and I went out to the Flushing Meadows fairground to look over the IBM pavilion, which had been designed by Eero Saarinen just before his death. The building was dominated by an elevated theater shaped like a giant egg with "IBM" imprinted in bas-relief all over it. Dick and I were touring this exhibit with some associates when the subject of computer circuits came up. I'd been hearing about a new machine, recently unveiled by a competitor, that incorporated an electronic chip, made of silicon, called a monolithic integrated circuit. Such chips are as common as table salt today, but I'd never heard of them, and our competitor was claiming they were far superior to the ceramic-and-metal integrated circuits in System/360 machines. Technology was Dick's area, so I asked him about it and he was totally mystified. "What are monolithics?" he said. I castigated him for that loudly, telling him he'd better make sure the 360 wasn't going to be obsolete before it was even delivered. We later found that our scientists had been working on monolithics for years, so there was no real danger. Such incidents drove Dick and me apart.

Now I began to worry about Al's impending retirement. His fifty-fifth birthday was less than two years away, and he seemed more serious than ever about leaving. I told him I didn't think IBM could spare him, and I tried everything I could think of to make him to change his mind. I even offered to step aside and let him run the company, telling him he had done so much to build IBM that I would be proud to serve under him for the rest of my career. Al knew I really meant it. If he'd agreed, I'd have announced that I was turning over the helm to Al Williams who was going to be chief executive and president, and that I was going to stay on as chairman. But Al didn't want the job.

By some miracle hundreds of medium-size 360s were delivered on time in 1965. But that gave me no comfort, because behind the scenes I could see we were losing ground. The quality and performance of the early computers were below the standards we'd set, and we'd actually been skipping some of the most rigorous tests. For months we had the chief testing engineer come to the Monday morning meeting. I'd ask, "How are those machines performing?" and he'd say, "They're not making it." He'd set up his charts and show where we were going wrong. Production kept getting held up by shortages. At one point we ran out of little copper electrical contacts without which our mighty computers couldn't function: our usual suppliers just couldn't keep up with our factories. We solved that through old-fashioned IBM heroics —engineers flying around the country to all the suppliers they could find, scooping up copper contacts, and rushing them back to IBM. To make matters worse we were delivering the new machines without the crucial software; customers were forced to use temporary programs much more rudimentary than what we'd promised, which meant that they couldn't get the full benefit of their new machines. Yet customers were still ordering 360s faster than we could build them. With billions of dollars of machines already in our backlog, we were telling people that they'd have to wait two or three years for computers they needed. A lot of customers were unhappy about that, and I was worried that the slightest additional delay in shipments would drive them into our competitors' arms.

Meanwhile the friction between Dick and Vin got completely out of hand. Their jobs were supposed to be complementary, but instead of supporting each other they were running a race. Vin did a superb job at rallying the sales force and convincing customers to make the transition to the 360. But he was constantly asking my brother for changes and enhancements in the machines to make them sell better still. He'd say, "If we can't have this feature, it'll be very difficult to sell to the aircraft industry, and if we can't have that feature, it'll be very difficult to sell to department stores." I'd told him to do that, of course, but if there hadn't been this feeling of rivalry and resentment, I doubt he would have pushed so hard. Vin was an experienced production man and could see that the engineering staff was badly overloaded. Dick, for his part, had a go-for-broke attitude. He said yes too many times when he should have told Vin, "I am freezing the production specifications now. You'll just have to sell the machines the way we build them." Dick would instead just turn around and put even more pressure on the engineers.

That autumn everything looked black, black, black. Everybody was pessimistic about the program. We were clinging to our production schedule but morale was going down. Some sections of our factories had been working sixty-hour weeks for six months, and the employees were worn out. The stress on technicians in the field was steadily increasing as they tried to install more and more of the new machines. The engineers were in the worst shape of all. I remember going up to Poughkeepsie to check on the software problem. We had a huge building filled with programmers, and their manager was a fellow named Don Gavis. He'd never been to college but he really knew programming. I went to his office and found him sitting at a desk with a rumpled cot next to it where he slept. I said, "Why can't you get this programming out faster?"

He didn't give a damn that I was chairman. He snarled, "Well, if you'd get the hell out of here and leave us alone, we would!" I made a hasty retreat.

Dick wasn't doing too well under such tremendous pressure. Another of his problems, in addition to Vin, was Dick's own subordinates, who were not serving him well. His top lieutenant was an imperturbable fellow who never failed to irritate me. We talked pretty forcefully at those Monday morning meetings, but this guy would come in week after week and report horrible production problems in a monotone. Sometimes I'd lose patience and explode at him, and when Dick intervened to protect his man, I'd explode at Dick too.

In mid October, Dick told us that a metallurgical problem at our new integrated circuit factory was going to cut production in half for the immediate future. The consequence was what we'd all feared: we were going to have to delay our computer shipments. "How far are we going to miss these deliveries?" I asked Dick. It wasn't a week or two weeks; it was three months.

I panicked. Never in its history had IBM missed a shipment date by that far, and with so much riding on System/360 we couldn't afford to now. When I realized I had no confidence that there wouldn't be further delays, my thinking became very self-protective. I was fifty-one years old, I had nine years of fantastic success behind me, and I didn't want my career to be wrecked by an announcement that the whole new product line was never going to fly at all. Under these circumstances, sparing my brother's feelings was the last thing on my mind.

We mobilized the best people we had and ordered them to find out what was wrong on the manufacturing side of the house. Al and I teamed up. Red LaMotte had retired, but we asked him to come back in and give us his perspective. Those were terrible days, because the more we dug into it, the worse the situation looked—which is always what happens in a crisis.

Al, whose usual role was to counsel restraint and put

problems into perspective, saw no reason for calm this time. He was frantic about IBM's finances. We had always been a tower of financial stability, and we had figured the 360 delay wouldn't have much impact on our revenues, at least in the short run, because we were cushioned by our enormous rental income. But Williams was nervous about something else: it was time to think about closing the books for 1965, and he didn't know where all the money was. The particular headache was a balance-sheet item called work-in-process inventory. This figure was supposed to represent the millions of parts and thousands of machines currently under production in our factories. What we didn't realize was that our accounting system was an anachronism, left over from the days when IBM had just a few plants and each was responsible for its own set of products. With the 360 the plants had become interdependent—about two thirds of all our factory shipments were unfinished goods that went on to other factories for more work. We had no system for keeping tabs on this inventory moving around the company. Al guessed that the amount in question might be $150 million—but the data he was getting were so vague as to be useless.

The man he assigned to the problem was John Opel, at that point a fast-rising young executive in the Data Products Division. "Find out what the damn inventory is," Williams told him. Opel knew about manufacturing and had a reputation as a brilliant analyst. He polled all the plants but he couldn't get the numbers to add up either. He'd give an estimate to Al only to find out within twenty-four hours that he'd not only missed, but missed by fifty million dollars. Opel finally got so frustrated that he insisted that each factory manager take a physical inventory—which means clerks with clipboards walking through the factories counting things. We'd never had to do that before. But that was how Opel finally discovered that the accounting system had gone completely out of whack. We had almost *six hundred million dollars* of work-in-process inventory, and none of the factory managers wanted to claim it. They were squabbling with Opel about who was responsible for what.

This state of affairs made Al frantic, because understating the inventory made it seem as though IBM had more cash on hand than we actually had. In reality the 360 had soaked up all our funds. In another few weeks we'd have needed emergency loans to meet the payroll. Here was Al, ready to retire after a long and distinguished career, and in the whole history of IBM we'd never had a problem like that—IBM had always been swimming in cash from the enormous flow of rental payments. We didn't tell the public about our cash shortage, but it was the big reason we unexpectedly sold another $370 million of stock that spring.

Dick and I were hardly talking at all. The more problems we turned up, the quieter he became, just as he had in the old days when Dad and I argued. By now I knew that my plan for bringing him into the domestic company had been a horrible blunder, bad for Dick's career and for our personal relationship. I thought I was giving Dick an opportunity in an area where he would be an outstanding success. Instead I had handed him a stacked deck. He couldn't hold his own against the demands put on him by Learson. Dick knew how to rally the engineers when they were almost too exhausted to go on, but he had little experience in running a rapidly changing engineering and development operation, and it was hard for him to manage the day-to-day particulars of the business. I would have had the same problem, except that I'd always surrounded myself with competent detail men. The people working for Dick weren't serving him well.

Everybody was scared. Al and I agreed that if the 360 program was ever to get off the ground, we had to put it under a single manager, a dictator, and we knew it had to be Learson. Over the years Vin had proven again and again that he knew how to take hold of a troubled project and bring it off. I agonized about the effect this would have on my brother. I called Dick into my office on a gray December afternoon. "I've got to tell you some things that are not very pleasant," I said. "The future of the business depends on this 360. It looks bad now, and I'm going to have to take the whole project and put it under the person I believe is most competent to bring it out of the woods." I told him it was going to be Vin, and that Dick would shift over to be chief of the corporate staff, with no line management responsibility. He was absolutely furious. "In other words," he said, "control of this entire business goes to him, and I'm left with some crumbs."

In the following months we began to feel our way out of the manufacturing crisis. The machines weren't very good at the outset, but our service people kept them running in the field, and the more computers we built, the higher the quality became. Then the long-delayed software finally began to come and suddenly the rose was blossoming. At the end of 1966 we had over four billion dollars in revenues, something like seven or eight thousand systems installed—and a billion dollars in pre-tax profits.

The board of directors elected Vin Learson president of IBM on January 26, 1966. Al Williams, taking the first step into early retirement, moved up to head the board's executive committee. We made Dick vice chairman, and he remained chairman of World Trade and a member of the executive committee. But for months afterward he came to the office only sporadically and kept to himself; his confidence seemed shaken. I felt nothing but shame and frustration at the way I'd treated him. There were so many other ways to have managed things. Perhaps the wisest course would have been to leave Dick in World Trade. He would have been known as the great IBM internationalist, and that, I think, would have been equal in honor to serving as chief executive for five or ten years. As it was, we remade the computer industry with the System/360, and objectively it was the greatest triumph of my business career. But whenever I look back on it, I think about the brother I injured, and the dream of my father's that I could never make come right.

CHAPTER 28

A little later that winter my mother died. She was eighty-two and had been ill for months, so we had a chance to get ready for her death. It was very hard on Dick. As her youngest child he had been closest to her, and her death came only a few weeks after his responsibility for manufacturing and engineering at IBM was taken away. I mourned her by retreating with Olive to Colorado, where I hand-wrote acknowledgments to literally hundreds of condolences from people inside and outside IBM all over the world. We stayed for almost two weeks, which wasn't nearly enough time, but I couldn't get away from work for any longer. While our management crisis had been resolved, we still had to make good on our commitment to deliver billions of dollars of new computers. The urgency of my work was as great as always—the difference now was that the joy I'd felt in running the company had disappeared. With Mother gone, Dick on the sidelines, and Al Williams working a reduced schedule in preparation for his retirement, I found myself more isolated than I ever imagined possible.

By promoting Learson, I'd kicked myself upstairs. I was still chief executive, of course, but I was out of the day-to-day operation of the business. All the other key executives, line and staff men alike, reported to Vin. There was no question that he deserved this job. The team he'd assembled for the System/360 project—people like Bob Evans, Fred Brooks, and Gene Amdahl—may have been the best collection of engineering-management talent in IBM history. In spite of his toughness as a boss, Vin had won their loyalty and respect. He called them "the boys," and with the future of the company riding on the new computers, they got the job done.

It took me a long time to reconcile myself to having him as my number two, however. I resented the rough way he had treated my brother. But even in the best of circumstances, the difference in our temperaments would have made it hard for Vin and me to build a trusting relationship like the one I had with Al Williams. Al and I talked about everything together, from corporate strategy to child-rearing. We'd made many of IBM's important decisions in relaxed discussions with our feet up on the coffee table. In contrast, Vin worked best by himself, and despite his great intelligence, decisiveness, and drive, he was not at all contemplative or methodical like Al. He ducked meetings whenever he could, put very little store in staff work, and favored executives like John Opel who knew how to take shortcuts across organizational lines. I'd worked with Vin for fifteen years and he had hated office procedures from the very beginning. Back in the early '50s, when Al was treasurer and Vin was general sales manager, Al had learned this the hard way. In those days Vin was big on a kind of memo that Al called "floopers" because of the way they'd float over the transom and onto Al's desk without his really noticing. By sending floopers Vin could always claim to have informed Al of whatever it was he was going to do. Then if Al challenged him he'd say, "You knew all about that. I told you in a memo on the twenty-eighth of October!"

"I never got such a memo!" Al would say, but he'd look in the pile on his desk and sure enough, there it would be. After Dad held Al responsible for several of Vin's expenditures that Al hadn't approved, Al finally told Vin he'd disavow any memo he sent that he hadn't read and put his initial on.

While Al and I had been in and out of each other's office constantly, Vin and I usually met only at sessions of the Management Review Committee four or five times each month. Each meeting was a tightly scheduled series of presentations by line executives and staff experts—budgets, pricing decisions, product strategies, and per-

sonnel policies all passed before us for review. It was a
textbook example of the precision management style for
which IBM was famous. Yet I ran those meetings in a
way that would have surprised most business school professors, because it was anything but scientific. I used the
committee to probe the business and to stir things up,
much as Dad used to do by buzzing people into his office
and arbitrarily assigning tasks. For example, if there was
a story in the newspaper that morning about a physicist
at Bell Labs winning the Nobel Prize, I might disrupt the
agenda and demand to know why no IBM scientist had
ever won. As Dad always had, I tried constantly to make
the executives aim a little higher.

This practice had worked fine as long as Al was president. He functioned like the ideal ground controller when
I went off on these flights: if I was headed in the wrong
direction, he had an easy, comfortable way of straighten-
ing me out, but he also knew how to follow up when I
had a point. With Vin as president, however, the atmosphere in the committee changed. He was skeptical and
impatient, less inclined to take a broad view. He was
never exactly insubordinate, but he often seemed to think
I was second-guessing decisions he had already made, or
wasting time on concerns that had nothing to do with
running IBM.

Vin, like Al, had too much self-discipline and good
sense to enter a contest he couldn't win, so he never challenged me directly at the company. Instead he fought it
out with me on the high seas. My hobby was ocean racing, and the year I made him president Vin entered the
Newport-to-Bermuda race, where I'd been competing for
years. He didn't have much deep-water experience, but
he was a good sailor, expert in small-boat tactics. I told
him jokingly at a Management Review Committee meeting that he'd better not win if he expected to stay at IBM,
but Vin made it no secret that he intended to beat me and
everybody else. He bought a boat called a Cal 40 with a
radical new design, and enlisted its architect as a member
of his crew. He studied the history of the race and found
a navigator who had been on a winning boat three differ-

ent times. When we raced to Bermuda that June, my *Palawan* placed twenty-fourth on corrected time—and his *Thunderbird* came in first.

That may have stung me more than I realized, because at the next Bermuda race two years later I inadvertently provoked a blow-up with Vin. By then yachts like his had become quite common, although they were still controversial. They were fast, and their owners found ways to make them faster each year, but there was a whole school of traditionalists like me who thought the new designs were risking seaworthiness and safety in the pursuit of speed. Two nights before the race was due to start, I took a walk along the docks in Newport with Olin Stephens, the dean of American yacht designers, who was also chairman of the International Ocean-Racing Rules Committee.

"You're letting people modify their boats too radically," I told him. There was a Cal 40 like Vin's sitting out of the water nearby, so that you could see the silhouette of its unorthodox keel and rudder. I gestured toward it. "Look at that boat. It's designed specifically to take advantage of the fine print in the rules."

Olin, who is a very mild man, said, "Well, yes, that's a clever design, but why do you object to it? It's perfectly seaworthy."

"Because if we keep fiddling with these rule-beaters," I said, "they are going to evolve until finally they become *un*seaworthy and somebody is going to get hurt." What I didn't realize was that the particular Cal 40 I'd picked to criticize was actually Learson's. Suddenly I heard an enraged voice shout, *"What did you say?"* and from the shadows behind the hull emerged Vin, looking nine feet tall, with his fists clenched. "My boat's a rule-beater? What do you mean by that!"

"Oh, no, Vin," I said. "I didn't even know this was your boat. I've just been talking to Olin here about the way his committee is permitting boats to move more and more in unusual directions. I'm sort of a conventionalist—"

"Hah!" he said. "You're trying to knock me off and you have no right to do that!"

The next day I went to Vin at a pre-race meeting and told him he'd completely misunderstood the bit of conversation he'd overheard. He ignored me and walked away. Olin Stephens tried to tell him the same thing and also got ignored. The spectacle of the two top executives of IBM feuding over their sailboats must have been titillating for people who liked gossip. I wish I could have stopped it, but we both had our pride involved and were both overreacting. We raced—and *Thunderbird* beat *Palawan* again, finishing thirteenth in the fleet against *Palawan*'s twentieth. But when we got back to the office the following week, Vin still wasn't talking. I heard nothing from him for several days; he didn't even return my phone calls. It took about a week before he'd cooled off enough to remember we were running a big business and somehow the chairman and president had to communicate. I don't think he ever believed my explanation, even with Olin's corroboration, but finally he accepted a phone call from me and agreed that the matter ought to be dropped.

If there had been any more episodes like this, Vin and I might have parted company. But IBM did fantastically well during that period—thanks largely to his skill as a manager and his success with System/360. After the doldrums of the early 1960s the company was growing again by nearly 30 percent per year—a growth rate more like that of an entrepreneurial start-up company and absolutely unprecedented for a multi-billion-dollar corporation. By 1965 we were among the ten largest industrial companies in America, and two years later the market value of our stock was greater than that of General Motors. I was proud of our achievement, but I felt as if I'd seen it all before: great success, huge growth, frequent reorganization, constant hiring and training on an ever increasing scale. The tension at the top of the business really wore on me, and while my life was more frenetically busy than ever, I began to find it impossible to tend the store as single-mindedly as I did right after Dad died.

I might have been indispensable to IBM, but the work wasn't as fulfilling.

I felt for the first time that my life was going out of control. I'd always been able to find the right answer in any crisis I'd ever faced, and I'd come to believe it was possible to achieve a truly perfect career. By using all the tools at my disposal—money, power, prestige—I knew I could influence events to a greater degree than most people, and I had jumped to the conclusion that with enough effort I could make everything turn out right for myself, my family, and IBM. The complexities I now ran into caught me completely unawares; suddenly nothing was simple, nothing came out quite right.

I wasn't the only IBM executive sorting out personal problems in the aftermath of the 360 crisis. Divorce was becoming much more common at IBM—it had been practically unheard of among our senior managers in Dad's day. Many of the men were also having difficulties with their teenagers, trying in vain to shield the kids from the social ferment of the late '60s. Drugs caused some real tragedies. One executive's son was a troubled boy who read that LSD enables you to understand yourself. He figured that if one dose is good, two or three must be better, so he took way too much and destroyed his mind. There was nothing his father could do; the boy had to be committed to an institution.

I had problems with my own teenagers, though not nearly as grave. In the spring of 1966 one of my daughters announced that she wanted to drop out of boarding school. For a couple of months I spent a day each week running IBM from the backseat of a limousine as I rode up to New England, trying to persuade her to stay. Ultimately I was successful: she finally graduated and went on to college. But even as I was pressuring this child, part of me understood the confusion of the younger generation. I'd had such a hard time finding my own direction as a young man that I felt sympathy for kids who weren't conventional achievers. I decided that one of the most important things a college can do is give such people a chance to find their own way. In 1968 I got my brother

and sisters to back me in establishing an unusual fellow-
ship program. The Watson fellowships—which are
named after my father and financed with money from my
parents' estate—are really a reflection of the kind of kid
I'd been, and an expression of my gratitude at not being
written off by my father or the administration at Brown.
Each year the program picks seventy-five graduating seniors from small liberal arts colleges around the country.
Instead of looking for straight-A scholars, we ask colleges to nominate young people whose character, interests, and creative potential make them worth taking a
chance on. We pay their way abroad for a year, with very
few strings attached, to pursue their own projects, which
can be as ambitious as they want. That first year, for
example, we had a Watson fellow in Paris doing painting,
another tracing cultural vestiges of the legal system of
ancient Greece, and another studying the impact of
American medical aid on countries in Asia and South
America. The choices reflected the extraordinary insight
and imagination of Robert Schulze, a former dean at
Brown, who was the program's first executive director.

I felt proud that we'd come up with a creative response to the generation gap. But I had to admit that this
program was very modest compared with the vast disaf-
fection of millions of young people in the 1960s. There
were signs of trouble everywhere—on TV you saw college kids taking over campuses and calling for revolution.
These protests were very upsetting—it seemed as though
our democratic process was on the verge of breaking
down—but they also made me stop and think about the
social ills that caused them. As a liberal Democrat I felt a
duty to solve such problems—but I didn't know how. I
kept looking for ways to make myself relevant on a much
wider scale, and for a while even toyed with the idea of
jumping into politics. At various times the Kennedy family and other prominent Democrats sounded me out on
running for office. Eunice and Sargent Shriver came to
visit us in Vermont at one point and Eunice said, "Tom,
you know us all and you're a natural-born politician. I've
seen you charm people and you can be tough as nails.

Why not get involved?" Bobby, who was now a senator from New York, tried to convince me to run against Nelson Rockefeller for governor in 1966, and the following year Ted Kennedy introduced me to influential New England Democrats as a possible senatorial candidate. But each time such an opportunity came up, I'd talk it over with Olive and decide to hold off. I was reluctant to leave IBM and didn't think I had the fire in the belly you need to go out and win votes.

Yet if Bobby Kennedy had made it to the White House, I'd have been willing to put my career at stake—either by running for office during his administration or serving as an appointee—to try to help put the country back on track. I pledged my support to him in the summer of 1967, even though the possibility of his becoming president seemed at least five years away. Lyndon Johnson was still firmly in command, and no one expected Bobby to run until 1972. I told him that the nation was not making the kind of progress I had hoped, that I thought he would make the best president, and that I wanted to back him in any way I could. I'm sure he was hearing the same thing from a lot of people. He simply said, "It means a great deal to me to hear that," and beyond that he was noncommittal.

I saw a lot of Bobby. He came to visit each winter in Stowe and each summer in North Haven. I used to lend him the *Palawan* for a week each year, and he and his friends would stay at North Haven for one or two nights before sailing off. Every bedroom in the house would be filled and it was always an exciting group—people like Sander Vanocur, the television reporter; Rowland Evans, the columnist; and John Glenn.

To me it seemed that Lyndon Johnson's animosity was the best thing that had ever happened to Bobby. As soon as it had become obvious that Johnson didn't want him as a running mate in 1964, Bobby had begun to mature at a rapid rate. During his years as senator he became a great force, much greater than he'd have been as vice president. He fascinated me, though he was not always an easy guy to be around and could be terribly abrupt. I remember taking a walk with him on our North Haven farm. As we chatted it began to mist a little bit, but I paid no attention until he said rather brusquely, "When are you going to turn around?"

"What do you mean?"

"Well, it's raining!"

"We wouldn't call this rain."

"*I* call it rain. Let's go back to the house."

I could imagine having a cozy talk with Jack Kennedy, but never Bobby. He was terrific with little kids, but in conversation with adults he was always serious-minded, more conscious than most people of his duty to his country, and he never let down the bars. I don't think he was very comfortable with me, either. But soon after he became a senator he made a recommendation that had a far-reaching effect on IBM. We were at my ski lodge at Stowe, and during a quiet moment Bobby said, "You've done a lot for the Kennedys, Tom. Is there anything we can do for you?"

I'd never thought about it, but intuitively I knew what to say. Bobby's team at the Justice Department was disbanding, and he had brilliant men. "Can you recommend a lawyer who might be willing to come to IBM as our general counsel?" I said. Given IBM's size and dominance of the computer business, I felt sure we would eventually face more antitrust problems.

"There are only two people you'd want to consider," Bobby said. "Burke Marshall and Nicholas Katzenbach. If you can get either of them, you'll do very well." Katzenbach had succeeded Bob as attorney general, and Marshall had been head of the Justice Department's Civil Rights Division and played a key role in the desegregation of schools in the South. I went to Washington, talked to both men, and both ended up joining IBM, Marshall right away, and Katzenbach a few years later, after working for Johnson as attorney general and as undersecretary of state.

As a senator representing New York, Bobby was interested in cultivating the business community. That was a hopeless cause, but I dutifully gathered up all the moderates I could find and held dinners and lunches for him in New York. These occasions never worked particularly well, because Bob was at his best when he felt sympathy for his audience, and when it came to businessmen, there wasn't much sympathy on either side. The only time I ever saw him attract business backing was in 1966 when he decided to tackle Brooklyn's Bedford-Stuyvesant ghetto. It was the worst slum in New York, bigger and more neglected than Harlem and in many ways a tougher and more frightening place. There had been race riots in the Watts section of Los Angeles the previous summer, and nobody wanted the violence to spread.

Bobby's idea was to have a committee of white business leaders work in partnership with a black community board, providing managerial advice and access to capital, and when Bobby felt passionately about something, people rallied to him. He persuaded both Mayor Lindsay and Senator Javits to pitch in, and then recruited a bipartisan team of top businessmen, including me, Bill Paley of CBS, Andrew Heiskell of Time Inc., George Moore, the chairman of First National City Bank, André Meyer, a senior partner at Lazard Frères, Benno Schmidt of the Wall Street firm J. H. Whitney, and others. Bobby would fly up from Washington to New York for our meetings, and unlike other blue-ribbon committees, this one worked. The white and black groups put together a combination of new jobs, housing renovations, and social services that gave Bedford-Stuyvesant a bit of new life. It was a modest success—but in the context of all the other failed efforts to revive ghetto communities, that was quite a remarkable accomplishment. During the "long hot summer" of 1967, when there were race riots in dozens of cities, Bedford-Stuyvesant was quiet, and Bobby deserves some credit for that.

IBM made the biggest contribution of all to the effort in Brooklyn: we put a new plant there. People in the late 1960s had begun to talk in terms of "corporate social responsibility"—the use of the economic power of big business to right some of the country's wrongs—and there was no question in my mind that IBM ought to extend itself. No one expects much in the way of corporate citizenship from a company that makes only a few million dollars a year, but when you make hundreds of millions, you ignore public opinion at your own peril. I'd already enlisted IBM in President Johnson's War on Poverty a couple of years earlier. Through a subsidiary we were running a major Job Corps center at Camp Rodman, an abandoned army base in New Bedford, Massachusetts. The idea was to train seven hundred fifty "hard-core unemployed" each year—black high school dropouts from the inner city who had never held jobs. We ran Camp Rodman for several years, and the experience caused us some real soul-searching, because there were more problems than we anticipated. Groups of Job Corps trainees started roaming around New Bedford at night, getting into fights with local gangs. The incidents became worse and worse until there was one in which six policemen got hurt and the city council petitioned President Johnson to close the camp. We changed directors and improved the discipline, but we never solved the basic problem: the Job Corps trainees had spent so many years out of work and in many cases drinking and taking drugs that they had no real motivation, and therefore it was virtually impossible for them to learn. IBM ended up hiring very few Camp Rodman "graduates," and I doubt any other company did either. Other Job Corps camps had the same difficulty, and the government finally closed down the entire project.

It seemed clear that to have any impact on unemployment, we would have to get to people before they reached the Job Corps stage—and that meant improving the slums in which they were growing up. I'd gone to the inner cities as a member of Johnson's anti-poverty commission, and the riots of 1967 didn't surprise me because I could see why people would want to tear up those slums. Many of my business peers still thought that in America if you worked hard you reached the top. But it was obvious to me that in the ghetto, if you worked hard, the chances were you'd still be at the bottom when you died. Somehow we had to reestablish the relationship in those communities between effort and personal integrity —and reward. That was the philosophy behind the Bedford-Stuyvesant plant. Talking to Bobby Kennedy, I became convinced that what the ghettos needed were plants in which people could acquire skills, earn decent wages and benefits, and develop a sense of pride in their achievement. If IBM could prove such a plant could be operated, other companies might follow our lead and eventually enough might happen in the ghetto to make a real difference.

We leased the biggest building we could find, a grimy eight-story stone and brick warehouse on Nostrand Avenue in the very center of Bedford-Stuyvesant. Our plan was to employ around five hundred workers—not as unskilled labor, but in real IBM jobs, with good wages, benefits, training programs, and the chance to advance and even move out of the ghetto by transferring to other IBM plants. Five hundred was a small number compared with, say, our plant in Rochester, Minnesota, where thirty-five hundred people worked, but we were in uncharted territory and the handful of other corporations that were trying to run inner-city factories were having a terrible time. Aerojet-General in California, for example, hired unskilled youths in Watts and put them to work making tents for the Vietnam War, a business it knew nothing about. The factory lost millions of dollars and the company finally had to lay people off.

To reduce the risk of similar embarrassments, we decided we'd stick to making products we understood—cables and other parts for our computers—and that we'd rely on experienced IBM managers. The man I picked to run the project was Ernest Friedli, the assistant manager of our giant Kingston plant. Friedli was white but he'd grown up in an immigrant family in a tough section of Brooklyn, and he called Bedford-Stuyvesant "my old neighborhood." He could be pretty blunt. At one point in the planning process I questioned whether we ought to air-condition the plant. No other business in Bedford-Stuyvesant was air-conditioned, and I didn't want it to look as if we were overdoing it. Friedli came right back at me by saying, "Put yourself in the place of a factory worker. Suppose you had to go up to Endicott for training and found air-conditioning there, and came back to a sleazy, non-air-conditioned building; wouldn't that be bad?" I immediately agreed that the last thing we wanted was to make people feel like second-class citizens. Friedli was a real leader. He went around the company and recruited a team of supervisors, four black and two white, asking them to take the transfer with no immediate raise, because this was a job that required dedication. All six said they'd like to go.

The toughest call I had to make was whether to put IBM's name over the door. We could have worked through a middleman—one idea was for us to find a black entrepreneur and offer him financing and a contract to serve as an IBM supplier. Our studies showed that a middleman could turn a profit after just one year, if he was frugal and did without a lot of IBM extras—such as a community relations manager, a plant psychologist, a big personnel staff, maybe even a plant receptionist. Vin Learson and other executives were for this approach, and so was I at first, because it was much safer and cheaper. But I changed my mind because I noticed that other companies were taking middleman approaches to the inner city, and I thought this would only reinforce the residents' feeling that nobody wanted to bet on them. I thought the courageous thing to do was to accept the risk and make it an IBM plant.

We gave the project a lot of scrutiny at IBM, and probably the smartest thing we did was to analyze it thoroughly as a business proposition. We decided to go ahead in Bedford-Stuyvesant only after studying other ghettos we might have gone into, for example, and my involvement in the community was only one of many factors in the final decision. Kennedy himself never asked for a plant, nor did I tell him of the plan until we'd decided to go ahead. We also studied whether it made sense to start the plant with hard-core unemployed like the young men from Camp Rodman—and the answer was no. As Friedli pointed out, our primary goal was to establish a factory that worked, not to take on so many social burdens that the operation went broke. Of the first two hundred Bedford-Stuyvesant residents he hired, one hundred twelve were unemployed and forty had police records, but he rejected the applicants with very serious problems, such as alcohol and drugs. Friedli's judgment must have been just about right, because the factory worked better than we'd hoped. While we'd expected it to be almost a nonprofit operation, we found we could make cables and other components there at slightly lower cost than at our other plants, and Bedford-Stuyvesant became a permanent part of the IBM system.

Bobby Kennedy would have been proud to see the project succeed, but even before it was publicly announced, in April 1968, he had turned his attention away from New York politics and entered the presidential race. My last few meetings with him had to do with that. I remember most vividly the day in late February when he came to my office to sound me out on the issues. We talked for an hour, mostly about Vietnam. This was in the wake of the Tet offensive which had swung public opinion against the war. I asked him what he thought the United States should do.

He said, "Tom, there is no sensible, easy solution. Just none. The only possible thing to do is to get our people out."

"How?"

"I'd get out in any possible way. I think it is an absolute disaster. Being there is much worse than any of the shame or difficulty one would engender internationally by getting out. So, with whatever kind of apologies and with whatever grace I could conjure up, I'd get out of there in six months with all of the troops the U.S. has."

I was shocked by that; his thinking was much more radical than mine. I was still transfixed by the question of how to deal with our South Vietnamese allies and all the promises we'd made them. But Bobby really wasn't interested in discussing the particulars of withdrawal—he said that no matter how we did it, it was going to be chaotic. To him that was all of secondary importance, because he had the long vision to see what the war was doing to our country.

Three months after he announced his candidacy, early on the morning after the California primary, an IBM executive called to tell me Bobby had been shot. I couldn't believe that two brothers could die in the same way, so I assumed he'd only been slightly wounded. I was scheduled to make a business trip to the West Coast that day with Burke Marshall, and Burke, who was very close to Bobby, was really shaken. He said, "Should I call the family office and see if we can give anybody a lift on our plane?" I said yes, and he found out that Jackie and her brother-in-law Stas Radziwill wanted a ride. So I arranged a car to take Jackie from the city to Kennedy airport, where Stas was arriving from London. As it happened the assistant manager at JFK was a fellow who had flown with me during the war. I called him and said, "This is a tragedy. I've got to take Jackie to California with me. I'm going to get her on board and then we want to taxi right up under the wing of Stas's airplane and pick him up."

I got them both into the airplane, and since I was flying we hardly spoke. We made a rest stop at Grand Island, Nebraska, the exact center of the country, and ran into Tom McCabe of Scott Paper and a bunch of Republicans who were just coming back from having helped Nelson Rockefeller campaign in Oregon. It still wasn't clear to any of us that Bobby's condition was serious. But when we landed in Los Angeles, Chuck Spalding, a close friend of the Kennedy family, met us and rode with us into town. Jackie said, "Chuck, what's the story? I want it straight."

Chuck said, "Well, Jackie, he's dying." Then we knew it was all over.

That was the end of the Kennedy era, although the family has a fantastic ability to rise above tragedy and go on. They even sized me up briefly as a replacement for Bobby in the Democratic race. Not long after the assassination I went to visit at Hyannis, and when I stepped off the airplane a crowd of little Kennedys came running across the tarmac wearing yellow sweatshirts that said "Tom Watson for President." Jackie had had them made up for the kids. I got in a car with her and Ethel and said, "Are you serious?"

"Why not? Why not?" they said. But we all knew I'd never stand a chance, and when a columnist friend of the family called a few days later to ask if I was indeed going to run in Bobby's place, I told him I'd already gotten over my vague aspirations to elective office.

It took two more years of upheaval on the college campuses for me to come around to Bobby's position on Vietnam. In June 1970 I was called to testify before the Senate Foreign Relations Committee; they wanted to explore the effect of the war on the U.S. economy, but I decided to use that platform to make the strongest possible case for pulling out of Vietnam right away. I said that as long as the war was allowed to go on, it would demoralize our young, erode our prestige abroad, make the economy unhealthy, and ultimately cause our society irreparable harm. "It's impossible to figure out an efficient, orderly, and dignified way of getting out," I said. "We must end this tragedy before it overwhelms us." I did nothing more than echo what Bobby had told me long before—but it was still so unusual for a prominent person to speak bluntly about withdrawal that the *New York Times* quoted me on the front page. That was how far ahead of us Bobby Kennedy had been.

CHAPTER 29

The last working day of the Johnson administration, January 17, 1969, was Black Friday at IBM. The Justice Department filed a massive antitrust complaint, accusing us of monopolizing the computer industry and asking the courts to break IBM into pieces. It was one of the biggest antitrust cases ever brought, comparable to the one in 1911 when the U.S. took apart Rockefeller's Standard Oil trust. The government objected to virtually our entire way of doing business, from our use of total system sales—supplying customers with complete installations including hardware, software, engineering help, training, and maintenance—to the big discounts we gave universities.

Strangely, none of these practices was illegal per se. We'd used them to build a fantastic industry, and all of our competitors did business the same way. But that was irrelevant, the government said; the point was that in the hands of a company of our size and strength, these marketing tools became weapons that crushed competition. The Justice Department asked the court to force us to change these practices, and added an ominous request for "relief by way of divorcement, divestiture, and reorganization . . . to dissipate the effects of the defendant's unlawful activities."

We'd seen this suit coming because we'd been under investigation by the Justice Department for two years. But what really alarmed me was the precipitous way in which the complaint was brought. Since the Johnson administration was almost over, I had thought the Justice Department would hold off and let the incoming Nixon administration decide how to handle the case. That would have been reasonable, and I had no cause to expect the government to act otherwise. The Antitrust Division had called IBM to task before, in 1935 and 1952, and they'd always been fair. We'd avoided a showdown in the courts on both occasions, and had been able to compromise with consent decrees that gave IBM plenty of room to grow. To me it seemed natural for the Justice Department to keep an eye on us because we dominated an important industry, and in the early 1960s I even gave speeches acknowledging the need for the Sherman and Clayton antitrust acts. I saw our dealing with the Antitrust Division as part of a healthy process of regulation to protect the public good. Nothing in my experience prepared me for how treacherous the legal process can be when it gets out of hand.

We tried in every way to head off the suit. Burke Marshall and I had even gone to Washington at the last minute to make a personal appeal to Attorney General Ramsey Clark. That meeting was one of the most uncanny experiences of my life. I'd been witness to an almost identical scene as a young executive seventeen years before. It was 1951, the Justice Department was about to sue us for monopolizing the punch-card industry, and Dad and I had gone to Washington to meet with the attorney general on that case—Tom Clark, Ramsey's father. The argument that Dad had used on Tom Clark was not terribly different from the one I used on Ramsey. I pointed out that the data processing field was very broad, and that the competition IBM faced was strong and increasing thanks to the constant evolution of technology, which no one had a monopoly on.

Like his father before him, Ramsey was impervious to these arguments. He refused to budge even when I appealed to him as a fellow Democrat. I told him, "I've been loyal to this party all my life, and my father was a loyal Democrat before me, and it makes me ashamed for an administration to behave the way you are behaving. You have less than a week left in office and if you'd really wanted to pursue the matter, you could have brought the suit a year ago. The only reason you're doing it now is that the Republicans have won and you want to dump a big problem into their laps."

"The facts are the facts," Ramsey said. "We think you're guilty and it is my duty as attorney general to bring this suit." I thought that was pompous and started to lose my temper, so I left.

I'd always thought Dad was irrational for refusing to face the realities of antitrust law. But now that I was confronted by similar accusations twenty years later, I had exactly the same reaction. My first public response to the suit echoed a move Dad had made: I declared our innocence in the newspapers. This was accomplished with typical IBM drama, by taking out double-page ads in eighty newspapers all over the United States. "Has IBM Spoiled the Computer Business for Others? Let's look at the record" was the way the ads began, and to show how the company had drawn together and was acting like a team, we had the IBM branch manager in each city hand-deliver the copy to the local daily. Those ads cost IBM three quarters of a million dollars—almost as much as our entire annual corporate-advertising budget —but I thought they were worth it because I wanted to reassure our customers, shareholders, and employees that IBM had a strong case.

My own private impulse, after being spurned by Ramsey Clark, was to forget the niceties and fight like hell to protect IBM. It was like some primitive instinct—as though Ramsey Clark were threatening my child. This powerful feeling came over me again and again through the years as our antitrust problems unfolded. When I sat down with our lawyers I'd be perfectly conscious of the difference between righteousness and greed one minute, and the next minute I'd be plotting defensive strategy with a totally unfettered and lawless mind. Only after I'd figured out what tactic I wanted to use would I go back and think about its legality. There was something wrong with that thought process: perhaps it is the best explanation for why antitrust law is necessary in the first place. I realized now how Dad must have felt during all those years I urged him to knuckle under and settle.

I struggled to put the government case in perspective. Remarkably, in spite of the sweeping changes and heavy penalty asked for by the government, the reaction on Wall Street was mild. Our stock, which was selling at around three hundred dollars a share before the complaint was filed, dropped only about eight points, and investors seemed to figure there was no use worrying since the case would take years to resolve. That was reassuring news, and it confirmed my sense that the case never should have been brought. I had been working for years to keep IBMers from taking unfair advantage of our position in the industry. IBM machines accounted for about 70 percent of all the computers sold, and one of the challenges senior management faced was not to exaggerate threats or overreact to competition, particularly in the 1960s as we began to come up against smaller companies. As early as 1961 I circulated a standard of ethics about what our people could and could not do. There were rules against bare-knuckle selling practices, such as disparaging other companies' products or leaking information about machines we hadn't yet announced in order to block a competitor from making a sale. Perhaps most important, I told the salesmen that in fighting for orders they had to show a sense of fair play:

Turn the situation around. Suppose that you were a competitor—small, precariously financed, without a large support organization, and without a big reputation in the field—but with a good product. How would you feel if the big IBM Company took the action which you propose to take? Would you regard the IBM Company as taking unfair advantage of you? Would you consider that the IBM Company was using a sales tactic which IBM possessed solely because of its size and reputation, and which, therefore, was unavailable to you? . . . We simply cannot shoulder people around or give the appearance of doing so.

Each year every salesman was required to sign a statement that he understood the rules. I wanted our record kept clean because IBM already had a great business. We had no reason to monopolize, no reason to be predatory in our actions. It would have been stupid.

In spite of all our efforts, we often found it hard to pull our punches, especially against companies who jumped into the business to piggyback on our success. In the late '60s a whole crop of new businesses sprang up, specializing in cut-rate disk drives, terminals, and other peripherals designed to plug into System/360 equipment. These so-called plug-compatible manufacturers, or PCMs, took business away from some of the most lucrative segments of our product line, and were a constant annoyance. Because they were parasites, they were terribly vulnerable to any move we made, and we faced a legal and customer-relations dilemma whenever it was time for us to update our designs or lower our prices. Say, for example, IBM's engineers wrote an improved piece of software—could we introduce it if, as a side effect, it would cause our computers to reject data that were being stored on a Brand X disk? Could we introduce it even if this, in turn, might put the Brand X Disk Corporation out of business? It was a very gray area of the law. We were forever asking our lawyers for opinions and getting mystifying answers like, "If you release the product that way, you have a forty percent risk of getting in trouble." This made the business very difficult to manage, and in addition to the Justice Department complaint we were slapped with more than a half dozen additional antitrust suits by plug-compatible manufacturers, computer leasing firms, and other companies all claiming we'd tried to do them in. The most important of these was a suit filed by Control Data, a Minneapolis computer maker, whose lawyers worked in close cooperation with the Justice Department.

Republicans have never been known as trustbusters, and it wasn't clear that the administration would take a hard line, although Nixon's new antitrust chief told reporters that he would pursue the case vigorously. We tried to mollify them by cleaning up our act voluntarily. Six months after the suit was filed, we made the drastic move of abandoning an age-old marketing practice known as bundling, a key element in our total-sales approach. It had always been our custom, whenever we rented or sold a machine, to lump everything together in a single price—hardware, software, engineering help, maintenance, and even training sessions for the customer's staff. This practice dated all the way back to the days of Herman Hollerith, the inventor of the punch-card machine, and it had been a powerful method for making customers feel secure enough to try computers when the technology was still new and hard to understand. Burke Marshall, however, was shocked to find IBM doing business in this way. He saw bundling as a glaring violation of antitrust law known as a "tie-in sale," such as when a local electric company tries to dictate the appliances you buy for your house. By requiring customers to buy our products by the bundle, we were making it almost impossible for independent companies specializing, say, in software to break into the business. At first people at IBM had trouble grasping this. No one could understand what Marshall objected to—bundling was like the Apostles' Creed at IBM, and since we looked at what we were doing as selling a service, it seemed perfectly natural that there should be one all-inclusive price.

Burke Marshall is a mild man, but as the public officials of Mississippi and Alabama learned from his work at the Civil Rights Division, he also has a precise mind and an unbendable will. In 1968 he stood up at an executive conference and told us that things had to change. We were going to have to undo the bundle and price each of our goods and services separately.

"But why?" people kept asking. "Why change now?"

He went through his explanation again and again until finally he lost his temper. "Because you've got a tie, goddamnit, you've got a tie! It's illegal! If you try to defend it in court, you'll lose!" He was shouting in a voice an octave above normal.

I went back to my room with Learson and a couple of

others. "The guy really means this," somebody said, and I decided that we ought to follow Burke's advice rather than risk a showdown in court. In June 1969, after months of hectic preparation under the apt code name "New World," we announced à la carte prices for our systems engineering services, customer training, and some of our software. Some executives thought we were giving up our birthright, that unbundling meant the death of the systems-selling technique on which my father had built IBM. But to me the bundle was simply another tradition that had to go, just as we had agreed in 1956 to sell our machines as well as rent them, and to license our patents to other companies. There had been doomsayers before those moves as well, but IBM had prospered—which made the antitrust laws easier for me to accept.

We wanted a quick settlement with the government, and might have succeeded if the Justice Department hadn't found the perfect ally in its plan to litigate against IBM. It was Control Data, which in December 1968 had filed a massive antitrust suit against us that closely paralleled Uncle Sam's. Of all IBM's competitors in all my years of management, Control Data was the worst thorn in my side. It had been founded in 1957 by a team of electronics engineers who had worked together since the war, including a number of years at Remington Rand. Their leader was an entrepreneur named William Norris and their top computer architect was Seymour Cray, a skinny, reclusive fellow who quickly became an industry legend. Norris's skill as a businessman and Cray's genius had made Control Data one of the industry's great success stories, growing in six years from nothing to annual sales of more than sixty million dollars. Their specialty was building big, ultra-fast machines for the scientific market—what people now call supercomputers. These products appealed to the same clientele that gave the computer industry its impetus in the first place—weapons labs, airplane and rocket manufacturers, elite universities —customers who were willing to fork over millions of dollars for the fastest state-of-the-art processors.

Before Control Data came along, IBM had been at the top of the supercomputing game. Our flagship project in the late '50s was a machine called STRETCH that grew out of a contract with the weapons lab at Los Alamos. STRETCH was the brainchild of an engineer named Stephen Dunwell and was going to be IBM's masterpiece: it was a daring design, with all sorts of exotic innovations. We promised customers that it would perform a hundred times as fast as our biggest commercial processor. Looking back, I think STRETCH was so ambitious that it is a wonder we got it built at all. But when it came out in 1961, behind schedule and only 60 percent as powerful as planned, I was disappointed and irate. I thought our engineers needed to be taught a lesson about not letting customers down. So, in the course of a press conference at an industry convention, I announced that the new computer had failed to meet specifications, and that I was hereby cutting the price on the machine from $13.5 million to $8 million to reflect its performance. We couldn't make any money at that price, and before long the project got shelved.

Making an example out of STRETCH shook up the engineers all right, but it turned out to be a grievous mistake. The engineers understood me to be saying, "No more of those big machines around here," and it was true that I would have snapped at anybody who brought up the subject. So for two years IBM did almost nothing in supercomputing, leaving the field wide open for Norris and his men.

In August 1963 came their bombshell: a machine called the 6600 that everyone recognized as a triumph of engineering. For seven million dollars, it delivered three times the power of STRETCH. Word of the new machine made me furious, because I thought the distinction of building the world's fastest computer should belong to IBM. At that point the System/360 was the most advanced set of designs we had, and nothing in that whole product plan was even remotely comparable to the 6600. On August 28, 1963, I sent my top men a memo:

Last week Control Data had a press conference during which they officially announced their 6600 system. I understand that in the laboratory developing this system there are only 34 people, including the janitor. Of these, 14 are engineers and 4 are programmers, and only one person has a Ph.D., a relatively junior programmer.

Contrasting this modest effort with our own vast development activities, I fail to understand why we have lost our industry leadership position by letting someone else offer the world's most powerful computer.

This note, eventually introduced as evidence in the antitrust suit, became famous as the "janitor memorandum." It wasn't illegal but it was where our troubles began, because the moves IBM made in response to my anger were too close to the limits of the law. Even though our engineering staff was overloaded, we tried to catch up with Control Data, and at the System/360 unveiling the following April, we said we would bring out a supercomputer at the top of the line that would leapfrog Control Data's machine. Control Data hadn't yet delivered its first 6600, and the effect of this announcement was to put a chill on its market: suddenly it became hard for their salesmen to close deals. Even though our supercomputer didn't exist yet, a lot of customers decided to hold off until they could get a look. In those days virtually every computer company used this tactic of announcing "paper machines" to keep a competitor from getting too far ahead, but it was exactly the kind of thing I'd told our salesmen to be careful about because of IBM's great size. The impact of our announcement on Control Data was so great that Norris cut his prices in a panic, and the company plunged into the red.

As it turned out, IBM was never able to beat the Cray design. Within two years Control Data was back on its feet; scores of 6600s had been installed and its salesmen were dropping hints about even faster machines being built in Seymour Cray's lab; meanwhile we had embarrassed ourselves by announcing four different versions of our supercomputer and still not delivering a one. Finally my business sense overcame my pride and I belatedly figured out that we couldn't compete with Control Data for the same reason that General Motors can't compete with Ferrari in building two-hundred-mile-an-hour sports cars. Supercomputers had become so highly specialized that even if we came up with a design equal to theirs, it would never fit in with the rest of our product line, our style of selling, our volume and profit targets, and so on. I was afraid to twist IBM inside out, trying to capture what was actually a small segment of the market. Control Data outsold us more than fifteen to one, and in the end we canceled our supercomputer program after delivering only a limited number of machines.

Because my temper was partly to blame for IBM's erratic behavior in the supercomputer market, I felt personally responsible for the Control Data lawsuit. Norris wanted compensation for the ordeal we had put his company through. His salesmen had kept detailed records of IBM's tactics as we fought for supercomputer accounts, and the suit listed no fewer than thirty-seven different ways in which we had supposedly abused our market power. The suit was so detailed and specific that industry wags nicknamed it the "IBM Sales Manual." The most famous accusation, which came directly from the supercomputer race, was that IBM had marketed "paper machines and phantom computers" in order to block Control Data from winning orders. I never met Norris, but he was a formidable adversary because of his understanding of the industry—and the depth of his antagonism for IBM. He shared everything he knew with federal investigators, and his case and the government's became intimately entwined.

The wheels of justice slowly began to turn. First came the discovery process, in which each side requisitions documents from the other and takes depositions from witnesses. Control Data demanded the records of sixty IBM departments and the memos and files of over one hundred executives. We had an entire warehouse near

Nyack, New York, where hundreds of clerks and parale-
gals did nothing but process paper for the case. The first
batch of material they put together consisted of seventeen
million documents—enough to fill a file drawer two miles
long. Control Data's lawyers reviewed forty million IBM
memos and documents in all, decided that a million of
them were relevant to the case, and had them micro-
filmed. Then they winnowed this collection down to
eighty thousand key documents and used a computer to
build a sophisticated electronic index. It was set up
to support the allegations that IBM was a monopolist.
You could push a button and show, for example, a whole
pattern of instances in which we had allegedly offered
preferential discounts to keep customers loyal. Control
Data's index marked the first time computer power had
ever been applied to a lawsuit on a massive scale—and
Norris made the system available to both the Justice Department and the other companies that were taking us to
court.

One of the journalists covering these developments
pointed out that without Control Data's help the government wouldn't have "discovered" very much about IBM
or the computer industry at all. The Justice Department
could only afford to assign twenty-five people to its case,
so it relied on Norris and his staff to do most of the work.
The government's suit went along this way for three
years or so, with papers going back and forth among the
various parties, but little visible progress toward either a
settlement or a trial. Finally in 1972 David Edelstein, the
judge who had signed our consent decree in 1956 and
who was now the chief judge of the Southern District of
New York, assigned himself to the case. He wanted to
push rapidly toward a trial, and he also seemed determined to make *U.S.* v. *I.B.M.* into a landmark of juris-
prudence. Talking to reporters about the case, he said
"its universality, its complexity, and its sheer volume of
documentation beggar the imagination. . . . It's not like
'A' suing 'B.' This case involves the world and the public."

Our annual legal bill went up into the tens of millions

of dollars. We had the best lawyers—within IBM we had both Marshall and Nick Katzenbach, who arrived just after the suit was filed; and for our outside counsel we used the firm of Cravath Swaine & Moore, led by Bruce Bromley, the seventy-nine-year-old retired judge who had guided us to the 1956 settlement. Perhaps I should have been more optimistic, but it depressed me to see IBM back in the lawyers' hands. The antitrust case began to color everything we did. For years every executive decision, even ones that were fairly routine, had to be made with one eye on how it might affect the lawsuit. To keep damning evidence to a minimum, the lawyers even dictated what we could and couldn't say at meetings. There were all sorts of code words and strange uses of language: for example, the executives in our computer divisions were told to avoid military metaphors when talking about beating the competition, and if IBM had more than fifty percent of a given market, they were supposed to use the phrase "market leadership" instead of "market share." This sort of mealymouthing went against my instincts. I wanted IBM to be the best in everything and recognized as such, which meant making no apologies and capturing more market share than anybody else. Instead we were slowly tying ourselves in knots. In 1969 and 1970, because of the double drag of the lawsuits and a recession, IBM's annual growth slumped to less than five percent—down from the nearly thirty percent we'd achieved in each of the two previous years.

All my life my answer to complicated circumstances has been to make a dramatic and decisive move, but this time there were no such moves to make. I remember agonizing over how we could settle the Justice Department suit and avoid the risk of going into court. The 1956 consent decree that ended our previous case had been reasonable, and my inclination was to make another deal. But all the Justice Department was offering us this time was the death penalty. They wanted to dismantle our company, so that instead of one $7 billion-a-year company, IBM would become seven $1 billion companies. That was something I couldn't accept. At the beginning I was willing to split IBM in two, with one half devoted to making large computers and the other to small; we could have operated that way even though the split would have been traumatic. But the Justice Department wasn't interested, and over the course of the suit, increasing competition from Japan weighed against any divestiture at all because we needed all of our mass and might to fight competitors such as Fujitsu and NEC. Our only choice was to let the case drag on.

Four years later I finally had an opportunity to move decisively. In late 1972, the pretrial maneuvering in the Control Data suit was finally coming to a close, and the lawyers at Cravath recommended that we'd be wise to settle out of court. Vin Learson negotiated the deal, which cost IBM a small fortune. It involved selling Norris our Service Bureau Corporation subsidiary for a fraction of its real worth. This was a $63 million-a-year business that did data processing jobs for customers whose own computers were overloaded or who didn't have computers of their own. Control Data operated a pretty large service bureau of its own, and the addition of ours made them the world's largest supplier of computer services. We also gave Norris a package of cash and contracts worth $101 million, including $15 million to cover his legal fees.

In spite of the expense, this settlement was a brilliant tactical stroke on the part of Cravath. Because of all the work Control Data had done in analyzing and indexing our documents, their suit was the master link in all the other antitrust suits against IBM. That computerized index now became the property of IBM, because it is customary in out-of-court settlements for the two sides to exchange their lawyers' paperwork as a way of burying the hatchet. We got the so-called work product from their lawyers and gave them ours, and that night Bruce Bromley came to my office.

"You've got to destroy that index right away," he said.

"My God, isn't that illegal?" I said.

"It's perfectly legal. We've spent millions of dollars to

get them to drop the suit, and we get the work product as part of the settlement. It belongs to us now."

"I can understand that we own the work product. But it seems to me there is something wrong about destroying evidence. Aren't there laws against that?"

"Yes, but this isn't evidence and it never was. Technically speaking, it's nothing more than a set of files that used to belong to their lawyers and now belongs to you. You can do whatever you want with it."

We both knew full well that the index could eventually be used to marshal evidence in the other lawsuits that were still pending. Business sense dictated my answer. If I didn't take the lawyers' advice, I would be placing IBM under a terrific handicap. I had no choice. "Burn it," I said.

They destroyed the index that very night. A few days later there was a flurry about this in the newspapers, because the Justice Department and a lot of people in the industry felt that destroying the index was improper. But there was nothing they could do, and their investigations were hobbled after that. I never was totally comfortable about that decision. Even though I had a fiduciary responsibility to protect the investment of IBM shareholders, and even though the best lawyers money could buy assured me I wasn't breaking any law, it made me feel uneasy.

Without Control Data around to help, the Justice Department's case deteriorated into a courthouse mess. Judge Edelstein let things get completely out of hand. He refused to set limits—either on the issues the Justice Department was allowed to add as the case progressed, or the amount of evidence or witnesses we could use to respond. He left crucial motions undecided for months and made arbitrary rulings that shocked lawyers on both sides—such as insisting that depositions be taken in court rather than at the office or home of the witness as is customary. The lawyers had to spend months reading depositions into the court record with Judge Edelstein mostly absent from the bench. I sometimes thought he was overwhelmed and afraid to come to grips with the case. As time went by he became so hostile toward our lawyers and witnesses that we tried to have him removed.

The case dragged on for twelve years, until the Reagan administration finally dropped it in 1981. Looking back, I see a lot of sad irony in the whole affair. I think a lot of people would agree that at the outset the Justice Department's complaint had merit. IBM was clearly in a commanding position in the market, and some of our tactics had been harsh. We eliminated many of these practices ourselves, and our overall record during the case was pretty clean. But I've always thought that if Judge Edelstein had carried the suit along rapidly, we'd likely have ended up with a consent decree in which we might have formally agreed to hold back from announcing our machines until we were a little further along with their development, to loosen our grip on the educational market, and so on. Instead, the case stretched on unresolved for so long that before it was over history showed my argument to Ramsey Clark to have been right. IBM kept growing, but the computer industry grew even more, and the natural forces of technological change etched away whatever monopoly we may have had.

CHAPTER 30

Enough was going wrong by 1970 that I started to daydream about a very different kind of life. In the top drawer of my desk, mixed in with memos about key business issues and old letters from Dad, I had a secret list that I'd take out and look at when nobody was around. On it were adventures I wanted to have: climbing the Matterhorn was first, then learning to fly a helicopter, going on safari, sailing to the Arctic and around Cape Horn, and making a singlehanded voyage— to anywhere. I also wanted time to enjoy myself with my wife and my children. My zest for business was evaporating fast. We'd built IBM into a seven-billion-dollar-a-year giant, and in my heart of hearts I felt that I'd taken it as far as I wanted to go. I was fifty-six years old, and my life was a constant punch, punch, punch of making decisions and pushing IBM ahead—running from crisis to crisis, going to company dinners, visiting plants. Each year was filled with hundreds of meetings and speeches and public appearances, so that I was doing something practically every night and spending as much time on the road as at home. I'd lived this way for more than fifteen years, and Dad had kept it up all his life, but I was bone-tired and fooling myself that the fast pace didn't bother me. During one hectic week I flew to Chicago to give a speech, and in the half hour I had to myself beforehand the thought suddenly came to me: "I can't keep this up. Something is going to break." But I pushed the idea out of my mind.

The Nixon recession, which started in mid-1969, was longer and deeper than anybody had predicted, and IBM hit the first serious downturn of my career. Not only did our sales stay flat, but profits actually began to *sink* for the first time since the war, giving Wall Street the idea that IBM's glory days might finally be over. In the first eight months of 1970 our stock fell and fell, losing almost half its value. Try as I might to get the company revved up, things looked worse and worse as the year progressed.

At the same time as the company struggled, my sense of isolation increased. Dick resigned from IBM in March to become U.S. ambassador to France. His good feeling about the company had never been restored after the events surrounding System/360. I knew the ambassadorship was something Dad would have been proud of—it took a weight off my heart to see my brother rise, despite my mismanagement, to the highest stature anyone in our family had attained. Still, at the same time, it was painful for me to think that when I stepped down, there would be no Watson to pass the business to. Meanwhile Jane, our sister, was slowly dying of cancer. It metastasized and in the spring she needed surgery to remove a tumor from her brain. From then on she was in a decline, in and out of the hospital every couple of months.

I hadn't had much to do with Jane since she'd sold her IBM stock, but her illness made hurt pride irrelevant, and I got in the habit of visiting her several times each week. She was a solid, thoughtful, tough gal, and she really fought the cancer, staying active socially and giving dinner parties even though she was almost bedridden. When Nixon appointed her husband undersecretary of state, Jane was too sick to move to Washington, but she knew how much the job meant to Jack and urged him to grab it. She was happy that I came to see her, and in those final months we developed a warm relationship. Being there day after day was the best way I had to tell her that in spite of our past differences, I admired her and loved her and felt sorrow that she was dying.

All these problems piled up on me and there was no escape. If I had been a drinker in those days, I'd have quickly killed myself. Vacations didn't help. I threw myself into skiing—we must have gone on a dozen ski trips in 1969 alone—and when the weather was warm I raced my sailboat. But afterward I'd go back to IBM with my nerves just as taut as before. By fall 1970 my discouragement showed. People who worked around me say that I became more and more volatile, flying into rages over petty details like the way snow was plowed in the parking lot. Late on a Wednesday afternoon in mid-November, I was in my office and Jane Cahill, my executive assistant, started to come in the door. Then she stopped cold, because I had my head down on the desk. "Are you all right?" she said.

"I'm fine. I'm tired," I said. Jane offered to drive me home, but I told her I'd drive myself. My sister's condition was much worse, and the day before I'd learned of the death of my best friend from college, Nick Lunken. He'd been ill for years but I remembered him as a merry guy who loved to play practical jokes and always got me to laugh. I was supposed to go to his funeral the following morning.

That night I woke up with a pain in my chest. It wasn't very intense but it wouldn't go away. Olive was in the Caribbean with friends, so I drove myself to the emergency room at Greenwich Hospital, where they put me on a monitor. By morning I'd convinced myself I was fine, and told the internist who came to examine me that I wanted to leave. He said, "You're not going anywhere. You're having a heart attack."

"Impossible!" I thought. "Dad never had a heart attack." But they wheeled me into intensive care and put me into an oxygen tent. Next the doctor tried to stick an IV into my arm, the needle broke, and he yelled at the nurse to get another one. I thought he was acting awfully tense. More doctors trooped in. There was a speaker inside the oxygen tent and I said, "Why are all you fellows gathering around here?" My voice was weak because I was slowly losing consciousness. Then I said, "Oh, I know—so each of you can render my estate a bill. Ha ha . . ." and I was out.

If my father had ever been struck down in this way, IBM would have been paralyzed because it was a one-man show. But when I got sick, business went on pretty smoothly. Vin Learson came to the intensive care unit and I put IBM in his hands until I could get healthy again; I didn't want to make decisions from a hospital bed. Then I called Al Williams, who was the senior member of the board, and told him we had it all arranged.

Dr. Newberg, the internist, was an energetic, attractive man. Over the next three weeks he had long talks with me about what a heart attack is, how serious mine had been, how long I'd need to recuperate, and so forth. Finally he said, "You know more about heart attacks than any patient I ever had."

"I'm trying to avoid having another one," I said.

"Well, as long as we're on the subject, what are you planning to do when you get out of here?"

I said, "I don't know—go back, and maybe retire in a few years."

Newberg looked me right in the eye and said, "Why don't you get out right now?"

I was so stunned by this suggestion that I couldn't think about anything else for the rest of the day. I realized that the strain of running IBM had taken a huge toll. Now I was being offered a way to step down with honor.

The next morning I saw the sun coming up outside my window and felt better than I had in decades. I decided that as long as I was in the hospital I'd stop worrying about IBM. I sent for the secret list of adventures that had been in my desk drawer for years. Most of the items on the list were too arduous for a recovering heart-attack victim to consider, but I thought I could sail. Before long I was happily immersed in plans for a new sailboat designed for voyaging rather than speed. I got Olin Stephens, the yacht designer, to come to the hospital with Paul Wolter, *Palawan*'s professional captain, and we spread sketches out on the bed. I started rereading the journals of Captain Cook, which I'd loved as a boy, and I was amused to find a comment I could almost have written myself. It was from Cook's letter to a friend upon being retired to a desk job in Greenwich, England, after a decade of roaming the seas:

My fate drives me from one extreme to another; a few months ago the whole Southern hemisphere was hardly big enough for me, and now I am going to be confined within the limits of Greenwich, which are far too small for an active mind like mine. I must however confess it is a fine retreat and a pretty income, but whether I can bring myself to like ease and retirement, time will shew.

Less than a year after Cook wrote this complaint, he managed to obtain the command of two ships and was off on his third and last great voyage. If Cook could fight his way out of the doldrums of retirement and take to the sea, so could I, I thought. Knowing of my ambitions, my brother sent me a very large oil painting of a 19th-century English sailing ship entering Portsmouth harbor after a long voyage. The note said, "I hope this is the biggest get-well card you'll receive." IBM seemed very far away indeed.

I came home thirty days after the heart attack, and the first thing I had to do was go to my sister's funeral. She died on the last day of the year. She was only fifty-five, but I guess everyone in our family felt reconciled to her death because it had been expected and we'd all been able to say good-bye. After that I had to face the slow ordeal of recuperating physically and emotionally from my illness. When you have a heart attack, you realize how fragile your body is. I felt that mine had let me down, damn near entirely, and for several months I had very volatile reactions to insignificant things. Olive bore the brunt of my anger and bitterness. She had fixed up a very comfortable room for me on the ground floor of our house because I wasn't supposed to climb stairs. She put books in there that she knew I'd like, paintings, and so on. When I first walked in I saw she even had a miniature air horn on the nightstand, a small version of the kind of horn they use to call time-out at basketball games. "What's that for?" I said.

"That's in case you feel bad. You blow that and we'll come."

I tried it and the valve must have been clogged because it just went *boop*. I don't know why I got so mad, but I said, "Goddamnit, Olive, you'd never hear this!" I made a big stink about it, which was awful of me. She'd obviously put a lot of time and thought into preparing that room, and I should have been grateful instead of acting like an angry fool.

I kept to myself during the weeks that followed, working on my plans for the new boat. In the barn behind our house Paul Wolter built full-size mockups of sections of the hull. I wasn't supposed to get out of bed, but I'd sneak out there and look at the mock-ups for hours, imagining what the boat would be like, and debating with Paul about the changes we ought to make.

Finally, after a couple of months had passed, I went back to IBM and told people I was thinking of getting out. The board of directors did everything in the world to keep me in the company. They came to me individually and as a group. "You're so valuable to the business," they said. "Can't you just arrange your schedule so you're under less stress?" IBM has one of the best boards in the world, but all boards have a common failing. If the chief executive has done well, they won't push for a successor to be designated until something goes wrong—and then they often end up hiring a new man pell-mell from outside. All the same, I tried it their way for a little while. The doctor had told me to do a lot of walking to build up my heart. So I'd leave my office and pace endlessly around the grounds of our headquarters. The doctor also ordered me to lie down for an hour or two after lunch. So each day I'd eat and then lie down. But you can't run a big company like that. I'd get up from my couch and look into the outer office and I'd see people with important problems sitting there cooling their heels. That wasn't the example I wanted to set. After two months I finally went to the board and told them it wasn't going to work. I knew I was doing the right thing. I wanted to live more than I wanted to run IBM. It was a choice my father never would have made, but I think he would have respected it.

I wrestled with the question of who was to run the company after me. A year earlier, when Dick left for Paris, I'd decided on Frank Cary as my successor. Frank was really everybody's choice. He was head of IBM's computer divisions in the U.S., and had emerged as a natural leader even though his management style was utterly different from mine. Frank was a brilliant business analyst, cool, impartial, and totally self-confident. He rarely spoke up at meetings, and it wasn't his style to step in and save the day the way Learson and I did. He didn't make heroic moves and he didn't make glaring mistakes; when he ran into a problem he simply figured out how to fix it. A lot of people attributed Frank's muted style to the fact that he came from California—he was one of the talented young managers Al Williams had turned up in 1955 when he scoured the company for MBAs. At one point Frank was a district manager in Chicago, and I'd flown out to look him over. He seemed unprepossessing at first sight, but talking to me didn't appear to intimidate him in the least. When I bored in with questions his answers were straightforward and calm. I called Williams and said, "We've got to bring this guy East." As soon as Frank got to New York he began to shine, and that was without Al or me championing him. He started at about the fourth echelon of management, and passed muster with a lot of other bosses before he got to us.

The heart attack threw my Frank Cary plan into disarray, because it hinged on the assumption that I'd be around three more years until I turned sixty, the retirement age all the senior executives had agreed upon. If I'd made it that far, Vin, who was older, would have retired first, and Frank would have had a clear path to the top. But when I decided to step down, Vin was only fifty-eight, with a year and a half to go before his retirement. Even though Cary was the man we'd picked to run the company long-term, Vin was ending a long and dramatic career and clearly had a claim on the top job. I resolved the question by naming him chairman and chief executive for that eighteen-month span.

I gave the board my letter of resignation at the end of

June, agreeing to stay on as head of the board's executive committee, just as Al Williams had in the first stage of his retirement. Bill Moore, the chairman of Bankers Trust and head of the compensation committee, asked, "What do you want to be paid?" and I laughed because it was so much easier to negotiate my salary now than it had been after Dad's death. I told him I'd finish the current year at full salary, that the next year I'd take half pay, and that in the final year I'd work but take no pay at all. I fully intended to let my responsibilities taper off, and I didn't want to feel any obligation to show up at the office.

Finally I went sailing, as I'd been longing to do. I don't think I understood at the time why I felt so compelled to sail, or the depth of the emotional turmoil I was in. So much of what was important to me had suddenly been taken away—my IBM career was over, my license to fly airplanes suspended because of the heart attack—and lurking underneath was my terror at realizing my life, instead of being long like Dad's, might be short like Jane's. Only in retrospect can I see how panicked I was. But at the time I knew instinctively that sailing would rescue me. Dr. Newberg had said, "You're either going to be a heart-attack invalid, always trying to be near a hospital so you can check in for the next one; or you can try to forget about hospitals altogether." I wanted to forget, and my solution was to head for a remote place where no hospitals were. I got Paul Wolter and we took the *Palawan* up around the island of Newfoundland.

We brought a crew of young men to do the heavy work, and an old friend named Ed Thorne who was a great companion and excellent seaman. Ed knew he was going sailing with a captain who might drop dead at any minute, but he was game. Before we left he went to see Dr. Newberg, who took an orange and taught him how to give an emergency injection of morphine. I carried morphine along because I knew heart pain could be excruciating. When we put out to sea I worried each night when I went to bed that I might wake up dying and have no doctor around. As it happened one day we anchored in front of the Grenfell Mission Hospital on Newfoundland's Great Northern Peninsula, and it crossed my mind that this might be my last chance to get off the *Palawan* alive. But then I put the fear behind me and I'm glad I did, because it would have been awful to live with that kind of dependency. The weather was rough, but we kept pounding along for a month, and the trip worked out better than I had a right to expect. In reality I was still pretty frail.

Olive was waiting for me when we got back to North Haven, but the way I'd behaved since my heart attack had taken a terrible toll on our marriage. I must have thought that I had to get better all by myself, because I'd done everything I could to push her away. I'd been self-absorbed, unappreciative, and rude—a fairly common re-action among heart-attack victims, I've been told. Olive was constantly trying to keep me amused, but if some-thing wasn't to my liking I'd snap, "Don't you know I can't do that with my heart condition?" When I came back from the Newfoundland voyage our marriage was hanging by a thread. Nine months of frustration came boiling out in a bitter fight, and Olive finally said, "I can't stand this anymore!"

"Fine," I said. "I can't either." I left and went out West with some friends.

As far as Olive was concerned, that was the last straw. We'd been married almost thirty years, she had made tremendous efforts to cope with my temper, and it had all come to naught. It looked like retirement was only going to make my disposition worse. She was ready for a di-vorce.

It took me a couple of weeks to realize that I was making the worst mistake of my life. By the time I raced back East to ask her to change her mind, she had moved out of our Greenwich house and gotten an apartment in Manhattan. The friends I confided in were pessimistic. "She'll never come back, so don't waste any effort," one told me. Another one saw how sick I was about losing her and said, "She's a great girl. Give it everything you've got."

I couldn't reach her. She wouldn't answer the letters I

wrote, or pick up the telephone when I tried to call. Soon the news of our separation appeared in the gossip columns, which made it pretty official, and Olive hired a woman divorce lawyer who was one of the best in the business. I knew I had to do something drastic. So I went to the lawyer and asked for her help. "Olive can't be sure about this thing, and I want her back," I said. "Could you be our intermediary?"

The lawyer was down-to-earth. "I feel as though I owe you a favor, and I'll tell you why," she said. "I met your father once. When I was a young associate just starting out, I was sent to deliver some papers to him at home in New York. It was snowing that night. After he signed the papers, he walked me to the front door, called his limousine, and put me in it. Then he arranged a blanket on my knees and told the driver to take me home. So for your father's sake, I'll talk to your wife." Olive was madder than hell when she found all this out, but the lawyer did serve as a go-between.

I was as desperate as a teenager to have Olive back. More weeks went by, the matter still wasn't resolved, and I went with my sister Helen to visit England. One night we took a walk on the Strand and suddenly I felt faint. It was totally psychosomatic but I thought I was going to die. I checked out of the hotel and came straight back to the United States and to Greenwich Hospital, where I actually told the doctor that I had a broken heart. "I guess you really miss your wife," he said.

I sent my secretary to tell Olive I was sick. She was skeptical. "Will he live?" she said.

"I think he'll live all right, Mrs. Watson, but he's seriously ill." So she came straight to my bedside and that was the beginning of our reconciliation. Within two days we were on our way to Europe and I sent a cable to the IBM board that said, "Reports of our divorce are greatly exaggerated. We are leaving for Sweden on a second honeymoon. Olive and Tom."

We had a tough time putting our marriage back together. There were blow-ups, mainly caused by me. At one point when it looked like we might separate again, I decided I had to try a psychiatrist, the only time in my life I've ever gone. "We need help," I told him, "but there's no point in bringing Olive in here because she doesn't like to analyze emotional matters."

He said, "Tell me about you and what your problems are." So I gave him a short rundown of my life. Then I talked about our marriage and occasionally he'd throw in a question such as, "Did you ever have an argument at breakfast?" or "Did you ever have arguments over the children?" We'd had terrible arguments over the children, so I concentrated on that. Around the middle of the third session I said, "I guess what you're trying to tell me is that the woman is doing her damnedest to get things right, and I never give her any credit. I keep trying to win every fight. I guess I've got to lose some."

"That sounds about right," he said. I had a lot to learn about how to be a reasonable husband, but I was finally getting the message that I couldn't run my life like IBM.

The Nixon recession ended and during Vin Learson's short term as chief executive IBM had good results. By the time Frank Cary took over in January 1973, the company was growing rapidly again, and annual revenues were up near the ten-billion-dollar mark. I was preoccupied with recuperating, and as long as Vin was on top, I hardly felt as if I'd given up my power over the company; he made operating decisions pretty much as I would have. But when Cary came in I really had to contend with the fact that the Watson dynasty, after almost six decades, was over. Frank was fifty-two; therefore he was likely to be chief executive for eight years, and from my own experience I knew that is more than enough time for a boss to change a company forever.

When Frank started his new job I asked him to spend a couple of days alone with me at my ski house in Vermont. I told him there were things I wanted to pass along that I thought he might not know in spite of his MBA. No textbook in the world can tell you how to be the chief executive of IBM, and the most important lessons had been drilled into my head by Dad. Not surprisingly,

Frank seemed a little reluctant to go at first. I'm sure he expected a bunch of homilies; I'd sometimes felt the same way around my father. But then he agreed, and in the middle of March we flew up to Stowe. The ski season was over and nobody was at the lodge; it was the perfect place to get away.

I had no fixed agenda; I simply gave him every bit of advice that came into my head. I told him a saying of Dad's, about how the head of business should behave: "Act like a beggar, feel like a king," the idea being that in your dealings with others you should be empathic and humble, yet utterly self-reliant and confident within. Frank Cary behaved that way instinctively, and this was my way of telling him he was doing the right thing.

I told him the real test of his leadership would be whether he could keep IBM, as immense as it now was, from becoming cold and impersonal. I was concerned that he continue to make the small gestures that had been so important to me and Dad: sending flowers to wives, books on birthdays, handwritten notes to tell employees that you recognized and appreciated what they'd done. "These things aren't luxuries, they're good business," I said. "IBM is a service company, and the more personal the tone, the more your employees and customers will respond."

We covered everything from the IBM dress code to the question of how to lobby Congress. Cultivating people is something a chief executive has to do, cultivating not only politicians but anyone of influence, including newspaper publishers and other businessmen. I told Frank that the most graceful and effective way to do this is in person, and that probably the worst way is to have a Washington office staffed with professional lobbyists.

The one area where I thought Frank might be weak was representing IBM to the outside world. His success so far had been very much within the confines of the company, and I wanted him to realize he was now a public figure. I felt very strongly—and my father did too —that businessmen have a responsibility to do good in the community, not just stay in the office and coin money. Despite a few lonely nights spent on camping trips in the Palisades as head of the New York area Boy Scouts, I'd gotten great satisfaction from my public work. I told Frank that upholding this tradition of service was a key part of his job, and I told him how to approach it. "You're a big shot now," I said. "You'll be asked to join everything. Pick two or three public organizations that you think really have meaning and take the time to work hard on these. You have to earn your position in the outside world, just like you earned your position at IBM." But pretty soon it became obvious that Frank wasn't interested in the national spotlight. Instead he joined the boards of a handful of powerful companies and became an important figure in the Business Roundtable and other insider groups. I was disappointed at first, but I knew Frank had a tough job to do, running IBM in not only my shadow but the old man's, and I came to accept the fact that he was going to do it his own way. Trying to make himself famous was what any Watson would have done, but it wasn't Frank Cary's style, and the fact was that for eight years he ran IBM as well as it had ever been run.

CHAPTER 31

I woke in my bunk to the heavy sound of *Palawan*'s engine. My watch showed 4:00 A.M. but the portholes were bright with daylight. It was August 1974, and we were cruising the icy waters off the coast of Greenland, more than five hundred miles above the Arctic Circle. In my heavy pajamas and a coat I stepped on deck, where the temperature was just below 40 degrees with a light mist blowing from the northeast. Here and there I could make out the dim shapes of large icebergs, which are as common as clouds at that latitude, only harder to ignore. At the helm on this watch was Jimmy Madden, my friend from childhood who had sailed in the Arctic once as a college boy. Above, in the lookout ring at the crosstrees, was Nick Scheu, an eighteen-year-old sailing novice. I was glad he seemed alert. Yachts manned by amateurs almost never venture this far north. The waters of the Greenland coast are known for all sorts of ice, from icebergs more than a mile long to large, almost entirely submerged masses of "blue band ice" that are difficult to spot and that can send a thin-hulled vessel quickly to the bottom. Somewhere ahead lay Smith Sound and our destination, the deserted Eskimo settlement of Etah where Admiral Peary in 1909 began his eight-hundred-mile trek to discover the North Pole.

This was the first major voyage of the boat I'd dreamed of—and then planned—in my bed at Greenwich Hospital. The new *Palawan* was a sturdy blue sixty-eight-foot ketch, not huge as yachts go, but the biggest boat I'd ever owned and exactly suited to the kind of voyaging I had in mind for my retirement. I'd designed her with the idea of being able to sail to remote corners of the earth, in reasonable safety and comfort, with enough friends to keep things interesting. The boat was simple enough for me to sail with the help of a single professional if Olive and I wanted privacy, yet capable of sustaining eight people at sea for sixty days and four thousand miles. When she was brand-new in 1973 I'd sailed her across the Atlantic from Bremen, where she was built, getting to know her quirks. Later that year we'd cruised around the Caribbean and along the coast of Maine. But those trips were mere preparation: I'd nearly died; I'd stepped down from IBM; and I was looking for an adventure that those recent events in my life wouldn't totally overshadow. I wanted to make a journey to a seldom-traveled place with real risk. The plan was to take the *Palawan* as far north as possible, despite the warning of George B. Drake, a marine architect friend of Jimmy Madden's who had been up the Greenland coast aboard a cargo ship the year before. When he heard we were planning this voyage he wrote Jimmy a letter that said:

> I do not recommend this trip on a yacht. We found heavy ice, and the weather deteriorates as you go north. Overcast most of the time, sudden squalls out of nowhere that last quite a while, and fog coming in at odd times, quite different from the fog we experience even off the coast of Maine. The motor vessel on which we sailed was a replacement for one that was lost, presumably by hitting an iceberg. . . . Our ship was on her second bow, as in spite of her having two radars she smacked an iceberg and folded in her original bow.

Early in the summer we'd set out from Camden, Maine, cruising to Newfoundland and then to Greenland across the Davis Strait, taking a circuitous route to avoid ice near Labrador's coast. The crew I'd assembled for this ambitious project was hardly what you'd expect for an arctic expedition: a mixture of young and old, men and women, with only two professional sailors, neither of whom had any arctic experience. The weather was frigid, overcast, and often foggy, and we charted our course mainly by radio navigation instead of the sun. After a cold week we had a spectacular landfall at Godthaab, Greenland's capital. We were in dense fog as we drew near, and I thought we'd have to stop because there was no way to find the harbor entrance. But suddenly the fog blew away, revealing brilliant blue skies and a spectacular view of the town at the foot of low snowy mountains, with the high peaks of the ice cap in the distance beyond. Greenland is five sixths covered by ice all year round, but in the region of Godthaab in summer there are lovely fields, wildflowers, and even a few small trees. During our layover in Godthaab, Olive and one of our friends flew up to join the crew; I also recruited an Eskimo ice pilot named Lars Jensen who had just graduated from shipmaster school. Lars was only twenty-eight years old, but he'd been at sea all his life. He was skeptical about joining the crew of a pleasure boat, and wouldn't sign on until he'd sailed with us a couple of days, checking our seamanship and making sure we weren't going to treat him as a servant.

Lars turned out to be a wonderful crewmate. He didn't talk much, but was extremely competent and had a wry sense of humor that helped in the tight spots. A few days after we left Godthaab I clumsily scraped *Palawan*'s centerboard on the bottom during a passage through a shallow strait. Lars was playing gin rummy down below, and I expected to see him come erupting out onto the deck in alarm, but there was no sign of him. Afterward one of the crew told me that as the sound of aluminum grating on rock was heard in the cabin, Lars simply flipped another card onto the table and proclaimed, "The dangerous waters of Greenland!"

We gradually worked our way up the coast toward Disko Island, once a rendezvous for whalers, following the great arctic explorers whose adventures had intrigued me as a boy—men like John Cabot, Martin Frobisher, Jens Munk, and Henry Hudson, going all the way back to Eric the Red. The conditions we ran into were better than Jimmy's naval architect friend had predicted, and on July 12 we crossed the Arctic Circle within sight of spectacular glaciers and fjords.

A tragedy at home interrupted the voyage. Early on July 18, as we got ready to leave the tiny harbor of Egedesminde, a messenger came to the dock with a telegram from my secretary at IBM: my brother had had a serious fall in his house in New Canaan. There were no details about Dick's condition; the telegram simply said, "YOU MUST COME HOME."

I knew when I read it that Dick was going to die. Though he was only fifty-five years old he'd been in poor health, and was recovering from a heart attack the year before. Olive and I were able to get a helicopter to fetch us from an airport one hundred fifty miles away, and we flew from there to Connecticut to stand by helplessly at the hospital. Dick died a week later without ever regaining consciousness. After his funeral Olive stayed behind to console Nancy, Dick's wife, but I went directly back to the boat. I was in no state to be of help to anybody, and I was afraid to sit idle because I knew my brother's death was going to haunt me. We had never fully healed our relationship after the System/360 crisis. I'd taken actions that had derailed Dick's IBM career, and I blamed myself. Hard feelings had darkened our relationship for nine years, even though we were the sons of a man who taught his children never to let the sun set on a family argument. Now I saw the terrible wisdom of Dad's belief. My brother had died, and my feelings were so tangled that I didn't know how to mourn him. Being responsible for the *Palawan* and its crew in that harsh landscape helped me come to terms gradually with what had happened.

By early August we were far north of where any pleasure boat had ever gone. I'd competed in so many ocean races that most seagoing conditions were familiar to me, but I'd never seen anything like what we now encountered. The sea was black and very still except for little patches rippled by wind. There were lots of birds—terns, ducks, and big sea birds like gannets. We cruised among icebergs that in the light of the midnight sun would turn a translucent blue. The calm was broken by the weird sound of what fishermen call "growlers," room-sized chunks of submerged ice grinding against each other in the swell. Once in a while the *Palawan* would be rocked by a three- or four-foot wave that came from an iceberg rolling over many miles away. Our weather was mostly clear, and in the middle of the night crew members would sit in the cockpit looking at the sun, an orb low on the horizon, radiating eerie shades of red on the clouds above the black sea. There were always two people on watch, the rule being three hours on, six hours off, and there was a standing order to call me if anyone saw ice fields, or if the weather began to deteriorate. If we had gotten into trouble help would have been a long way off, and we surely would have been told that we shouldn't have been there in the first place.

The Etah settlement where Peary's expedition began was 150 miles ahead, but Lars Jensen took a long look from the mast and saw that ice had completely choked the passage through Smith Sound. We decided to turn eastward, toward the tiny Eskimo village of Qanaq, perhaps the most northerly on earth, where he knew some of the residents. We inched our way along for twelve hours, with *Palawan*'s bow gently nudging aside giant ice cakes as the sky turned gray and it started to mist. Finally, about six miles southwest of Qanaq, with the huts of the town dimly in view, we ran into such heavy ice that the boat stopped. Lars kept saying, "I'll get us in there, I'll get us in," but I thought about our unshielded propeller, only three feet below the surface, and our unreinforced hull, made of aluminum only a quarter-inch thick, and decided we should turn around.

The ice was shifting, and for a while we could go neither forward nor back as the wind from the west became stronger and rain and sleet pelted us. If a westerly gale springs up along the Greenland coast it's possible to be pinned in the ice or "beset," as the old-timers say; the ice can pile up and easily crush a boat like ours. I had visions of various arctic explorers frozen in over a winter; visions of myself trying to explain to other yachtsmen what had happened to my beautiful new boat; visions of a helicopter having to come rescue us from Thule Air Force Base to the south; visions of dealing at close quarters with water temperatures of 33 degrees—all sorts of unpleasant visions of being considered not intrepid explorers but foolish troublemakers. We carefully backed into better water, and after three hours of work we were able to turn around and make our way out to sea. We'd come within about 770 miles of the Pole. We cruised southward toward the Thule air base and the following afternoon moored at the supply dock next to a large tanker. The guard on duty was amazed to see a yacht. "If I had a boat like that, I'd be in the Caribbean," he said. Pretty soon the base commander and a couple of Danish officials showed up and welcomed us, which was a relief because I hadn't been sure what kind of reception we'd get. Although I'd kept the Danish authorities aware of our run northward, I also never stayed anywhere long enough to give them a chance to tell us to turn back.

The voyage accomplished what I'd hoped—it helped me to let go of IBM. Not that I'd ever seriously considered reversing my decision to retire, because as far as I was concerned that wasn't an option: I'd had a heart attack, been told not to run the company anymore, and was never so stupid as to say, "Doctor, I must go back, they really need me." So I was on my own and retirement was a disconcerting prospect, because I wasn't sure I could live at peace with myself without IBM. I stayed active on a number of boards, including Time, Pan American, Bankers Trust, the Mayo Foundation, the Smithsonian Institution, and Caltech—so my calendar typically included a couple of high-level meetings per week. But I didn't like just being a director; I felt terribly underutilized and had to fight off the impulse to try to dominate some of those meetings.

The process of weaning myself from IBM took years. I stayed chairman of the executive committee until 1979 and at first I did a fair amount behind the scenes, counseling with other directors to make sure IBM was steady as we moved through Vin Learson's brief tenure, and then helping Frank Cary get smoothly launched. When I turned sixty and formally retired in January 1974, I told Frank I would not come into the building for one hundred days. Having a former chief executive hanging around only undermines the new guy's authority; my father had died, so he wasn't around to interfere with me, and I had no intention of interfering with Cary. It was hard to do, but one hundred days passed and I didn't show my face. Then I had to struggle to get used to being a retiree. Before my eyes IBM was evolving into an enterprise far different from the one I had run. It was already 50 percent larger than when I'd stepped aside as chief executive, with revenues of eleven billion dollars in 1973, and Cary and his team were instituting major changes. They'd found that whenever we launched a new product our factories couldn't build machines fast enough to satisfy the demand. The entire industry was accelerating, and Frank worried that IBM's relatively stately pace of production left us vulnerable. We were still losing business to the plug-compatible manufacturers, who got better and better at zeroing in on customers who didn't want to wait for IBM deliveries.

But it wasn't just the PCMs that Frank was worried about; it was the Japanese. By now they had used their manufacturing power to invade the U.S. markets for steel, automobiles, and consumer electronics, and everybody knew that the computer industry was next on their list. Frank had no intention of letting IBM go the way of U.S. Steel, so he made a plan to build vast new automated plants and beat Japan at its own game. The board agreed that this strategy was sound, but the cost of the factories was staggering. Even though I knew that technology was changing and that the U.S. was in a period of high inflation, I could hardly believe the bills that were coming through. I remember asking Frank over and over the same questions that my directors had always asked me: "Are you sure you need all this? Have you gotten competitive bids? We don't want these factories to be lavish, you know." The rebuilding took six years and ended up costing over ten billion dollars, but it enabled IBM to stave off Japan, which today controls a smaller fraction of the computer market than it otherwise would have.

In spite of Frank's success, he made a few decisions that caused me to wish I was still running the show. In particular I was alarmed when he and his eventual successor John Opel rapidly phased out the rental system, shifting billions of dollars' worth of business to outright sales. They did this partly because the life span of the machines had gotten quite short and partly to free up capital that would otherwise have been tied up in rental machines. But it bothered me because rentals traditionally had been crucial to IBM's success. Rental contracts wedded us to our customers, gave us a powerful incentive to keep service top-notch, and made IBM stable and essentially depressionproof. Once the stream of rental payments dried up, IBM became far more volatile and vulnerable to fluctuations in demand. I felt the same uneasiness Dad must have felt in the 1950s, when Williams and I insisted on increasing IBM's debt. He'd gone along with us even though his instincts told him that debt was bad; the debate must have been a painful reminder to him that IBM was no longer entirely his business. It was painful for me to realize now that it was no longer mine.

I probably would have become deeply depressed if IBM had been the only outlet for my energy. Fortunately, I knew not only how to sail, but how to fly. Aviation was my earliest passion, and while IBM had replaced it at the center of my life, my desire to be airborne had never disappeared. When the Federal Aviation Administration restored my unrestricted pilot's license two years after my heart attack, my first present to myself was helicopter lessons. I wasn't sure that life outside of IBM was going to be worthwhile, but the idea of mastering a new form of flying excited me. So in the spring of 1974 I enrolled at a helicopter training center near Boston. Each day I'd fly an hour in the morning, spend a couple of hours in bed, and fly another hour in the afternoon. I fancied myself a talented pilot, but keeping a helicopter steady is like trying to stand at attention on top of a medicine ball. After about thirty-five hours in the air, I despaired of ever learning how. I told the instructor, "I think it's about time I gave this whole thing up."

"Not at all! You can solo anytime you want."

His confidence surprised me, and without giving myself a chance to think I said, "Well, let's do it right now." I closed the door and off I went. The practice area was a forest where a lumber company had cut large swathes. For forty-five minutes I flew up and down those cuts, which were at least fifty yards wide but seemed much narrower to me, until I felt the beginnings of mastery, and a couple of weeks later I proudly qualified for my license. A lot of veteran fliers shy away from helicopters because of the gruesome way the early ones used to crash. Typically, one rotor blade would fly off, then the other, and the pilot would find himself in a fragile little capsule plunging to earth. That prospect terrified me too, so after careful research I bought a Bell Jet Ranger, the helicopter with the longest and best safety record, better than most small planes.

I picked up my flying career where I'd left off at the end of the war. While I'd flown several thousand hours during my years at IBM, it was always for business and I never felt that I was getting enough solo time or variety. As a young man I'd flown every airplane I could get my hands on: fifteen different types during college and thirty more during the war, including bombers, fighters, transport planes, and even the big O-38 biplanes that were still part of the army's inventory. Aviation in those days was very informal: I'd go up to a sergeant on the flight line and say, "I've read the tech order on the C-47, and if you'd just stand behind me and show me where the switches are, I'd like to fly it." And he'd say, "Sure, Major." It always satisfied me just to get the new airplane up and down; I had a reputation for knowing what I was doing because I never tried crazy stunts and never had a crack-up. Flying after the war became increasingly technical, with more and more FAA rules, but unlike many pilots of my generation I didn't mind—following procedures became part of the challenge. I love piloting jets, which is the most technical flying of all, and after I got my helicopter license I bought a Learjet and became certified to fly that as well.

I've experimented with just about every form of aviation except space flight. I wanted to try a hang glider at one point, after a friend's son demonstrated one in Stowe. There seemed to be no reason why a sixty-year-old couldn't learn, so I asked the young man for the name of the best instructor in the United States. I called, and the secretary at the hang gliding school said he wasn't in. I called again and again for a couple of weeks, but could never get hold of the guy. Finally I said to the secretary, "Is he dead?"

She said, "Yes."

"Was he killed by a hang glider?"

"Yes." That was the end of hang gliding for me.

It's quite a challenge, to be able to shift from one type of flying machine to another, and not necessarily the safest thing in the world. In spite of my best efforts I occasionally had a close call. A lot of people who knew me must have been saying, "That old bird is going to kill himself in an airplane." But flying is vital to me, and in the first five years of my retirement I logged two thousand hours, not much less than the average corporate pilot. I found that it sharpened me to take new challenges, and I was constantly trying to program my time so I stayed a little overcommitted. That was how I'd lived at IBM, and my worst fear in retirement was of being dead in the water.

CHAPTER 32

I n the summer of 1977, Jimmy Carter's first year as
president, I was sitting in my study at North Haven
making plans for a voyage around Cape Horn when
the phone rang. It was Harold Brown, the new secretary of defense. "Cy and I think you ought to come to
Washington and get busy," he said, referring to Secretary
of State Cyrus Vance. Brown and Vance had both been
directors of IBM when I retired and knew me well.

"Harold," I said, "I'm sitting in a comfortable chair
looking out a picture window at beautiful spruce trees
and Penobscot Bay. Why would I want to come to Washington?"

"President Carter wants you to be chairman of the
General Advisory Committee on Arms Control and Disarmament."

I'd never heard of this group before, but Harold explained that it was a blue-ribbon commission whose purpose is to give the president independent advice on
nuclear strategy. It was established when Kennedy was in
the White House, reports directly to the president, and is
a way for prominent citizens to get behind the curtain of
military secrecy and understand what is really going on
in the arms race. Brown and Vance thought I was an
obvious choice to lead the GAC, as it is called. I was a
liberal whose whole professional life involved high technology. And I'd spent enough time in Russia, first as a
military man and later as a businessman, that the Soviet
way of thinking was not a total mystery to me. I saw the
Soviets as responsible people, as interested as we are in
preventing World War III, so that negotiating arms reduction treaties with them made sense.

Surprising myself a little, I jumped at the opportunity.

Before my heart attack I'd always turned down offers from Washington. It never seemed right to leave IBM, and I wasn't willing to risk making a fool of myself in some new area where I didn't know the ropes. But now I was retired and I'd been having adventures for several years. Here was a Democratic administration—the first in a long time—giving me a chance to do something important. Like many Americans I hadn't given much thought to World War III since the early 1960s. I remembered those terrifying days when everybody huddled by their radios and TV sets waiting for news about the Cuban missile crisis. I'd built a fallout shelter for my own family during that period, and had started a Family Shelter Loan Program at IBM, so that any employee who wanted a shelter could afford one. But as more and more people built shelters, the less and less sense it seemed to make. You would stay in your shelter for thirty days, but when you came out, what would you meet? A savage world with a lot of predatory people to threaten your family. We all equipped our shelters with pistols and rifles, but the whole thing began to seem insane. Soon people seemed to decide that if nuclear war ever happened, there would be no point in trying to survive.

When Harold Brown called, I hadn't been downstairs to replenish the supplies in my shelter for many years. Psychologically it had been easier to push out of my mind the danger of the arms race—even while I knew it was still going on and IBM was supplying computers for weapons labs. The race had gone through several rounds of escalation. The U.S. had built a whole new generation of intercontinental ballistic missiles called Minutemen; we'd surrounded the Soviet Union with Polaris submarines; we'd added multiple warheads to all our missiles; and of course the Russians had matched every move. The arms-control effort, which lagged far behind, now seemed to be nearing a crisis. The first SALT treaty limiting nuclear missiles had lapsed, SALT II was still on the negotiating table, and meanwhile the U.S. and Russia were on the verge of another escalation of the arms race.

I put away my charts of Patagonia. For the next six

months, leading up to the first meeting of the GAC, I shuttled back and forth to Washington and learned everything I could about treaties, politics, and nuclear weapons. I was briefed by the Arms Control and Disarmament Agency, the State Department, the CIA, the Defense Department's internal security agency, and the office of the Joint Chiefs of Staff. I spent hours listening to military analysts talk in hypothetical terms about attacks, counterattacks, and tens and hundreds of millions of casualties. It was staggering. These people used a form of jargon that made it possible to discuss nuclear holocaust for hours without ever mentioning a human death. I thought their whole way of looking at things was perverse. I felt intimidated by the sheer volume of information that I had to master. But at the same time that I struggled to assimilate the technical content of what I was hearing, I was determined not to let the true meaning escape me. It seemed to me that we ought not to be making preparations to destroy civilization. I guess the military would argue that if we are always prepared, it will never happen. But that concept was driving the arms race. I was sure the experts who spent their lives immersed in the intricacies of strategic planning would consider my point of view simplistic, so I tried to keep it to myself. But using plain common sense was the whole premise for an advisory board like the GAC. In any technology field, especially one as dangerous as this, you need to counterbalance the narrow focus of the experts.

The White House didn't ask my advice on whom to appoint to the GAC—the members had been chosen before I arrived in Washington—but it was an interesting and competent group. Carter had named Republicans and Democrats, scientists and businessmen, lawyers, a churchman, and a labor leader—a dozen people in all. Half were prominent citizens who knew almost nothing about nuclear weapons; the other half were defense and foreign-policy experts; but almost all the members made the GAC a top priority. We had McGeorge Bundy, who'd been national security adviser for Kennedy and Johnson; Brent Scowcroft, the national security adviser to Gerald Ford; and Harold Agnew, the current head of the Los Alamos lab. Wolfgang Panofsky and Paul Doty were prominent scientists who had been in and out of government for years. The "civilians" included Owen Cooper of the Southern Baptist Leadership Conference; Margaret Wilson of the NAACP; Bert Combs, a federal judge and former governor of Kentucky; and Arthur Krim, the head of United Artists and a tremendous power in the Democratic Party. Lane Kirkland, the secretary-treasurer of the AFL-CIO, was our biggest hawk.

During the first few months I must have called on forty senators, building the network we were going to need if the committee were to have any effect. I had a lot of help from Bill Jackson, the GAC's executive director, who had been Senator Alan Cranston's chief legislative assistant in the areas of foreign policy and defense, and really knew how to get things done on Capitol Hill. Jackson was a short peppery guy about forty years old with a huge briefcase, and so energetic that he often failed to organize his ideas or express them succinctly—not exactly the IBM style. But he had brass and great political instincts, so I turned off my IBM approach and did things his way. Jackson had me making courtesy calls on everybody from liberals like Frank Church to hard-liners like Scoop Jackson. I also made a point of seeking advice from veterans of U.S.-Soviet relations, such as Averell Harriman and John J. McCloy, who had been the founding chairman of my committee in 1961.

I didn't know how to politick, but I began to realize that in some ways it isn't much different from being a salesman. Rules of thumb that I'd learned selling punchcard machines also worked here, such as never wasting a customer's time and always making friends with the secretaries.

The committee had so much ground to cover that Bill Jackson and I decided it should meet each month for a full two days. That is a lot of time to ask of volunteers, and I measured my success by the number of people who showed up at each meeting. I'd send out teasers, saying for example that four physicists who'd helped design the first atom bomb were coming to talk to us. We always got ten or eleven attendees out of a possible thirteen, which indicated that people were interested. Each meeting was a challenge for me because I'd been on the sidelines for seven years, and there were enough experts on the committee that I felt I could ruin my credibility by making two or three really stupid remarks. Before each meeting Jackson and I would meet in a hotel and he'd spend a whole day throwing questions at me. When the meeting began I'd have detailed notes to keep me going and keep the pace fast. I never concentrated so hard in my life.

Running the GAC was not at all like running IBM. Toward the end of my career I had a well-deserved reputation for swarming all over people at meetings, but this was an advisory panel, not a team of IBM executives, and my job was to develop a consensus. So I was constantly holding myself back. I'd sit in those briefings and write notes to myself that said, "Don't talk too much. Make sure everybody has a chance to speak. Ask for ideas from those who haven't said anything yet."

My goal was to take that diverse group and somehow weld it into a team. I knew it was hard for laymen not to feel intimidated by someone as brilliant and experienced as McGeorge Bundy, who was at Kennedy's side during the Cuban missile crisis. So I made it clear to the professionals that they'd have to let other committee members catch up. In the meantime I thought it would be worthwhile to confront the professionals with a radically different viewpoint on the bomb. So I set up a private screening for the committee of Stanley Kubrick's brilliant satire *Dr. Strangelove*. When Brent Scowcroft, one of the top military strategists in the country, heard that the film might be shown to the committee, he said, "How can you show such an unrealistic picture to people who are seriously trying to understand nuclear weapons!" I admitted that the scene of the pilot riding the H-bomb and wearing his cowboy hat was a little farfetched. But I thought there was a ring of truth to the rest of the movie—all those safeguards going wrong. It makes the point that the

people with their fingers on the triggers are human, and
that accidents can happen.

The GAC usually met at the State Department, in a
secure conference room with a big oval table, brown pan-
eling, green carpet, and fluorescent lights. When the
high-level briefings on weapons began, the first reactions
of people like Arthur Krim and Bert Combs and Margaret Wilson were emotional. There would be a coffee break
in the middle of a Defense Department presentation on
cruise missiles or the neutron bomb, and committee
members would come up to me glassy-eyed and say,
"Can you imagine the position these people have worked
us into? We're paying taxes, and they've got us in a sce-
nario where everybody dies!" Nobody on the committee
was for unilateral or total disarmament, however. Most
of us simply wanted to find ways to make the standoff
with the Russians a lot less tense and cut down the arsenals on both sides.

Before long the real thinkers in the group began to
emerge. Wolfgang Panofsky pointed out a frightening
paradox in arms control: technology moves faster than
the treaty-making process, so that we are perpetually
making treaties about obsolete weapons while racing to
build modern ones. Arthur Krim, one of the most farsighted men I've ever met, suggested that it was fallacy to
think that we could invent weapons that the Russians
couldn't somehow match. Again and again the U.S. had
escalated the arms race, thinking we were pulling decisively ahead, only to have the Russians catch up a few
years later. This made sense to me because the computer
industry is also a game of technological leapfrog, only
nonlethal.

I didn't think the committee could function intelligently unless we saw the weapons for ourselves. So Jackson and I took the group to New Mexico, where we
visited Los Alamos, the birthplace of the atom bomb, and
the Sandia National Laboratories in Albuquerque, which
are run by AT&T and are where bomb components are
developed today. We saw a Department of Energy histor-

ical exhibit that included full-size replicas of Little Boy, the bomb dropped on Hiroshima, and Fat Man, the one dropped on Nagasaki. Then we went to a sort of warehouse at Sandia, where we sat as a variety of nuclear weapons were rolled out on silent, rubber-tired dollies for us to see. The technicians pushing these dollies were clothed like IBMers, in dark gray suits, white shirts, and dark shoes. The bombs themselves were little modern things, cylinders maybe six feet long, but some of them were tens or hundreds of times more powerful than the Fat Man upstairs. I'll never forget one weapon called the Dial-a-Yield. Why you would want to adjust the explosion of a nuclear weapon I don't know, nor how you would find the time or inclination to do it in the middle of a nuclear war. But some engineer, in an effort to be logical, had probably said, "Well, we don't just want to blow everything to kingdom come. Let's design a Dial-a-Yield. If we dial it down, it will only do so much, and if we dial it up, it'll do so much more." The whole committee was brought up short by seeing such things, even Lane Kirkland and the other hard-liners. When you sit across a room from a nuclear weapon you can't help but feel afraid of the future.

After hearing dozens of presentations by high-ranking officers, many of us came to the conclusion that military men aren't capable of imagining nuclear war as a rational civilian might. They talk about it, they make plans for it, and yet they avoid thinking about what would really happen in nuclear war. The people on our committee would ask, "What do you think the survival rate of the United States might be?" Some estimates were as low as 10 percent and some as high as 50 percent. When we questioned whether there would be an America left that resembled the one we live in now, the answer would be, "Well, we could breed the race back from there."

I thought our first report to Carter ought to be unanimous, but there was such a range of opinions on the committee that this was no easy feat. Most members were in favor of reversing the arms race through treaties. Lane Kirkland, on the other hand, was always puffing out black smoke. "Treaties with those bastards aren't worth a damn," he'd say. He was pretty close to Scoop Jackson, a senior member of the Senate Armed Services Committee, and thought the U.S. should simply arm up and stand firm. Harold Agnew, the director of the Los Alamos lab, was a kind of gadfly—full of criticism but impossible to pin down. He'd sit quietly through a meeting, suddenly make a caustic remark about an idea we were working on, and then go back in his shell. Scowcroft was hard to read too, although he was brilliant and the clearest-minded military man I ever met.

There were plenty of issues on which we all disagreed, but we finally found a common cause when the Air Force showed up to present its proposal for the new MX missile, which amounted to yet another escalation of the arms race. They wanted to dig thousands of silos in the desert and move the rockets around so they'd be hard for the Russians to attack. Out of every twenty silos only one would have a real missile, and the rest would be decoys. The cost of this giant shell game was going to be something like fifty billion dollars, to cover three hundred new MXes with ten warheads each, hundreds of giant tractors to haul them around, fifty-seven hundred dummy rockets, and six thousand silos. We heard briefings on the MX throughout the summer of 1978. The State Department was against it and the CIA sent a man to tell us how ridiculous the proposed basing schemes were. "We know a little bit about deception," he said, "and those decoys aren't going to fool anybody."

For every criticism that was made, the Air Force would come back with some new improvisation. I would never have tolerated such half-baked thinking at IBM, and the rest of the GAC felt the same way. At the end of September we reported to the president that the MX scheme was impractical and should not be pursued. I think Carter had already reached the same conclusion. He kept the plan around as a bargaining chip, but as long as he was in the White House the new missiles were never built.

Carter seemed to find our work useful, and late in

1978 he asked us to come up with ideas for new reductions of nuclear arms. Even though SALT II hadn't yet been signed and was also going to face a tough battle for approval in the Senate, he was looking forward to SALT III. Critics of the administration would have dismissed this as typical Carter idealism, but to me he seemed to be acting from a realistic sense of how dangerous the nuclear arsenals are and how technological advances make agreements obsolete. We gave him a long list of proposals, such as the phasing out of rockets with multiple warheads. But our most important point was that the treaty-making process was too slow. It had taken three administrations six years to work out SALT II; meanwhile, weapons laboratories had given the world new generations of missiles, bombers, and the neutron bomb. We told Carter that the only answer was for the heads of both countries to streamline arms negotiations by taking an active, continuous, and direct role themselves.

By the spring of 1979 the GAC had branched out into many other projects. Panofsky wrote a highly classified study for the White House on the future of ICBMs, and Arthur Krim began agitating among prominent Democrats for a treaty banning all new weapons. Our meetings became an important arms-control forum, and we heard from prominent people all across the ideological spectrum—hawks like Fred Iklé and advocates of détente like Averell Harriman and the State Department's Marshall Shulman. All of this was done without a single leak to the press, which was one reason so many people were willing to talk to us. Another reason was that we were known to have Carter's ear. When Stansfield Turner, the director of the CIA, wanted to alert the president that the United States was down to only one spare spy satellite, he came to the GAC to make his case. Even the Russians noticed that we were around: in March I got an invitation, which I declined, to visit Moscow and discuss the future of arms control at a Soviet foreign-policy institute.

Carter seemed to share our faith in personal leadership. When he went to the Vienna summit conference to sign SALT II the following June, he made a set of dramatic proposals to Leonid Brezhnev on speeding up SALT III. He gave the premier a handwritten list of major arms cuts both countries might pursue, and told Brezhnev that the United States would be willing to put into effect each element of the next treaty as it was agreed on, instead of waiting for the entire package. This must have given the Russians a lot to think about, but we never had a chance to learn their response. Instead, increasing tensions between our countries and Senate objections to SALT caused the whole treaty-making process to collapse.

I liked running the GAC and would gladly have stayed with it for the rest of the Carter administration. Olive was pleased with the effect the job had on me; she said it made me happier and easier to live with than anything I'd done since leaving IBM. But in May 1979 a report appeared in the *New York Times* that Malcolm Toon, the U.S. ambassador to Moscow, was about to retire, and that Averell Harriman was advocating me as his replacement. Olive spotted it first and got very upset. "What's this about us going to Russia?" she said. The thought of having to move to a foreign country and being separated from our children and grandchildren was really alarming to her. "Let me see that!" I said. "That's ridiculous! We're not going to Moscow. Nobody's mentioned it to me."

A couple of days later Vance called and said I was indeed going to be Carter's choice. It turned out that the administration had the idea that I could make things go more smoothly in Moscow. Toon, the current ambassador, was a holdover from the Ford administration and an advocate of toughness toward the Soviets. I'd met him when I was getting ready to run the GAC and thought he had an odd, abrasive style. When he talked about Russia he usually had reasonable ideas, but he'd lead off with a hostile aside like, "Well, of course, I hate the sons of bitches." He was critical of SALT II and skeptical about the future of détente. The Russians didn't like him and Carter wanted me to take his place.

As flattering as the offer was, I had no diplomatic

experience and knew I'd again be going in over my head. Furthermore, I didn't disagree with Toon that much on the basic issues, although I was less inclined to be polemical. There was another factor as well: I wasn't sure I was being fair to Olive. She was really downcast—the more she heard about Moscow, the less she liked the idea, although she perked up a bit when Gay Vance called and told all about Spaso House, the magnificent ambassador's residence, saying how easy it would be for us to have friends and grandchildren come visit. Olive and I discussed the matter a great deal, and I finally said I wanted to go ahead. I really was hoping to advance U.S.-Soviet relations and arms control, and I told Olive that would be the best thing for the grandchildren—ours and everybody else's.

Long before my appointment was made official, I found myself the object of a big controversy. A lot of foreign policy experts thought that I was the wrong choice, that the Moscow job called for a veteran, Russian-speaking diplomat like Toon, instead of an amateur with good intentions. Moscow is generally seen as one of the most demanding diplomatic posts, and for thirty years it had been filled by professionals. There were reports that powerful members of the Senate Foreign Relations Committee were going to challenge my appointment if Carter went through with it. Some critics didn't know I had experience in arms control; they thought Carter had suddenly gone soft on Russia and was sending the chairman of IBM to throw open the gates of trade between our two countries. My proponents tried to counteract all this with a lobbying campaign. They publicized my work on the GAC and my various trips to Moscow, and suggested that I belonged in the great tradition of business statesmen like Harriman, who had been our Moscow ambassador during the war.

Things were looking very promising, although while all this was going on I made an embarrassing mistake. In July, just before my appointment was to be officially announced, I attended the Vienna summit conference as chairman of the GAC with Carter. I got a call in my hotel from a newspaper reporter I knew slightly. He said, "I'm down in the lobby with a colleague of mine, and we want to talk to you about your nomination for the ambassadorship."

"I haven't heard that I've been officially appointed," I said, "so I don't think I am in a position to say anything."

"Well, how about letting us come up and talk to you for background?"

"Oh, I don't mind that," I said. I wanted to be friendly but wasn't thinking very clearly; the GAC had avoided publicity completely, and for years at IBM we'd been very careful in our dealings with the press. The interview lasted fifteen minutes, went very well, and the reporters agreed to put it down only as background. Then just as they were getting ready to leave one of them said, "What's that on your thumb?"

As it happened, I was going to the opera that night, and I wanted to remind myself to look for Ambassador Toon there. So I had written on my thumb, in small letters, t-o-o-n.

"Oh, that!" I said. "My youngest daughter does the same thing. She calls it scratch memory. I'm going to the opera tonight and I want to make sure I look for Ambassador Toon."

I could never find out which of the two reporters spread the story around. But pretty soon an article came out that I was an old man with a lousy memory. I didn't think the story was devastating, just annoying. But when I got back to Washington, Marshall Shulman called me in. He was the top State Department authority on U.S.-Soviet relations and one of the people drumming up Senate support for my appointment. He said, "That article is really going to hurt your chances."

"You've got to be kidding," I said. "I could have a smudge on my nose someday and someone could write about that. If that's going to make or break me as ambassador, I'm in the wrong game." I came on strong because I didn't want to admit how naive I'd been to talk to those two reporters. Shulman didn't back down an inch. He told me off, and I was quite relieved when my appointment finally went through.

When I left the GAC, Arthur Krim and his wife Mathilde gave me a party in their magnificent townhouse in New York. Mac Bundy made the send-off speech and presented me with a set of colonial pewter spoons on behalf of the group. I'll never forget the funny thing he said: "When you look at these spoons, Tom, you'll notice that they are too long to use at a banquet with friends—and too short to sup with the Devil. So perhaps they'll be just the right length for you to use in Moscow, and be reminded of the great affection in which everyone in this room holds you." It was the nicest send-off I could have had.

CHAPTER 33

There were already signs of the coming winter when we arrived in Moscow in October. The city's dingy buildings and grim skies reminded me of the four months I'd spent in Russia as a young pilot and aide to General Follett Bradley during the war. While I had no affection whatsoever for the Communist system, the experience of Russia in wartime had left a deep impression on me. On the Bradley mission we'd worked in the old U.S. chancellery on Mokhavaya Street, right across from the Kremlin, with the German armies less than thirty miles away. We'd flown across the vast outer provinces and gotten stuck for a week in the middle of Siberia. Turning back Hitler's invasion was one of the great triumphs of Soviet history, and I was proud to have witnessed it and to a small degree participated. But I didn't fool myself into thinking that nostalgia was going to make me an effective ambassador. Even though I felt connected to Russia because of the war, I was quite aware of the reality of U.S.-Soviet affairs. In 1979, détente was working poorly, and the signing of SALT II had been the only positive development in a long time.

My mission from Carter and Vance was clear-cut: they wanted me to right the tremendous imbalance that had developed between the treatment of the American ambassador in Moscow and the treatment of Ambassador Anatoly Dobrynin in Washington. Dobrynin had been the Soviet envoy in America for twenty years and was so well established that he could get to see the president just by picking up the phone. He was even allowed to park in the State Department garage. Our ambassadors, by contrast, had had little access to the Kremlin for more than ten years. During the SALT negotiations the Carter administration had done the expedient thing and used Dobrynin to convey its thinking to Moscow, shunting Malcolm Toon aside. But now that the treaty was signed, Carter wanted the prestige of the American embassy restored.

I had yet to learn the nuts and bolts of my new job, but I already knew what sort of ambassador I wanted to be. My ambition was to model myself after my good friend Llewellyn Thompson, the ambassador to Moscow under Presidents Eisenhower, Kennedy, and Johnson. I'd met Thompson in Moscow in 1942, when he was a junior diplomat. Most of the embassy staff had been sent to the town of Kuybyshev five hundred miles to the rear, but Tommy, as he was called, had been assigned to keep an eye on our Moscow facilities. One of my first tasks had been to fly him all the way to Teheran to pick up provisions for the staff, because all over Russia food was scarce. We loaded the bomb bay with two tons of supplies —not fancy food like you'd expect for an embassy but wartime staples such as KLIM, a kind of condensed milk, and beans in cans. I came to know Tommy well and looked up to him the way a young man admires someone ten years older. He was a tall, slim fellow, fluent in Russian, naturally a bit shy and reserved, but he didn't let that stop him. As ambassador he traveled all over Russia and rubbed elbows socially with high-ranking Soviets almost every day. He and his wife knew how to create a warm ambiance and made Spaso House, his official residence, a magnet for hundreds of important Soviets from Politburo members to ballerinas—it was one of the few "decadent" places where high-ranking Soviets could openly go. Nikita Khrushchev liked Tommy so much that they used to talk together for hours on end.

Thompson wasn't a brilliant theorist like George Kennan, but he understood Soviet motivations and in 1962 that knowledge may have helped save everybody's life. At the peak of the Cuban missile crisis Khrushchev sent Kennedy two conflicting messages. The first was conciliatory and made it clear that the premier wanted to avoid nuclear war; the second was belligerent and almost dared Kennedy to take the confrontation another step. Kennedy and his men were baffled until Thompson advised that the first message was probably closer to what Khrushchev felt, and that the Russians were worried not so much about putting missiles in Cuba as about obtaining a bargaining position on other matters. On that basis Bobby Kennedy came up with an astonishingly simple idea: ignore the second message and answer only the first, with an offer to try to build détente between East and West if the missiles were removed. That's what the president did, and Khrushchev ordered the missiles taken out the following day.

My life had come full circle to Spaso House. I'd first set foot there as a kid just out of college, seeing the world before I had to start work at IBM. During the war I'd shaken hands with Winston Churchill at a Spaso House reception. I'd visited Thompson there as head of IBM. Now, at age sixty-five, I was coming back as ambassador myself, eager to see what I could make my long acquaintance with Russia add up to.

The house was grander by far than any place Olive and I had ever lived. It is an extraordinary stucco mansion, about two miles from the Kremlin, built by a czarist sugar magnate just before World War I. By the time the house was finished, there were signs of revolution, and the sugar magnate was too afraid to move in, although he gave parties there. Under Lenin the building was broken up into apartments for bureaucrats, and that's the way it stayed until 1933, when Roosevelt opened relations with the Soviets. His ambassador, William Bullitt, picked Spaso House from among a half dozen buildings the Russians proposed, probably because it has capitalist prosperity written all over it. The place is organized around a huge, elegant room, with ornate pillars, archways, balconies, and a massive crystal chandelier hanging from a domed ceiling three stories high. Alcoves lead from this hall to a state dining room, living quarters for the ambassador and his family, libraries, sitting rooms, and numerous bedrooms for guests. Beyond the dining room is a ballroom, added by the Americans, where two hundred people can be seated for movies or lectures. The house stands on a broad lawn behind wrought-iron gates, and with all its windows lit on a frosty Moscow night, it seems elegant and totally inviting.

An ambassador's first task when he arrives in the country where he is to serve is to present his credentials. This involves a formal meeting with the chief of state or his deputy, and the Soviets know how to carry off such ceremonial occasions with utmost grandeur. I was escorted in a motorcade from Spaso House to the Kremlin on Monday, October 29. Every bit of traffic along the route stopped, and policemen saluted me at every corner. Then I walked in a procession through tremendous halls with gifts given to the czars and artifacts from the Russian Revolution laid out in glass cases along both sides. We reached a great room, where I'd been told to walk up to the point of a diamond on a rug. From the opposite end of the hall came a little gentleman, the Soviet vice president V. V. Kuznetsov, saying things in Russian. Then the chief of protocol whispered to me, "Now read your speech," which I did, and there was clapping and handshaking and champagne was passed around. I felt a tremendous thrill. After the ceremony, Vice President Kuznetsov took me into his office and said in American English, "What would you like—coffee or Scotch?"

"What are you going to have, Mr. Vice President?" I said.

"Coffee."

"I'll join you. Sir, you speak amazingly good English."

"I went to Carnegie Tech in Pittsburgh and then worked for the Ford Motor Company for three years. In the early days just after Lenin took over, he wanted some of us young technocrats to learn American ways and I was one of the lucky ones to be sent to your country. I remember it extremely well."

As I look back on my visit with Kuznetsov, the ceremony, and the idea of my standing there proudly in the Kremlin, I'm reminded of my father. He was so proud to attend the first morning reception of King George VI, in

1937. I have to admit that the Watson love of being a celebrity hasn't entirely passed me by.

There were over one hundred Americans on the embassy staff, and I went to work right away to win their support. They'd all read those newspaper stories about my having to write Toon's name on my thumb, and I knew they must be wondering what they were getting. I met the issue of my inexperience head on. I called a general meeting and after explaining my work on the GAC that had led to the ambassadorship, I put myself in their hands. "Ambassador Toon made the point many times that this post needs professional leadership," I said. "Obviously I'm not a professional—and that means I am grateful for your competence." Adding a little IBM touch, I said that the door to my office would always be open to anyone with problems, suggestions, or new ideas. They seemed to respond to that, and also to my mission of restoring the embassy's prestige. It helped that there was a big difference between Toon's style and mine. His was more aloof. I concentrated on the same things I would have at IBM—cultivating loyalty and boosting morale. The following week Olive and I had a reception for all the embassy personnel and their families, and it was the first time many of them had seen the inside of Spaso House.

The Soviets for their part seemed happy to see a new face. My first visit was with foreign minister Andrei Gromyko, whom I originally met in 1959 when Khrushchev toured the IBM plant. In those days Russian officials were known for wearing badly cut suits, and I remembered how Gromyko had stood out because he was well dressed. A man of deep intellect and impeccable manners, he had gradually taught his comrades the way diplomats ought to act. His nickname at the State Department was Old Stoneface but I thought of him as a great actor. He was impassive only when it suited his purpose; at other times he'd become interested in something you said and you could watch a half dozen different expressions cross his face. When I saw him officially in Moscow the routine was always the same. I'd call to make an appointment—one day's notice was usually enough—and we'd meet at the Foreign Ministry in a little conference room next to his office. He'd come in, we'd each take a glass of mineral water, and we'd talk about arranging exit visas for Jews, getting on with permission to build our new chancellery, speeding up action on SALT II in the U.S. Senate, or whatever our business was that day.

My first hope of a diplomatic success came during a meeting with Brezhnev's assistant Aleksandrov. He was telling me how fondly they remembered Tommy Thompson, and I took the opportunity to remind him that unlike recent ambassadors, Thompson had been given full access to the Politburo. "That is a goal of mine," I said. "I'd like to chat with each member of the Politburo. If I succeed in that, I will have done some good for my country and maybe for your country, and I will also be showing my boss Cy Vance that I am active here, not just sitting around reading Tolstoy."

Aleksandrov was a little man with a loud voice. He laughed and said, "*Personally,* I think that would be an excellent idea!" It was unclear whether anyone else would, but to Mark Garrison, our embassy's deputy chief of mission, the fact that I got even that far without a rebuff was intriguing. Garrison was a Sovietologist and career foreign-service officer, a remarkably level-headed man with whom I became good friends. I think he was simultaneously curious and skeptical about my chances, but he coached me patiently in the basics of being an ambassador, and I relied on him heavily, just as I'd depended on Bill Jackson at the GAC. My other coach was Robert German, our political counselor, who was constantly by my side as I moved in official circles. Bob is a soft-spoken Texan, a lawyer by training, and he helped me avoid gaffes. I always asked him for a blunt critique of my performance, but he was too much of a diplomat for that. When he had something to say it would filter back to me through Garrison.

I hadn't even been on the job a month when we began getting reports of Red Army units building up along the border with Afghanistan. Probably the U.S. should have paid more attention, but the White House and State Department were preoccupied with the hostage crisis in Iran. Even though the Kremlin was known to be irritated with Afghanistan's president Amin for not suppressing the Islamic rebels in his country, nobody on our side really thought the Soviets would invade. They had never used their own troops anywhere outside the Warsaw Pact countries since World War II. For me an invasion was doubly hard to imagine because, by an odd coincidence, I knew something about Afghanistan. I'd been there with my daughter Jeannette only four years before. We'd stayed in Kabul and then journeyed up into the hills along the ancient trade routes, sleeping in tents and primitive inns. We'd get up at dawn to go to the camel market and haggle for rugs. The trip had given me a sense of the tenacity of the people and the desolate beauty of the land.

It was Christmas, and Spaso House was filled with our children and grandchildren who had come to visit from the United States. The embassy had two days of warnings that the troop movements had accelerated, and then came a call in the evening of December 27 that battalions of paratroopers were landing at Kabul airport. I stayed up all that night reading intelligence reports. Thousands of Russian soldiers were involved, and I felt the weight of the world on my heart: instead of building bridges to the Russians I found myself faced with the most serious crisis since the days of Kennedy and Khrushchev. Before dawn I got orders from Washington to demand an explanation from the Kremlin. We asked for an appointment with Gromyko, but the Foreign Ministry said he was away. The only official available was a deputy foreign minister named Maltsev whom I'd never met. After talking to him that morning I nicknamed him Minister No, because he was a rude and taciturn man, a real throwback to the worst days of the cold war. He said that there was no point in explaining the invasion because it wasn't the United States' affair. Afghanistan was a neighboring country with which the U.S.S.R. had a treaty; Amin had asked for help against rebels who were threatening his government, and Russia had responded. Then Maltsev said, "Anyway, it's all in this memorandum," and handed me an envelope.

"Your position sounds hard to believe," I said, "but thank you very much."

I started to get up but I heard Bob German say, "I think the ambassador would like to have the memorandum read." He was saving me from a major error, because if I had left without reading the memo it would have implied that the United States accepted the Soviets' explanation. The memo was in English, and it simply repeated the poppycock Maltsev had just given me. I told him on behalf of my government that it was unacceptable. The following morning we got word that two entire Red Army divisions had crossed the border, and the grim facts of the invasion soon came out. The Russians had overthrown the government, assassinated President Amin, and put in an Afghan puppet leader who had been hiding in the Soviet Union and who was flown in with Russian airborne troops.

Our embassy became a pressure cooker. Everybody went without sleep for a couple of days. I was a novice, and not a young man, and Garrison and German and the rest of the staff were working on pure adrenaline, exchanging telexes with Washington so fast that I couldn't keep up. I said, "Look, you guys know all about this, but I'm the fellow who is really responsible here, so if you don't mind I'd like to follow along." But they kept hurrying ahead until I got mad. I told Garrison, "I don't know whether I'm going to be able to get along with you in this embassy."

Garrison knew I could have him relieved, but that didn't intimidate him in the slightest. He came right back at me and said, "The point is not whether you and I can get along; the point is what we can do for our country today. Later on there'll be time to sort out whether we can work together." I quieted down right away. We finally sent a long advisory to the State Department giving our analysis of the invasion. We called it "a serious and unacceptable change in Soviet policy" and suggested that our government "make the political cost to them so high that they will find a way to withdraw their troops." That same day President Carter sent Brezhnev a message on the hot line telling him to withdraw his forces or jeopardize U.S.-Soviet relations.

The uproar in the Kremlin must have been even worse than on our side. They'd made their biggest foreign-policy mistake in more than a decade. Historians are still debating why they decided to invade, but whatever their motives, they failed completely to anticipate the U.S. response. We saw the invasion as the possible first step of a strategy to expand into the Persian Gulf. That was the logic behind Carter's hot-line message, and I soon got a call from the Foreign Ministry saying Gromyko was available to see me. We met in that same little conference room next to his office. "I can't understand what you've done," I said. "I've talked to Minister Maltsev, as you know, but I can't understand the explanation he gave. It just seems impossible to me."

"Why?" said Gromyko.

"Well, I'm not a professional diplomat. But the fellow who calls for help under your treaty is dead the minute you get there, and the new leader of the country comes in on your military aircraft. That doesn't sound like a change of government caused by events internal to the country."

I'd never seen Gromyko with so much as a hair out of place. But now he leaped up and screamed, literally screamed, "Who told you that? Who told you that?" Then he came at me across the floor and said, "Your president is shouting at the clouds, and his voice is coming back as an echo, and he thinks it is the voice of God!"

This was all through an interpreter. I was stunned and said nothing for a few seconds. Then I told him, "I guess that's all there is to talk about, Mr. Minister."

And he said, "I guess so, Mr. Ambassador." I got up and started walking toward the door, but my mind was racing. I thought, "I've got to work with this man, I'm on my own here, so do I really want to walk out?" I stopped about three feet short of the door and said to the interpreter, "Tell the minister that when I saw him in the Kremlin a few weeks ago, he asked me if I was starting to learn to swim a little bit as a new ambassador." The interpreter translated that and Gromyko, looking stormy, said, "Da."

"Tell him that, after talking with him in this fashion, he makes me think I'm drowning."

Gromyko burst into the loudest laugh, walked over and put his arm around me, and said, "Don't drown. Kick your feet, strike out with your arms, this is just a job. You're doing your job, I'm doing my job, don't let it get you down!" He laughed again, pumped my hand up and down, and out I went.

A few days later the president called me back to Washington, and I joined the White House consultations about how the United States should respond. Carter was determined to make the Soviets pay for their aggression, but in fact there was very little we could do. This wasn't a drop-the-bomb situation, or one in which we'd send in troops. The White House and State Department made up a long list of possible anti-Soviet moves—my own embassy contributed a number of suggestions—and in the end the president decided to adopt almost every one. This meant taking apart practically all the cooperative arrangements we had with the Russians under détente, from art exhibitions to new sales of grain, and boycotting the Moscow Olympics. There wasn't much I could add to the discussion; the only time I spoke up was to object to particular trade sanctions that went too far. For example, American companies had delivered manufacturing equipment to Russia, and now they weren't even going to be allowed to send spare parts to fix equipment that was still under warranty. I told the president this didn't make sense: if you want to declare war or have a boycott, fine, but breaking a commitment to a customer is always wrong. President Carter overrode me and I guess that was the point: he wanted to show the Russians that they'd made it impossible for business to continue as usual.

I didn't know the president very well, and I was a little surprised at how vehemently he reacted. I could understand his anger, because the Afghanistan invasion ruined SALT II, which was so vital to the world's safety and on which both sides had worked so hard—there was no way the Senate would approve the treaty now. The change in U.S.-Soviet relations really shook me. I was still trying to get the feel of my job, and now people started saying again that the embassy needed a hard-nosed professional to deal with the new cold war. After talking to the president I told my staff, "I feel like a chameleon. I'm going to have to change color." The first time I saw Gromyko after my return I made a desperate stab at breaking the impasse our countries had reached. It was a personal appeal. I told him, "I don't have any instructions on this, but it is time to talk about what to do. Why not find some way to put this thing behind us?"

"It's too bad you don't have any instructions," he said. "It's too bad that your government doesn't feel the way you do." I'd never felt so hopeless. Gromyko in this instance was icy, as if to say, "I have better things to do than sit here exchanging unofficial opinions with you."

I went back to my embassy in the late afternoon darkness. I was deeply depressed because I was going to have to stay in this jail for a year. There was no way to leave gracefully before the end of President Carter's term. I was sixty-six years old, a hell of a time to be losing a year out of my life. I felt like a rat caught in a trap.

Life at the embassy settled into a dreary routine. Every morning I'd go to my office and find between fifty and two hundred cables waiting on my desk, and dozens more would come in during the day. They covered everything going on all over the world, and I was supposed to read them. Foreign service people learn to skim cables early in the game, but fast reading was not one of my skills, and I could never get through them. From time to time American politicians would visit—congressional delegations, they were called, or Codels. Welcoming them was my job, but sometimes it seemed that all they were interested in was having their pictures taken for the newspapers back home. The first thing every politician would ask to do was talk to the Pentecostals in the embassy basement. These were a handful of religious dissidents who had taken refuge there two years earlier and were trying to pressure the Kremlin into granting them exit visas. I'd explain to the congressmen that the more attention we drew to these people, the less likely the Soviet government would be to budge. But the congressmen couldn't resist the easy publicity. One guy even had a picture of himself with the Pentecostals put on his Christmas card.

When I got absolutely beside myself with boredom, I'd go out with my camera and take pictures. I walked all over Moscow, sometimes on embassy time and sometimes on my own. Once I stumbled across an outdoor pet market, a free market, which was still pretty unusual in Moscow in those days. They sold hedgehogs and fat guinea pigs, cats, dogs, and even tropical fish, which you'd never think of finding within thousands of miles of Moscow in February. I could speak Russian a little by then, and met a lot of ordinary people in my wanderings. Some of them were pretty feisty—local shopkeepers who'd yell, "Get away from there, you're second in line," and old ladies who'd grab my sleeve on the street and say, *"Shapka, shapka, kholodno, kholodno!"* Meaning, put on your hat, it's cold. The children always looked extremely happy—I'd always been struck by how kind the Soviets were to their little ones, even during the hardships of World War II. But by age seventeen or eighteen the young people start looking oppressed. You hear about the awful drunkenness in Russia, but you rarely see it in public. The way people drink is to go into a room on a Saturday afternoon with a girlfriend or wife or group of friends and close the door. The vodka bottles don't have corks—once you tear off the metal cap, you drink till it's gone. So they empty as many of those bottles as they want, and they do it to achieve oblivion.

Despite the frustrations of the Moscow assignment, there were unexpected personal rewards for Olive and me. Our children were grown, and we were able to spend more time together than we had since our courtship. As I'd expected, Olive made Spaso House a cheerful, hospitable place, and we made many friends in the diplomatic community. This was the first time Olive and I had ever worked intensively together, and we found we were a pretty good team. There was a lot to be done to boost the morale of the American community and embassy staff. We brought over a caller for a square dance, arranged lectures on Russian history and art, and hosted visits by Bob Hope and the great radio broadcaster Lowell Thomas, who was an old friend of Dad's. Olive and I also traveled together, showing the American flag in every corner of the Soviet Union. We went over to Leningrad a couple of times, of course. We flew down to Georgia, and explored the town of Baku, which had been a stop on an ancient caravan route to the Orient. We took a steamer from Odessa along the Black Sea coast, to Yalta and the industrial city of Batumi, right on the Turkish border. Then we went all the way north, to Murmansk, a city of nearly a half million people above the Arctic Circle, and to the arctic seaport Archangel. We traveled to Irkutsk, a city deep in Siberia that was originally settled by Cossacks. The farther we got from Moscow, the friendlier local officials seemed, and the less concerned about the recent disputes between Washington and Moscow. I saw again and again how powerfully World War II still affected their lives. Near Irkutsk, Olive and I met a woman whose father had run the fishery on Lake Baikal that had supplied Stalin's army with food. That lake is almost four hundred miles long and the deepest in the world, yet between 1941 and 1944 they'd depleted the fish population dangerously to keep the soldiers alive. The fact that I had been in Russia helping the war effort meant a great deal to these people, and I was frustrated not to be able to turn this goodwill to account.

It gnawed at me that I was so much less effective at this job than I had been at the GAC. All I could do was sit back, the pawn of events much bigger than I, and watch as President Carter's star declined. By the time the election came in November, I wasn't sure he could beat Ronald Reagan. I was at a conference of ambassadors in Brussels having to do with human rights, and I went to bed on election night thinking it was going to be close. When I woke up Reagan had won by a landslide. I felt frustrated, depressed, disappointed—and relieved. I thought, "Just two months to go and I can get out."

When it came time for me to leave Moscow, the Russians got sentimental. I think they were reluctant to see me go at such a low point in U.S.-Soviet relations because they have such great reverence for old soldiers. Korniyenko, Gromyko's deputy, said, "Can we do something for you? Is there a gesture we can make?"

I said the first thing that came into my head. "The best gesture would be for you to let me go out on my airplane with the Pentecostals. How about that?"

Korniyenko looked shocked. "Well, I'll talk to the foreign minister about it. But to tell the truth, I don't think we should do that. And I don't think *you* would really want us to do that, either."

I had to admit he was right. It would cause a horde of people to descend on our embassy hoping to get to the United States. The Foreign Ministry gave a small lunch in my honor instead. On the afternoon of January 15, 1981, Olive and I stepped onto a U.S. Air Force jet at Sheremetyevo airport, and my short, unhappy tour as a diplomat came to an end.

CHAPTER 34

When I came back from Moscow that January it was the tenth anniversary of my decision to step down at IBM. I'd been disappointed in my dream of being the ambassador to help end the cold war, but taking stock of those ten years I felt extraordinarily lucky. I'd succeeded in regaining my health, weaning myself from business, gratifying my urge for adventure, and adding honor to the family name with the sort of public service my father never had time for.

It was astonishing the degree to which my life and his had diverged. When I was young I wasn't sure there would ever be any comparison between us: he was a giant and I didn't think I was cut out for business at all. It took me a long time to commit myself to an IBM career, but then I became a success and for twenty years the company consumed my life and my family's. When I was forced to retire much younger than most men, it was traumatic to have to walk away. Yet if I'd stayed on the job until normal retirement age—not to mention as long as Dad, who was still putting on his business suit every morning at age eighty—I'd have missed the chance to go beyond IBM in any significant way.

I knew it was now time to come to grips with the fact that I was old. My great fear was that there wouldn't be enough to do—that my brain would atrophy and life would lose its shape. While I didn't want to take on anything as hard anymore as running the General Advisory Committee, I'd already made elaborate preparations before leaving Moscow for keeping myself sharp. I intended to stay up-to-date in the field of U.S.-Soviet affairs, and at Brown University I helped found a new Center for Foreign Policy Development specializing in the subject. To my delight, Mark Garrison, my deputy at the Moscow embassy, elected to leave the Foreign Service and head the center. I couldn't have found a better man. But, in spite of this, I felt low when Olive and I moved back to Greenwich. She said, "Why not just take it easy? See your grandchildren, go to the Caribbean!" That's pretty much what I did for a couple of months, worrying all the while that I might be losing my relevance.

I still missed the power that went with being head of IBM, although I was glad to see the company growing under Frank Cary. By 1980 it had almost quadrupled in size from the time I ran it, to twenty-six billion dollars in sales. The business was now so huge that I found it hard to imagine how any chief executive could ever manage. But Cary had done fine in his quiet, competent way, and he was scheduled to hand the company over to John Opel that spring. Opel urged me to rejoin the IBM board. I'd resigned when I became ambassador, and I told him I thought it made more sense to stay away, but he said, "You are too much a part of the history of this business not to come back," and pointed out that I was only sixty-seven. So back I went, with the proviso that I would be called chairman emeritus. (A few years later, when I turned seventy, I insisted on retiring from the board like any other IBM director. I'd made that rule myself and felt very strongly about it.)

The thing that got me moving again, oddly enough, was giving the commencement speech at Harvard in June 1981. Harvard has a tradition of picking speakers who are in the news, not necessarily highbrows, and I was immensely pleased and flattered that out of all the people on the national scene they picked me. I got the invitation at the end of February and went right to work. My father and brother were natural public speakers but to this day I find it hard to face an audience. I compensate by scrupulous preparation—I'll rewrite a speech over and over, run it past two or three experts, practice it with a tape recorder in the cellar, and finally try it out on Olive, who is always a patient listener. By late March I was in a fever of anxiety—never mind that graduation was still ten

weeks away. Then came a telephone call from my friend
Andrew Heiskell, the retired chairman of Time Inc., who
was a member of the Harvard Corporation, one of
Harvard's two governing boards. "Your speech is off," he
said. "We've asked President Reagan and he has accepted."

I suppose I should have been insulted, but actually I
was grateful for the reprieve. Besides, it's hard to complain when you're being upstaged by the president of the
United States. "Just think of it, Olive," I said. "Isn't it
wonderful? I was having fits trying to get this speech into
my head, and now I don't have to do it!" But then, about
three weeks before graduation, Heiskell called again.
"You're back on," he said. There had been a big misun-
derstanding with the White House. Reagan had apparently accepted the invitation because he thought he was
going to get an honorary degree, but Harvard rarely gives
honorary degrees to American public officials who are in
office. After Reagan's staff found that out, they told Harvard he wasn't going to do it. It didn't make any difference to me—not only was I not in office, but, as it
happened, I already had an honorary degree from Harvard.

So on June 4, 1981, I found myself sitting on the
speaker's platform in Harvard Yard with other person-
ages like Cy Vance, Ansel Adams, and Jorge Luis Borges.
Derek Bok, the university president, gave the first address, and while he spoke I looked around, letting my
mind wander. I thought about how old Harvard Yard is
—how it had already been there for over a hundred years
when undergraduates walked out the gate to join the
Minutemen at Concord. Finally I heard Bok get around
to introducing me. But as I stepped up next to him at the
lectern there was a roll of thunder and a horrific
cloudburst. The speakers' platform was covered, but the
podium was not, and the poor graduating class was sitting out on the grass on folding chairs. Some of the seniors got up and filed away into the surrounding
dormitories, where there were TV monitors set up to
carry the ceremony. But Derek kept everything on hold

for a few minutes, hoping the rain would let up. Finally I said to him, "This rain looks like it's going to last awhile."

"Do you mean you just want to belt it out now?" he said.

"Yes!" I said. So I talked, and meanwhile more seniors trickled away into the dorms. I suppose the thunder and downpour were appropriate, because my subject was nuclear war. What I tried to do was get across to the young people the most important lesson I'd learned in my jobs in Washington and Moscow. It was very different from what they would have heard from President Reagan:

> The result of any use of nuclear weapons would not be victory. It would be all-out war and total destruction. We have to confront the illusion of softheadedness—that anyone who favors an end to the arms race must be soft on U.S. defense or even soft on Communism. The illusion of softheadedness is thermonuclear McCarthyism. Because the search for a way out of this morass—the search for an avenue of negotiation and survival instead of confrontation and weaponry—has a long and honorable heritage. Our imperative is to change our course and to take the only road which offers a viable hope for the future: not a road to unilateral action of any kind, but a road to a long series of mutually verifiable treaties.

The rain let up, and the students came back to their seats, clapping with great enthusiasm. My speech was very well received. The Harvard *Crimson* ran a flattering story entitled "A Capitalist for Disarmament." *Time* magazine and the Boston newspapers also quoted things I'd said. Soon more speaking invitations came in, and I found myself transformed into a voice for arms control. I hadn't paid much attention to the nuclear-freeze movement before that, but my skepticism about nuclear weapons dovetailed nicely, so to speak, with the interests of antinuclear groups that were popping up all over.

At places like Harvard and Brown, it was easy to get people enthusiastic because they were students. Convincing anybody with real power was another matter. My first chance to win the hearts and minds of influential people came in 1982, when I was asked to give a speech at the Bohemian Grove. This is a private summer retreat for two thousand of the country's richest and most powerful men. People like Richard Nixon, George Bush, Henry Kissinger, and Leonard K. Firestone all belong, as well as scientists, artists, and entertainers who help keep things lively. It's not the kind of scene I like, because it requires lots of meeting and talking with strangers. But when I was young my father had told me that the Grove was a gorgeous place and that I should go if I had the opportunity, because I would never find that kind of atmosphere anywhere else.

Someone put me up for membership in 1957, the year after my father died. But unless you had a special in, it took about twenty years to get to the head of the waiting list, so I ended up going as the guest of Dad's old friend Lowell Thomas. The Grove is on the Russian River about seventy miles north of San Francisco, and is only open for sixteen days each July. It is organized into more than a hundred "camps," with offbeat names like Tunerville, Aviary, and Poison Oak. Thomas belonged to Cave Man, which was one of the largest and whose members included Eddie Rickenbacker and old Herbert Hoover.

Coming into the Grove was impressive. You drive past "private property" signs to an area where there are long platforms posted with the names of the camps. You never find out where all the camps are, because they're tucked away in twenty-seven hundred acres of steep hills and stupendous trees, some of which date back to the time of Christ. Each camp has its own kitchen and a campfire area where the men can sit and talk. The entire Grove is crisscrossed with catwalks and bridges, and as you walk around you bump into a lot of well-known people. Most members go there to get away from business; in fact, the

Bohemian Grove motto is a line out of *A Midsummer Night's Dream:* "Weaving spiders come not here."

I went to the Grove as a guest seven or eight times while I ran IBM, but I didn't actually join until I came back from Moscow in 1981. The following summer came the invitation to give a speech. The Grove has a tradition of so-called lakeside talks—they set up a microphone after lunch and members sit all the way around the lake, with comfortable chairs reserved for the very old fellows. When I got up to speak I could see before me in the audience such dignitaries as Henry Kissinger.

It was my big chance to pitch bilateral reduction of nuclear arms, and I gave it everything I had. Like any good salesman I was really sure that I could win them over. My thinking had developed during the year since my Harvard speech, and I felt confident that my ideas on national security were comprehensive and realistic enough to make sense even to veteran policy-makers. Not only could I demonstrate why we had to reduce our blind dependence on atomic weapons, but I was able to paint a picture of how the United States might defend its interests without them. I took the position that, given the strength of the Soviet military, we couldn't cut back our nuclear arsenal without beefing up conventional forces—even if this meant reinstating the draft and raising taxes. Then I suggested that antinuclear protesters had a point—they were ordinary Americans applying common sense to the fact that we had more nuclear weapons than we needed. I told the Bohemians what I'd learned as head of the General Advisory Committee—that nuclear strategy, like any national issue, benefits from open public debate:

> Everything necessary to make decisions on nuclear weapons and our relations with the Soviet Union is in the public domain. There are no secrets, and every one of us can and must participate in deciding our country's fate. Never believe this subject is so complex and so secret that we laymen must leave it to others. It's vital that all of us add our American

common sense to the inputs of military strategists and technicians.

There was plenty of applause when I finished, but I was looking for something more—maybe people jumping up and sending cables to Reagan, or turning to the senators in the audience and saying, "Watson's right! What are we going to do about it?" Of course that didn't happen. Later that afternoon I overheard a conversation between two Bohemians. "Did you listen to Watson?" said the first.

"No," said the second. "How was it?"

"It was terrific, absolutely terrific."

I was just starting to swell with pride when the second Bohemian asked, "Well, did you learn anything you didn't already know?" And there was no reply. I felt as though I'd been dropping pebbles down a well.

I talked to other tough audiences after that—the midshipmen at Annapolis, the students at the Naval War College at Newport, Rhode Island—and they were just as unmoved. Eventually I realized how the conservatives viewed me: as an elder statesman who'd been to Russia and knew his stuff, but was a bit kooked on nuclear weapons. I had the consolation that many other prominent people were also advocating arms cuts and that within a few years there was a massive mobilization of public opinion against the arms race. In the year Reagan took office, 70 percent of the population favored an increase in the defense budget, but by his second term that percentage was reversed—only a small minority wanted more arms and 77 percent were in favor of an immediate, bilateral nuclear freeze.

Once the word was out about nuclear arms I let my speaking taper off; I thought going further wouldn't accomplish anything except to make me sour. I shifted my energies back to airplanes and boats, starting with a single-handed voyage across the Caribbean. It was only a thousand miles, but enough to acquaint me with the tedium and fear of sailing alone, neither of which I liked. So I went back to organizing voyages with amateur crews. Late in 1985 I finally made my long-postponed trip around Cape Horn, and the following summer I took the *Palawan* north again, along the Labrador coast and into the far reaches of Hudson Bay. I was proud to be able to pull off such adventures, but the glow of accomplishment never lasted long. I'd no sooner be back from one voyage than I felt compelled to start planning the next.

Occasionally I'd interrupt these projects to give a speech or write an op-ed piece on arms control or the state of U.S.-Soviet affairs. But I was sure no one in the Reagan administration would be asking my advice on the Soviet Union. Oddly, it was Mikhail Gorbachev who made it possible for me to continue my involvement in relations between our two countries. Many years earlier I'd asked the Soviets for permission to retrace the flight I made across Siberia with General Bradley during the war. This request was so unusual that Georgi Arbatov, the senior Soviet official I first discussed it with, had a hard time understanding what I meant. He thought I simply wanted to fly a private plane along the commercial air route that goes from Moscow to Tokyo. Lufthansa and Air France use that corridor all the time and Arbatov said it would be simple to work out. When I finally took out a map and showed him the old Lend-Lease ferry route across Siberia, Arbatov got a long face. "This will not be easy," he said. That was back in 1979; my request disappeared into the Russian bureaucracy until Gorbachev came into power and started looking for ways to warm up relations with the West. I ran into Arbatov in the spring of 1987 at a meeting of the Council on Foreign Relations. "Tom, you can do it," he said. "You can fly your airplane along the old ferry route. Just get in touch with Aeroflot to arrange for jet fuel."

They gave me only six weeks to put the trip together. Several years earlier I'd bought a Learjet that could comfortably accommodate a half dozen passengers and two pilots on a long flight. My copilot was Bob Philpott, who had been one of IBM's top pilots for many years. I wanted Olive to come but she was forced to stay home because of a family illness. I brought my sixteen-year-old grandson Willy, who is my son's only son, Mark Garrison and his wife, and Strobe Talbott, *Time* magazine's top correspondent on arms control. We took off from the Westchester County airport on July 5, 1987, and two days later, after spending nights in Reykjavik and Helsinki, we crossed into the Soviet Union heading for Moscow.

Arbatov had sent a cable asking me not to arrive until 5:30 in the afternoon, and I worked things out so that I put the Lear down at precisely that time at the Moscow airport. As we taxied in from the runway, we were met by a small car that led us to a special parking spot. Then out stepped Arbatov and General Ilya Mazuruk, a legendary pilot and Hero of the Soviet Union who had been the commander of the Alaska-Siberia ferry route during the war. He was grizzled and bent and more than eighty years old. The Lend-Lease operation had been one of the high points of his life, and as he walked toward my airplane tears poured down his face. He put his arms around me and kissed me on both cheeks. Until that moment I hadn't felt nostalgic at all, but I got teary-eyed too. We drank champagne and that night there was a dinner where several people stood up and overstated my wartime accomplishments.

We stayed in Moscow a week, making sure all the necessary arrangements for the trip were in place, and I had a chance to meet with Andrei Gromyko. By this time Gorbachev had elevated him to the presidency of the Soviet Union, which was a largely honorary post. He was much more relaxed than I'd ever seen him. We had a long, amiable talk, and finally he dispensed with his interpreter and spoke to me in English. "Do you know," he said, "I felt sorry that you had a difficult time as ambassador. We had looked forward to your being here. You were here in the war, we see you as a fellow soldier, and there are many things we could have accomplished. It is a pity that you came at the time you did." It was kind of him to say this, because it made me feel as though my ambassadorship had not been an entire waste.

On Monday, July 13, we finally left for Siberia. We flew four or five hours each day, stopping nights in remote places like Novosibirsk in the western lowlands. Just as in the war, I had a Soviet navigator on board to make sure we didn't stray into restricted areas, but in other ways there were astonishing contrasts between the trip now and the one in 1942. The B-24 bomber I'd flown then cruised at about 180 mph, compared with 600 mph for the Learjet. The bomber's heaters had been broken, and in spite of our shearling flying suits we'd been in a near stupor from the cold. I'll never forget the sight of General Bradley wiping the windshield with vodka to keep frost from building up. But the Lear was designed to handle extreme cold—it is always Siberian winter at the high altitude at which a modern jet flies.

During idle periods in the cockpit I gazed out the window at the ground below, amazed once again at the vast expanse of Russia. Maybe once an hour we'd see smoke and a big industrial installation, but there were almost no roads or villages. I was reminded of Alexis de Tocqueville's meditation on the untamed American wilderness, and his prediction in the 1830s that the United States and Russia would become the world's two great powers. At each airport we were greeted by local officials and old soldiers from World War II. They'd give us a little welcoming ceremony in a hangar, with food and soft drinks and speeches about U.S.-Soviet friendship as demonstrated on this ferry route.

Finally we reached Yakutsk, the little tundra outpost where we'd nearly crashed in a snowstorm during the war. It had become a bright and bustling city, with ten-story buildings that the Soviets have learned to erect on top of the permafrost. From the air we could see the booming port facility on the Lena River nearby. I put the Lear into final approach and marveled at how the airport had changed. In 1942 it had been nothing more than an open field with a single tar runway, but now it was a major hub of Aeroflot, with masses of concrete and tremendous numbers of planes.

The mayor met us at the airport and we toured the

town. The old wooden shacks I remembered were mostly gone, there was no trace of the prison camp, and the weather was warm. The local museum hadn't changed, however, and walking into that place with its modest displays of drawings and native artifacts and bones was one of the strangest experiences of my life. In advance of our trip I'd supplied the old lady who ran the museum with photos from the Lend-Lease mission. She'd made a little exhibit, and I found myself standing in front of a picture of me and my war buddies in the same room with a mastodon skeleton and the mummy of an Eskimo princess.

Before the afternoon ended, I took an hour and walked alone on the bank of the Lena thinking about my life. Yakutsk was where I'd gained my self-confidence as a young man—where General Bradley had promoted me and where the crew had finally accepted me as their leader. I looked across that great river, which I was seeing unfrozen for the first time. The thought came to me that, whether my life went on many more years or ended tomorrow, I'd accomplished something just by seeing the place again.

In my honor the Soviets had located eight or nine veterans who had served in the Lend-Lease operation. I remembered some of them right away, including a stout little mechanic who had arranged for General Bradley's entire crew to get fur-lined thigh-high boots like the native Yakuts wore. Those boots had saved my feet from frostbite, and I still felt grateful to him forty-five years later. We had a wonderful feast, and I went to bed happy that night. I understood this might be my last great air adventure but for the moment that didn't make me restless at all.

ACKNOWLEDGMENTS

I would never have written this book had it not been for my friend Andrew Heiskell, retired chairman of Time Inc. When I returned from my ambassadorship to Moscow in 1981, Andrew began urging me to tell my story, and it was Andrew who, six years later, escorted me to *Fortune* magazine and introduced me to Marshall Loeb, the managing editor, and to my eventual coauthor Peter Petre. Throughout a long and demanding project, Andrew remained an important source of encouragement, and I hope the final product gives him satisfaction.

John Akers, IBM's chairman, backed this project with understanding and generosity. He put the IBM archive at our disposal, granted access to company personnel, and most important, enabled us to call on the talents of Richard Wight, retired director of corporate communications. Dick's research has been invaluable. We have drawn freely on the facts and insights in two unpublished works of IBM history he has written in recent years, and to the extent that this memoir contributes to the story of American business, Dick Wight deserves much of the credit.

In some respects, this book began in the pages of *Fortune,* in which the first product of my collaboration with Peter Petre, a 1987 article, appeared. Marshall Loeb gave our book enthusiastic support, granting Peter a generous leave of absence, and then patiently extending it when the project took longer than expected. The imprint of Mr. Loeb's editorial imagination appears on the cover of this volume: he gave us the title *Father, Son & Co.*

This book does not pretend to be a comprehensive history of the computer industry, or IBM, or even of the Watson family. But it would have been much *less* complete without the friends and colleagues who helped reconstruct the events we describe. As I worked on the project I turned back to some of those I'd depended on at IBM. In particular, I want to thank six of my former executive assistants who later went on to become officers of the company: Dean McKay, who did masterful work in shaping IBM's corporate image through design; Bob Hubner, one of the most effective and empathetic managers I ever met; Spike Beitzel, a particularly shrewd adviser; Dean Phypers, my confidant in the 1960s when IBM was under enormous strain; Jane Cahill Pfeiffer, who saw me through the difficult year in which I had a heart attack; and David McKinney, who aided me in the sometimes painful process of disengaging from the business.

I was fortunate to have had first-rate associates outside IBM, as well. When I went to Washington to work for President Carter, Bill Jackson, executive director of the General Advisory Committee on Arms Control and Disarmament, was immensely helpful in teaching me the ropes. During my ambassadorship in Moscow, when the Afghanistan crisis broke, I'd have been lost without Mark Garrison, the deputy chief of mission at the U.S. embassy. Both men dug into their files and contributed to this book.

Many friends and former colleagues took time to sit for interviews, and some shared writings of their own. They include James Birkenstock, Tina Brandt, Harold Brown, Richard Bullen, Frank Cary, Charles De Carlo, F. L. Dunn, Keith Funston, Jean McEwen Hughes, John J. Kenney, Burke Marshall, H. Wisner Miller, John Opel, Clair Vough, Barney Wiegard, and Dan Wright. Also James Brown Jr., Isabelle Markwald Bushnell, Jeannette Cammen, Richard Day, Robert Galvin, Robert German, Arthur Krim, Eleanor Lazarus, Molly Noyes, Senator Charles Percy, James Robison, Tyge Rothe, Eunice Shriver, Erma Swenson, Edwin Thorne, and Strobe Talbott. I also want to thank the people of the IBM archive —Barbara Henninger, Donald Kenney, John Maloney, and Robert Pokorak, in particular. The staff of IBM's secretary assembled personnel information we requested, and the staff of the comptroller provided financial data. Finally, Robert Djurdjevic and Bro Uttal provided my coauthor with independent perspectives on the computer industry.

Publishing was an unfamiliar world when I started this project. I consider myself extraordinarily lucky to have had the help of our agent, Kathy Robbins. She is tactful, attentive, and as smart a businessperson as I've ever known. Linda Grey, our publisher, understood from the very beginning exactly what the book was meant to be, and has been a great source of encouragement. Our editor, Beverly Lewis, worked hard to give the text its final polish. A number of veteran journalists assisted us at various stages and in various ways: Louis Banks and John McDonald with editorial advice; Lorraine Carson, George McNeill, Vicki Sufian, Carolyn Tasker, and Linda Williams with research; and Katherine Bourbeau with photo research. We were also fortunate to have had the logistical help of Diane Chiquette, Elizabeth Corrigan, Kim Dramer, Alicia Hill, Jean Kidd, and Ellen Miller.

Two families supported the book. Peter Petre's wife, Ann Banks, is a gifted writer who edited our earliest drafts and gave important advice all along the way. My own Olive, who has backed me loyally in everything I've done for the past forty-eight years, willingly put up with even this project. My sister, Helen Buckner, gave us wonderful reminiscences of Dad and of scrapes she saw me get into as a boy; and my eldest daughter, Jeannette Sanger, contributed funny, revealing stories about growing up in our household. Finally, I'd like to make a special acknowledgment to my grandson, Thomas William Watson, whom everyone knows as Willy. He has been a wonderful companion to me during voyages to the Arctic and Antarctic, and I hope he'll find in these pages a few stories he hasn't already heard during our long nights at sea.

SELECTED
BIBLIOGRAPHY

IBM did not always welcome efforts by journalists to probe the company or my family. Ironically, the best account of my father's life is a book IBM refused to cooperate with—William Rodgers's *THINK: A Biography of the Watsons and IBM*. The best layman's account of computer-industry history in the years spanned by my career is Katharine Davis Fishman's *The Computer Establishment*. Both books contain insights that helped us in writing this one. We also relied heavily on three works backed by the company: *IBM's Early Computers*, a comprehensive and meticulously researched technical history; *IBM and the U.S. Data Processing Industry: An Economic History*, which is based on the case we made in our 1969 antitrust suit; and my father's authorized biography, *The Lengthening Shadow*.

Banfield, Edward C. "An Act of Corporate Citizenship," *Programs to Employ the Disadvantaged*, Peter B. Doeringer, ed. New York: Prentice-Hall, 1969.

Bashe, Charles J., et al. *IBM's Early Computers*. Cambridge, Mass.: MIT Press, 1986.

Belden, Thomas and Marva. *The Lengthening Shadow: The Life of Thomas J. Watson*. Boston: Little, Brown, 1962.

Brock, Gerald W. *The U.S. Computer Industry: A Study of Market Power*. Cambridge, Mass.: Ballinger, 1975.

Brooks, Frederick P. Jr. *The Mythical Man-Month*. Reading, Mass.: Addison-Wesley, 1975.

Fisher, Franklin M., et al. *IBM and the U.S. Data Processing Industry: An Economic History*. New York: Praeger, 1983.

Fishman, Katharine Davis. *The Computer Establishment.* New York: Harper & Row, 1981.

Levinson, Harry, and Stuart Rosenthal. *CEO: Corporate Leadership in Action.* New York: Basic Books, 1984.

Malik, Rex. *And Tomorrow . . . The World?: Inside IBM.* London: Millington, 1975.

Rodgers, William. *THINK: A Biography of the Watsons and IBM.* New York: Stein and Day, 1969.

Thirty Years of Management Briefings: 1958 to 1988. Armonk, New York: IBM, 1988.

Watson, Thomas J. *"As A Man Thinks": The Man and His Philosophy of Life As Expressed in His Editorials.* New York: IBM, 1954.

Watson, Thomas J. *Men, Minutes, Money: A Collection of Excerpts from Talks and Messages Delivered and Written at Various Times.* New York: IBM, 1934.

Watson, Thomas J. Jr. *A Business and Its Beliefs: The Ideas That Helped Build IBM.* New York: McGraw-Hill, 1963.

Watson, Thomas J. Jr. *Addresses and Articles of Thomas J. Watson, Jr.* Armonk, New York: IBM, n.d.

Finally, we want to thank, for prompt answers to our questions, the Boston Computer Museum, the Jimmy Carter Library, the John Fitzgerald Kennedy Library, the Lyndon Baines Johnson Library, the Mystic Seaport Museum, and the National Security Archive.

INDEX

About the Authors

THOMAS J. WATSON JR. was chief executive officer of IBM from 1956 to 1971. Today he is chairman emeritus and a member of the company's advisory board. He remains active in U.S.-Soviet affairs. Mr. Watson lives with his wife, Olive, in Connecticut.

PETER PETRE is a member of the editorial board at *Fortune* magazine. He lives with his wife, Ann Banks, and their daughter, Kate, in New York.

We Deliver!
And So Do These Bestsellers.